# WAR IN DARFUR

# WAR IN DARFUR

## AND THE SEARCH FOR PEACE

**Alex de Waal**
Editor

GLOBAL EQUITY INITIATIVE
HARVARD UNIVERSITY

Justice Africa

2007

Library of Congress Cataloging-in-Publication Data

A copy of the Cataloging-in-Publication (CIP) Data
is available from the Library of Congress.
ISBN 978-0-674-02367-3
ISBN 0-674-02367-6

Design and composition by Hanley|Jones Art + Design

# CONTENTS

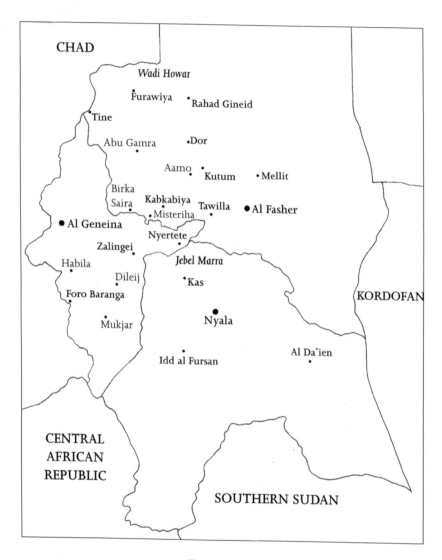

DARFUR

SUDAN

# PREFACE

DARFUR IS VIOLENTLY CONTESTED. The land is locus of a bloody war that gained international attention in 2003, though hostilities had in fact been conducted over many previous years. The people, their identities, and political allegiances are bitterly disputed. And the concept of Darfur itself, the significance of the conflict there, and the position of Darfur within Sudan are also contested. The authors of the essays in this collection provide different perspectives on the origin and escalation of Darfur's war and the search for peace. What unites the diverse contributions is a concern with the under-documented and complex history of Darfur, in its local, national, and regional contexts, and an impulse to reflect upon the African Union's efforts to reach a peace settlement in Abuja.

This collection began as a series of papers commissioned by the Conflict Prevention and Peace Forum and Justice Africa to provide background analyses of Darfur for the African Union mediation, by both Sudanese and international scholars. The dossier was delivered to the AU in early 2005. The contributions by Musa Abdul-Jalil and colleagues, Ali Haggar, Roland Marchal, and Adam Azzain Mohammed arose from that exercise. Hafiz Mohamed was instrumental in this project and has continued to have a leading role in organizing the Sudanese contributions to this volume. Some of those involved in initiating this project met again, under CPPF auspices, in July 2006, less than three months after the conclusion of the AU's mediation of the "Inter-Sudanese Peace Talks on the Conflict in Darfur." That meeting provided the opportunity for the essays by Dawit Toga and Laurie Nathan, as well as the concluding reflections by Alex de Waal. The contributions by Deborah Murphy and by Rebecca Hamilton and Chad Hazlett were organized through Harvard Global Equity Initiative and the Harvard student activism around Darfur.

This collection seeks detail and focus in preference to comprehensiveness. There are many gaps, which arise solely because of constraints of space and time. We would have liked to have included chapters on sexual violence during the conflict, the government's conduct of the war, attempts at local conflict resolution, the impact of the war on livelihoods, the emergence of a war economy, and the humanitarian crisis and assistance efforts. These must wait for another occasion.

Mohamed el Amin translated Ali Haggar's chapter from Arabic and Victor Tanner translated Jerome Tubiana's chapter from French. Copyediting was done by Alana Devich, the bibliography was finalized by Ginger Tanton, Tim Jones of Hanley|Jones Art + Design did the cover design and text layout, proofreading was done by Anne McGuire, and Erin Judge steered the production process through the Global Equity Initiative and Harvard University Press. The costs of production were borne by a grant from Justice Africa.

# CHRONOLOGY

1990, Dec. Idriss Déby takes power in Chad

1991 Darfur becomes a state within a federal system

1991, Dec. SPLA incursion into Darfur headed by Daud Bolad

1994 Darfur divided into three states; Native Administration reintroduced

1995, Mar. Nine "amirs" appointed for the Arabs in Western Darfur

1995–99 Arab-Masalit conflict

1999 Split in ruling National Congress Party

2000, May Publication of the *Black Book* detailing marginalization of Darfur

2001 Organization of armed opposition in Darfur

2002 Conferences at Nyertete and Kass to try to mediate the conflict SPLA makes contact with SLA and provides assistance

2002, Dec. Vice President Ali Osman warns Darfur not to follow the path of the South

### 2003

Feb. SLA announces its existence and publishes manifesto

March JEM announces its existence

April Rebels attack al Fashir airport

May Rebel attacks on Kutum, Mellit, Tina

July Janjawiid counteroffensive begins in earnest

September Government-SLA ceasefire talks in Abéché, Chad

### 2004

January Major government offensive

March UN Coordinator Mukesh Kapila calls Darfur "the world's worst humanitarian crisis" and makes a comparison to Rwanda

April Government-SLA/JEM talks in N'djamena agree on a ceasefire and disarmament of the Janjawiid

May First AMIS forces arrive in Darfur

June U.S. Congress described Darfur as "genocide"

July UN Security Council gives Khartoum 30 days to disarm the Janjawiid and facilitate humanitarian assistance

August Government and rebels meet in Abuja, Nigeria, under AU auspices

September U.S. Secretary of State Colin Powell declares Darfur to be "genocide" and the UN Security Council sets up an Independent Commission of Inquiry into Darfur

Oct-Nov Third round of peace talks in Abuja

December Fourth round of peace talks in Abuja

### 2005

January 9 Comprehensive Peace Agreement signed between Government of Sudan and SPLM

January  ICID delivers its report
March  UN Security Council refers Darfur to the International Criminal Court
May  First discussion of handing over AMIS to the UN
July  Government of National Unity consisting of NCP, SPLM, and others formed; John Garang dies in a helicopter crash
July  Government and SLM/JEM agree on a Declaration of Principles for resolving the Darfur conflict at fifth round of Abuja talks
Sept.–Oct.  Sixth round of peace talks in Abuja
October  SLM-Minawi holds conference in Haskanita
November  U.S. attempts to reunify the SLM
November  Seventh round of peace talks opens in Abuja
December  Chadian rebels attack the town of Adré and Chad declares it is in a state of war with Sudan

### 2006

January  President Bashir is blocked from becoming President of the African Union at the Khartoum Summit
March  Vice President Ali Osman Taha indicates that Sudan will consider favorably a transition from AMIS to the UN in the event of a peace agreement for Darfur
March  AU Peace and Security Council votes to hand over AMIS to a UN force in six months' time
April  UN Security Council votes to hand over AMIS to a UN force and gives a deadline for the Abuja talks to complete by the end of the month
Chadian rebels attack N'djamena, JEM is engaged in its defense
May  Darfur Peace Agreement concluded and signed by Sudan government and SLM-Minawi, not by SLM-Abdel Wahid and JEM
June  National Redemption Front formed in Asmara, Eritrea
July  Ahmed Abdel Shafi announces the dismissal of Abdel Wahid al Nur
August  Minni Minawi becomes Senior Assistant to the President
AU expels the non-signatories from the Ceasefire Commission
August  UN Security Council passes Resolution 1706 requesting Sudan to consent to a UN peacekeeping force
November  UN Secretary General Kofi Annan proposes a "hybrid" AU-UN force, and the Sudan government agrees to this proposal in principle though not in detail

### 2007

February  ICC issues summons to appear to a government minister and Janjawiid commander suspected of war crimes

# GLOSSARY

| | |
|---|---|
| *Abbala* | camel herders |
| *Amir* | "Prince": Arab tribal leader under 1995 local government system |
| AMIS | African Union Mission in Sudan |
| *Ansar* | Followers of the Mahdi |
| AU | African Union |
| *Baggara* | cattle herders |
| CAR | Central African Republic |
| CDR | Conseil Démocratique Révolutionairre, Chadian opposition front |
| CPA | Comprehensive Peace Agreement |
| DDDC | Darfur-Darfur Dialogue and Consultation |
| DPA | Darfur Peace Agreement |
| *Fursha* | middle-ranking administrative chief in Dar Masalit |
| *Fursan* | horsemen, used to refer to the militia of the Beni Halba |
| G-19 | Group of Nineteen SLA commanders who opposed Abdel Wahid al Nur |
| GI-net | Genocide Intervention Network |
| *Hakura* | land grant under the Fur Sultanate |
| ICC | International Criminal Court |
| ICID | International Commission of Inquiry into Darfur |
| IDP | internally displaced person |
| IGAD | Inter-Governmental Authority on Development |
| Islamic Legion | Libyan-established international brigade for Sahelian countries and Sudan |
| JEM | Justice and Equality Movement |
| *Masar* | livestock migration route |
| *Murahaliin* | *Baggara* militia |
| *Nazir* | paramount chief, usually of an Arab tribe |
| NCP | National Congress Party |

| | |
|---|---|
| NDA | National Democratic Alliance, umbrella opposition group |
| NIF | National Islamic Front |
| NMRD | National Movement for Reform and Democracy |
| NRF | National Redemption Front |
| *Omda* | middle-ranking administrative chief |
| PCP | Popular Congress Party |
| PDF | Popular Defense Forces, government paramilitaries |
| PSC | Peace and Security Council (of the African Union) |
| Qoreish | tribe of the Prophet Mohamed |
| *Shartai* | senior chief in the Fur hierarchy |
| *Sheikh* | lowest-ranking tribal leader |
| SLA | Sudan Liberation Army |
| SLM | Sudan Liberation Movement |
| SPLA | Sudan People's Liberation Army |
| SPLM | Sudan People's Liberation Movement |
| STAND | Students Taking Action Now: Darfur |
| *Wadi* | seasonal watercourse |

# CONTRIBUTORS

ABDUL-JABBAR ABDULLAH FADUL is a development specialist who has lived and worked in Darfur all his life. He has degrees from the University of Khartoum and East Anglia, UK. He headed Darfur's Agricultural Planning Unit and is senior lecturer in environmental sciences and natural resources at the University of al Fashir.

ADAM AZZAIN MOHAMMED is a former local government officer in Darfur and professor at the Institute for the Study of Public Administration and Federal Governance, University of Khartoum.

AHMED KAMAL EL-DIN is a lawyer with degrees from the University of Khartoum and Leeds, UK. He has many years of experience as a leading journalist, public servant, and political activist. He is an independent Islamist working in support of peace in Sudan.

AHMED A. YOUSUF is a retired local government officer in the Sudan civil service and a former commissioner of Mellit, North Darfur.

ALI HAGGAR is a senior researcher at the University of Omdurman who is active in the search for peace in Darfur.

ALEX DE WAAL is program director at the Social Science Research Council, a fellow of the Global Equity Initiative, Harvard University, and a director of Justice Africa. He is author of *Famine that Kills: Darfur, Sudan, 1984-1985* (Clarendon Press 1989) and co-author, with Julie Flint, of *Darfur: A Short History of a Long War* (Zed Books 2005).

REBECCA HAMILTON earned a J.D. from Harvard Law School and a Master in Public Policy from the John F. Kennedy School of Government, Harvard University, in 2007. She has worked with internally displaced populations in Sudan and speaks throughout the United States about advocacy for Darfur.

CHAD HAZLETT earned a Master in Public Policy from Harvard University and is Field Officer and Advocacy Associate at the Genocide Intervention Network.

DEBORAH MURPHY is a recent graduate of the John F. Kennedy School of Government at Harvard University. She has worked for Africare, the U.S. State Department, and the World Resources Institute.

MUSA ABDEL JALIL is professor of social anthropology and head of the Department of Sociology and Social Anthropology at the University of Khartoum.

ROLAND MARCHAL is senior research fellow at the, Centre d'Études et de Récherches Internationales, Paris.

JULIE FLINT is a journalist with long experience of Sudan and the Middle East. She is the author of *Darfur Destroyed,* for Human Rights Watch, and is co-author, with Alex de Waal, of *Darfur: A Short History of a Long War* (Zed Books, 2005).

LAURIE NATHAN is a research fellow in the Crisis States Research Centre at the London School of Economics and in the Department for Environmental and Geographical Sciences at the University of Cape Town. He was a member of the AU mediation team in Abuja.

VICTOR TANNER is an adjunct member of faculty at the School of Advanced International Studies at Johns Hopkins University. He first lived and worked in Darfur in 1988 and has conducted research on aid programs and conflict dynamics there since 2002.

DAWIT TOGA holds a Ph.D. from Columbia University, and is political analyst in the Conflict Management Division at the African Union in charge of Sudan/Darfur. He participated at the North-South Naivasha Talks, which resulted in the signing of the Comprehensive Peace Agreement between the Government of the Sudan and the SPLM/A, and was also a member of the AU team at the Abuja talks.

JÉRÔME TUBIANA is a Ph.D. in African Studies of the Institut National des Langues et Civilisations Orientales in Paris. He has worked in Chad, Sudan, and Niger as a researcher, journalist, and photographer.

# WAR IN DARFUR

# I

# Sudan: The Turbulent State

ALEX DE WAAL

## Contesting Darfur and Sudan

THE WAR IN DARFUR is the most recent manifestation of a pattern of extreme political violence that has afflicted the peripheries of the Sudanese state over many generations. Until the 1980s, this form of violence was specific to the Sudanese state's southern frontier but for twenty years it has afflicted most of the southern, eastern, and western borderlands. Darfur's war also compels us to re-examine assumptions about the origins and nature of Sudan's political dysfunction and how it can be overcome.

A generation of Sudanese politicians and scholars has located the country's unresolved national question along the north-south axis of the Nile valley. Sudanese and foreign writers alike have blamed divergent identities as the root of the country's recurrent north-south wars (Hasan 1971; Ruay 1994; Deng 1995; Lesch 1999; Jok 2001). The simplified version of this analysis identifies the north as "Arab" and Muslim and the south as "African." The Comprehensive Peace Agreement (CPA), signed between the "northern" government in Khartoum and the "southern" Sudan People's Liberation Movement/Army (SPLM/A) in Nairobi in January 2005 is framed by this polarity: its basic formula is one country (for the interim) with two distinct systems of governance

for north and south respectively, to be followed by an option for the southerners to vote on the separation of Southern Sudan. Self-determination is a solution that reproduces the same oppositional categories that were nurtured by
decades of war, and most probably the southerners will take it.

The eruption of the war in Darfur obliges academics and policymakers to
reconsider the primacy of the north-south identity polarity in Sudan.
Elsewhere I have criticized Sudanese political science for its "Nilocentrism"
and argued that there is a neglected east-west axis along which Sudanese
national identity also needs to be analyzed (de Waal 2005a)—an axis which
gives different meanings to the words "African" and "Arab." Darfur's historic
identity has been both "African" and "Arab" with no sense of contradiction
between the two. Sean O'Fahey (1980) notes how Darfur possessed a strong
sense of regional identity from the seventeenth to the twentieth centuries,
ruled by a state bilingual in Fur and Arabic. In their contribution to this volume, Abdul-Jabbar Fadul and Victor Tanner refer to the contemporary manifestation of this as the "Darfur consensus." No commensurate "Sudan
consensus" exists. In principle Darfur's contribution to Sudan's national
debate should enable northern and southern Sudanese to transcend the
polarizing terms in which the current debate on national identity is conducted. Sadly, the timetable of the CPA means that Sudan's basic national
questions need to be definitively addressed very soon. The failure of the
Darfur Peace Agreement (DPA) means that this historic conjuncture will
occur before Darfurians have the opportunity to participate fully in the
national debate and make their distinctive inputs.

Darfur's war has not only set Darfurians against one another but has
allowed the region's identity to be defined by the racial labels preferred by a
small minority of extremists. Much media commentary has cut the "African"
and "Arab" labels from the north-south conflict and uncritically pasted them
onto Darfur—while simultaneously neglecting the similarities between the
Darfur war and the wars in the south and the southern marchlands of northern Sudan, namely the Nuba Mountains and Blue Nile.[1] This labeling is
rejected by all Darfurian political leaders save the ideologues of the Arab
Gathering. Despite their historic and ethnographic inappropriateness for
Darfur, the labels "African" and "Arab" have gained political currency among

Darfurians, and may yet supplant the Darfur consensus as the determining political trajectory for the region. The logic of the north-south "Arab"-"African" polarity, as translated into the provision for southern self-determination in the CPA, is leading Sudan inexorably towards partition. Any contested separation of Southern Sudan is likely to be accompanied by immense human tragedy but at least the outcome maps onto a discernible geographical boundary. The same pseudo-racial logic cannot be transferred to Darfur without setting in motion the complete dismemberment of Darfurian society with no solution in sight. Darfurians' fear of southern separatism is fuelled both by an apprehension of their collective abandonment by the southerners, whom they see as strategic allies in counterbalancing the power of the northern elites, and the fearful implications of the "Arab"-"African" polarity on their home region.

The war in Darfur should compel us to attend more closely to the ways in which identity conflicts are, in significant ways, a byproduct of the political structure of the Sudanese polity. There is a strong tradition within Sudanese social and political science which holds that the country's fundamental political problem is the excessive power held by a disproportionately wealthy elite in Khartoum which relentlessly exploits and subjugates the country's provinces. According to this paradigm, Sudan's conflicts arise from the ruthless ways in which the center preys on the peripheries, with racial, ethnic, and religious conflicts being secondary to these dynamics. The most influential exponent of this analysis was the late John Garang, commander in chief of the Sudan People's Liberation Army (SPLA) from 1983 to 2005 and, briefly, first vice president. A subordinate theme of the CPA is an attempt to build a united democratic Sudan based on the equality of all its citizens, a project that seems in eclipse following the death of Garang in July 2005 and the continuation of the war in Darfur.

The major part of this introductory chapter elaborates on the center-periphery paradigm, combining it with another genre of Sudanese political history that focuses on persistent instability at the center of power. Although a hyper-dominant center may seem incompatible with an unstable center, this chapter seeks to show that no contradiction in fact exists. To the contrary, many of the most malignant aspects of the Sudanese crisis arise precisely from this combination of traits. Local ethnic or tribal conflict, the militarization of tribal administration, the opportunistic behavior of provincial political elites, violent disputes over natural resources, and the brutalization of society, can all be traced back to the impacts of this intractable political pattern.

## Three Persistent Realities

THE HYPER-DOMINANCE of the national capital is the single most important reality in Sudan today. Khartoum and its environs consist of a middle-income enclave surrounded by provinces that are not only poor but in important respects are suffering from development processes running in reverse. The center possesses immense private wealth, a class of skilled professionals, and a political culture that has a strong liberal tradition. The peripheries, by contrast, are not only poor but are subject to processes of subjugation and exploitation which mean that even peaceable development leaves them disadvantaged.

Many leading Sudanese political scientists have attributed their country's crisis to the central elite's greed and grip on power. Leading figures in the country's insurgencies—among them former professors of the social sciences—have claimed to be fighting to remedy the exploitation of the peripheries by the center. Among this group of social scientists-turned-revolutionaries are Ahmed Diraige, Taisir Ahmed, Malik Agar, and Sharif Harir. The *Black Book*, published in 2000[2] by members of the Islamist movement who went on to found the Justice and Equality Movement (JEM) and take up arms in Darfur, expounds a similar critique of central power.

The second most persistent fact in Sudanese political history is the inability of any one elite faction to establish unchallenged political dominance over the state. The center possesses sufficient economic, social, cultural, and political infrastructure that it can support not one but multiple elite groups. After independence, these contending groups competed for power, but none of them was able to dominate the others, leading to chronic political instability. The country switched between civilian and military rule and parliamentary coalitions were invariably fragile. Even when a president displayed remarkably longevity, as with Jaafar Nimeiri, personal continuity at the top masked many internal twists and turns. This has been the central theme of histories of the Sudanese state (e.g., Woodward 1990). Since the 1989 coup, continuity of military men in power has masked multiple competing power centers in Khartoum and frequent reconfigurations within the ruling group.

The lack of internal political cohesion among the northern establishment has not been an impediment to that establishment maintaining its sociocultural and economic dominance in Sudan and its collective control over the country's political and economic institutions. But it has prevented the emergence of a coalition in Khartoum that is sufficiently strong to exercise the leadership necessary to achieve peace or sustain a consistent set of economic and governance strategies. This instability has been projected into Sudan's peripheries and has made it impossible to build or sustain any stable mechanism of provincial governance. The provincial elites have been unable to establish the political infrastructure necessary to mount a sustained challenge to the dominance of the center, and have also been unable to establish stable clientelistic relations with a center that is always in flux. As the center has been unable to pursue any long-term political strategy, individuals and institutions within the government have become skilled at the default option of short-term crisis management. Economic policy, foreign relations, administrative reform, and counterinsurgency have all been conducted as crisis management. Commonly, different parts of the government and ruling party will be conducting different and competing policies in parallel. In turn this has given greatest latitude to those ready to adopt low-cost, ad hoc approaches to managing security, notably the security officers who run the "militia strategy" of fostering tribal irregulars.

In the 1990s scholars of war began to analyze the phenonema of "new wars" and wars in which the belligerent parties conducted violence against the civilian population in preference to one another (Kaldor 1999; Keen 2005). Extreme ethnically-targeted violence conducted by a combination of regular army units and tribally-mobilized paramilitaries, often in pursuit of economic goals, was a feature of Sudan's civil war from the mid-1980s. This is the third striking and persistent fact of contemporary Sudan. Some of the most appalling episodes warrant cataloguing here, for the reader unacquainted with the sorry precursors of Darfur's tragedy.

In 1987, Ushari Mahmoud and Suleiman Baldo documented a massacre in the Darfurian town of ed Da'ien and enslavement in Bahr el Ghazal by the *murahaliin* militia drawn from the Baggara Rizeigat (Mahmoud and Baldo 1987). Two years later, a report by Amnesty International documented a wider pattern of killings by the Rizeigat and Misiriya *murahaliin* and army in northern Bahr el Ghazal (Amnesty International 1989). At the time of preparing this report, human rights researchers debated whether to use the word "genocide." Army commanders deliberately starved the displaced population (de Waal 1994b; Keen 1994). The previous year (1988) an anonymous report, "Sudan's Secret Slaughter," detailed ethnically-targeted mass killings in the city of Wau, carried out by the army and a proxy militia drawn from the Fertit, targeting Dinka civilians and policemen suspected of supporting the SPLA. A comparable series of massacres was carried out in the city of Juba in 1992 after the SPLA briefly overran the southern capital before withdrawing. Again, the culprits were military intelligence, certain army units, and local militia mobilized on a tribal basis. The Sudan government's assault on the Nuba Mountains in 1992–1993 was a new departure in the conduct of the war, in that the objectives of the campaign including not only crushing the rebellion and its civilian supporters, but also forcibly relocating the entire Nuba population out of their ancestral homeland to "peace camps" where they would take on a new identity (African Rights 1995). Although tribal militia had been raised in the Nuba Mountains as early as 1985, the main instruments of this onslaught were the army and *mujahidiin* units raised in the name of jihad, and local government (de Waal and Abdel Salam 2004). The systematic use of sexual violence was also documented in the Nuba, as a deliberate tool of destroying communities with the aim of creating a generation with a new identity. This campaign, mounted by a revolutionary government at the height of its ideological hubris, represented a more far-reaching attempt at violent social re-engineering than anything attempted before or since (de Waal 2007). It re-ignited the debate among human rights researchers as to whether to use the term "genocide." Subsequent counter-insurgency campaigns in Bahr el Ghazal (Human Rights Watch 1999) and the Southern Sudanese oil fields (Human Rights Watch 2003) were also mounted with a combination of indiscriminate violence and scorched earth tactics.

The government's counterinsurgency in Darfur follows a very well-established pattern.

Long wars are usually brutal. But Sudan's civil wars have been peculiar in the persistence of a particular pattern of extreme brutality, with tribal militia as a vanguard force. In contrast to the voluminous literature on the causes of Sudan's wars, the phenomenon of the tribal militia has gained remarkably little attention from scholars. Apart from the human rights literature cited above, the most-cited sources on this topic are two brief anthropological essays (Salih and Harir 1994; de Waal 1994a). This is a remarkable gap. It is as though having explained the reasons for war, scholars and policymakers were content to regard its atrocious conduct as needing no additional explanation. But there are important questions needing to be answered. Tribal militias were identified as a threat to national stability as early as the 1980s—indeed the army chief of staff wrote to the prime minister on this subject in February 1989. Yet, counter to predictions, they have not yet led to the disintegration of central authority in Sudan. All those who have studied the militia note that they have been supported by the army and military intelligence. Yet this is an ambivalent relationship marked by mutual distrust. Militias that were created at one point in the war—notably as the *murahaliin* armed in the mid-1980s to fight the SPLA—have later shown independence from their former sponsors. The militia and their propensity for savagery deserve explanation beyond noting that they are part of the war. The argument developed in this chapter is that tribal militias are more than a cheap tool of counterinsurgency—they are also a facet of the central strategy for governing the peripheries.

Describing the Sudanese state as either "strong" or "weak" fails to do justice to this complicated reality. It leads to the paradoxical situation in which the state is failing to deliver on basic governance functions for most Sudanese citizens, while the establishment demonstrates an astonishing capacity to not only survive but also prosper. The prospects of dislodging the dominant elite groups, however fractious they may be, are remote. Like a gyroscope, the Sudanese system of rule is never stationary yet has not fallen over. Whether the ruling elites can continue to preside over such disastrous contradictions remains to be seen. The following sections develop the framework of the well-endowed but unstable center dominating the provinces, exploring how this helps explain other manifestations of the Sudanese crisis.

## Center and Periphery

SUDAN IS ONE OF THE MOST UNEQUAL countries in the world. National economic statistics are unreliable but the best estimates are that about half the nation's income and assets are in the capital, which contained about 8 percent of the population in the 1980s and 20 percent today. About three-quarters of the country's health professionals are located there. The country consists of a middle-income capital city and immediate surroundings, which enjoy a booming economy. The hinterland qualifies as a "least developed country" in which the majority of the people live in absolute poverty.

The stronger version of the center-periphery hypothesis is that there exists a deliberate and consistent conspiracy by an administrative, military, and commercial establishment to exploit the provinces. The country's wars are a logical continuation of historic processes of asset stripping and proletarianization of the rural populace, which began in the nineteenth century, and which has continued during war and peace alike. War is but a continuation of primary accumulation including land seizure using military organizations. The weaker version argues that extreme center-periphery inequalities are the logical outcome of the historic imbalance of power and wealth in the country, inherited from colonial times. There is no conspiracy as such, but rather the operation of merchant capital according to its own iron laws, which means that those who already have accumulated capital will continue to do so, at the expense of those who have only their labor to rely on, lacking even recognized title to their own lands.

Fatima Babiker (1984) has explored how Sudan's merchant classes (commonly known as *Jellaba*) function, extracting profits from the peripheries and investing them in the center. Tony Barnett and Abbas Abdelkarim (1988) analyze the extreme disparities in investment and wealth between Khartoum and its environs (roughly including the Gezira, the White Nile to Kosti, the Gedaref's mechanized farming schemes, the Nile northward to Atbara, and the towns of el Obeid, Kassala, and Port Sudan) and the rest of the country. Mustafa Babiker Ahmed (1988) and Mohamed Salih (1999) have studied mechanized farming and its role in generating further inequality through the expropriation of smallholder farmers and pastoralists to make way for agricultural "mining" of the central rangelands and other ecological niches. They show how land laws that benefit the elites brush aside the customary land-tenure systems. Mark Duffield's analysis of the labor market, and specifically the need of the Gezira scheme and mechanized farms for a large supply of workers at less-than-subsistence rates, concludes with demonstrating how war-related displacement and modest humanitarian assistance has further entrenched this pattern (Duffield 2001, ch. 8–9; also Alsikainga 1996).

The migration of much of Sudan's professional class to the Gulf States from the 1970s onward has accentuated inequality. By the late 1980s, the earnings of those expatriates were equivalent to more than half of Sudan's GDP, and remittances from expatriate workers (mostly outside the official banking system and unrecorded) were by far the largest source of foreign exchange (Brown 1992). This inflow of hard currency financed a real estate and consumer boom in the major towns of northern Sudan and generated considerable profits for those traders able to supply these new demands. Given that most expatriates hailed from the existing elites, remittances from the Gulf further exacerbated internal inequalities.

The economic hyper-dominance of the center has far-reaching social, cultural, and political implications. The social values prevailing in Khartoum are the standard for the rest of the country. All the leading educational and cultural institutions and all the country's electronic and print media are Khartoum-based. Provincial universities (with the exception of Gezira) and radio stations are pale echoes of their counterparts in Khartoum. Only the national capital has the infrastructure to support a modern political party.

Most of those who have developed center-periphery political-economic analyses note the changing nature of the interests of the center and the controlling elites, but tend not to theorize the divisions within those ruling elites. These disputes over who controls state power and the associated ability to dispense patronage are regarded as internal squabbles within an elite that remains essentially cohesive. The core of the hypothesis is that the central

elite seeks control over the resources of the country by exploiting the natural resources of the periphery (farmland, oil) and the labor of its inhabitants,
also gaining profits from trade in the provinces, while investing its capital
only in the center.

Important theaters of the 1983–2005 war began with, and were sustained
by, violent mechanisms of seizing land and livestock and gaining control of a
labor force, subjugating communities by destroying their capacity for independent organization and, ultimately, their distinct ethnic identities. This was
markedly the case in the Nuba Mountains (African Rights 1995; Salih 1999),
and in parts of Blue Nile and Upper Nile, which comprised a frontier of
expanding commercial farming where the confiscation of land from small
farmers drove many villagers to support the SPLA. More remote regions
such as Equatoria and Darfur have historically been characterized principally
by social and economic neglect, which has compelled impoverished villagers
to become migrant laborers. Land conflicts in Darfur have followed a different trajectory[3] but it is possible that the mass displacement brought about by
the war will in turn lead to agricultural "development" strategies that bring
a central Sudanese system of commercial farming to the region.

The center-periphery dynamic is generating some significant challenges
for the Sudanese establishment. The most significant of these is mass migration to the cities. In the decades up to the 1980s, the economy of the center
was based on agriculture, which relied on cheap migrant labor. Withholding
full citizenship rights from Nigerian-origin laborers and withholding full
land-tenure rights from all migrants including those from Darfur kept down
the cost of labor. Eritrean and Ethiopian refugees and displaced southerners
augmented this labor force in the 1970s and 1980s. The 1980s saw an important change in which the main demand for cheap labor began to be located
in the towns, especially the fast-expanding capital. While benefiting from
their cheap labor, the government saw migrants as a security threat and a
burden on services (Karadawi 1999). But the scale of migration was such
that migrants were becoming increasingly hard to manage, let alone assimilate, with far-reaching electoral and security implications. The votes of
recent migrants to Khartoum decided the 1986 elections in several constituencies, to the dismay of the National Islamic Front and the traditional

sectarian parties. As noted by Adam Azzain Mohammed in this volume, urban unrest has brought down governments in the past, and the prospect of most urbanites hailing from the far peripheries including the south was alarming to the northern elites. Government leaders began to speak fearfully of the "black belt" surrounding the capital city. The 1990s witnessed titanic urban replanning and relocation schemes intended to resolve this tension. These efforts have worked up to a point: Khartoum remains a remarkably orderly and calm city. But the capital has swelled to seven million inhabitants. It is vast and, as the riots following the death of Garang showed, potentially unruly.

## Instability at the Center

FROM THE 1950S TO THE 1980S, the political intrigues of the contending elites in Khartoum were largely in plain view, the subject of unending commentary in the press. In the 1990s, the competition within the regime—here defined as the state and the ruling Islamist party—was largely hidden from public scrutiny until the conflict between President Omer al Bashir and the sheikh of the Islamists, Hassan al Turabi, became very open in 1999. Only then did the extent and acrimony of the internal disputes stretching back to the very earliest days of the Islamist regime come to light (de Waal and Abdel Salam 2004). The configuration of power within the ruling coalition of security chiefs and party bosses was the focus of intense interest by foreign diplomats during the peace processes that led to an end to the war in the South (the Machakos-Naivasha process, named after the two Kenyan towns in which most of the talks were conducted during 2001–20004) and the attempted resolution of the Darfur conflict (the Abuja process, 2004–2006). But in recent years it is rare that a political scientist has developed an analysis of Sudan based upon these perpetually unresolved power struggles.

The leading academic exponent of the inter-elite competition view is Peter Woodward, whose book *Sudan 1898–1989: The Unstable State* takes the story up to 1989, but whose analysis remains valid for the years following. Building on Woodward, five central elite blocs can be identified throughout the ninety years preceding Bashir's coup. The first two are the two dominant sectarian parties: one is the Mahdist movement and its associated Umma Party, traditionally linked to landowning interests in the central region and the rural aristocracy of western Sudan; and the other is the Khatmiyya sect and the Unionist Party, associated with trade interests and the rural aristocracy of the northern and eastern regions. These two elite blocs dominated each of Sudan's parliamentary periods. Another pair includes the "modern" forces: the administrative elite including the military, and the independent trade unions, professional associations, and the Communist Party, historically aligned with the left. Members of these groups are drawn from the same social strata as the traditional sectarian elite (especially the Khatmiyya) and have overlapping interests and loyalties. Despite his fervent attempts to create a modern Sudan with new loyalties, Nimeiri failed to displace these blocs, which re-surfaced in the late 1970s as distinct power centers within his single party, the Sudan Socialist Union, and then re-emerged as fully-formed parties immediately after his overthrow in 1985.

One by-product of the concentration of power and wealth in a middle-income enclave is that it intermittently supports a liberal political culture. During Sudan's parliamentary periods, each elite group can sustain its own party infrastructure, its own media, and its own constituencies complete with business interests fully in the open. The remarkably mutual civility that Sudan's elites (mostly) exhibit also arises because every individual (or family) is a potential future ally.

The elites are not only contenders for power but are business enterprises too. Historically, the Umma Party was based on agriculture and the Democratic Unionist Party on commerce. The remittance economy and the associated expansion of the urban and informal economies have benefited the Islamists most, but all establishment groups have shared in some of the profits. In 1982, the army formally entered commerce with the establishment of the Military Economic Board. Although the formal ownership of private sector companies by the army was short-lived, the principle of merchant-officer partnerships has continued and has been a feature of the war.

During both conservative and radical periods, the institutions of state suffered. The sectarian parties distrusted secular state institutions (including the army) which they feared were nurturing modern political forces that would consign them to history. Radical governments (after the 1964 popular uprising and again in the early years of Nimeiri's rule) tried to dismantle and reconstitute most administrative institutions.[4] In trying to use the state as the engine of sociopolitical transformation, Nimeiri only succeeded in bankrupting it. To save his own political skin he turned in 1977 to "national reconciliation" which was a form of accommodating the old power blocs.

The Islamists emerged as an elite group themselves in the late 1970s. The Islamists drew their membership from each of the above groups, their finance from the diaspora and the associated remittance-driven consumer sector and Islamic financial institutions and their clients, and their ideology from a project of national sociopolitical transformation. After seizing power in 1989, the National Islamic Front (NIF) sought to replace the fractious loyalties of Sudanese Muslims with a new adherence to a monolithic and transformative political Islam. Although—as with Nimeiri's radical secular effort two decades earlier—the Islamist project did not succeed, it did have an important impact on Sudanese political life.

Since Bashir's coup, there has been remarkable continuity among the individuals at the zenith of state power, especially the security officials close to president Bashir. Superficially, it appears that the Islamists succeeded in consolidating control over the state. The Islamists' aim was that their transformative project would supplant the sectarian divisions of earlier decades. They accurately diagnosed the weakness of their predecessors and believed that the combination of legitimacy through Islam and greater resolve could create a new, transformed Sudanese identity. One guiding political principle for the NIF was *tamkiin* ("hegemony") which entailed putting Islamists in charge of all the key institutions of state. Another pivotal project was the *da'wa al shamla* ("comprehensive call to God") which sought to transform all social, economic, and administrative institutions into agents of Islamization. The strength of Islamism lay in the way in which it could win the assent of so many Sudanese Muslims. That was also a weakness: for most Islamists, loyalty to the NIF supplemented rather than supplanted other allegiances. The Islamists did succeed in eroding formerly-solid elite blocs, but at the cost of bringing a broader spectrum of individuals into its ranks. The National

Congress Party (NCP) which replaced the NIF as the public face of political Islam as the regime began a tentative civilianization in the mid-1990s, was intended to serve as the sole political party. Many members have multiple and overlapping loyalties: one person can simultaneously be a ranking member of the NCP, possess a family loyalty to the Khatmiyya, have served in a trade union or in the army, and also have sympathies to leading figures among opposition Islamists.

The continuity at the top masks the reality of multiple power centers in Khartoum. Consistently from the earliest days of the Islamist government, the most important politics to the regime has been the internal tussles for power, between the security apparatus and the civilian cadres, and among different leading individuals in the government. The splits were highlighted in August 1990 when President Bashir promised the Kuwaitis, Egyptians, and Saudis that Sudan would stand with them against Iraq, only to be countermanded by Turabi's declaration of support for Saddam Hussein. The next major crisis occurred in June 1995, when a militant group present in Sudan tried to assassinate Egyptian President Hosni Mubarak without the knowledge of Bashir. Finally, the rifts became unbridgeable in 1999, when it seemed as though Turabi was about to concentrate power in his own hands, leaving Bashir as a figurehead. At the last moment, Bashir struck, using his power to dismiss Turabi and later imprison him. But although Bashir decisively won that round, he is still fearful of the potential for an Islamist coalition to unseat him. He was unable to prevent Turabi from forming an opposition Islamist party, the Popular Congress Party (PCP). Bashir's greatest fear is Turabi. This partly accounts for the ferocity of the offensives in Darfur following the formation of the Justice and Equality Movement (JEM), which has links to prominent Islamists aligned against Bashir. A consistent rule of thumb in assessing politics in Khartoum is to look for the adversary closest to home. The actions of the most powerful men in the government are chiefly driven by the need to outmaneuver a rival within the ruling circle itself.

While Sudan's previous rulers had either neglected state institutions or tried to bend them to their own interests, the Islamist government went much further in deliberately eviscerating them in pursuit of a party agenda. At the height of the Islamists' revolutionary project in the early 1990s, they sought to turn local government into a branch of jihadist mobilization, to put social services in the hands of Islamist philanthropic agencies, and even to privatize tax collection on the model of the Islamic tithe, *zakat*. This not only weakened the state but over time also brought the internal party disputes into the state's own administrative organs. As the Islamists' ambitions ran into their own inescapable limitations and contradictions (de Waal and Abdel Salam 2004), the project of revolutionary transformation morphed into the politics of exhaustion. Meanwhile, Bashir and his cabal discovered that the fragmentation of administrative institutions is in fact an asset to their project of staying in power. It is difficult for rivals to organize to take power in a system with multiple power centers. The NCP's grip on power largely stems from its power of patronage.

Symptomatic of the failure to consolidate the state has been the unpopularity and lack of respect for Sudan's rulers. For this reason, they have sought to find legitimacy in various forms of populist mobilization and particularly in invoking Islam. Sudan has some committed and even visionary Islamists, notably Hassan al Turabi, who have pursued a long-term agenda of creating an Islamic state with tactical acumen. But each stage in the progress in the adoption of political Islam as a state ideology is better accounted for by paying attention to the political maneuvers of the contending elite factions. A succession of tactical maneuvers, each of which was intended to create or consolidate a political alliance, has entrenched political Islam. The principal reason that Nimeiri invited the Islamists into the government in 1977 and adopted Islamic law in 1983 was to try to win over Islamist constituencies in northern Sudan and outflank his political rivals. Subsequently, Sadiq el Mahdi was unable to suspend Islamic law because he needed the NIF as a coalition partner. Both Nimeiri and Sadiq realized that Islamic law was a crucial impediment to making peace with the SPLA, but could not abandon it because of fear that they would not survive the resulting instability among the central elite factions. The radicalization of the NIF regime in 1990 had much to do with Turabi's determination to upstage Bashir over the Gulf War, and the subsequent embrace of international jihadism was in part born of financial necessity because of the cutbacks in international aid following Turabi's declaration of support for Saddam Hussein. The embrace of political Islam is less a cause of the conflict than a consequence of an underlying structural weakness that left Sudan vulnerable to instability.

The failure of the Islamist project leaves the intra-elite power struggle naked for all to see. Sudan today is ruled by overlapping cliques held together by a common interest in holding onto state power. They are superbly skilled at ensuring that their internal disagreements do not jeopardize their collective hold on power, symbolized by the presidency of Bashir. It is unlikely that they can do more than sit atop a paralyzed state system, making money, dispensing patronage, and managing their recurrent crises.

## Paying for the State and the War

UNDERSTANDING STATE FINANCE is essential to an analysis of Sudan's turbulence. Since the late 1970s, Sudanese governments have faced a permanent financial crisis, brought about by the government's inability to pay the interest due on its debts. In fact, in a classic case of uncoordinated government, the Ministry of Finance did not even know what debts had been incurred by the Palace and by ministers acting on their own authority, and had to hire a foreign accounting firm to track down the country's debt obligations (Khalid 1985, 135).

In both peace and war the problem is essentially similar: how to pay for the military and grease the wheels of a patronage machine. Sudan's domestic revenue collection is inefficient and, in addition, it has never been able to capture anything but a tiny fraction of the remittances from expatriate workers. National budgets have been under austere discipline since 1978, and in the late 1990s had shrunk to about $900 million per annum. These funds were simply not enough to finance a war. In the late 1980s the combined expenditure on the army and security was about $450–$500 million per year, which the army insisted was insufficient for its needs. In 1999, officially gazetted defense spending was a meager $240 million.

Successive governments have pursued three main strategies to pay for the war. The first is seeking external finance (Brown 1992; African Rights 1997, ch. 2). During the first years of the financial crisis (1978–1985) Nimeiri exploited his position as a Cold War ally of Washington to extract concessions from the U.S. Treasury and the IMF. Sudan's debt was rescheduled a record eight times during these years. Nimeiri expertly played the U.S. State Department against the Treasury, banking his strategic loyalty. But the IMF's economic medicine did not work and in 1985 the U.S. Treasury balked at bailing out Nimeiri another time, a decision that contributed to his overthrow in April that year. His successors could not find the funds to pay their dues either and in February 1986, the IMF suspended Sudan for nonpayment of its arrears. But over the next three years the newly installed Sadiq el Mahdi government still managed to attract about $900 million in foreign assistance each year while simply refusing to pay more than 5 percent of the interest due on its rapidly mounting debts. The stratagem was simple: to warn the U.S. that without generous assistance the regime would face a choice between defecting to the Libyan camp and collapsing. This worked until January 1989 when James Baker moved from the Treasury to the State Department and called Sadiq's bluff. For a few months there was progress on humanitarian aid (Operation Lifeline Sudan was set up) and a peace process—and then there was a military coup. The incoming Islamist regime did not have much of a chance to establish a new working relationship with its creditors before Turabi's declaration of support for Saddam Hussein in August 1990 sent aid to Sudan into a tailspin. Official development assistance to Sudan shrank from about $900 million in 1988–1989 to about $200 million in the late 1990s, mostly in the form of emergency aid to the South, with a minuscule $15 million routed through the national budget.

Strategy number two has been to find alternative sources of foreign money. This was pursued from the earliest days of the war, when Nimeiri canvassed the option of oil companies directly financing militia and mercenaries in their areas of operation. In 1987, Sadiq el Mahdi traveled to Arab countries to seek both governmental and private contributions for the armed forces' mobilization to recapture Kurmuk in Blue Nile, which had fallen to the SPLA. But the most significant and sustained efforts were by the Islamists from 1990 onward, when Sudan opened its doors to Arab and Islamic non-state organizations. Usama bin Laden was the best known, though not the most significant in monetary terms, of those who assisted in Sudan's refinancing. A range of Islamist philanthropic organizations, Islamic banks, and private companies (some of them acting on behalf of governments including Iran and Iraq) provided extensive support to military training, weapons purchase and manufacture, infrastructural development, and military operations. This made it possible for the regime to sustain a major military mobilization despite a stagnant or shrinking official military budget.

In turn this had several important implications for how the war was fought. Non-state finance meant that the party and associated organizations created a power base with considerable independence from the official institutions of state, which in turn contributed to the tensions between Turabi and Bashir. Also, the foreign engagement had a price in terms of requiring the Sudanese regime to support specific ideological and commercial interests. This strategy proved politically dangerous and economically unsustainable. Politically, it generated major tensions within the regime. One striking case was the parallel foreign policies operated by the Palace and Ministry of Foreign Affairs on one hand, and the Arab and Islamic Bureau and off-budget security agencies on the other. The latter supported a number of foreign jihadist adventures including the attempted assassination of Egypt's president, Hosni Mubarak, in Addis Ababa in June 1995. This operation was conducted without the knowledge of President Bashir who was furious when it was carried out. Even though Bashir succeeded in reining in many of the excesses of the jihadists on Sudanese soil over the following three years, he could not dispense with the non-state funding that sustained his own military effort. When Bashir moved against Turabi in 1999, the latter complained that it was his independent efforts that had built up the military industries and institutions that the president was now relying upon.

The parallel financial track also had economic problems: the numbers did not add up. The Islamization of the economy was based on the expectation of a miracle—the Islamists promised that the enthusiasm and virtue unleashed by faith-based governance would swell the coffers of both state and Islamist institutions. The miracle didn't occur. By the end of the 1990s, a series of liquidity crises and corruption scandals affected Sudan's Islamic banks. Some of these scandals were engineered by members of the regime seeking to discredit their adversaries, but the underlying financial crisis was real.

The third approach to war finance has been privatization—fighting the war in a cheap and self-financing manner, using militias and support from local business interests. This has had profound implications for the nature of the war and has also had important consequences for the cohesion and viability of the state. The militia strategy—dubbed "counterinsurgency on the cheap" (de Waal 2004)—has directly resulted in massive and repeated violations of human rights in each of the war zones. It has also locked the central government's war strategy into the agendas of local armed groups including armed factions that originate from outside Sudan, as discussed by Ali Haggar in this volume. The financing of joint operations by the militia and army created a similar dynamic in which militia leaders, merchants, and military officers worked together to profit from the war, by raiding cattle, selling timber, smuggling ivory, and making windfall returns from the inflated price of grain and other essentials in garrison towns. While the army has relied on the militias to do much of the fighting, it has also distrusted their loyalties. In February 1989, the chief of staff wrote to the prime minister expressing his fear that the militia strategy would undermine the state. These fears have not been laid to rest. During 2005–2006, the Janjawiid of Western Darfur emerged as a parallel military authority able to challenge the army and hold the government hostage to its agendas.

The cost of the war, both in terms of military expenditure and in terms of revenues foregone (especially in the oil sector) should, logically, have impelled the government to seek peace. But instead, privatization of war finance made the war more difficult to resolve. Arming militia leaves the dynamics of conflict outside the control of central government. Using certain subgroups of the elite—such as merchant-officer partnerships in the war zones—to control sectors of the war also allowed these local coalitions to pursue their own political and economic interests in sustaining local war economies, even overruling edicts sent from the central government. Over the years, these strategies have created an unmanageable set of problems in the peripheries, and so deepened antagonisms that reaching any political settlement has become hugely more complicated.

The advent of oil revenues has enabled the Sudan government to escape from its liquidity crisis. Since the country began exporting oil in 1999, the national budget has risen from under $900 million to over $11 billion. In turn this has allowed a substantial increase in official spending on the army. But the new funds have not resolved the underlying problems of the Sudanese state. The immediate prospect of oil revenues sharpened the rivalry between state and party over who should control regime finances. The state executive won, but not without having to make significant compromises with some of the quasi-independent power centers within the regime, such as off-budget security agencies. For Bashir to keep the different elite factions within the ruling coalition happy means he must allow them to control substantial revenue streams. Although Turabi's challenge to Bashir was seen off, the state is no more stable and consolidated than it was a decade ago. In addition, oil revenues are insufficient to the state's basic economic plight. While Sudan's gross external debt remains over $26 billion, oil income is insufficient to achieve solvency.

## Center-Periphery Political Bargaining

SUDAN'S HYPER-DOMINANT but unstable political center determines a particular pattern of center-periphery political bargaining that in turn helps to explain the pattern and persistence of violence in Sudan's provinces. This pattern is similar during both parliamentary and authoritarian regimes, a fact that helps explain the provincial elites' ambivalence towards electoral democracy. While the center can sustain not one but multiple contending elites, by contrast, the provincial elite groups between them cannot muster sufficient economic, cultural, and social resources to form a bloc that can mount a serious challenge for power at the center. The Southerners, united by race and anti-Islamism, have a head start on the elites from Darfur, Kordofan, and the east, but the level of economic development and infrastructure in the South is a fraction of what is available to even one of Khartoum's elite groups.

At the core of Garang's argument for a united Sudan was the observation that the autonomous Southern region of 1972–1981 was never truly autonomous because it remained financially dependent on funds remitted from Khartoum, and hence the solution to the marginalization of the south and other peripheries was to obtain, through military and constitutional guarantees, sufficient representation in Khartoum to ensure that the peripheries received their fair share. Failing to achieve this goal, Garang settled for secondary political standing in Khartoum (this, he hoped, would be an interim measure only) with the reserve option of a center of quasi-state power in Juba, where a government of Southern Sudan would have direct control over half the country's oil revenue and could also receive foreign aid directly and manage its own economic affairs. This is the formula of the January 2005 Comprehensive Peace Agreement, and as Garang certainly knew, it is an unsatisfactory compromise.

The core of Garang's analysis was adopted by many radical provincial leaders across northern Sudan. The manifesto of JEM is a striking case: the movement's initial position was to demand six Sudanese regions with the presidency (later vice presidency) rotating among them, each of which would on its own be a formidable counterweight to the center. One reason that Khalil Ibrahim of JEM and Abdel Wahid al Nur of Darfur's Sudan Liberation Army refused to sign the Darfur Peace Agreement in May 2006 was that the text did not contain an autonomous region for Darfur—the Transitional Darfur Regional Authority and the promise of a referendum on whether Darfur could establish a single region were not considered good enough. The history of regional politics in Sudan does not augur well for any effective restraints on the established pattern of center-dominated politics.

Conservative provincial leaders have tried to assimilate to the central elite family-by-family (Ahmed 2002). Most of the northern rural aristocracy has long-standing loyalty to the sectarian parties. Over time, the sons of leading provincial families have obtained an education and taken positions in the government bureaucracy and army. But their position remains marginal. The central executive has the legal authority to dismiss tribal chiefs and replace them with more pliable alternatives and in many cases can do so without sparking too much local resistance. Few tribal leaders can consider their positions secure.[5]

The central elite factions need the provincial elites for two things: votes and militia. Although economically insignificant, the provinces command the largest electorate, and whenever there is an election, their votes are needed to deliver a ruling majority. Because no central elite party can expect to generate support on account of its record on welfare or development, they seek votes through sectarian and ethnic allegiances. In parallel, the low-cost means of policing the peripheries and mounting counterinsurgency is through tribal militia. To pursue either of these strategies, the intermediary of a loyal, or at least dependable, provincial leader is required. This provincial leader's position is strengthened because of the competition among the contending central elite groups for votes and, to a lesser extent, militia. But most of the cards lie in the center. Central government controls the appointment of native administrators and can play on the rivalries between traditional and radical provincial elites. Few provincial politicians can obtain sufficient private means to secure their own autonomy, though most aspire to do this—usually at the expense of provincial development funds.

Meanwhile, what strategies have been followed by provincial politicians? The leaders of provincial parties, or rural blocs within national parties, repeatedly call for a grand union of the marginalized. Each time there is a democratic uprising, there is a brief flare-up of provincial solidarity, with the Beja, Nuba, Darfurians, Ingessena (from the Blue Nile), and southerners making common cause. In 1985 it operated under the name Rural Solidarity. Within a few months the coalition crumbles. In place of this recurrent and ever-unrealized vision, provincial leaders follow two strategies. By far the most common is to attach oneself to part of the central elite, cutting a deal in which votes and/or militia are delivered in return for a place in the administration and/or commercial opportunities. Following the career of a provincial politician it is common to see him attaching himself to a succession of elite blocs, looking for the best deal. Darfurians have bounced from the Umma Party to the army to the Islamists, in different sequence, and occasionally have also attached themselves to the Unionist bloc, the "modern forces," and the SPLM. Easterners have aligned themselves with all of the above. This strategy has the inevitable result that the provincial elite members fail to organize a common platform, become corrupt, and become politically discredited.

A second strategy, used chiefly during war, is to seek the sponsorship of a foreign government.[6] Thus the SPLM has been backed at different times by

Ethiopia, Uganda, Eritrea, and the U.S.; the Beja Congress[7] by Eritrea; and the Darfurian rebels have obtained support from Chad, Libya, and Eritrea, as well as the SPLA, the latter acting as a state-like actor and also a conduit for foreign sponsorship.[8] This strategy also has the disadvantage that it severely compromises the autonomy of the client provincial leader. The SPLM was badly burned on account of its overreliance on Ethiopia when the Ethiopian government was overthrown in 1991 and sought to diversify its foreign patronage thereafter. The Beja Congress is deeply vulnerable to the political calculations of Eritrea. The Darfur rebels have slightly wider options, but for several factions their freedom of political maneuver is circumscribed by Chad.

Center-periphery patterns of political bargaining are similar during peace and war. The pattern can be described as the circulation of provincial elite members (Bayart 1993), or as a "divide and rule" strategy by the government, or as opportunistic political-survival strategies by fragmented and dependent rural elite leaders. It also has neo-patrimonial characteristics (Schatzberg 2001) and is quite consistent with the hypothesis that African states instrumentalize disorder (Chabal and Daloz 1999). Each of these descriptions is equally accurate and each of them applies during peacetime, conflict, and peace negotiations. Any description is, of course, incomplete without also referring to the shifting coalitions within the center. This combination of instability in the central elite coalition and dependence among the provincial elites creates the flux and indeterminacy for which Sudanese politics is famous. Literally, nobody is in control. This has many consequences, but one is particularly grave: it is almost impossible to make peace.

The peacemaking process to end a Sudanese provincial conflict does not resemble the standard model of a negotiating forum, with a cohesive government on one side and a cohesive rebel group on the other.[9] Rather, it takes the form of a series of overlapping political bargaining sessions, with each faction within the regime trying to locate its preferred client among the rebels, and each rebel leader trying to maximize his chances with the different central blocs, while keeping an eye on his rivals to make sure he is not outflanked. In short, peace negotiations are a continuation of the patterns of political bargaining outlined above. The purpose of negotiating is less to find a compromise on substantive issues than to haggle over the price of the deal and to weigh up the political clout of each player so as best to calculate when and where to jump. In order to cut any final peace deal, it is not sufficient for two leaders to make a decision. It is necessary to negotiate painstakingly to obtain the consent of not only the different elite blocs at the center, but also to neutralize potential spoilers in the provinces. Meanwhile, the provincial rebels will hesitate to strike a deal with any central elite faction leader because the configuration of power at the center may shift, either offering them a better deal or leaving them stranded if they have made an alliance with the wrong group. And if the provincial rebels have foreign patronage, they may also hope for a new regional dynamic that will boost their patron and give them a more powerful bargaining position, or they may be fearful that signing a deal without the clear backing of that foreign patron will leave them stranded.

This particular configuration of explanations has the special attraction that it explains a persistent feature of Sudanese political life, namely that everything is always open for negotiation, and that the leaders who have risen to the top are uniquely skilled in manipulation. Sudanese governments are routinely accused of perfidy and bad faith. This should be taken less as a judgment about the character of the individuals who rule Sudan than as recognition that such indeterminacy is a structural condition of Sudanese governance, so that any contract will be honored for only as long as power relations do not change. To some observers from abroad, the regime's maneuvers seem to demonstrate supernatural Machiavellian cunning at outwitting the international community. From close up, the Sudanese state appears deeply dysfunctional, often as unpredictable to its own members as it is to outsiders.

The analytical framework propounded in this chapter has no simple label. For the sake of simplicity we will call it the "turbulent state" hypothesis. The remainder of this introductory chapter further develops this hypothesis, seeking to demonstrate how it provides insights into the nature of ethnic and identity politics in Sudan, the nature of conflicts over dwindling natural resources, and "brute causes" accounts of the Sudanese wars.

## Identity Change

SUCCESSIVE GOVERNMENTS in Khartoum have adopted "Arab" and "Islamic" identities reflexively, regularly making Arabization and Islamization into designed political projects. However, the most powerful engine of sociocultural change is not official policy but the sheer imbalance in power, wealth, and cultural assets between center and periphery. The provinces with their disparate, low-status, uncodified cultural archives are no match for central "Sudanese" culture backed by the media, educational institutions and curricula, Islamic missionaries, and traders and administrators with their money and power. Paul Doornbos's essay, "On Becoming Sudanese" (1988), documents the process of cultural change in two small towns in western Darfur, as the mores of the Sudanese elite penetrate and take over local cultural traditions. Doornbos was concerned with a peaceful period in which the main mechanisms for cultural change were the intrusion of the market economy (and associated tastes in food and clothing) and the attempts by itinerant neo-fundamentalist preachers to cultivate an Islamic "orthodoxy" among rural people who were devout and tolerant followers of the Sufi tradition.

Racial discrimination and prejudice are among the most sensitive issues in Sudan (Abdel Salam and de Waal 2000). Sociocultural classification based on skin color corresponds closely with power and wealth, and that members of the northern establishment justify their dominance with reference to racial categories.

Comparable processes of sociocultural change have been accelerated with the use of force during the war. In the early and mid-1990s, "peace camps" in which youth were inculcated with the Islamist values of the regime, losing their prior identities, served as an instrument of both militant mobilization and cultural change. Mass displacement of rural populations has led to a generation of young people losing much of their parents' culture. However, the extent of forced urbanization during the war may contain within it the seeds of a different trajectory of social change. During the last twenty years, the sheer number of displaced people moving to northern cities has meant that they can no longer be readily assimilated into the dominant culture. At the same time, clumsy and violent attempts to impose cultural change have generated resistance, notably widespread adoption of evangelical Christianity among displaced southerners. Through these means, urban centers including greater Khartoum are becoming "Africanized," a process which may yet bring about different patterns of sociocultural change at the heart of modern Sudan.

Some provincial leaders have grounded their resistance in the need to sustain local culture. A leading example is the late Yousif Kuwa Mekki, who led a Nuba cultural renaissance before joining the SPLA, and continued to sponsor a revival of Nuba traditional cultural practices while he was SPLA governor of the Nuba Mountains (Mekki 2002). At its height in the late 1980s, SPLA radio ran regular programs in vernacular languages, with the aim of encouraging a renaissance of local cultures that would in turn contribute to popular resistance against the government.

Many of Sudan's Islamists have been acutely aware of the dilemmas of Islam in Africa.[10] From the 1960s, the Sudanese Muslim Brothers knew that if they followed the lead of their Egyptian parent organization and unreflectively equated Islam with Arab culture, they would stand little chance of broadening their appeal beyond the elites of the north. The Islamists' main political competitors were the sectarian parties (Umma and DUP) which already possessed an Islamic identity based on Sufism—a specifically "African" form of Islam. Turabi saw the Umma Party in particular as raw material for a future nationwide Islamist front (El-Affendi 1991). This had particular relevance to Darfur, as a populous and devout Muslim region. Turabi's deputy was a Darfurian, Ali al Haj Mohamed, who tried to build a popular base for the NIF in the region, promising that common Islamic faith would be a route to national emancipation. Turabi indicated that a color-blind Islamism should trump Arabism. As leading Islamist cadres subsequently conceded, this approach never commanded assent across the NIF leadership. When the Islamist movement splintered in 1999–2000, many leading Darfurians went into opposition. The men who went on to create JEM wrote and circulated the *Black Book*, criticizing both government and Islamists for their bias towards the center and their neglect of the regions.

Darfurian Islamists concluded that they were "too black" to be regarded as equals in the Islamist project.[11]

## Tribalism as Peripheral Governance

ADMINISTRATIVE TRIBALISM has long been the cheapest and most convenient way for a ruler to govern the vast territories of Sudan.[12] The British codified the existing systems in the 1920s into the native administration system. Despite several attempts to abolish tribal administration, successive central governments have repeatedly rediscovered its value. It combines an economical means of local administration, a mechanism for turning out votes and a security strategy.

Across northern Sudan, including Darfur, tribal chiefs and native administrators are civil servants, appointed by the sovereign. Their task is the exercise of power (Asad 1970). Government intrusion into this system is age-old, and the formal hierarchies of local government have come to coexist with the tribal system. The rural aristocracy is conservative and will tend to support the government of the day. Over time, its members have obtained an education and become assimilated into the central elite (Ahmed 2002), so that it is common to see retired civil servants and army officers serving as tribal chiefs. The system almost always serves the interests of the state. But it also has its own logic which gives a measure of independence to chiefs, who cannot escape the fact that they need the support, or at least acquiescence, of the members of their tribe. They live locally and interact with them each day. A tribal leader is also a symbol of his people's aspirations to autonomy. Each tribal chief is expected to possess a legitimate claim to chieftaincy through his lineage. In local lore, memories of better government are associated with a supposedly-traditional system based upon tribe—tribalism can become the vehicle for expressing resistance to the central state.

In addition, intertribal mediation has become the preferred mechanism for conflict resolution, and reconciliation is achieved through the collective payment of *diya* (blood money). This is notably the case in Darfur. Hence the very process of ending the conflict defines it as a tribal dispute and compels individuals to identify with tribes (Abdul-Jalil 1984).

The main challenge to native administration arises from radical provincial leaders who see their rise obstructed by conservative chiefs who support the government. However, they have rarely managed to loosen the grip of the native administration system. What happens is that conservative and radical provincial elites end up competing in trying to offer the same political goods to potential patrons at the center. Those goods are votes and militia. Rural voting patterns tend to follow tribal lines and virtually every militia organized since the 1980s has been based on a tribal or lineage identity. Once conflict has broken out and social trust breaks down, ethnic ties commonly become a stronger basis for organization.

Provincial leaders who become insurgents commonly end up with tribal organization as well, despite their avowed intentions to organize across ethnic groups. The reasons for this include the fact that the government has mobilized their enemies on the basis of tribe, and their own limited options for building support in a society in which tribe has become the main organizing principle, especially for military mobilization.

In passing, it is worth noting that the strategy of sponsoring tribal militias crosses Sudan's international borders. Instigating ethnic conflict has its own logic, so that wars tend to spread. Also, the insurgent strategy of seeking support from a neighboring state leads to tit-for-tat reciprocal destabilization. Sudan military intelligence is implicated in supporting militias in Chad, Central African Republic, Uganda, Ethiopia, and Eritrea.

### Fighting for Survival

NO SCHOLAR WHO HAS DONE FIELD RESEARCH in Sudan subscribes to the simple hypothesis that drought and ecological degradation directly create conflict.[13] But once the crucial intermediate factors of the functioning of mechanisms for conflict management, the management of commercial investment in agriculture, and the control of local administration are taken into account, the links come into sharp focus.

Disputes are inevitable whenever different communities share the same natural resources. Whether and how they are transformed into violent conflict depends upon the means of peripheral governance adopted. The 1970s migration of Zaghawa communities from the desert edge to much more productive areas of eastern and southern Darfur was managed at first with relatively little tension (de Waal 1989, ch. 4), despite the potential threats posed by the diversification of Zaghawa livelihoods and large-scale settlement in areas traditionally controlled by other ethnic groups. Meanwhile, just to the south, in an area of much more plentiful natural resources and little change in either livelihoods or migration patterns, armed conflict did erupt. This instance concerned access to the grazing and water shared between Baggara and Dinka herders along their common border, which is also the north-south border (Keen 1994; de Waal 1994a). The mechanism of intertribal meetings for dispute resolution had broken down by the early 1980s, to be supplanted by active efforts by central government to mobilize the Baggara as a proxy force to fight the Dinka who were suspected of supporting the SPLA.

Subsequently in the 1990s, Darfur suffered the fatal combination of significant immigration from Chad, principally of Arab tribes seeking land,[14] continued internal migration with increasing demands on the land and water resources of key localities, and the deliberate manipulation of the tribal administrative system to augment the power of some groups at the expense of others. The driving force for Darfur's resource competition has been land hunger by camel-herding Arab groups in North Darfur and of Chadian origin. Their weak claims to both rangeland and farmland derive from the historical anomaly that the sultans of Dar Fur did not award them land grants in the eighteenth century, and the relatively recent arrival of the Chadians. Disputes over pasture and pastoral migration routes arise from a number of causes, including increased competition for a small number of migration corridors ill-supplied with water, the growth of irrigated agriculture along seasonal rivers that blocks migration routes, the southward drift of camel herders following the ecological degradation of the desert edge, and the determination of recent Chadian immigrants to open up new pastoral migration routes. Disputes over farmland arise in part because impoverished former nomads looking for land to cultivate find that all the best land is already taken.[15] Land jurisdiction is vested in native administrators, so that the hierarchy of chiefs and the identities of the men in each post have important implications for who can have access to land. Control over land is both the aim of armed conflict and the mechanism whereby warfare is conducted.

This analysis brings us back to militarized tribalism as a mechanism for peripheral governance. Tribal administration was always politicized and militarized—those who try to hark back to a golden era in which tribal authority was fully accepted and pacific are overlooking the long and sorry history of how local authority was constituted and manipulated from time immemorial. However, under the current government, the militarization of local authority has reached new heights. In the Nuba Mountains, chiefs were given jihadist military titles in 1992, and some of them came to operate private police forces and prisons (African Rights 1995). In the segmentary lineage systems of the Nilotic areas, chiefly authority was always contested but corporate action based on lineage solidarity could readily be mobilized. After more than two decades of conflict, authority has passed in large measure to war leaders (Hutchinson 1996). In Darfur, the rebel movements similarly built their mobilizing structures around local *aga'id* (village-defense leaders), marginalizing the chiefs.[16] In the case of the Janjawiid, military organization and lineage authority began to fuse as early as the late 1980s, not least because the structure of intertribal peace talks and compensation payments identified lineages as the responsible entities. Since 2003, the government's mobilization in Darfur has militarized most tribal authority structures. For the colonial authorities, native administration was local government on the cheap; for the NIF, the militia strategy is counterinsurgency on the cheap (de Waal 2004).

What makes militarized tribalism into such a brutally effective engine of conflict and displacement is that the key resource dispensed by tribal leaders is land. Once the government has adopted tribalism as its mode of control, the contest is fought out over livelihoods. It is a war for survival.

Darfur and Southern Sudan constitute Khartoum's "outer periphery" where the ruling elites have modest economic interests. In Kordofan, eastern Sudan, Blue Nile and the immediately adjoining areas of Upper Nile—the "inner periphery"—groups within the elite possess mercantile interest in land. In eastern Sudan, specifically along the seasonal rivers that provide rich irrigable land as well as dry-season pastures for the Beja pastoralists, and in the Nuba Mountains, the location of some of the most fertile soils in the country appropriate for rain-fed plow cultivation, alliances of administrators and merchants have systematically sought to wrest control of land from local herders and smallholders (African Rights 1995; Salih 1999). Land is the asset most essential for rural people's livelihoods, and its forcible expropriation is cause of famine, crime, and armed resistance.

State-driven land seizure is also a major cause of ecological degradation (Ahmed 1988). Mechanized farms are typically established on land that was formerly managed by smallholders and pastoralists. In the search for a quick return, commercial farmers mine the land, harvesting good yields for a few years until the soil is exhausted and infestation by parasitic weeds such as *Striga* have set in. Meanwhile, the dispossessed farmers are compelled to seek more marginal land for their own cultivation, and herders are driven further afield in search of pastures.

In every area in which land has been seized from smallholders and pastoralists, incidents of banditry and vandalism are common. Anticipating violent resistance, the police or army usually conducts land seizures, and those who resist are jailed. Local leaders are also bought off with their own land leases (granted on favorable terms), the authority to organize militias, and even private prisons. In several instances, land expropriations have led directly to rural insurgency. This was the case for the Beja and the Nuba. In both those cases, the insurgencies have been contained and perhaps defeated, but there is a likelihood of recurrent rebellions wherever land confiscations take place. This is also a struggle for survival in which the hand of the government is undisguised.

### "Brute Causes"

POLITICAL SCIENTISTS NATURALLY TEND to favor structural explanations for conflict—"root causes" (cf. Johnson 2003). Those who are close to the action and intent on immediate responses tend to focus on the responsibilities of individuals. The "brute causes" hypothesis originated as a riposte to the focus on root causes and as an argument that, to the contrary, contingency and individual decision—especially bad or malign individual decision—can play a major role in creating conflict. The "brute causes" approach also focuses on how and why political and social conflict becomes violent or sustains high levels of violence.

There are three main variants to the "brute causes" hypothesis. The first is that those who run the country are brutish: they are criminals and necessarily behave as such. This is a logical elaboration of the "bad men do bad things" approach that sometimes serves as the policy derivative of reporting of human rights violations. Human rights organizations (and latterly the Chief Prosecutor of the International Criminal Court) focus professionally upon individual accountability for actions, and hope that accountability for such crimes will help resolve Sudan's crisis. Some activists go further, elevating criminal responsibility to a basic organizing principle, whereby President Bashir and the members of his inner circle are cast as irredeemable criminals who cannot be reformed, intent on genocide, enslavement, and other crimes against humanity. This is the liberal echo of the moral universe constructed by President George W. Bush and the other architects of the "war on terror."

The "turbulent state" paradigm does not obviate individual responsibility for human rights violations, but it does help explain why successive Sudanese governments have ended up in much the same predicament and charged with much the same abuses. The secular nationalist Jaafar Nimeiri, sectarian parliamentarian Sadiq el Mahdi, Islamist visionary Hassan al Turabi, and authoritarian soldier Omer al Bashir have converged on the same mixture of presiding over an unstable regime that endorses extreme violence. We should not have much confidence that simply changing the men in charge will alter this tendency. This is not to excuse criminality, but rather to ask, what is it about trying to rule Sudan that causes its leaders to behave in such a way? Part of the answer must lie in the structure of the Sudanese polity. Another part lies in the fact that the Sudanese political condition selectively permits those with certain skills and proclivities to rise to the top.

There is a less judgmental variant to the "brute causes" hypothesis, which emphasizes the role of individual agency, but points to the structural and cultural determinants of the choices that individuals make. The focus shifts to the decisions made to initiate, escalate, or prolong a war. In the Sudanese case, the core argument would be that because of the difficulty in obtaining a consensus for any bold, sustained, or proactive policy, the default option prevails, which is to allow those groups within the power structure that are ready to act to have a free hand to deal with the immediate manifestations of the problem without regard to the long-term consequences. This structural feature of Sudanese governance would then lead to a pattern whereby the most ruthless and/or opportunistic individuals repeatedly hold the initiative. Although the majority can see the folly of this approach, they are unable to muster the means to bring it to an end. One might call it the "rampage of folly" (cf. Tuchman 1984).

Thus, for example, the decision to formalize the militia strategy in South Kordofan and South Darfur in July 1985 had very far-reaching consequences for how the war was fought. It was an opportunistic action taken in the heat of circumstance, under a transitional government with no plan that looked further ahead than a few months thence. In turn, the decision to prosecute the war using deniable intermediaries fed into a climate of impunity, in which war zones were "ethics-free zones" (de Waal 1994b) and which allowed violent and ruthless individuals to rise. Sudan may not possess more individuals with a tendency to extreme violence than other countries, but the conditions that have prevailed over the last twenty-five years have given plentiful opportunity for such people to exercise their grisly talents and gain reward and recognition. Sudan's political culture has meanwhile become militarized, from the level of communities up to the national leadership and the media. At the apex of political power in Khartoum are men who would find it difficult to survive, let alone thrive, in a transparent and democratic system.

Much the same is true of the leaders of the opposition. Starting and sustaining insurgency is an immense personal gamble. Only those with certain character traits—an outsize ego and sense of personal destiny—will try to start an insurrection, and only those with a high degree of ruthlessness will sustain their leadership of an armed rebellion. John Garang's personal qualities of egotism, vision, and single-mindedness were stamped on the SPLA for twenty-two years. His concerns over maintaining personal supremacy within the SPLA contributed to some critical military decisions which prolonged the conflict, for example the decision not to press home the near-victorious assault on Juba in July 1992. Abdel Wahid al Nur's vanity helped him found the SLA and also stopped him from making the political compromises needed to achieve peace. Minni Minawi's tactical adroitness and readiness to strike first and hardest ensured he rose to the top of the SLA but left him without the political skills and constituency to lead Darfur.

Counterexamples to these traits are found mainly among the civic elites of Khartoum and some of the tribal chiefs of the provinces. The northern establishment has intermittently sustained a remarkable liberal political culture, marked by tolerance and pluralism. Even during the depths of civil war in the late 1980s, Khartoum supported a free press, liberal universities, and open debates in parliament. This metropolitan liberalism is the social truce among the contending elite factions, none of whom can politically dominate the others. The rural aristocrats, especially those with sectarian affiliations, are honorary members of this liberal civic consensus. Twice in Sudan's independent history (in 1964 and 1985), non-violent action by civic activists intent on peace and democracy has brought down military governments. In neither case did the arena of civility extend to the war zones, as the "modern forces" that spearheaded the protests were unable to press their agenda onto their coalition partners, the sectarian parties, and no stable government resulted.

Under "brute causes" we can also include the hypothesis that war creates war. It does so through both supply and demand. Wars result in plentiful availability of small arms and established markets and supply routes for weaponry. More significantly, every war creates a supply of men trained in the use of weapons, at least some of whom have gained some personal satisfaction and material gain from a career in organized violence. Post-war programs for disarmament, demobilization, and reintegration rarely cater adequately to more than a fraction of these men, who are left with their frustrations and grievances. As well as "war before," there is the "war next door" factor: armed conflict in an adjoining country also provides a supply of weaponry and soldiers.

On the demand side, previous wars and nearby wars create motives for armed conflict. Every war and every peace deal leaves a legacy of unresolved grievance. A next-door war generates motives for both insurgents and counterinsurgents for involving the country across the border. In Sudan's case, the second civil war was clearly related to the failures to implement the peace agreement ending the first, and the militia strategy was related to the failure to properly demobilize the National Front fighters after the 1976 invasion. The wars in next-door Eritrea/Ethiopia, Uganda, and Libya/Chad also contributed hugely to the outbreak and recurrence of wars in various parts of the country. Indeed, Darfur's war began in 1987 as an import from Chad. The 1990s Islamist insurgency in Egypt contributed to Sudan taking on the role of sponsor of al Qa'ida. If Ethiopia had been at peace in 1983, it is unlikely that its government would have supported the SPLA, which it did in retribution for Sudanese backing for Ethiopian and Eritrean insurgents. In the opposite direction, the war in southern Sudan contributed to conflict in northern Uganda, and the Darfur conflict has contributed to violence in Chad and the Central African Republic. In short, the "brute causes" approach demonstrates how conflict so readily generates the conditions for its own perpetuation. It is not a competing hypothesis for explaining Sudan's dysfunction as much as a description of what has happened as the years have passed and successive governments have failed to find a political solution to the conflicts they face. As failure has piled on failure, Sudan's crisis has become overdetermined: a thicket of complementary and intersecting reasons why wars continue, ignite in new locations, and reignite in places where a settlement had temporarily been gained.

### War in Darfur and the Future of Sudan

THE WAR, DESTRUCTION, MASSACRE, and mass displacement in Darfur over recent years is unprecedented only in the international attention it has gained. Sudan's peripheries have experienced similar disasters over recent decades, some of them just as horrific, many of them more protracted. Given the structural turbulence of the Sudanese polity, perhaps the only surprise is that Darfur did not plunge into outright war earlier on. That escape was probably due to a sequence of events that left Darfur without the leadership needed for coordinated insurrection. The SPLA tried but failed to instigate rebellion in 1991, and its failure decapitated the region's radical leadership. Thereafter, resistance by Fur, Masalit, and Zaghawa was poorly coordinated. The pact between N'djamena and Khartoum whereby Idriss Déby denied Darfurian rebels any support from Chad held during the 1990s.[17] And many Darfurians continued to hope that the Islamists would offer them political emancipation.

The war in Darfur reveals many unsavory characteristics of the Sudanese polity. It reaffirms what was repeatedly demonstrated in the south, namely that disorder in the peripheries does not pose a threat, either economically or politically, to the class that prospers at the center of Sudan. The country possesses a deep historical pattern, which reached its extreme in the mid-nineteenth century but which has older roots and newer manifestations, in which the Sudanese state has a dominant but factionalized core, an inner periphery of relative stability but highly exploitative relations of production, and an outer periphery or frontier marked by extreme violence and disorder. This pattern has proved durable: it has succeeded in managing (though not resolving) its problems of inter-elite competition and financial crisis without collapsing. Whatever coalition of central elite groups happens to be running the country, the wider establishment of merchants, soldiers, and administrators continues to prosper. Sudan's elites possess a cultural cohesion that belies its political fragmentation. For this group, Sudan's crisis has become a way of life. Doubtless they would prefer peace and stability, but the existing configuration remains manageable.

The governing establishment's main vulnerability is military. The central elites' dominance of the economy has not translated into establishing effective state institutions that exercise effective coercion across all Sudanese territory. The immediate consequence is that the ruling elites are always fearful that a rebellion could run out of control. In turn, those men who promise to maintain the security of the regime have been granted immense power and impunity. The nervous paranoia of Khartoum's security chiefs helps explain their habit of over-reacting to provincial military threats.

Sudan's governing elites are expert at managing multiple crises. This is their modus operandi: they manage bankruptcy and debt, war, and international isolation, while all the time remaining focused on the primary task of outmaneuvering their closest allies and adversaries in Khartoum. The ruling establishment is facing new challenges that it has not yet learned how to manage, such as the huge number of provincial migrants to the center, the unintended consequence of its ravaging of the marchlands. If greater Khartoum is unable to sustain its prosperity and relative social peace, the chickens will have come home to roost. But this has not happened yet, and the government is working on the problem. Short of urban, armed conflict, it is difficult to see how the central elite can be seriously threatened by any continuing disorder and conflict in the peripheries. Even the separation of southern Sudan and the loss of much oil revenue would not be an irreparable loss: Khartoum's clientelism has long extended over its international borders and its influence would doubtless continue in an independent Southern Sudan.

Provincial leaders have long recognized their weakness vis-à-vis the center and their inability to resolve this structural impasse. Many placed their hopes in John Garang's vision of a "New Sudan." Garang held that defining the Sudanese problem in racial terms was to surrender the terms of the debate to the enemy, and the structural crisis should be seen for what it truly was— the political dominance of a small elite. Garang's rival idea was a "New Sudan" that would bring real political and economic equality for the marginalized provinces. The political momentum behind this idea died with Garang in the mountains of northern Uganda on July 30, 2005, but it is improbable that, even had he lived, that the SPLM Chairman would have been able to translate his manifesto into a political reality. Garang's key insight was that the road to stability and democracy in the peripheries lay through Khartoum, and he was late and reluctant in embracing self-determination, the South's opt-out clause. The problem of how to organize and represent the peripheries remains unsolved, and should the South separate, Darfur's difficulties will only intensify.

The "turbulent state" hypothesis, as elaborated in this chapter, has pessimistic implications for the inhabitants of Sudan's provinces. It indicates that provincial war and destabilization is the habitual modus operandi of the Khartoum elites, and implies that Sudan will most probably continue to function in the fashion of a deadly gyroscope, its balance achieved at the price of deadly disorder in its peripheries. It implies that international efforts to achieve peace and democracy are likely to succeed only insofar as they are molded to the modest aims of making the dominance of Khartoum's elites less wantonly violent and exploitative.

This analysis further implies that the CPA, while more fragile than its proponents would hope, does at least hold out the hope of providing a foundation for the southern elites to organize to represent the interests of the south, with the further hope that Sudan's other marginalized peoples will see that joining in this experiment is their least bad option. However, the referendum is due in 2011, so that the remaining time for organizing Sudan's provincial elites into a cohesive bloc is desperately limited—the next few years are perhaps the last hope. Many southern Sudanese recognize a kinship of the oppressed with the Darfurians, but still more fear that the war in Darfur proves only that the northern elites have not changed character and can never be trusted. Along with the slow implementation of the CPA and other signs of bad faith from Khartoum, ongoing war in Darfur nourishes southern separatism, and should the southern Sudanese opt for independence, the options for Darfur will be narrow indeed. The likelihood of an equitable solution to Darfur's war reduces with each passing year along with the increasing likelihood of national partition. Without peace in Darfur, Sudanese can never resolve either the structural impasse of their state or their complex challenge of identity. Sudanese need urgently to reflect on the implications of the wars in their country before their incomplete attempts at solutions further tear the country apart.

# 2

# Native Administration and Local Governance in Darfur: Past and Future

Musa A. Abdul-Jalil, Adam Azzain Mohammed, and Ahmed A. Yousuf

RIBAL AND/OR ETHNIC LEADERSHIP and local government are two types of decentralized governance. Since 1922–1932 in Sudan, the former has come to be known as "native administration." It was so called by the colonial government (1898–1955) to differentiate it from administration by expatriates. It has retained the same name even after Sudan achieved its political independence in 1956 and all levels of government fell into the hands of Sudanese nationals. As most of the population of Sudan lives in rural areas and remains predominately tribal or ethnic, native administration should have been labeled as tribal or ethnic administration.

The ethnic pattern of decentralized governance is best suited for identity groups at the "traditional stage" of development: when identity groups are isolated spatially and intellectually and live in a state of insecurity; when communities are physically isolated by natural barriers (rivers, mountains, deserts, etc.) that impair communal interaction; additionally, they are intellectually isolated and characterized by widespread illiteracy, which impairs intercommunal communication. These traditional societies have lived in a state of insecurity as modern government institutions responsible for the protection of individual's life and property do not exist or are inefficient. Such communities developed their own systems of grassroots administration for the provision of security and communal solidarity. As such, tribal and/or ethnic leadership preceded the colonial era of 1898–1955, but it did not have a consistent type of governance. The different local communities had diverse structures and functions for political leadership.

The new role of the native administration, being one of protecting life and property for individuals, sharply contrasts with a previous role of leading one's identity group (i.e., tribe) to war, attacking other identity groups, or defending one's identity group when attacked by others. The Islamic sultanates (the Funj in Central Sudan, Mussabbaat in Kordofan, and Fur in Darfur) are examples of kingships established by dominating identity groups through the use of force. The current situation in Darfur, in which tribal and ethnic militias attack one another to establish dominance, is not a totally new phenomenon: the same pattern prevailed prior to the colonial rule. It is the phenomenon of leading one's identity group against others. A word needs to be said about the previous leadership patterns as exemplified by the Darfur sultanate, which existed long before its annexation into the larger Sudan.

## Consolidation of the State: The Dar Fur Sultanate

SULAYMAN SOLONG (1650–1680) established the Fur sultanate in around the mid-seventeenth century. Solong also founded the Keira dynasty with which the sultanate is associated. Prior to that, the kingdom was dominated by the rule of the Daju and Tunjur dynasties, though its history remains unknown. Following the emergence of the Fur sultanate from Jebel Marra into the central areas of the region (the richest and most stable parts in terms of soil and water) its growth and expansion was achieved through a combination of peaceful and coercive incorporation of territorial and ethnic groups. In 1787 the seventh sultan, Mohamed Tayrab, extended the Fur sultanate to the Nile by conquering the Funj province of Kordofan to the east and opening Darfur to the expanding commerce of the seventeenth and eighteenth centuries.

Strategically located between the White Nile and West Africa, there was a constant flow of migration to the region from the west and east. In addition, a central strategy of the Darfur sultanate was to encourage immigrants' movement into Darfur to meet the pressing need for manpower. Immigrants came from West Africa, the Nile Valley, and other locations and included holy men (*fuqara*), scholars (*ulama*), and traveling merchants (*jallaba*), as well as poor immigrants seeking to improve their livelihoods.

Another factor that contributed to the expansion and internal consolidation of Dar Fur sultanate was trade. Four major routes converged on the Fur sultanate:

- The route from western *Bilad al Sudan* and going through Barnu, Wadai, Darfur, and the Funj Kingdom to the Red Sea ports and the Hijaz.
- The famous *Darb al Arbain*, or Forty-Days Road, beginning at Kobbei (twenty-five miles north of al Fashir) in Darfur and travelling to and from Egypt. The route passed through Jebel Meidob, crossed the Libyan desert through Bir Natrun, and continued on to Laqiyya, Salima, al Shaff, Kharja, and to Asyut in Egypt. In total it traversed nearly 1,100 miles of desert and took forty days to march, which is how it got its name. The route carried commerce of slaves and ivory from Chad and Darfur to Egypt for over one thousand years.
- A north-westerly route to Tripoli and Tunisia via Fezzan.
- Around 1810 a fourth trade route opened up from Benghazi in northern Libya through the Kufra oasis to Wadai as a result of the decline of the caravan routes in the west. This route thrived after the Islamic reformer and entrepreneur, the Grand Sanusi, established religious hostels (*zawiyas*) and sanctuaries from Kufra in southeast Libya to Wadai in Chad for merchants and pilgrims.

Following the emergence of the Keira sultanate in the central areas of the region, the sultans began organizing the land through the granting of *hakuras* (concessions or estates). The granting of the *hakura* included rights over the territory of the *hakura* and the people living within it. *Hakuras* were granted by the sultan to reward the notables for maintaining control over areas, or granted as a means of attracting newcomers to the sparsely populated kingdom, as well as to provide an income for members of the royal clan. The *hakura* system was part of the political development of the state that reflected the attempt by the center to consolidate its power over the regions. R. S. O'Fahey argued that the estate system arose in response to a need for the sultans to provide for a burgeoning elite within an increasingly centralized state. He has correctly noticed that "the estate system undoubtedly had some impact on the tribal system by substituting a quasi-exploitative relationship for a communal and kinship one, by replacing chiefs 'drawn from the people' by nominees from the centre" (O'Fahey 1980, 68).

### The Administrative System in the Precolonial Era

THE DAR FUR SULTANATES adopted a three-tier system of administration whereby people were ruled largely by their own chiefs. According to this system the administration was based upon four provinces, each divided into a number of district chiefdoms or *shartayas*. Each *shartaya* was further divided into a varying number of local chiefdoms or *dimlijiyyas* administered by a *dimlij*. Some of the larger *shartayas* had chiefs called *sembi* who acted as agents for the *shartays* to control the *dimlijs*. The *shartai* was the sultan's representative and was mainly concerned with justice and taxation. The appointment of the *shartai* was either made or confirmed by the sultan. It was usually made from among the brothers of the previous officeholder. The village sheikhs comprised the third layer of the system. They were responsible for the direct administration of land, tax collection, settlement of small disputes, and all ceremonial activities concerning the upper level of the administrative system.

The Keira sultanate maintained its independence until it was overthrown in 1874 by the Ottoman Empire (Turco-Egyptian rule), who invaded and occupied the northern part of Sudan by 1821. The Turco-Egyptians remained in Darfur until they were defeated by the Mahdist troops in 1883. The brief period of Turco-Egyptian rule was marked by sporadic revolts by the Fur and the turbulent Baggara tribes to the south, for whom the coming of the Mahdi promised the destruction of a hated foreign regime. In 1883 Muhammad Ahmad declared himself as the *Mahdi*, "the awaited one" who had come to restore Islam to its initial purity. His followers, known as the

Ansar, gathered from all over Sudan, and in 1885 the Mahdist forces conquered Khartoum, overthrowing the Turco-Egyptian regime.

The Khalifa Abdullahi, from the Ta'aisha tribe in Darfur, succeeded the Mahdi. From 1885 to 1888 there was a series of revolts against Mahdist rule in Darfur, first by the Rizeigat and then by the Fur. There was also opposition to the Mahdists on the western frontier lead by a *faqi* ("holy man"), from Dar Tama. During this period the Khalifa was wrestling with the challenges of pacification and disputes in Darfur. In addition the state was involved in a policy of the forced migration of the Baggara from their homeland in Darfur to Omdurman. The Baggara did not respond willingly to the call of the Khalifa and they resisted both the threats and promises. However, by 1888 and under the pain of destruction and dispersion by the military power of the Khalifa, the great tribal migrations of the Baggara started. The Mahdist rulers did not retain the administrative structure they found in Darfur; instead they created a system of their own. Since it did not last long enough, the Mahdist system of administration did not affect the time-tested system developed by the Keira sultans.

In 1898 Darfur regained its independence under Ali Dinar, a prominent Fur loyalist from the Keira royal family who was serving the Khalifa in Omdurman until the British troops captured it in 1898. He returned to Darfur and appointed himself sultan, intending to restore the Fur sultanate. Under Ali Dinar, Darfur reverted to its previous system of administration, albeit with a few innovations. By 1916, Darfur was just emerging from a very severe famine, characterized by massive depopulation, localized civil disturbance, and unrest. Although in 1898 an Anglo-Egyptian army under General Horatio Herbert Kitchener reconquered Khartoum, it was not until 1916 that the British annexed Darfur by force, defeating and killing Sultan Ali Dinar.

### The Anglo-Egyptian Condominium Rule and the Introduction of Native Administration

AS A PREREQUISITE to imposing a colonial type of economy in Sudan, the "condominium rule" was imposed for the pacification and consolidation of colonial power. In the case of Darfur, condominium rule meant the reorganization and management of the different tribes by defining the territories and retaining their tribal leaders (wherever that was possible) to avoid weakening them so that the existing systems should not be disturbed. In other words, there was an adoption of a soft-landing policy in which old orders gave way to new, and the new deferred to the old.

The colonial government abolished the Fur sultanate, but retained many of the institutions from the old regime. However, the colonial administration introduced major changes for the entire system: First, the whole system came to be labeled "native administration" (*idara ahlia*). Second and, more importantly, the primary function of the native administrators became that of maintaining law and order within one's identity group, and between it and other identity groups. This responsibility of protecting individuals' life and property is, of course, the primary responsibility of a modern government. However, it would have been extremely costly for the colonial state to provide security institutions for every village and every nomadic camp, so the central government delegated that task to the native administrators. Therefore the system enjoyed the full support of the central government. Third, besides providing a cheap type of administrative machinery, the native administrators were also responsible for tax assessment and collection, the protection of the environment, and the settlement of disputes. Hence, they were supported by a system of "native courts" that ruled according to customs and traditions rather than according to a modern state system of criminal law and civil suit.

The British relied upon a form of indirect rule based on a model developed by Frederick Lugard, the British high commissioner in Nigeria. The Lugardian model, as discussed by AbuShouk and Bjørkelo and reported by Young et al., was a practical form of administration and control that would leave the local population free to manage their own affairs through their own rulers, but under the guidance of the British staff and subject to the laws and policy of the administration (Young et al. 2005). It is based on the following fundamentals:

- A political hierarchy of local chiefs that would derive their power from the central government and be in charge of the maintenance of law and order, organization of labor, and collection of local taxes;

- A parallel hierarchy of native courts, which would deal with minor criminal, civil, and personal cases in terms of customary law and general principals of justice;
- A native treasury that would manage local revenues and pay out the necessary expenses of local authorities and social services; and
- A team of local staff, which would carry out its duties under the guidance of British field officers and remain subject to the laws and policy of administration.

The application of this model in Sudan meant that the British opted for the incorporation of traditional tribal and village leaders into the structure of the government. The native or tribal administration was based on an earlier system of magdumates divided into recognized dars, or tribal homelands. Accordingly *shartais, maliks, nazirs, omdas,* or sheikhs were entrusted with administrative, judicial, and police matters within their territorial domains.

The native administration system was gradually developed and finally legalized after a series of ordinances in 1922, 1925, 1927, and 1928. It was eventually consolidated in the Native Courts Ordinance of 1932, which regulated the administrative and judicial powers of tribal sheikhs and established a hierarchy of local courts in the Anglo-Egyptian Sudan (Abdul-Jalil 1985). This system provided security with minimal staff and finance. The model was modified over time: the local government framework was introduced in 1932, and municipalities, townships, and rural councils were created in 1937. However, traditional tribal leaders with their executive, financial, and legislative powers remained an integral part of the reformed system.

A further development took place in 1951 with the establishment of the Local Government Ordinance. According to this new arrangement the *nazirs* and other tribal leaders assumed an honorary role in the newly established local councils that took over the financial and executive powers previously held by tribal leaders.

The new role of the native administration was to:

- Assure good management of tribal community affairs;
- Allocate land for agriculture and grazing;
- Maintain security;

- Communicate with the local council, and the province- and state-level governments;
- Collect taxes and other levies;
- Settle conflicts related to land tenure;
- Mobilize communities; and
- Chair tribal and subtribal courts.

For the Fur ethnic group, the establishment of the native administration system, which coincided with the end of the independent Fur sultanate, reduced their status to that of just another ethnic group or tribe, which meant their particular economic and administrative privileges were abolished. But for many other ethnic groups this change meant an increase in influence and authority. For more than half a century the native administration provided a system of local governance that managed the use of natural resources and allowed various groups to live in relative peace and stability.

## The Structure of Native Administration

THE NATIVE ADMINISTRATION system consists of three administrative tiers. The uppermost tier is occupied as the paramount chief, although, as we will see below, there have been variations in the title during Darfur's experiments with native administration. The paramount chief is in charge of an entire tribe, and is assisted in most cases by *omdas,* who are usually heads of the tribal subsections, which comprise the middle tier of the administrative structure. At the bottom tier are the sheikhs, who are village or camp heads. All these native administrators are granted the legal powers to maintain law and order and to collect taxes in their respective communities. But in addition the paramount chiefs and some *omdas* may also be given legal powers to settle disputes among individual followers.

A chain of command is maintained so that family heads are responsible to their respective sheikhs who in turn are responsible to the *omdas,* and the latter are accountable to the paramount chief. The system has been particularly efficient in maintaining law and order because every tier knows everything about members of the lower tier(s). When crime is committed, the paramount chief would immediately know about it using the *omda*, the sheikh, and family heads as informants. In Sudan, land tenure is based on communal ownership generally referred to as tribal (i.e., dars). When a crime is committed, it must have been committed within the territory of a communal head, who would then report the crime up the chain. This makes it possible for the paramount chief to maintain law and order within an entire territory.

The system of native administration that exists in Darfur today does not manifest homogeneity of titles or administrative structure. At the uppermost level, usually called the paramount chief, there are eight titles: *maqdum, dimingawi, nazir,* sultan, *malik, shartai, omda,* and sheikh. Many of the titles do not indicate a rank order among them; the significance of the post depends on other factors such as tribal wealth, population size, and dar significance. It is neither internally consistent nor consistent with other hierarchies of chiefs elsewhere in Sudan or Chad. Here is a brief description of each of the native administration titles:

### The Maqdum

The *maqdum* goes back to Fur sultanate times. It identifies an area rather than tribal administration. Today there are two *maqdumates*—one in Nyala and the other in Kutum. The *maqdumates* presumably supervise all other posts in the area, but recently some tribal units, such as the Birgid and the Tarjam tribes of Nyala *maqdumate*, have attained their independence and established their own paramount chiefs. Since this change, Kutum *maqdumate* has not been reinstated and chiefs of tribal groupings in the area, called *maliks*, are acting independently.

### The Dimingawi

This is also a historical title that dates back to the times of the Fur sultanate. It is limited to the Fur homeland of Zalingei. Below the *dimingawi* there are three tiers of native administration: *shartai, omda,* and sheikh.

## The Nazir

The Baggara tribes of southern Darfur use this title, as do the Berti of eastern Darfur. Below the Berti *nazir* there are three tiers: *shartai, omda,* and sheikh. Below the nazir of the Baggara tribes there are only two levels, *omda* and sheikh.

## The Sultan

Today there are three paramount chiefs with the title of sultan in Darfur: that of the Masalit in Geneina, the Gimir in Kulbus, and the Kobe Zaghawa of Tine. While the Masalit and Gimir sultans have the two tiers of *omda* and sheikh below them, there is only one tier below the sultan of the Kobe Zaghawa: sheikh.

## The Malik

The *malik* title is found in al Fashir, among the Berti tribe of Mellit, the Meidob tribe to their north, and the Zaghawa tribes. Previously the Kutum *maqdumate* was supervising the native administration for the whole area but when it was dissolved, tribal *maliks* acted as paramount chiefs. Both the Berti and the Midob *maliks* have two tiers, *omda* and sheikh, below them. Below the *malik* of al Fashir there are generally three tiers: *shartai, omda,* and then sheikh. The al Fashir *malik* is analogous to the Nyala and Kutum *maqdums* in that the *malik* represents an administrative rather than a tribal leadership. Like the Nyala and Kutum *maqdums,* the al Fashir *malik* is in control of administrative units for different tribes.

## The Shartai

The *shartai* title is widely used in the Darfur system of native administration, but in most cases it comes as a second tier in the administrative ladder. It does, however, exist as a paramount chief in the Kabkabiya (Fur) area, below which are two tiers: *omda* and sheikh. However, for practical purposes most of the *shartais* around Nyala and al Fashir act independently of the upper tier of the *maqdum* or the *malik,* respectively.

## The Omda

The *omda* is an intermediary between the village head and the paramount chief. The title was based on an Egyptian model and introduced by the condominium government. Its usage is the same among all tribal groupings. In most places the *omda* is a head of a tribal subsection (lineage) and commands several sheikhs.

## The Sheikh

As a rule the sheikh title is reserved for the village or camp head. But the Zayadiya tribe of North Darfur also use the title to designate the position of their paramount chief. Below the Zayadiya sheikh are two tiers: *omdas* and sheikhs. The northern Rizeigat nomadic tribes also use this title with two tiers below it.

## Native Administration after Independence

IF PROPERLY MAINTAINED, the colonial native administration could have worked successfully to maintain law and order in any traditional communities. The system, however, has been politicized and its function has been changed so that it is no longer serving the purpose of maintaining law and order. In the first place, the leaders of the nationalist movement, who were attempting to liberate Sudan from colonial rule, did not welcome the system. They perceived native administrators to be colonial stooges—created by the colonial government to perpetuate its governance. In the second place, and following the emergence of political parties in the Sudan, the radical political parties, particularly the leftists, regarded the native administrators (especially the paramount chiefs) as the supporters of the reactionary political parties—the Umma Party and the National Unionist Party. Both nationalists and radicals acted relentlessly to attack the native administrators and undermine their leadership position. This gave rise to resistance to native administration at the local level by the newly emerging educated and politically conscious segments of local communities.

The most serious blows to native administration came in 1964 and 1970. Following the October 1964 uprising, a resolution was made by the leftist-dominated caretaker government to abolish the system. However, this government was short-lived. The resolution was not implemented because national elections brought a conservative government, which ignored it. But another radical government ascended to power in 1969 and it was this government that removed most of the paramount chiefs in northern Sudan from office. Since 1964 the demoralized native administrators have become less effective in carrying out their traditional roles of maintaining law and order and resolving disputes among individuals. They were further weakened by the central government's tampering with the native courts under the pretext of separating legal and administrative tasks. This separation has introduced a more contemporary type of administration in which specific institutions are created to perform specific functions. In traditional administration a single ruler performed all functions (i.e., administration, law, governance, and financial responsibilities).

In 1971, President Jaafar Nimeiri's military regime passed the People's Local Government Act, which divided the region into regional, district, and area councils. This local administration replaced the native administration and abolished the jurisdiction and administrative authority of the tribal leaders. Some say this reorganization was the first factor that triggered wide-scale tribal conflicts in Darfur. In southern Darfur province alone, sixteen different rural-council border disputes and conflicts occurred soon after the implementation of this act. This act meant that one tribe could control a locality belonging to another. The government had thus promoted tribal competition. James Morton also argues that the weakening of the native administration has contributed significantly to increased conflict in Darfur (Morton 2004). The critical weakness in modernizing administration lay in the change of emphasis from its previous judicial role (maintaining law and order) to its newer administrative role—a role to which political mobilization has lately been added. Additional rural police stations were established, but the government did not provide the resources necessary for them to operate effectively.

In practice, however, tribal leaders continued to be the acknowledged heads of their groups, and the tribe became a political base to promote its members to senior positions in local councils, as well as members of the regional and national assemblies. Ethnic allegiance and increasing polarization are said to have permeated every corner of government office, as members of the group are considered to be representatives of their tribes and are supposed to work for the interests of their tribal folk. This has been termed "vertical ethnic expansion" by people from the local level to the regional, and even national, levels.

Prior to abolishing native administration, the Nimeiri regime had already dissolved all political parties in the Sudan. The vacuum was filled with an emerging social and political force—the Sudanese Socialist Union, which was then the only recognized party. Both the party and the new local government structures were led by the rural elite such as teachers, small traders, and government employees who occupied the scene in Darfur, resulting in the emergence of new leadership. This leadership played a critical role in shaping the political scene in Darfur in the years following the promulgation of the Regional Government Act of 1980. The leadership was given responsibility for services in Darfur but was provided with wholly inadequate resources.

In 1987, during the second democratic era, native administration was reestablished. This period was short lived and by 1989 the National Islamic Front seized power in Sudan through a military coup of the National Salvation Revolution. Since then the native administration has been subject to structural and mandatory changes to conform to the Islamic orientation of the state. In this respect an Islamic title of *amir* (Arabic for "prince") has been used instead of sultan, *shartai,* and *nazir.* The amir is now a *mujahid* ("religious warrior") leading the tribe to protect the Islamic religion and the country and to maintain the *shari'a* values along the same tracks as the first Muslims during the Prophet Mohammed's era.

A final drastic change for the system was introduced in 1995 by the incumbent government. In the famous Naeema Congress, the role of the native administrator was redefined to be one of a religious leader for each identity group, not only leading them in prayer but more importantly to prepare the youth to go to jihad (holy war) in the south. Instead of curbing identity groups' attacks on each other, native administrators were told to do just the opposite, leading their followers to war. At the local level such as in Darfur, the government has been turning a blind eye to what its new allies are doing with their government-supplied firearms. Instead of directing them against the rebels in the south, they were directing them against local identity groups to settle local scores (e.g., grabbing land).

## Evolution of Local Government in Sudan

TO A LARGE EXTENT the 1922–1932 native administration acts created an efficient system of local government, if the system is defined as the transfer of inherent powers to locally accepted institutions. The inherent powers conferred on the system included judiciary, administrative, and financial responsibilities. Their followers on the whole accepted native administrators, even though they were not popularly elected. In most areas the administrators were relatives of customarily recognized leaders. But the typical system of local government in its council forms has also been experienced by Sudan. Native administration has become an issue of debate among Sudanese intellectuals and is related to the evolution of local governance. Some intellectuals, however, regard native administration as irrelevant and outdated. Others see it as suited to Sudan regardless of societal change. In fact, however, it will have to be viewed as closely related to societal change. Sudan has become transitional rather than purely traditional or purely modern. Native administration must be reformed in order to accommodate the changes that the Sudanese societies (including Darfurian) have undergone so far.

Sudan, more than most African countries, has legislated multiple acts of local government (e.g., 1937, 1951, 1960, 1971, 1981, 1991, 1994). The phenomenon has more to do with the desire of the central government to manipulate the system to serve the political ends of incumbent governments than with the genuine goal of serving the interests of local communities.

The first politically negotiated attempt to change the local government was made in 1937, when the local councils for the municipalities (big cities, townships, and small cities) and rural councils were founded. The colonial government wanted to reconcile the newly emerging elites (mostly leaders of the nationalist movement) and the native administrators so they would sit side by side in local councils and make local decisions rather than letting the elites use their resources to attack both the foreign rule and native administrators. The tribal leaders dominated such councils by being appointed as chairpersons, and most rural councils bore tribal names. The elites were dissatisfied with the experiment and the system was brought to an end in 1971.

A more serious attempt was made in 1951. A local government act was passed based on a 1948–1949 "Marshall Report." A. H. Marshall was a British local-government finance specialist who was commissioned to come to Sudan and assist the government in designing a local government that would best suit Sudan. He spent six months touring almost every Sudanese locality and came up with a system that in many respects is regarded the best system of local government the Sudan has ever had. He divided local councils into five categories according to local communities' "preparedness" to shoulder the responsibility of local governance. Stage five would be a local council with full autonomy. It would be a corporate body that can sue and be sued, own land, have its own stamp, elect its own chair, and be a budgetary unit. By 1960, eighty-six local councils qualified to be full-fledged councils at this stage. Most of them were remarkably successful in practicing real grassroots democracy by freely electing their local councilors and delivering goods and services to their local communities. For instance, the Bahri (North Khartoum) municipality established a sewage system that still exists.

Local communities have introduced a modern system of administration that contrasts with native administration. Whereas in native administration one structure performed all functions, in the local councils different committees within the council performed specialized functions. Moreover, the notion of the elected councilors having supremacy over the bureaucrats was well established. The bureaucrats were there to implement policies adopted by the elected councilors. In other words, the local government system of 1951 was a true training for the local population in practicing a real democracy even before Sudan got its independence. It is the frequent military takeovers in Sudan that have thwarted an otherwise successful earlier experience with a democratic rule.

In 1960 the Provincial Government Act was legislated by the first military government, bringing to an end the provisions of the 1951 democratic local governance. For the most part, council boundaries and council competencies remained the same, but councilors ceased to be popularly and freely elected. Other important landmarks for local government in Sudan include the 1980 Regional Government Act and after 1990 there were several legislations meant to transform Sudan into a federal governance. As authoritarian governments had made all those attempts, no genuine grassroots local government has emerged. Instead, local government institutions remained as long arms of the central government. Another cause of their ineffectiveness is lack of adequate financial resources. Home produced revenues would amount to less than 10 percent of state/region expenditures, since tax bases are spare for most states, which are at a subsistence stage of economy. Central transfers were also meager, amounting to less than 10 percent of the centrally collected revenue. The sound revenue-sharing system created by the Comprehensive Peace Agreement (CPA), which was signed in Naivasha (January 9, 2005), could lead to a solution for the state's finance problems if the CPA is implemented faithfully.

### *Structural Relationship between Local Government and Native Administration*

This chart shows the current organizational structure of the government and native administration.

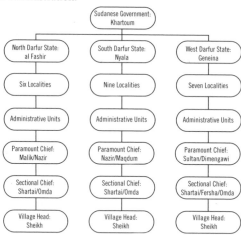

## The Historical Development of the Structure of Local Government Units in Darfur

The table below shows the local government structure of Darfur and the major changes that have occurred since 1916.

| One province with six districts/ rural councils 1917–1974 | Two separate provinces and area councils 1974–1980 | One region with two provinces and area councils 1980–1995 | Three separate states and provinces (date established) 1995–2003 | Three separate states and localities 2003–2005 |
|---|---|---|---|---|
| Darfur province districts:<br><br>Al Fashir<br>Um Kaddada<br>Kutum<br>Nyala<br>Zalingei<br>Geneina | North Darfur province area councils:<br><br>Al Fashir<br>Um Kaddada<br>Kutum<br>Geneina | North Darfur province area councils:<br><br>Al Fashir<br>Um Kaddada<br>Kutum<br>Geneina<br>Mellit | Northern Darfur state provinces:<br><br>Al Fashir<br>Um Kaddada<br>Kutum<br>Kabkabiya (1996)<br>Mellit (2000)<br>Tine (2002)<br>Waha (2003) | Northern Darfur state localities:<br><br>Al Fashir<br>Um Kaddada<br>Kutum<br>Kabkabiya<br>Mellit<br>Tine<br>Waha |
| | South Darfur province area councils:<br><br>Nyala<br>Zalingei<br>Al Da'ien<br>Buram<br>Wadi Saleh | South Darfur province area councils:<br><br>Nyala<br>Al Da'ien<br>Buram<br>Id Al Ghanam<br>Zalingei<br>Wadi Saleh<br>Jebel Marra | Southern Darfur state provinces:<br><br>Nyala<br>Al Da'ien<br>Buram<br>Id Al Fursan<br>Adila (1998)<br>Rihaid Al Birdi<br>Tulus (2000)<br>Kas (2000)<br>Sheiriya (2000) | Southern Darfur state localities:<br><br>Nyala<br>Al Da'ien<br>Buram<br>Id Al Fursan<br>Adila<br>Rihaid Al Birdi<br>Tulus<br>Kas<br>Sheiriya |
| | | | Western Darfur state provinces:<br><br>Geneina<br>Zalingei<br>Jebel Marra<br>Wadi Saleh<br>Habila<br>Kulbus (1996)<br>Mukjar (2000) | Western Darfur state localities:<br><br>Geneina<br>Zalingei<br>Jebel Marra<br>Wadi Saleh<br>Habila<br>Kulbus<br>Mukjar |

## Administrative Changes and the Current Crisis in Darfur

A BRIEF DESCRIPTION of the evolution of territorial administrative structure in Darfur is needed so that the current situation may be better understood. Following the establishment of the colonial rule in 1898, Sudan's territorial area was divided into provinces. Darfur as a province has existed only since 1916, when its last Fur sultan, Ali Dinar, was defeated and killed by the colonial troops. The province was then further subdivided into the districts of al Fashir, Kutum (in the north), Nyala (in the south), Um Kaddada (in the east), Zalingei (in the southwest), and Geneina (in the extreme west). As with all provinces, Darfur province was first administrated by military rulers. This leadership followed the hierarchical structure of the governor-general in Khartoum, who was assisted by a regional governor in al Fashir, and a district commissioner in each district. Later, civil administrators replaced the military cadre, but territorial divisions and rulers' tasks remained the same throughout the colonial era (1916–1955). Both native administration and local government operate within this larger structure of governance; however, following the political independence in 1956, continuous changes of administrative boundaries and titles at both the regional and local levels have been the rule rather than exception. Some of these changes are closely associated with the disturbances that the region has been experiencing.

In 1995 the government further intervened in the administration of Darfur by redividing Darfur into three states, despite fierce opposition and protests from the people of Darfur. This is widely believed to have weakened the social infrastructure and the integrity of the region. As a result of this division, the Fur homelands have been dispersed among the three emerging states. It is no wonder that Fur politicians have considered the restructuring a deliberate attempt to undermine their chances of governing the region. At the same time the government introduced what are known as "emirates" in some dars, appointing supporters as *amirs*. The *amirs* were political appointees who performed the tasks of the native administration. In fact it is an attempt to substitute old titles with new ones. Probably the objective behind such appointments is to get the support and loyalty of the native administrators that the regime failed to mobilize through other methods.

In 1995 there were dramatic changes to the previous systems in West Darfur, when the governor reorganized the state into thirty-four emirates, each one headed by a government-appointed amir. As a result of this, the homeland of the Masalit sultanate was divided into thirteen emirates, including six emirates that were allocated to the Arab tribes in the area, mostly recent immigrants from Chad. This meant the demotion of the authority of the historical Masalit sultanate, which resulted in a devastating ethnic conflict between the Masalit and the Arabs. Tampering with the administrative structure of tribal homelands thus introduced two types of conflict that are interconnected: conflicts over the land itself (mainly between pastoralists and farmers) and conflicts over local governance or local power struggles.

As mentioned earlier, when the British colonized Darfur they opted for a system that would stabilize and pacify the region; namely the indirect rule and the tribal landholdings that were based on the already existing system of the Fur sultanate. That is to say, land in Darfur is divided up into tribal dars. However, this is misleading as it implies that the tribal homeland is an ethnically homogenous territory, which it is not. Members, and even groups of members (other tribal communities with their own sheikh), are found in the homeland of another tribe. For example, a Gimir settlement could be found in Kabkabiya, far from their tribal homeland near Kulbus or Zaghawa in southern Darfur.

The tribal homeland policy favored the larger tribes for which a nazir, shartai, or sultan was appointed to be responsible for the land as well as the people. That meant small tribal groupings and their chiefs came under the administration of these large tribal chiefdoms with or without their consent. The Ma'aliya tribe, for example, came under the administration of the Rizeigat. Many of the small tribes struggled for their own tribal entity and land. The "claim" for an independent tribal administration is linked to ownership of a separate dar because according to customary law, a tribe could not have its own independent administration without having its own dar.

The independent administration includes the native administration as well as modern leadership positions and representation in local, regional, or national institutions. It follows that the majority tribes usually resist the claim for a separate dar by minority tribes as this would lead to the fragmentation of the dar. These situations have been a major source of tribal conflicts in the region, for example, the Ma'aliya-Rizeigat conflict in 1968.

However, these types of local conflicts have escalated when the government has supported the division of the dar. The 1995 decision to divide Dar Masalit into thirteen emirates meant the demotion of the authority of the Masalit sultan. This resulted in a devastating ethnic conflict, which led to widespread insecurity. Moreover it threw the region into a grassroots-administration vacuum. As a result the West Darfur state was declared an area of emergency from 1995 to 1999.

Southern Darfur state has recently witnessed the founding of five independent native administration units (of the level of paramount chieftainship), which, in effect, means a separation from the existing ones. As an example, the Tarjam nazir and the Beigo sultan have been separated from Nyala maqdumate, which has meant the reduction of the authority of the maqdum, who belongs to a Fur royal family. The incumbent maqdum, Ahmed Rijal, was dismissed from office by the *wali* (governor) and replaced by a cousin, Salah Mohamed al Fadul. Additionally, a new emirate has been established for a number of tribes in Kas, which includes African and Arab tribes. The new amir is a prominent Fur named Mansour Abdel Gadir, who seems to be in the favor of the government. And finally, the Ma'aliya have finally managed to win their independence from the Rizeigat as part of a deal to settle their most recent conflict. The deal involved setting free eighty-one Rizeigat men who had been convicted and sentenced to death following the mass killing of Ma'aliya. It is doubtful whether such a settlement will create sustainable peace and finally eliminate conflicts between the two groups.

A parallel critical issue is that the northern Rizeigat who are camel pastoralists (*abbala*) do not have their own dars. This was in part because the granting of tribal dars favored larger tribes, and also because at the time land was not an issue—there were no land shortages and the prosperity of Arab tribes depended on transhumant pastoralism and trade, not land ownership. Recently in western Darfur, there have been additional pressures from the influx of Chadian Arab groups. Many of these groups have close ties with the

Sudanese nomadic groups. This is mainly the case in West Darfur, which has been severely damaged compared to the other states.

The dar issue became more critical following the pressures on the natural resources as a result of the ecological degradation combined with expanding rain-fed wadi cultivation. One researcher has put it clearly, "With the pressure of the drought and in their quest for pasture and water, pastoralists violated customary arrangements that organize access to pasture and their passage during seasonal movements. While peasant and commercial farming expansion (both goz and wadi cultivation) encroached on pastoralist and transhumant grazing rights, pastoralists also have tended to deviate from defined and agreed upon seasonal movements routes, grazed on farms, and damaged crops. Competition over resources created conflict among pastoralists on the one hand and between farming communities and pastoralists on the other, with negative implications for the environment and social peace within and between communities" (El Amin 1992, 82).

The case of Waha locality needs some explanation because it looks like an anomaly in the administrative structure of North Darfur state. Its story goes back to the year 1982, when a "Nomads' Rural Council" was created within the Kutum area council to cater to the special needs of the Arab camel-herding nomads. It incorporated the native administrative units representing the subsections of Mahamid, Mahariya, Ereigat, Etaifat, and Awlad Rashid. The Nomads' Rural Council was responsible for tax collection, supervision of migration routes (*maraheel*), and distribution of sugar rations. The council did not have any geographical boundaries because it operated wherever the camel nomads moved within the whole of Darfur. When Darfur was divided into three separate states in 1995, the Nomads' Rural Council became part of Kutum province in North Darfur state. In practice, this limited its area of jurisdiction to North Darfur. However, in 2003, local government units were reorganized and many local councils were recombined to form larger units under the title of "locality." At this point the Nomads' Local Council was promoted to the level of a locality under the name "Waha."

Waha locality's regulations say that it supervises more than twenty-one nomadic camps (*damrat*) and eleven animal migration routes, and coordinates some services relating to basic schools and small health units (i.e., dress-

ing stations). The new locality headquarters is in al Fashir, where a commissioner and his staff reside, away from the nomads themselves. It soon became
clear that the reasons behind the creation of the Waha locality have more to
do with politics than with the need to provide services for the nomads. After
its inception the Arab nomads around Kutum became more hostile to the
surrounding communities, completely separating from them after the crisis.
The main mission of the Waha commissioner is to mobilize tribal support for
the government cause of fighting the new armed-opposition forces.

The central government has been responsible for the erosion of the native
administration's authority and capacity through various initiatives to reorganize local administration, including the 1971 Local Government Act and
the 1995 redivision of Darfur Region into three states (see table above). This
resulted in the politicization of the native administration, and the increasing
polarization between tribal groups in Darfur. Tribal administration became
closely linked with the political processes of government—particularly during elections to the regional and national assemblies.

## Other Factors Affecting the Role of Native Administration

APART FROM CHANGES due to administrative interventions,
native administration has been negatively affected by a host of other factors.
Although some of them have already been considered, it is worth mentioning all of them briefly:

- The spread of modern education has broken the intellectual isolation
  of local communities, paving the way for the adoption of new ideas.
- The flow of labor migration, triggered by the extreme underdevelopment of the region, has brought a considerable number of Darfurians
  into contact with city life and acquainted them with new forms of
  political relations.
- The political maneuvering by various central governments of the day
  (mainly the Nimeiri and Bashir regimes), which has been mainly
  driven by the need to get the support of native administrators to

mobilize rural masses in order to support government programs.

- Increased commercialization of economic activities and engagement in commerce with external centers has helped create a new local economic elite that is less amenable to control by native administrators.

- Environmental degradation has resulted in increased competition over natural resources, which has led in turn to the disregarding of and/or the change of customary land tenure, thus making it more difficult for native administrators to perform their traditional role of settling land-related disputes.

- Widespread armed robbery coupled with the proliferation of small arms has rendered native administrators helpless and dependent upon their poorly armed traditional guards.

- Since the inception of regional governance in 1980, regional politics has become increasingly based on ethnic polarization.

- The opposition groups whose leadership is drawn from young, educated Darfurians have recently further undermined the native administration system. These groups are often at odds with the tribal system because the traditional leadership is perceived as being allies of the government. Because of this, the rebel leaders have regarded most of them as their enemies, killing some and threatening others.

- The separation of many groups from their tribal leadership, due to displacement during the current crises, has weakened the authority of native administration.

- The conflict has also meant the loss of previous intertribal agreements and mutually beneficial arrangements.

This continual erosion of the native administration raises questions of its legitimacy and relevance in Darfur today.

## The Government-Attempted Reform: Can It Work?

AS WE HAVE seen, native administration was introduced by the colonial authorities with the aim of maintaining law and order in a vast country with a majority of its population living in the rural areas and participating in a traditional economy. Because the tribe was the most important political group an individual could identify with, it followed that tribal leaders became the focus for the new system, which developed from indirect rule to native administration. Since its inception in the early 1920s, the system has undergone many changes. Much of the time it oscillated back and forth according to the current political climate.

The system of local government was introduced later, in 1937, with the aim of gradually replacing native administration, which at the time constituted the lowest tier in the governmental structure. Subsequent events have shown the difficulty of dispensing with native administration. Modernist forces in Sudan were bent on doing away with it, but without any measurable success. The Ingaz regime has understood the difficulty of abolishing the system and accordingly worked to exploit it to serve its own political agenda. The current state of affairs in Darfur is a manifestation of the failure of the regime's plans in this regard.

The government has recently made a concerted effort to reform local government and native administration to better serve its own goals. Since 2003 a number of acts, provisional laws, and regulations relating to local government and native administration have been promulgated. Following the Naeema Congress of 1995, the national assembly passed the 2003 Local Government Act, which stipulates that one of the duties of local government bodies (i.e., localities) is to mobilize the public in order to defend "the faith and country."

As for native administration, the Ministry of Federal Governance produced a model of regulations, and each state was asked to enact its own regulations in line with it. In 2004, Northern Darfur state produced its own act for regulating the work of native administration. It also issued an act for regulating the provisions of the 2003 Local Government Act.

The judiciary also produced a 2004 act for town and rural courts, which deals mainly with customary law courts. Although judicial powers are supposed to be separate from administrative ones, in the case of native administrators they are allowed to combine the two. Appointments and accountability are all handled through the judiciary.

Although the general framework for the acts and regulations are structurally similar to what used to be practiced within administrative circles in Sudan, it seems that most of the provisions have been carefully phrased in order to facilitate the total manipulation of these institutions by the Ingaz regime. Some of these provisions warrant brief comments here for their relevance to native administration:

- All acts and bylaws include provisions for public mobilization that are easily manipulated by the ruling party to serve its political agenda. This means that even where elections are clearly stipulated, they cannot be conducted with reasonable transparency, that is, cannot be fair and free.
- The commissioner (*moutamad*) is a political appointee whose main duty is to support the central government. The *moutamad* is appointed by the *wali* in consultation with the president to supervise security matters. Security is generally defined as that of the regime and not of the people.
- The Local Government Act stipulates that 40 percent of the agricultural and livestock taxes are transferred to the state treasury. Given that the localities are responsible for providing basic services for the people (e.g., education, health, water) it looks very unfair. The state also receives funds from the center. It is clear that such an arrangement works to perpetuate the political system rather than enhance development (which the act considers one of the duties of localities). In fact, the failure to induce rural development has been one of the most striking shortcomings of local government in Sudan.
- Supervision of the formation of people's committees is also one of the duties of the commissioner. These councils are largely subordinate to the administrative unit. They are mainly concerned with the management of public affairs. The commissioner wields considerable authority over the committees.
- Although native administrators are supposed to help implement almost any government directive that comes from above, they do not directly participate in the locality councils or people's councils.

- The regulations stipulate that the native administrator shall help and supervise the distribution of land for the people within each dar. According to the customary-tenure system in Darfur, land managers (*sid-al-ardiya*) exercise the distribution of land on behalf of the *hakura* owners. The paramount chief of the area (or any level of native administration) sanctions these distributions and, most importantly, resolves land disputes. To entrust the paramount chiefs with land distribution is to open floodgates for new types of conflicts.

- The regulations also refer to the duty of the native administrators in public mobilization, which clearly signifies their political roles. Historically, native administrators did not act as supporters of political parties or systems, except illicitly. During parliamentary elections under democratic regimes, native administrators were supposed to be neutral. In cases where they chose to support a given party, it was considered a personal concern and the people were not obliged to follow suit. Under the current situation, the native administrators are required to mobilize tribe members to support the government party, using all possible means. Not doing so will cause the native administrators to fall into disfavor in the eyes of those who appointed them.

- The regulations also discuss training the native administrators, which in reality refers to their political reorientation. This is completely against the logic of accepting and preserving native administration, which is supposed to depend on customary practices to perform its main role of promoting order. Training means inculcating new values from outside the social system. Native administration is not meant to continue forever but rather to operate provisionally as a mechanism that serves rural communities in a transitional stage. If these societies are ready to depend solely on modern methods of participatory local government, there will no longer be any reason for keeping native administration.

- It is noticeable that appointments for native administration positions do not include any democratic procedure. The phrase "shall be appointed after consultations" frequently appears in various regulations and acts. It is clear that such unspecified consultations open the way for political maneuvering, which sometimes can be against the will of the majority of the people, who are the members of a given constituency, and whose opinion should matter most.

- The regulations of native administration do not specify the financial rewards for those holding posts at each level. Instead it leaves it for the governor and the commissioner to decide how to compensate native administrators. Evidently, the situation calls for manipulating the native administrator by material rewards or their denial.

- It is rather strange that the provisions of the Rural Courts Act exclude land ownership from the jurisdiction of such courts. In Darfur, many of the cases presented to customary-law courts dealt with land-related disputes. Land ownership in Darfur has a special meaning different from what evoked the 1970 unregistered land act. Customary ownership of land follows the *hakura* system, which was sanctioned by land charters, which were issued by Keira sultans. The government of Sudan does not seem to consider such charters valid documents. Access to land is a problematic issue in Darfur that needs a more careful approach.

It is obvious that the efforts made by the Ingaz regime regarding the reform of native administration cannot be expected to improve its role in stabilizing the situation in Darfur. The need grows for returning the region, as soon as possible, to its heritage of peaceful coexistence based on local conditions, rather than imposition by the incumbent government (Young et al. 2005).

### Prospects for Native Administration in the Stabilization of Governance

HAVING REVIEWED THE HISTORY of native administration in Darfur, its role in local government, and the changing conditions and difficulties facing it today, a few concluding remarks are in order regarding its future prospects.

Despite recent changes in Darfurian society, native administrators still command respect in many communities. It is important to remember that these communities are largely rural and still adhere to tribal values. As such, native administration is connected with tribal/ethnic identity. For this reason, when members of a given community are not happy with their leader, they think of replacing that leader rather than abolishing the system altogether.

Native administration has no doubt undergone considerable changes over the years; people's attitudes have also shifted. In order to cope with the need for modernization and communication with the outside world and with government circles in the urban centers, many groups have promoted young, educated leaders to hold posts in the system of native administration. As examples, the Habbaniya and Birgid have chosen retired generals as their paramount chiefs. The Mima have a university graduate as the deputy paramount chief.

Local governance and native administration in Darfur are not uniform, and there is an urgent need to learn lessons from different local approaches to reconciliation and maintenance of order.

The successes of native administration in the past were mostly felt in the area of conflict resolution and management. Most importantly, native administrators have been effective in using their native courts to settle land-related disputes. For this reason it is important that customary-law courts continue to function with the effective participation of native administrators, who should also be given jurisdiction to handle land-tenure and land-use cases according to known customs.

Native administrators are effective in processes of mediation regarding grassroots conflicts, but they are not effective in situations involving regional politics. In fact, the modern, educated elite and politicians can exploit the native administrators to support region-wide ethnic polarization, as illustrated by the conditions that led to the formation of Arab Gathering in 1987. As far as the conflict between the armed opposition groups and the central government is concerned, the involvement of native administrators seems irrelevant and out of place. The government effort to present native administrators as viable political leaders of Darfur in an effort to bypass modern educated elites is a fruitless exercise, and may be even counterproductive.

While understanding the fragile and limited capacity of native administration in many areas, the international-level talks should recognize and seek to enhance the function of the tribal leadership at the grassroots level. It is also important to recognize that native administration is not free from the political influence of the central government, which has its own political agenda. For this reason it is essential that its functions are depoliticized, clearly articulated, locally specific, and locally accepted by people at the grassroots.

It should be understood that native administration is not an ideal system for the distant future but it should be tolerated now for reasons of expediency. Therefore, a concerted effort should be exerted to make it more attractive to younger generations by making it more democratic, more transparent, less corrupt, and staffed by more-literate leaders whenever possible.

Lastly, Darfur needs a stable administration, both at the local and regional levels, that is capable of transforming conflict and embarking on reconstruction and development. In order for such a mission to succeed, the whole region should be reunited as one administrative unit in relation to the central government. Such a step is supported by multiple factors pertaining to history, ecology, economy, and politics.

# 3

## *Darfur: A Conflict for Land?*[1]

### Jérôme Tubiana

ON MAY 5, 2005, in the Nigerian capital of Abuja, the government of Sudan and one of two factions of the Sudan Liberation Army (SLA) signed the Darfur Peace Agreement (DPA). One of the more positive aspects of the DPA is its recognition of Darfur's traditional land-tenure system. The demand for this came from non-Arab and Arab traditional leaders alike, and was endorsed by the rebel negotiators. This was a major blow to the Janjawiid constituencies—the landless Arab camel-herding groups of northern Darfur. At the same time, however, the DPA remains vague on the overall question of land; it defers the final resolution of the issue to a set of negotiated processes that will take time to play out.

In the short term, the viability of peace in Darfur hinges on two intensely intertwined issues. The first is the disarmament of the Janjawiid militias. This is one of the points the DPA is clearest on. The second is the swift return of displaced populations—both internally displaced persons (IDPs) and refugees—to their pre-conflict land. This, too, depends on security, but it is less clearly spelled out in the agreement.

The extent of forced displacement over the past three and a half years has made the war in Darfur one of the worst human rights disasters in the world. There are no reliable figures, but in March 2005, the United Nations put the number of deaths at 180,000—multiplying an earlier World Health Organization estimate of ten thousand deaths per month by the eighteen months of conflict since October 2003, even though the conflict started in early 2003. Other estimates place the number of deaths closer to three or four hundred thousand, aggregating violence, disease, and malnutrition (International Crisis Group 2005a). The problem is that these estimates are not based on solid field data. All told, the figure that perhaps best illustrates the impact of the crisis is that of the two million people who have been forced from their villages—1.8 million displaced within the three states of North, West, and South Darfur, and two hundred thousand refugees in Chad. One in three Darfurians is displaced.[2]

Some observers have spoken of genocide, most notably high-ranking U.S. government officials. The UN Commission of Inquiry stopped short of a genocide determination, limiting its findings to "crimes against humanity" and "crimes of war" (United Nations 2005). Another term frequently heard in human rights and media reports is "ethnic cleansing." This term highlights the fact that civilians were forced off their land because of their ethnicity—their villages destroyed, their livestock and other belongings looted. Leaving aside the more spectacular testimonies of mass executions, the attacks of the Sudanese military and its Janjawiid militias on Darfur's non-Arab villages are arguably more striking because of the numbers of people that have been displaced rather than the numbers of people killed. The massive displacement is not merely a consequence of the attacks, but rather a central war aim of the attackers, who are clearing entire areas of their original inhabitants.

The Janjawiid recruit mostly from groups claiming an Arab identity, even though this belies the region's long history of intermarriage between ethnic groups. The majority of the militias' victims belong to fifteen or so "non-Arab" groups, including the Fur, the Masalit, the Zaghawa, the Tunjur, the Berti, the Daju, the Meidob, and the Birgid.[3] Some Arab groups have tried to remain more or less neutral, at least as far as tribal structures go. Conversely, a number of Arabized non-Arab tribes joined the government militias, for reasons both strategic and linked to identity—these include segments of the Tama and Gimir, the Kinneen (who are Tuaregs from the western Sahel), and some Fallata (who are mostly Pula and Hausa migrants from West Africa).[4] With the exception of the Gimir, many of these pro-Khartoum, non-Arab groups originally came from neighboring countries—especially Chad, because of successive wars in that country since its independence in 1960—as did some of the Arab groups involved in the violence.

The above exceptions notwithstanding, the war has both exposed and aggravated a feeling of difference between Arabs and non-Arabs. The divide between the two has probably never been as stark as it is today (Tubiana 2005, 165). The divide is not based on skin color. It is not based on religion—all of Darfur's ethnic groups are Muslim. Nor is it based on culture, as Arabs and non-Arabs share strong cultural traits and bonds. It is not based on language—non-Arab groups such as the Berti, Birgid, Beigo, Borgo, Mima, and Gimir speak Arabic as their native tongue even though they do not see themselves as Arab. Nor does the cleavage really represent a difference in way of life—most Arabs may indeed be nomadic or semi-nomadic herders, and most non-Arabs sedentary farmers, but there are non-Arab nomads—the Meidob, the Zaghawa, the Bideyat—as well as many Arab farmers. Rather, the basis for the cleavage is the claim to an Arab identity that has less to do with the above criteria than it does with often-fictional patrilineal lineages that lead back to mythical Arab forbearers. There may be little, if any, historical accuracy to these constructs. But to those who invoke them, they are fact and truth.[5]

One of the more striking early warning signs of the conflict was a dramatic increase in violent incidents between farmers and herders. One cause for these incidents was the cyclical droughts of the 1970s, 1980s, and 1990s, which forced the herders to encroach on the lands of the farmers. These clashes did not necessarily pit Arab versus non-Arab but they did lead, in 1987–1989, to a wide-ranging conflict between the sedentary Fur and a broad coalition of both cattle- and camel-herding Arab tribes. For the first time, nearly all the Arabs of Darfur came together, united by a new pro-Arab ideology, which was backed by Libya, and by successive governments in Khartoum from 1986. The central government's support for the Arabs continued even as the ruling parties in Khartoum—first the Umma Party and then the National Islamic Front (NIF)—sought and found support among non-Arab elites in Darfur (Harir 1994, 149–150).

It was during these conflicts that the term "Janjawiid" first appeared. A local Arabic word, it describes horsemen armed with Belgian G3 assault rifles. Today, they are known as Janjawiid—"devil-horsemen" (*jinn-jawad*)—though they themselves prefer to call themselves *fursan* (horsemen), *mujahidiin*, or, curiously, *bashmerga*, in reference to the Kurdish peshmerga militias of northern Iraq (Tubiana 2005, 174).

From 1994–1995 onward, the Masalit of western Darfur became the next victims of orchestrated Arab militias seeking access to land. By the time the two new rebel groups, the SLA and the Justice and Equality Movement (JEM), appeared in early 2003, widespread intercommunity violence over land had already begun taking place across Darfur. The two rebel groups made regional, and even national, claims that aimed to transcend ethnic cleavages with demands for a more equitable distribution of power and wealth for all of Sudan. But their base was for the most part non-Arab, with heavy representation from the Zaghawa, who provided many of the field commanders, and Fur. Deeply unsettled by the rebels' stunning early military successes—and in particular by the April 2003 raid on al Fashir—Khartoum mobilized militias from local Arab populations, a strategy that had served it well in South Sudan. It is hard to tell if Khartoum accused non-Arab groups of supporting the rebellion in the hope of cutting the rebels off from the civilian population. The violence physically and financially mauled non-Arab communities, but failed to remove the rebels from the areas they held. It also drove non-Arab civilians to join the rebels. At the same time, after more than a year of indifference in the face of mounting atrocities, reports of the violence finally attracted the attention of the international community (Tanner 2005b). Meanwhile, on the ground, the Janjawiid pursued their own agenda, forcing farmers from their villages then laying claim to their land.

The first field study carried out in Darfur during September and October 2004 showed that the prevailing opinion among both non-Arabs and Arabs was that the war was primarily a broad struggle for land that had grown out of earlier, more localized conflicts.[6]

In 2003, local conflicts in Darfur had started to spin out of control at the same time that talks between Khartoum and the southern Sudan People's Liberation Army (SPLA) were gaining momentum. Part of Darfur's non-Arab elite, a number of whom had recently followed Islamist leader Hassan al Turabi during his fall from power, decided they could no longer wait on the sidelines of the North-South negotiations. As a result, the new rebels received support from sources as varied as Turabi, the southern rebel leader John Garang, and Eritrea, as well as from some Zaghawa from Chad, especially within the military of Idriss Déby (Flint and de Waal 2005, 81–85, 92–96; Marchal 2004 and in this volume; Tubiana 2005, 177–181, 84–91).

The "land issue" only came politically to the fore in 2005. Until then, both the SLA and JEM had tended to ignore it, not wanting to mire their struggle in "tribal" issues, since their public focus was on national issues. Issues of land took second place to the overall development of Darfur. Part of the reason for this is that many of the rebel leaders were young urbanites who had lived outside Darfur for long stretches of time. They were educated in Arabic and sometimes in English, and were not always in tune with local issues. In addition, many did not belong to leading chieftaincy families, whose strong power is rooted in tradition. This is the case with the rival leaders of the SLA—Abdel Wahid Mohamed al Nur (a lawyer from the Fur tribe) and Minni Arkoy Minawi (a Zaghawa teacher)—as well as with the SLA's influential humanitarian coordinator, Suleiman Jamus (an engineer from the Zaghawa tribe), who opposed both Minawi and Abdel Wahid.[7] Until 2005, JEM and especially the SLA had been rather hostile to senior traditional leaders, whom they mostly viewed as stooges for Khartoum.[8] In 2004, the SLA (Minawi) even assassinated the Zaghawa *malik* of Um Buru. Nevertheless, some SLA and JEM leaders do come from traditional elites and they have somewhat succeeded in reconciling rebels and traditional leaders.[9]

Indeed, the SLA and JEM now seem to have come to the conclusion that tenure issues are important to local populations. Land became a leading issue during the negotiations in Abuja. Of course, land is not the only issue at stake in the conflict. Bringing peace to Darfur will also require progress on such issues as the disarmament of government militias and rebels alike, the prosecution of war criminals, power sharing at the local and national levels, wealth sharing arrangements, and reconciliation among communities. Movement on any of the above points, however, will require addressing the land issue.

## Land in Darfur

TO DATE, ANALYSES of the Darfur crisis have failed to focus on the issue of land. It is, however, a central driver of the conflict: the Janjawiid recruit mostly from the Arab camel herders of Northern Darfur who have never enjoyed traditional land rights, and who aim to gain access to the land they increasingly feel they need because of environmental pressure.

### The Uneven Distribution of Traditional Land Rights

Darfur's traditional land tenure system was developed under the Fur sultanate, a centralized state with effective bureaucratic and military systems that lasted from the seventeenth century until its destruction by the British in 1916. Masters of the land, the sultans distributed *hawakir* (territories with clear boundaries, singular, *hakura;* O'Fahey and Salim 1983, 12–21) to Fur leaders and dignitaries, to leaders from other groups who were their vassals, and to *faqis* (Muslim scholars). Often, the subjects and "guest-subjects" from other ethnic groups who also lived on the land in fact collectively assumed territories given through *hakura* to an individual. Thus the *hawakir* of a given chief would make up his people's dar (house, country, land). This would not prevent the other groups present from sharing in the land. The sultanate was known as Dar Fur—land of the Fur—but it was in fact a multi-ethnic patchwork of Fur territories and non-Fur dars.

The multi-ethnic nature of the sultanate and its land tenure system remains present in the memory of Darfurians today, but in different ways. Some regret the putative communal harmony of days gone by, while others view the dars as hard-and-fast ethnic territories. Both views are at odds with historical reality.

The sultans would sometimes allocate tenure rights—and the political authority that came with them—to the rivals of existing chiefs they deemed to have grown too independent. The new chiefs were often selected from the same ethnic group as the existing chief, sometimes from the same clan or even family. The sultanate was thus able to confirm its respect for the existing chieftaincies. The only notable exception to this was the Tunjur, who exerted paramount control over the region before being forced out by the Fur. The heart of the Tunjur kingdom, Dar Furnung, northeast of present-day Kutum, was "given" to the Falanga clan of the Fur, and the Tunjur royal clan had to move to Jebel Hires, near Shangal Tobay, south of al Fashir (Tubiana 1984).

Not everyone, however, has equal access to land. In southern Darfur, the main Arab and non-Arab communities enjoy similar tenure rights. The four main Arab groups—the Rizeigat, Habbaniya, Beni Halba, and Ta'aisha—have all had dars since the days of the sultanate, and as early as the eighteenth century for the Rizeigat. In the north and west, on the other hand, practically all of the non-Arab groups have land while most of the Arab groups do not, despite the fact that many of them were already present during the sultanate. Most farming communities have traditional tenure rights, while nomadic communities do not—the herders' highly mobile nature is part of the reason why they do not have, or did not need, dars or *hawakir*. The dar-less Arabs include the northern Rizeigat, or Rizeigat *shimaliya*, who are known otherwise as Rizeigat Abbala or Jammala (camel herders), and are distinct from the Rizeigat Baggara (cattle herders) of southern Darfur.

The northern Rizeigat and other groups only have *damrat* (singular: *damra*) inside non-Arab dars. In both Darfur and Chad, the word *damra* traditionally refers to "the habitual settlement place of [Arab] tribes, and often the location of dry-season farms"(Clanet 1994, 651) or "a small, temporary village that hosts those who cannot accompany the herds to their grazing grounds"(Jullien de Pommerol 1999, 363). In Darfur today, a *damra* describes semi-permanent and even permanent encampments where some services may be available, such as a school or a primary health center. These *damrat* groups are, in theory, under the authority of the non-Arab chiefs whose lands they live on, at least for part of the year. Beginning before the war, however, support from the Khartoum government had enabled these groups to establish a measure of independence from the non-Arabs.

The Arab groups that have dars—the Habbaniya, Beni Halba, Ta'aisha, and Rizeigat Baggara in southern Darfur, and the Beni Hussein in northern Darfur—have sought to remain neutral in the present conflict, at least as far as their tribal leaders are concerned.[10]

The Janjawiid have recruited most heavily among the tenure-less Arabs of northern and western Darfur. Several factors have, over the years, sharpened these groups' hunger for land—drought, growing livestock holdings, the encroachment of farms on dry-season pastures, and the desire to settle. The Janjawiid also recruited the landless Chadian Arabs who have settled in Sudan since the 1960s, fleeing drought, wars, and repressive regimes on their side of the border.

The rebels, on the other hand, found recruits among the Fur and Zaghawa militias that were set up by the various communities to defend their land against the predations of armed nomads.[11] Access to water and pasture was one reason the Zaghawa entered the conflict—a key point, as this led to the formation of the first organized rebel groups in 2002. The newly formed SLA and JEM then moved their demands from the local to the regional and national levels—from issues such as unpaid *diya* (blood money) to the construction of an all-weather road to the Nile Valley.[12]

## Contested Lands

TWO TYPES OF LAND are of interest to the dar-less Arabs. First are the water holes and pasturelands on the migratory routes of Darfur's northern belt. Second, to the south and southwest, are the richer, well-watered lands where a number of Arab groups would like to settle.

The first type of land is found mostly in two broad swathes that stretch north of Jebel Marra into the Sahara desert: the greater Kutum area and the territory between Mellit and the Kordofan border to the east.[13] Arab groups wish to establish sedentary camps in these areas, allowing them to access water, education, and health services. A certain number of such *damrat* exist in the Kutum area—camps that northern Rizeigat (Mahariya, Mahamid, and Etefat), Ereigat,[14] and Awlad Rashid[15] established at different points in the past. Mostly, non-Arab chiefs of the Tunjur, Fur, and Zaghawa tribes allocated these damrat to the Arabs. But over time, in the context of a weakened native administration, and with the active support of successive Sudanese governments, the *damrat* took on greater independence. Even before the current conflict, the NIF's government considered the damrat to be embryonic Arab dars, a policy that many non-Arab chiefs and rebel leaders see as one of the root causes of the violence.

Relations between the Arabs and their non-Arab hosts deteriorated as local clashes over resources intensified. Increasing divisions among the northern Rizeigat also contributed to their tensions with non-Arabs. The northern Rizeigat had first belonged to the greater Rizeigat Baggara group of southern Darfur. In 1925 they acquired their own chieftaincy, which the Mahariya controlled. The Awlad Rashid were attached to this chieftaincy because of their small numbers and common migration routes. Little by little, however, the different northern Rizeigat branches and the Awlad Rashid grew further removed from the Mahariya (Flint and de Waal 2005, 40–42). The growing number of northern Rizeigat chieftaincies led to an increase in clashes between Arabs and non-Arabs; clashes that proved harder and harder to resolve.[16] In the northern reaches of Dar Zaghawa, non-Arabs and Arabs have long been in competition over a string of critical water holes (e.g., Jineik, Hosh, and Wakheim), sometimes for decades (Tubiana 2006, 92; Flint and de Waal 2005, 7). The recurring nature of these clashes stems from the fact that, during migration, both Arab and non-Arab nomads (such as the Meidob and Zaghawa, and the Bideyat and Goran from Chad) cross paths. In 1996, some Rizeigat groups sought to seize land and settle in Jineik and Malemal-Zurug, near Malemal-Hosh. They had the support of two powerful officers in the Sudanese military, generals Abdalla Ali Safi al Nur and Hussein Abdalla Jibril, who reportedly organized a provocative meeting in the area that raised tension with the local Zaghawa. Many consider Jibril, now a member of National Assembly, and especially Safi al Nur to be the links between the Janjawiid and hardliners in the government, and, in particular, in the security apparatus (Human Rights Watch 2005, 12–13). Safi al Nur went on to become governor (*wali*) of North Darfur State in 2000–2001 and then a federal minister in Khartoum until 2005. In June 2004, U.S. Congress members, in a letter to President George W. Bush, described Safi al Nur as the "General Coordinator of Janjaweed" and Jibril as "supervising and controlling Janjaweed activities and operations" (*Africa Confidential* 2005). Jibril and Safi al Nur are both Ereigat, the first tribe associated with the northern Rizeigat to settle, which meant that they gained early access to education and, more than other groups, have individuals in the upper reaches of power (Flint and de Waal 2005, 43–45).

During the war, some damrat became Janjawiid camps where local Arab civilians and militiamen, some in uniform and others not, would join in defending garrison settlements and harassing surrounding non-Arab communities. Conversely, Arabs have abandoned many damrat in SLA-held areas for fear of rebel attacks—in Dar Zaghawa and Korma, for instance.

The northern migration spaces are far from being the only stakes in this conflict. Beginning in the early 1970s, drought and environmental degradation forced Arab groups to seek the more fertile lands of Jebel Marra and points south. The ensuing conflict with sedentary farmers, and the increase in drought-induced livestock losses, led the Arabs to the conclusion that they needed to gain control of land in the less arid areas. According to an interlocutor with close ties to the government, "the drought was especially severe in Darfur in 1979 to 1985. Fur areas, rich and less hard-hit by drought, were coveted by the Arabs."[17]

On the northern side of Jebel Marra, the rich lands of Wadi Barei and the Kabkabiya area were especially sought after by the Um Jalul sub-branch of the Mahamid—another branch of the northern Rizeigat—led by the now-notorious Musa Hilal. Some ten years earlier, he had moved south from the Kutum area, settling around Mistereha, west of Kabkabiya. Others joined from western Darfur and Chad, including various Rizeigat groups, Awlad Rashid, Mahadi, and others.

To the south, the small dar-less Arab groups of southern Darfur (e.g., Misiriya, Huttiya, Ta'alba, Tarjam, Sa'ada, Mahariya, and Bani Mansur), some of them from Chad, pressured various Fur, Birgid, and Daju areas south of Jebel Marra and around Nyala. Even Mahariya camel herders from northern Darfur started moving south, fleeing recurring drought.

In western Darfur, various Rizeigat Abbala branches, as well as Ta'alba and Mahadi Arabs, more or less recently arrived from Chad, went after the rich areas of Dar Masalit beginning in 1994, and Wadi Saleh—a Fur area—starting as early as 1987–1989 (Lesch 1998, 91–99; Vigilance Soudan 2000). Arab occupation surged anew from 2000–2001 on.[18]

### Land Tenure Law: Statutory Versus Customary[19]

THE LANDLESS ARAB GROUPS have sought to reinforce their landgrabs by calling into question the traditional tenure system. The rebels, on the other hand, want to see reaffirmed the so-called historical rights to land. The current crisis springs from these diverging interpretations of how to manage access to land.

#### Diverging Concepts of Land Tenure

There are two aspects to the landgrab attempts by dar-less Arabs: the first is the physical occupation of the lands, which is often preceded by the violent expulsion of the original inhabitants. The second involves establishing a legal claim to the land. This represents a fundamental challenge to the traditional tenure system, and is a central feature of the current conflict. Arab nomads began taking over lands well before the beginning of this war, which is part of what triggered it. That violence in turn made other, more numerous landgrabs possible. Meanwhile, the notion that this occupation should be legally sanctioned has taken root among the dar-less Arabs. This is, of course unacceptable to non-Arab leaders: "A piece of land to live off is not a problem. But today the Arabs want to register the land to their names."[20]

The Arab claim to non-Arab land sets up a clash between competing legal systems: on the one hand the statutory-tenure system of the Sudanese state, theoretically applicable to Darfur but never enforced, and on the other the traditional customary-tenure system, officially abolished but still in force in rural areas.

Historically, land in Sudan was either individually or communally "owned"—the former areas being mostly limited to the riverine areas of the Nile Valley from the Gezira downstream. After the reconquest of Sudan in 1898, the British implemented a number of policies to reinforce their control over the country and its land. They set up large state-owned irrigation schemes in the Gezira and the Tokar delta, empowered local chiefs through the creation or reaffirmation of tribal dars, and enforced wide-ranging grazing rights for nomads. After independence, these land policies changed. The military regime of Jaafar Nimeiri passed the Unregistered Land Act in 1970. This groundbreaking piece of legislation declared that all non-registered land was the property of the state—in practice this meant the majority of land in Sudan and almost all the land in Darfur. The Unregistered Land Act opened the door to widespread abuse of rural tenure rights across Sudan.[21]

Darfur, however, has to a large extent escaped these abuses because of a consensus in support of the hawakir and dar systems that brings together non-Arab groups and the main Arab groups.

In Darfur today, the main non-Arab and Arab groups generally favor the continuation of the customary system, while the landless Arabs demand that the modern system be enforced. A better understanding of the plight of the landless Arabs requires exploring how they fit into the traditional system of customary tenure. Theoretically, any individual, regardless of tribe, may come to the dar or hakura of any other group, and ask for permission to build a house, plant a farm, graze livestock, or simply pass through with animals and draw water. Interestingly, the SLA seems to want to preserve the flexibility of the traditional system: "as we see it, the traditional system gives land ownership to tribes, but the use of the land remains open to all."[22]

The request must be made to the local sheikh, or *omda*, who controls the land. The granting of usage rights—as opposed to ownership—implies acknowledgment of the authority of the local chiefs and adherence to specific rules: paying taxes on the harvest (*ushur*), accepting local leaders as adjudicators in case of conflict, and good neighborliness.

A further critical rule is the commitment to not leave the land fallow for more than three years, a principle that also exists in the modern Sudanese law (de Waal 1989, 47). Much has been said of this last provision, especially in the Western media—the fear being that the failure to plant for more than three years could, under customary or statutory law, cause villagers to lose access to their land, with the government reallocating it in keeping with statutory law. However, a global reallocation policy, whether through statutory or customary law, seems unlikely when it is overwhelming violence that forced people from their land—a point the displaced themselves often make (Tanner 2005a, 28).

The newcomer to the land is thus both a user and a guest. In return for following the rules that govern access to land, the newcomer enjoys the protection of the local leadership. In this context, the nomadic way of life of the dar-less Arabs in no way makes them inherently uncontrollable. But they are torn between competing allegiances. They must defer to their own traditional leaders, though the authority of the latter is often diluted by distance—elders often stay in the damrat, while the younger men travel with the herds. At the same time, they are subjects of the dar where they live. And finally, they are citizens of the Sudanese state. Interestingly, for groups that have clearly aligned themselves with the regime in Khartoum, it is this last allegiance that is the most problematic because of the government's woeful failure to invest in Darfur, and most notably in Arab nomad communities. Janjawiid Arabs and rebels are thus in agreement over a central point: the people of Darfur are second-class citizens in Sudan.

Nevertheless, the dar-less Arabs have turned to Khartoum in their bid to upend the traditional order. They have clamored for a modern tenure system that would allow any citizen to access land anywhere in the country by permission of the state, rather than that of the traditional authorities. Paradoxically, they are demanding that the statutory legal framework grant them a traditional right—collective ownership of land, not unlike dars and hawakir—while statutory law tends to favor individual ownership over that of the group.

Thus, the acquisition of Sudanese citizenship has become a way to escape allegiance to other groups—even if this allegiance is rather more symbolic than constraining. Calling into question the traditional tenure system also carries a powerful message of Arab emancipation. This merged with the Arab supremacist project propagated in 1970s and 1980s by a Libyan-backed organization called the Tajamu al Arabi, or Arab Gathering, which Khartoum furthered in the 1990s (Flint and de Waal 2005, 49–57).

## A Short History of a Legal Gray Zone

The British overran the Fur state in 1916. In so doing, they killed the sultan and abolished the sultanate, but they left its administrative and legal systems in place. Darfur became a model of the "indirect rule" policy. The only major territorial change made by the British was the creation of Dar Beni Hussein in the 1940s—and it was done through the traditional system. In fact, Darfurian elites, both non-Arab and Arab, often refer to Dar Beni Hussein as proof that land-poor groups can gain access to resources through negotiation—proof that the traditional system can be amended to accommodate new realities.

Another colonial innovation was the Land Settlement and Registration Act of 1925, which provides for the formal registration of tenure. But the act was only really applied in towns, and it never called into question the hawakir and dar systems (Food and Agriculture Organization 2004, 17). As the British confirmed existing tenure rights, they made changes in the so-called native administration (*idara ahlia*) that can still be felt today: they anointed the paramount chiefs of the leading Arab groups with titles that put them on a par with the sultans, *maliks,* and *shartais* of the non-Arabs.[23] That is how the four large Baggara groups of southern Darfur, as well as the Zayadiya and Bani Hussein of northern Darfur, acquired *nazirs.*[24]

Today, the landless Arabs hold fast to the idea that a *nazir* presides over a dar. In the past twelve years, the government has fueled and manipulated this notion, awarding numerous *nazirates* to small branches of the northern Rizeigat, as well as to the Ma'aliya, whose *nazirate* ambitions placed them on a collision course with the Rizeigat Baggara.

The post-independence undermining of traditional leaders started in earnest under Nimeiri, first with the 1925 Unregistered Land Act, and then with the abolition of the Native Administration Act and the People's Local Government Act, which actually rendered the native administration illegal (Food and Agriculture Organization 2004, 17; Ajawin and de Waal 2002). After the fall of the Nimeiri regime, the 1986 Native Administration Act restored some of the native administration's power. But the many traditional leaders interviewed for this research maintained that they have not recovered the authority they lost under Nimeiri.

As the government rebuilt the traditional administration from 1986 onward, it also sought to weaken the leading chieftaincies by creating new leaders and favoring landless Arabs. "The rebuilding of the system started with the precept that no new chiefs would be named. But the government, reacting to local pressures, started giving new titles and establishing new Arab administrations."[25] Khartoum named new nazirs and, especially, numerous new *amirs*. The British had given the title of *amir* to the descendents of sultans who pre-dated Sultan Ali Dinar—an effort to bolster the rivals of a feared family. From 1986 on, Khartoum applied the same divide-and-rule strategy, by elevating second-ranking Fur leaders. Before colonial times, the title of *amir* was given to Mahdist military chiefs. Today, other military chiefs in Darfur—Janjawiid leaders—carry the title.

From 1994 on, the government gave the title *amir* to a number of landless Arab leaders in Dar Masalit. "There was a time when only Sultan Bahr el Din of the Masalit would have carried the title of amir and it was respected by both the Masalit and the local Arabs. Then the government gave the title to Arab leaders in West Darfur. They were supposed to remain under the sultan, but believed they were now his equals, independent from his power. Recently, the title has even been given to Janjawiid leaders. They feel very proud."[26] As with the new *nazirates*, the creation of new emirates has allowed landless Arabs to challenge groups that have traditionally enjoyed access to land, and seek lands of their own.

On paper, then, the statutory system that the landless Arabs demand is already in place. Officially, traditional tenure rights are without value, dars and *hawakir* remain unregistered, and land in Darfur is the property of the state, which is, in theory, the only lawful arbiter of its allocation. But in practice, the statutory tenure never took hold. Successive governments in Khartoum quickly realized that even attempts to establish Arab *damrat* were enough to provoke local conflict.

Stakes are so high, in fact, that the state has refrained from ever clearly articulating how tenure in Darfur should work. "The government never registered the *hawakir*, but always acknowledged it was our land," says a Fur chief.[27] At the same time, a former non-Arab state official claims: "[before the war,] we had never heard of unhappiness with the traditional [land tenure] rights."[28] The consensus among non-Arabs interviewed for this research was adamant opposition to calling into question the traditional system. The dars and *hawakir* are deeply etched in communal memory, and these groups claim that, whatever happens, they will remember their tenure.

Having said that, the non-Arab leaders interviewed for this research do not rely on oral knowledge, but rather on written archives. Paramount leaders have documents dating back to the sultanate establishing their rights over a piece of territory and outlining its boundaries with great precision. The British endorsed these written claims and produced numerous documents and maps of their own. Over the years, post-independence governments have referred to both sultanic and colonial documents to resolve local disputes over land.

A number of the people interviewed have described the destruction of such documents in the current violence. It is hard to say whether the destruction was deliberate, or whether the papers were lost along with other belongings. But a Zaghawa close to the authorities told us, "These documents prove that such-and-such a territory belongs to this or that kingdom; this is relevant to future negotiations, and that is why the Arabs are destroying them."[29]

### Reaffirming the Traditional System

Negotiating in Abuja, the rebels succeeded, in July 2005, in getting Khartoum to recognize the traditional tenure system—implying the recognition of the historical dars, non-Arab and Arab alike.[30] "The hawakir system must be entered into Sudanese law, failing which there will be no peace," said Suleiman Jamus, the SLA humanitarian coordinator, in September 2005.[31] The DPA satisfies this demand. Paragraph 158, the most important point of the section on "Development and Management of Land and Natural Resources," is clear on this point: "Tribal land ownership rights (*hawakeer*), historical rights to land, traditional or customary livestock routes, and access to water, shall be recognised and protected. All levels of government shall institute a process to progressively develop and amend the relevant laws to incorporate customary laws and practices, international trends and practices and protect cultural heritage."

Not only does this agreement go against established Sudanese law, it spells doom for those Arabs who hoped to gain tenure rights in exchange for their participation with the Janjawiid. It also goes against part of the Khartoum government itself. In 2004, the deputy *wali* of South Darfur State, Adam Sileik, made the following statement: "Dars are nothing more than historical memories. Traditional leaders no longer have the right to allocate land. Only the government can give land. And it can give land to anyone it chooses."[32] This is the discourse of the Tajamu al Arabi ideologues. It is also that of Khartoum hardliners like General Safi al Nur (Flint and de Waal 2005, 58–59). On the ground, such talk is taken up by local officials like Sileik in South Darfur, and Mohamed Ibrahim Izzat, the foreign trade director in the North Darfur State Ministry of Finance, a Mahariya Arab close to Safi al Nur and who was chosen to represent the Arabs of North Darfur in future negotiations after a conflict resolution conference in Tripoli, Libya, in 2005. Izzat explains that Arab nomads need land so they can settle: "It's the only way we will be able to send our children to school and develop political leaders who can become minister or president, the way the Zaghawa have."[33]

Traditional Arab leaders also hold a similar line, such as *Omda* Mustafa Abu Noba, another North Darfur Mahariya close to Safi al Nur who has been sitting on Fur lands in South Darfur for the last fifteen years and who is considered a leading Janjawiid commander there.[34] "We nomads want to develop, export our camels and cows, and have villages where we can educate our children so that they can go to university. That is why we need land," he said in September 2004.[35] Over the years, Khartoum remained indifferent to the growing land-based conflicts in Darfur, which it saw as inherent to the region. This left the field open to the ideologues who were also a key constituency of the NIF regime.

There is, however, no consensus within the government. In 2004, a non-Arab Darfurian government official told us that challenging the traditional tenure system would only "lead to further conflict."[36] It is a little-recognized fact that the Darfur violence has proven a highly divisive issue for the regime (Tanner 2004, 726–727).

The focus on land issues may enable the rebels to capitalize on the precedent of the South Sudan Comprehensive Peace Agreement. According to a recent study, "the future leadership of south Sudan embraces customary law as the backbone for the [southern Sudanese] judiciary," as the "Naivasha Power Sharing Agreement provides a platform to develop parallel legal systems in north and south Sudan" (Food and Agriculture Organization 2004, 13, 17). The North-South model could open a door to a Darfur-specific tenure statute. The same report also states, however, that "it is not yet clear whether customary rules will take precedence over statutory regulations in all circumstances (evidence from urban areas demonstrates the latter)."[37]

The DPA contains the same ambiguity and potential contradictions on the issue of tenure. For instance, tension could arise between Paragraph 158, referred to above, and Paragraph 157, which guarantees the "rights in land owned by the GoS [Government of Sudan] within Darfur." This would renew the contradiction between the customary and statutory tenure systems. However, it is unlikely that the government will activate this contradiction given how clearly the traditional tenure rights have been reaffirmed. Government tenure rights will most likely remain confined to urban areas.

In practice, the DPA's reaffirmation of tenure rights will only become reality with the return of the displaced populations to their lands. The problem here is that the DPA is not sufficiently clear on what happens if the land that people return to has been occupied by others, and how these occupants would be dealt with. Numerous disputes may well arise that will be difficult and take a long time to resolve.

The DPA envisages Property Claims Committees and a Darfur Land Commission. The rebels groups are to name the chairperson of the land commission, which is to decide on traditional rights and adjudicate tenure clashes. The last sentence of Paragraph 166 is clear: "the outcome of the arbitration shall be binding on the contending parties and may be enforced in a court of competent jurisdiction." But Paragraph 169 is far more ambiguous: "In case of conflict between the findings and recommendations of the National Land Commission and the Darfur Land Commission, which cannot be resolved by agreement, the Commissions shall reconcile their positions. The matter shall be referred to the Constitutional Court for adjudication if the positions cannot be reconciled."

The DPA refers the land issue to yet-to-be-defined processes, such as the Land Commission and the "Darfur-Darfur Dialogue and Consultation" process, which is to include traditional leaders and local communities. Many criticized the weak participation of Darfurian "civilians" in Abuja. The Darfur-Darfur dialogue—or other future processes of consultation that may go beyond the government and the rebels—could be a chance to get the negotiations out of the rut that exists between parties that do little to represent the population. Just before the time of signing, Alex de Waal, a member of the mediating team, defended the Darfur-Darfur process in an open letter: "We know full well that a deal between Government and rebels cannot solve all Darfur's complex problems." So, he continued, the mediation proposed a Darfur-Darfur Dialogue and Consultation to be initiated within sixty days, "at which representatives of every group in the region can meet to begin the process of stitching the social fabric back together again, addressing problems such as land ownership and nomadic migration" (de Waal 2006b).

It was the rebels who wanted to defer some of the more sensitive issues, such as land, to slower-moving processes, so as to avoid further conflict. According to an SLA representative in Abuja: "We don't really want to get too specific with regards to land. The approach to the problem should be along traditional lines. That is why we suggested a land commission, to include traditional leaders, that would explore tenure systems. It would issue proposals to the government that could then be entered into law."[38] The land commission and the Darfur-Darfur dialogue will take time to get started, but a deliberate pace is needed to ensure a sustainable peace.

The rebels remain cautious because the traditionalist stance is not without problems for them. It shows up the Arab–non-Arab cleavage, while the rebels seek a pan-ethnic message. At the same time, however, focusing on the tenure issue has the advantage, for the rebels, of dividing the Arab groups. The dar-holding Arabs were fine with landgrabs as long as they were done by force—and even offered public support for their landless cousins. But the dar-holding Arabs cannot also strive to abolish traditional land rights. With numerous other groups on their land, and with the land itself subject to conflict, the land-holding Arabs need these rights to maintain their tenure.

### Land After the War: An Uncertain Future for All

THE RETURN OF THE DISPLACED is essential to long-lasting peace in Darfur. Yet a complete return to the old order is unrealistic. The conflict has heaped additional pressure on the nomadic way of life of many Arab groups, which forces the need for new solutions. The traditional tenure system is unlikely to ensure a return to pre-war multiethnic patterns.

### An End to the Pastoralist Way of Life?

The return of the displaced to their lands will give rise to lasting problems. Some Arab groups will not easily relinquish the lands they occupy and in some cases say they have "liberated." Others may find it hard to remain in non-Arab dars where local inhabitants sometimes say they no longer want to live side-by-side with certain Arab groups.

In Darfur, the rains come in June, July, and August. For both Arab and non-Arab camel herders, the destination for the migration that follows the rains are the Saharan pastures that stretch across the northern reaches of Dar Zaghawa around Wadi Howar. The problem is that this pastureland, and especially the routes that lead to it from the south, are under rebel control and therefore off-limits to Arab groups.

Arab cattle herders move north after the rains as well. Again, a number of strategic points along their migration routes are in the hands of the rebels. The result is that herds are forced to remain in the same place for longer periods of time, decreasing their food intake, and increasing illnesses and therefore death rates. Another result is overgrazing in areas that are already hard hit by endemic drought. The Arab nomads now want future negotiations to tackle the issue of migration corridors. Some groups, mindful of how threatened their nomadic ways are, may be willing to consider withdrawing from occupied lands in exchange for a reopening of the migration routes (International Crisis Group 2005b, 11).

But other Arab groups who have started settling—some began before the crisis, of their own free will, others were forced to settle because of the conflict—are clearly unwilling to return to nomadism. For instance, the conflict forced Awlad Rashid nomads to settle for long stretches of time in Bor-Said, a *damra* near Kutum, and they now have no intention of moving. "Before, we were nomads," says one of their leaders. "We chose this place because it was on our migration route. The war has forced us to remain here. Now we want to build a permanent settlement here. We cannot migrate anymore, it is better for us to stay here and educate our children."[39]

Some non-Arabs now claim to be opposed to any Arab migration through their dar. This is likely to accelerate the sedentarization of the nomads, and their need for land. Ending nomadism in a given place may resolve the conflict there, but it is likely to ignite new conflict in the areas where the nomads settle. The heyday of pastoralism may be behind us; as nomadism declines, so too will Darfur's multiethnic character.

### The Difficult Return to Multiethnicity

IN THE PAST, the dar system allowed for the coexistence of different ethnic groups in Darfur. Reaffirming the dar system may help bring about peace, but it will not be enough to restore multiethnicity.

For many non-Arabs in Darfur today, there are only two types of Arab groups: those who took part in the Janjawiid violence, and those who did not. They accept the latter as groups with whom they could live in the future, and who could even play some sort of mediation role—for instance the Rizeigat Baggara could use their ties to the Rizeigat Abbala of North and West Darfur (Tanner 2005a, 5, 22–23). But the Arabs who did take part in the violence as organized groups, most of them landless, will find the conflict has aggravated their lack of tenure. Non-Arabs will not want them in their dars, and some have even had to leave damrat in the Kutum area under SLA pressure. As the crisis drags on, these Arabs fear they will fail to hold on to land that is not theirs according to the traditional system, and feel that Khartoum may in fact turn on them. "The government made a deal with the Arab nomads: land against their participation in the Janjawiid. Now the government is finding it hard to deliver on this deal, and it is beginning to go back on it."[40] Today rebels and government allies alike see the government's commitment to restore traditional tenure rights as a sign that Arab land-grabs will not stand. This in turn could weaken government control over some Janjawiid groups.

If non-Arabs continue to prevent Arabs from settling in their dars, or even migrating through them, Arabs are likely to hold on to territory they have already taken over or make a move on other land. Only the dar-holding Arabs could agree to give land to the dar-less Arabs. But this would lead to a concentration of Arabs in South Darfur, and to an end to the pastoralist way of life of the northern camel herders who would settle there.

Whether this comes to pass or not, how Arabs and non-Arabs will coexist in the Arab dars of South Darfur remains a critical issue. Of particular concern is the Zaghawa. The Zaghawa have a dar in North Darfur, and some of them are defenders of the traditional system. But they are also migrants in South Darfur, forced southward by the droughts of the 1960s, 1970s, and 1980s. If Arab groups are forced from Zaghawa territory in the North, they are likely to enter into conflict with the Zaghawa on Arab territory in the South. The seeds for violence already exist, and the Zaghawa are likely targets this time around.

Since the end of 2005, the position of the Zaghawa has grown increasingly precarious. Most vulnerable are those Zaghawa who live on the lands of other groups, whether Arab or not. Our past research has shown that relations between Zaghawa newcomers and the non-Arabs present before (Fur, Berti, Birgid, and Tunjur) were good—rather better than relations between the same non-Arabs and Arab nomads. But the commercial and political success of the Zaghawa in southern Darfur, coupled with their prominence in the Chadian government of Idriss Déby since 1990, fueled fears that the Zaghawa would seek new, more autonomous chieftaincies— and new tenure rights. Since this war, a number of factors have exacerbated these fears. Khartoum propaganda describes the Zaghawa agenda as including a greater "Dar Zaghawa" reaching from the shores of Lake Chad to the Nile Valley. Also, the prominence of Zaghawa commanders in the SLA and the fact that these commanders hold sway over large non-Zaghawa areas, combined with abuses committed by Zaghawa rebels in non-Zaghawa areas has generated resentment. This is both cause and consequence of the tension between the Minawi (Zaghawa) and Abdel Wahid (Fur) factions of the SLA.

These issues are part of the reason the SLM-Minawi remained cautious about land in Abuja—moving slowly on the issue of "foreign" communities in existing dars was one way of protecting Zaghawa communities in non-Zaghawa areas.[41] This strategy clearly backfired as Minawi's signing has exacerbated anti-Zaghawa sentiment, especially among non-Arabs.

## Conclusion

THE MARGINALIZATION and underdevelopment suffered by all Darfurians, regardless of their ethnic background, are how the Darfur rebels explain taking up arms against the central government. True, non-Arabs are especially aware of their political underrepresentation. The Fur in particular, once powerful and independent, rue their peripheral status within Sudan, itself a recent and unstable creation. They have lost faith in the political parties that sought their support but never rewarded them in any way. But that is not what has transformed an anti-government rebellion into a broad clash between Arab and non-Arab groups across wide swaths of the region. Rather, the cause has been the proliferation of local conflicts over land and other resources combined with the unwillingness of the central government to mediate and—more recently and more ominously—its manipulation of land issues. Khartoum has used land not only to mobilize proxies among landless Arabs who saw an opportunity to renegotiate the terms of their access to tenure, but also to rekindle standing local conflicts from which it stood to gain. At the same time, the rebel groups played on the fears non-Arab's had about their land in order to attract support from those communities. This explains the new fracture that has appeared between landless Arabs, who want new land, and non-Arabs, who fear losing theirs.

The conflict made it possible for groups to take over land and then seek to legalize their landgrabs. This means that returning the land will not be enough to solve the conflict. Many forward-thinking Darfurians—again, both non-Arab and Arab—believe that "development," of which Darfur has been so starved, is the solution, not least because it could dampen the conflict over land. The reasoning includes the following: A more developed agriculture would free up land, while a modern livestock sector would encourage nomads to settle. More water holes would reduce tension over water. Finally, a better education system would dampen the war spirit of young people—the lack of education is often cited as the reason both rebels and Janjawiid manage to find so many recruits. But development projects, especially large ones, can also trigger conflict. New water holes, more intensive agriculture, increased livestock holdings, and the settling of pastoralist communities are all dangerous novelties in the context of Darfur's great political and environmental fragility. Development could very well lead to new clashes between nomads and farmers, or among competing herders (Lavergne 2005, 154–155; Tubiana 2005, 187–188).

It will be necessary to resolve the legal gray area that has characterized land tenure in Darfur for the last thirty-five years or so. This requires defining a tenure system that allows for the resolution of resource-based conflicts before they spin out of control. However, while a reaffirmation of traditional tenure rights may meet the approval of most non-Arabs and dar-holding Arabs, it will not ensure a return to a multiethnic Darfur. The violence has created lasting divisions between communities, and even altered the very notion of dar and *hawakir.*

Darfurians recall the dar and hakura systems as guarantees of stability because those systems allowed landless groups to live in or cross the territories of others. Today, however, the very terms "dar" and *"hakura"* seem to have lost that original meaning. The DPA merely defines *"hawakir"* as "tribal land ownership rights" (Paragraph 158), without further details; negotiators on all sides unanimously dismissed more historically informed interpretations. Non-Arabs and Arabs both use the terms *"hakura"* and "dar" to refer to collective, but mono-ethnic, rights to land—the very rights that the Arabs groups are trying to secure by upending the traditional system. And this despite there being no such thing as a mono-ethnic dar in Darfur, nor an instance of an ethnic group settled entirely in a single dar. Some Fur even use the term "Dar Fur" in its literal meaning of "land of the Fur"—a denial of the region's multiethnic history. If, as a result of the conflict, the dar system becomes a tool used to define tenure and exclude outsiders, it, too, will trigger injustice and conflict.

# 4

## Islam and Islamism in Darfur

AHMED KAMAL EL-DIN

T HE CALAMITIES THAT HAVE ENGULFED Darfur and its people since 2003 have given the region an unprecedented profile in the world's media. With the exception of historical records and
writings by visitors to the region, such as Mohamed al Tunisi, who visited
Darfur at the beginning of the nineteenth century,[1] followed by the account
of Gustav Nachtigal (1971) and the history written by Sean O'Fahey (1980)
and others, few around the globe knew much if anything about the western-
most Sudanese region. This began to change with the inception of armed
rebellion by dissident movements in Darfur against the power center in
Khartoum, after decades of underdevelopment, neglect, and marginalization, according to the political manifestos and slogans raised by these armed
groups.

Had it not been for the firsthand and critical media coverage of the atrocities, the suffering of Darfurians would have continued in near blackout due
to the physical remoteness and lack of political salience of the region, coupled with Sudan government's restrictive policies in relation to journalistic
and humanitarian workers' access to areas outside Khartoum, and Darfur in
particular. At one point, according to a local political newspaper editor, local
media in Sudan were ordered by security forces not to publish the word
"Darfur" or anything in relation to that region whatsoever. The international
outcry by rights activists, NGOs, and foreign media reporters, coupled with
a remorseful world conscience ten years after the genocide in Rwanda, all
contributed to the notable international political and diplomatic response

without which the crisis could have been even deeper, or could have developed to pass a point of no return.

On the other hand, world media reports have drawn a picture of Darfur quite different from the realities today and during the region's long history. First, the conflict has been portrayed as one between "Africans" and "Arabs," with many negative connotations attached to the two terms. Although such a division has in fact existed in the minds of some, and is even evidenced by increasing competition between nomad Bedouin tribes of mostly Arab origin and sedentary tribes of mostly "African" identity over pasture and tribal dominion over land in Darfur, the current conflict transcends all local tribal and other differences and represents political discord between the people of Darfur and the central authority in Khartoum.

Local ethnic divergences combined with conflict over means of subsistence have been a major reason behind the belated political revolt. For most of the years since Sudan's independence in 1956, local skirmishes have had the effect of confusing any unifying spirit in Darfur, which would have been required for the development of popular awareness among the people of the whole region of injustices which they suffered in common, which could in turn have fuelled organized dissension. Without such local differences which the government of Sudan covertly exploited but which it also claims to be *the* real cause of Darfur's ailments, the region could have exploded in rebellion far earlier than it actually did.

Secondly and unfortunately, the recent rush of reports has failed to portray Darfur as a historic entity of its own, which joined the current Sudan only ninety years ago, with deep-rooted dynastic history, full of seasoned local traditions and multifaceted cultures. This uniqueness is accompanied by a stronger Darfurian sentiment of belonging to a united and homogeneous region. Such sentiments include recognition of Darfur's own historic system of governance, complete with a traditional scheme of proverbs and other traditions serving as recognized legal maxims governing the people's lives at both public administrative and personal levels. This notion has found expression in Darfurians' common parlance when they talk of themselves as *hukkam* (singular, *hakim*), meaning people with a sense of ruling canons and etiquette. The word *hakkama*, denoting native female poet

whose popular verse focuses on words of wisdom, also has a similar meaning. An *ajwad* (plural, *ajaweed*) is a wise man, experienced and an elder, who
is an arbiter or member of a native arbitration forum in which individual or
intertribal conflicts are entertained and settled. Until recently the *ajaweed*
institution was widely used, with a great level of success, to tackle most
local conflicts of whatever origin. Another aspect of the political culture of
the region was the Canons of Dali, or Dali Code (*Qanoon* Dali),[2] which was
a consolidated compendium of Islamic rules of law, reminiscent of the
*Majalla* of the Ottoman era in Turkey.[3] Each of these legal, cultural, and
social institutions is only an example of the sociocultural richness of
Darfur. In searching for solutions to the crisis, these traditional Darfur institutions still hold much relevance. The need for a Darfur-Darfur dialogue,
recognized by all, as a complementary measure for better implementation
of any peace agreement, will put such traditional institutions in high
demand. Without drawing upon the rich cultural archive of Darfurian governance, including both its underlying ethos and its specific resources for
conflict resolution, little consensus can be arrived at in any intra-Darfurian
dialogue and consultation.

Thirdly, the media has neglected some basic facts concerning the Islamic
factor in Darfur, whether in relation to the local social structure or the orientation of the armed movements. The roles of Islam and Islamism in Darfur
are the topic of this chapter.

### Islam in Darfur

DARFURIANS ARE COMMONLY KNOWN for their dedicated incul-
cation of the Quran, the Muslim scripture, by heart. Traditional Quranic
schools, or *khalawi* (singular, *khalwa,* literally meaning a "solitary den"),
spread across the region and beyond, throughout the Sudanic belt stretching
from the Horn of Africa in the east to Mali and Senegal at the western coast
of the continent. Islam was most probably introduced to Darfur peacefully
and piecemeal, starting from the thirteenth century (Al Tayeb 1991) by
learned religious travelers and pilgrims mostly from west Africa, but also, to

a lesser degree, from north Africa and the Hejaz in Arabia. Among those was Ahmed al Ma'qour, who arrived to the region from Tunis, and later married a daughter of the then-sultan of Darfur, Shao Dor Sheit.[4] Other migrations came from west Africa, where several Muslim kingdoms (notably Kanem-Burno and Wadai) preceded the Fur Sultanate. The Hamawi historian, Yaqut, records that Islam reached Kanem by migrating Arabs before and especially after the demise of the Umayyad Caliphate in Baghdad at the hands of the Abbasids in 750 CE (132 AH), and by the end of the eleventh century an Islamic kingdom was established (Yaqut 1957, 432; Halim 1991). This immigrant faith was manifest in the form of Sufi (mystical) *tariqas* (orders), most importantly the Tijaniyya, established by Sidi Ahmed al Tijani, a native and dweller of the old city of Fez in Morocco,[5] from which came many Moroccan migrants to Sudan, including Darfur. The relatively small tribe, Magharba, living in al Fashir, North Darfur, relate to ancestors from Fez and other Moroccan localities, whose descendants kept irregular visits to their Darfurian next of kin during the Hajj (Muslim pilgrimage to Mecca) on their way back to Morocco. This author attended some of the gatherings arranged for Sheikh Ibn Omar of Fez in al Fashir, back in the 1960s, at the house of a famous Maghrabi Sufi, *Haj* Badawi Zein al Abideen, where rituals were uttered and dates and water distributed to the attendants, especially young children, at the end of the session, for the sake of gaining *baraka* or blessing, due to the presence of the Tijaniyya sheikh, according to Sufi beliefs.

The Sufi culture, in the form of Tijaniyya, suited the nature of Darfur people and tribes,[6] resulting in amicable reception of the faith of Islam and increasing devotion to its tenets. Parents used to send their children for years to centers of Islamic learning, where in many cases they spent much of their childhood and returned to their families only after learning the whole of the Quran by heart. During such a period a Quran student is called *muhajir*, or "migrant" for religious knowledge. For the purposes of more advanced learning Darfurians used to travel to centers in Egypt and north Africa, such as al Azhar mosque and university in Cairo where special chambers, known as Rewaq Dar Fur (or Darfur Vestibules) accommodated students from the region studying for their Ph. D.-equivalent and other degrees in Islamic studies, Arabic and the like. Rewaq Dar Fur still exists under the same name and for the same dedication.[7] Other destinations included al Zaitouna and al Qarawiyeen university-style mosques in Tunis. Most of the graduates from these institutes of Islamic learning finally returned to teach in Darfur, but some have ended up teaching in other places in west Africa, especially Nigeria. Some of the Cairo graduates have been key elements in importing the Muslim Brothers' movement to Darfur, which will be elaborated below.

Darfur received the Islamic faith in the form of easygoing and tolerant Sufism, with no force or violence involved, and consequently no resistance recorded, and from the bottom up, and by non-ruling elements, well before Sultan Suleiman Solong (1596-1616), first in his dynasty, adopted Islam as the official faith of his political dominion. These factors resulted in Islam becoming primarily part of the social structure in Darfur rather than a political order for the state. However, the marriage between Islam and the state in Darfur was established and remained over three centuries, from the first officially Muslim Sultanate of Suleiman Solonj to the death of the last Fur Sultan, Ali Dinar, in 1916.[8] The amicable linkage between the religion and local indigenous culture of the Darfur society led sometimes to popular confusion of certain practices with Islamic teachings, and vice versa. One striking example is an often narrated story where a native in Darfur watched how an expatriate European had to resort to a local brewing house for beer after he ran short of his imported alcoholic supply. The native then shouted out: the *khawwaja* (white foreigner) has embraced Islam! The episode resembles an expression of how drinking local beer was perceived, albeit erroneously, as an Islamic practice. That was due to the tolerant nature of the relationship between Islam and indigenous local customs. It is also an important feature to observe when studying the partial evolution of Islam into Islamism in Darfur, a process which has by no means been streamlined, uniform, or complete.

### "'Islam" and "Islamism"

THE FORM OF ISLAM that was historically introduced to Darfur has already been described above: a Sufi, tranquil, tolerant, and consequently popular Islam, which has been peacefully perceived and found its way deep into the social and cultural fabric and social components of the regional populace. Some distorted popular knowledge of Islam at the grassroots level could be a product of an emerging laxity. Nevertheless, when it comes to teaching the young, parents and guardians in general show much firmness, sometimes to the point of rigidity, which often demands personal sacrifices. The combination between strictness in teaching and inculcating the tenets of the religion, while being lax when with regard to practicing the same, has served to preserve and maintain Islamic teachings through generations, both in theory and in living practice.

Islam*ism*, by contrast, is not unproblematic. The term has been born in the West, with western culture's religious (Jewish/Christian) perceptions in the background. The term has been interchangeably used with "Islamic fundamentalism," "militant Islam," "radical Islam," and "political Islam," only to compound the imported confusion.

To Daniel Pipes, a western Arabist who studied Islam (including Sufism) and the Middle East and wrote abundantly on the topic, "Militant Islam derives from Islam but is a misanthropic, misogynist, triumphalist, millenarian, anti-modern, anti-Christian, anti-Semitic, terroristic, jihadistic, and suicidal version of it. Fortunately, it appeals to only about 10 percent to 15 percent of Muslims."[9] This depiction is useful in the sense that it covers most of the definitional components relevant to Islamism, together with most of the associated stereotypes. In historical reality, the modern Islamist movement that began in Egypt in the 1920s has been a force for modernism. In many of its manifestations it has been popular, progressive, and peaceable.

Although the semantics of Islam and Islamism is not a central theme of this essay, one necessary comment is relevant to the coming discussion of Islamism in Darfur. Islam, according to the Quran,[10] is a comprehensive way of life, simultaneously providing a vision for thought and guiding tools of behavior for its adherents. As such, it includes built-in rules that govern all aspects of life, including politics, albeit in very general terms. To view politics or behave politically under the guidance of Islamic doctrine constitutes nothing other than "Islam" proper, rather than any alienated concept with a distinguishing label, such as Islamism or Islamic fundamentalism, or any other term. There is no distinction between a private realm reserved for "Islam" as opposed to a public or political domain into which "Islamism" intrudes. Moreover, the use of violence in non-defensive manner and as a means of achieving Islamic ends—including political ends—finds no textual authority in Islam. And one is compelled, in the aftermath of several incidents of international terrorism, to argue that the unfortunate conceptual connection between violence and Islamic politics is due to erroneous interpretation of Islam into actions by the few. Western-oriented critics, however, refrain from judging these violent actions by the rules of the faith claimed to be behind them, in order to find out whether the psychology and intentions of the culprit or the authentic teachings of his faith are to blame.

When it comes to Darfur, given the manner it received Islam and reconciled with it both socially and culturally, the contrast between reality and perception about what Islam is becomes even more striking. Our use of the word "Islamism" or "Islamist" should henceforth be taken in that context, meaning the religion of a Muslim who, by definition, is also active in political life and is guided by Islam as a comprehensive way of life.

Although both the Umma Party and the Democratic Unionist Party (DUP)—the two most prominent traditional political parties of the Sudan—are based on Islamic Sufi sects and beliefs of the Ansar (followers of the Mahdi) and the Khatmiyya (followers of the Mirghanites) respectively, it is the Muslim Brotherhood, once operating under the title Islamic Charter Front (1965–1969) and later (in the mid-1970s) broadened into the National Islamic Front (NIF), which has always advocated the comprehensive implementation of Islamic teachings in political life and governance. The NIF has worked hard for that goal, in varying degrees and capacities, for the last half century. Accordingly, the NIF is much closer to the term "Islamists" which almost became another name for the movement (al Haraka al Islamiyya) throughout its history. Its student branch has been appropriately called al Ittijah al Islami (Islamic Trend). It should be noted, though, that both the UP and the DUP had their own versions of Islamist manifestos. The Umma Party campaigned under the slogan of an "Islamic Renaissance," while the DUP called for an "Islamic Republic." Both slogans were accentuated in the memories of Sudanese during the latest (1986) competitive election campaigns.

## The Islamic Movement in Darfur

THE FIRST EMERGENCE of a culture of modern political Islam in Darfur came with returning religious students who obtained their degrees in Egypt in the late 1940s and early 1950s, when Hassan al Banna's Islamic Brotherhood movement was in the ebb of its youth.

Among several veteran Islamists interviewed by this author, Dr. Ali al Haj Mohamed recalls several names of Darfurians who studied in Cairo's al Azhar and other Islamic and Arabic colleges, and later formed the first group of Muslim Brothers in Darfur. These include Sheikh Ibrahim Abdel Gader, Sheikh Abdel Hameed Dawelbeit, Mohamed and Ahmed al Sayyed Medani from al Fashir, and Abdel Muttaleb Ali al Sa'ati and Ahmed al Tijani Bukhari from Nyala. Among non-Azharites who were also early promoters of the movement in Darfur was late Suleiman Mustafa Abbakar who graduated as a professional teacher from Bakht al Ridha teachers' institute in the 1940s and was the prime name remembered by my personal sources to be the first Muslim Brother from Darfur. He was also the first ever to win elections on a Muslim Brotherhood ticket in any geographical constituency outside Sudan's urban center, in Kutum in 1965.

The span of the two decades from the late 1940s to the late 1960s witnessed three important phases in the development of political Islam in Darfur. During the first one, as we have seen, Darfurian students returned from Egypt, and through this process a culture of political Islam, to be distinguished from Darfur's dominant traditional Sufi Islam, was introduced into the urban centers of the region, paving the way for a more organized form. This Islamic culture differed from the historic Sufi form of Islam in Darfur in its insistence on strictly observing Quranic precepts, notably in the fields of rituals and in practices such as abstention from alcohol.

The second phase, from 1951,[11] was marked by the recruitment of members into the Muslim Brothers organization, which was then a loose affiliate

of the main movement of Egypt, in an ever-wavering relation which ultimately officially broke in 1988. Dr. Ali al Haj Mohamed, Turabi's current
deputy and top aide from Darfur, was recruited into the organization in 1953
while at intermediate level school, among a number of students from the
major cities, mainly al Fashir and Nyala. The third phase was heralded by the
first successful electoral campaign which took place in North Kutum, as a
sign of full-fledged political action in Darfur by a modern Islamic political
movement.

Ali Shammar is a veteran Darfur Islamist, recruited in 1961 and a graduate
in engineering from the University of Khartoum. He recalled to the author
how the electoral victory occurred. The constituency won by Suleiman
Mustafa Abbakar on behalf of the Muslim Brothers was North Kutum.
During the campaign it witnessed the first-ever political campaigning visit
from Khartoum by Sudan's Muslim Brothers leader Hassan al Turabi and his
senior aide Yassin Omar al Imam to boost their candidate. The Islamists'
campaign and their subsequent victory in the remote constituency dismayed
the Umma Party which had always considered most of Darfur, including
Kutum, to be "closed" constituencies for that party's candidates to easily win
in, regardless of any qualifications other than being nominated by the
Sayyed, or sect and party leader, then (and now) Sadiq al Mahdi. The
unprecedented win was also made possible, quite significantly, due to the
support lent by North Kutum's leading native chief at the time, late Ali
Mohamadein. Alliance between campaigning political forces and local traditional leadership has always been a crucial element for winning any election.
When the geographical constituency is inhabited by a majority tribe (the
Zaghawa in the case of North Kutum), it becomes even easier for the local
chief to guarantee sizeable support for his political ally.

The North Kutum election and other similar incidents later led the
Sudanese Islamists to believe that because of its deep-rooted Islamic orientation, Darfur could shift its political allegiances in their favor, at the expense of
its traditional vote winner, the Umma Party, whose followers (the *Ansar*)
mostly come from the western regions of Darfur and Kordofan. This has
since proved to be a near-myth by the evidence of the 1986 elections following the fall of General Jaafar al Nimeiri. The NIF lost most of the geographi-

cal constituencies it contested, compared to its landslide victory in each one of the twenty four "graduates college" constituencies throughout Sudan. This author visited Sudan and Darfur to report for the UK-based monthly, *Arabia*, in the summer of 1985, just before the beginning of the parliamentary election campaigns. At that time, many citizens in the streets of al Geneina had not even heard of Turabi, let alone considered voting for the NIF, while in Khartoum leading NIF members at the time anticipated they could win over most of Darfur, to their shock and surprise upon the vote count.

From the mid-1960s until today Islamism, in the sense adopted in this essay, has been the business of the Muslim Brothers (*al Ikhwan*), despite the emergence of several other Islamic groupings such as the *Wahhabi*-oriented *Ansar al Sunna* (advocators of the Traditions of the Prophet), the traditionalist *Ikwan* faction led by Sadiq Abdalla Abdel Majed, the *Jama'a Salafiya* (also pro-*Wahhabi*), and some unnamed *Takfiri* groups, one of which revealed its existence in a bloody massacre of worshippers inside a mosque in the al Jarrafa neighborhood of Omdurman in 1996. The first three movements have all participated in Sudan's current Government of National Unity, before any manifest political activity on their part, while the NIF's successor, the National Congress Party (NCP) split in 1999 into the ruling NCP and the newly-formed Popular Congress Party (PCP) led by Hassan al Turabi as the main political opposition force to the NCP-led government.

Among the Darfurian interviewees for this essay was Dr. Gibril Ibrahim Mohamed, a leading member of the JEM. He was also a member of the Sudanese Islamic movement until the 1999 split when he left the organization to participate in the establishment of JEM. On the relationship between Darfurians and the broadly Islamic forces of Sudan, he said:

> Although the Muslim Brotherhood is the main group to advocate
> Islamism, all the other major parties claim allegiance to Islam
> and do rally followers under its banner. It is very important, how-
> ever, that the Darfurians are not going any more to play the role
> of foot soldiers for any party, be it Islamist or not, internal or
> external. The degree of Darfurians' awareness of their fate and
> destiny is never as strong and clear as it is today. The armed

struggle, with all its tragedies, has contributed to, and accelerated the level of that awareness of deserved rights, as well as of the exploitation they have been subjected to for generations. They are not prepared to be fooled again.[12]

The accent of disenfranchisement and the content of this statement are shared by most leaders and grassroots of the current Darfurian armed and political movements. Those in different factions of the SLM are even more disenchanted about the traditional parties, and especially so about the Islamist or Islamic ones. As Muslims themselves, they consider these parties and their Islamic slogans as mere hypocritical manifestations of power-mongering and opportunism. It would be very difficult to argue against the validity of such expressions of disappointment in the light of Darfur's political experience with the Sudan's centrist partisan politics, which have so repeatedly disappointed them.

One striking expression of such causes can be found in an infamous paper presented before the economic committee of the ruling NCP in the fall of 2005. The eight-page paper, written in Arabic and entitled "The Future of Investment During the Interim Period," was prepared by Abdel Rahim Mohamed Hamdi, ex-minister of finance and national economy under the current regime and a leading economic advisor to the ruling party, who was also instrumental in introducing the free market economy during his tenure of office. Significantly relevant, in the 1960s Hamdi was the editor of the Islamic Charter Front's official partisan newspaper, *Al Mithaq*. The paper he presented, which now forms an integral part of the its ruling party documentation for its 2005 conference on the national economy,[13] called for government economic, particularly investment, efforts to be focused on and limited to a "Dongola-Sennar plus Kordofan Axis," an area which encompasses the Northern State, Khartoum, Medani, and Sennar, but which excludes Eastern Sudan, Darfur, and the South.

Hamdi's paper states that the purpose behind investment during the interim period, between the signing of the Comprehensive Peace Agreement (CPA) with the South and the national elections, is to cater for "the interest of the [National Congress] Party in utilizing the investment during the interim period for the realization of advantages that would guarantee its continuation in power, and a monopoly of abundant political authority." As Darfur and other areas not included in the paper's "Axis" do not, according to it, fit within such partisan interest, the easiest way is to exclude them from the investment axis. This was emphatically stated under a subtitle on "What Investment and Where in the Country?" in which the paper explicitly talked of "(1) A Northern Axis: (Sennar-Dongola plus Kordofan)," then "(2) It is possible to direct some investments to some other areas—Eastern Sudan and Darfur, conditional on the realization of political stability." Any doubt as to the exclusion of Darfur in the NCP's economic strategies was further dashed by the concluding remarks of the paper, which talked of "the Axis Area," "the Axial Sudan" or "the targeted communities and entities" as the sole beneficiaries of investment returns during the interim period. Again, the third among the paper's six "basic assumptions" states the following:

> The geopolitical mass in the Northern Region . . . which I shall
> call in short the "Dongola to Sennar plus Kordofan Axis" is more
> homogeneous. It practically encompasses the idea of Islamic/
> Arabic Sudan from the ancient Islamic kingdoms centuries ago.
> It is therefore easy to formulate a political Arabic/Islamic alliance
> which would accommodate it. . . [E]ven if others would secede
> from it, economically if not politically, by drawing away huge
> resources from them, this part [of the country] has the capability
> to survive as an effective state. This is true in a slightly different
> way even if Darfur would depart.[14]

It is hard to think of any other case in current history in which a national ruling party has been so blunt, in an authentic and official document, in stating its policies for discrimination among regions of its country. Both messages and deeds similar to this blatantly partisan policy paper lie behind the explosion of civil war in Darfur. Among the leaders of Darfur's armed movements, it is not surprising that the former Islamists are the most aware of these divisive policies, which were made so explicit in the 2005 NCP paper. Some of Darfur's Islamists urged the leaders of the national Islamic movement to take preemptive measures against such divisive policies but their valuable advice went unheeded. The main reason that their warnings were neglected is related to a partisan mentality within the ranks of Sudanese Islamic movement which is responsible for most of its own crises, and the ensuing national disasters.

It was precisely this critique of the dominance of Sudan's centrist elites in successive governments that prompted Darfurian members of the Islamic movement to compile the statistics on the division of leading positions in the country between individuals from different regions. The resulting compendium and critique, known as the *Black Book,* was intended by its authors to expose the "black record" of Sudan's centrist governments. It purports to provide an authentic presentation, in figures taken mainly from official records, of the disparities in power and wealth sharing in Sudan, as between the remote areas, including Darfur, and the center. For that purpose Khartoum was not the real "center," but rather a government forum dominated by people overwhelmingly originating from the Northern Region. Alongside some sharp commentary, most of the first volume of the *Black Book* included schedules and tables with figures recording statistical data such as the number of posts held, and the identity of those holding the posts, from 1954 when the countdown to independence commenced to the year 2000, the date of the book's clandestine publication in Khartoum. (Some later updates were published in the online version posted on JEM's website.) Besides the elite from the Northern State, whose population comprises less than five percent of Sudan but who have provided the vast majority of senior government officers, all others were grossly underrepresented. Because of the need to symbolically accommodate the South, a number of positions were awarded to Southerners. However, individuals from all the other provinces of Northern Sudan, and especially Darfur, were grossly underrepresented.

The first public comment by a government official was made by Dr. Majzoub al Khalifa, then Governor (*Wali*) of Khartoum State, who was later to lead the government negotiation team at the Darfur peace talks. He denounced the book in the press as "racist" and said it had been written by "racists." Ironically, a leading Islamist from Northern Sudan was the first to respond publicly to Dr. Khalifa. Dr. Lubaba al Fadl Abdel Hameed, ex-President of the Islamist Ra'idatunnahdah women's association, strongly supported the case for Darfurians as presented in the book. In fact, the *Black Book* was the most embarrassing written account for the government ever.

A thorough perusal of the *Black Book*'s figures, coupled with the absence of any objective official response to it so far, would leave little doubt that the book accurately represents the facts as they are in Sudan. For example, while Darfur Region (North, South, and Western Darfur) accommodates (by 2000) about one-fifth (19.2 percent) of the Sudanese population (5,992,000), and the Northern Region only 1.86 percent thereof (less than 10 percent of Darfurians), Darfurians got far less than their numerical proportion. This may be illustrated by the following figures excerpted from the *Black Book:*

| Region | Revolutionary Command Council members (15) | Presidents, Vice Presidents & Presidential Assistants (11) | Presidential Ministers (10) | Presidential Advisors (20) | Interior Ministers (8) |
|--------|--------------------------------------------|------------------------------------------------------------|------------------------------|-----------------------------|------------------------|
| Northern | 8 (53%) | 3 (27%) | 6 (60%) | 10 (50%) | 8 (100%) |
| Darfur | 2 (13%) | 0 (0%) | 0 (0%) | 2 (10%) | 0 (0%) |

The authors of the *Black Book,* who went on to become the founders of JEM, were critical not just of the secular and sectarian governments that had ruled Sudan until 1989, but also of the Islamic movement, from whose ranks they themselves were drawn. In their attempt to broaden the base of the Islamic movement, Hassan al Turabi and his deputy, Ali al Haj Mohamed, had appealed to Darfurians' historic piety and their discontent with the established parties, and promised that all Muslims, regardless of their color, could achieve emancipation through an Islamic revolution. However, as one of JEM's members, Prof. Abdullahi al Tom (not himself an Islamist) later commented, Darfurians were "too black for the Islamist movement" in Sudan. Despite the presence of Ali al Haj, himself a Darfurian, in a senior position in the party, the promise of a color-blind Islamism turned out to be a sham.

However, the policies of Turabi and Ali al Haj favored Darfur and other non-Khartoum and remote populations more than those of their rivals in the ruling NCP. It was partly for that reason that Turabi himself was victimized by his ruling ex-disciples. This division became obvious during the year pre-ceding the December 1999 split of the NCP, when Turabi, then speaker of the National Assembly, led a constitutional amendment initiative in parlia-ment whereby regional governors (*walis*) were to be directly elected by their respective regional constituencies, instead of being appointed by the President, as it has been the case under Sudan's 1998 constitution. Turabi insisted on proceeding with the amendment despite an explicit, written request by President Omar Hassan al Bashir. The move, which triggered the dissolution of the National Assembly in a prelude to full Islamist division, was hailed by regionalists, among whom Darfurians and other western Sudanese form a sizeable majority in parliament. Later on the fight was resumed in a 10,000-strong NCP general assembly in which their vote on the issue came in favor of Turabi's proposed amendment, only to lead to the sec-ond leg of the division, four months later, when Turabi was ousted from his top party position, as secretary general, by a presidential decree. It was a pre-emptive act by al Bashir to avoid a possible major and strategic shift of power to Turabi through elected governors in a twenty-six state, one million square mile country—a recipe for real loss of central control.

Darfur has also been victimized by the Islamic movement's security men-tality, which has arisen from its over-reliance on a small urban constituency, and its fear that it will be vulnerable to other Sudanese political forces which were either well-represented in the military or had their own sectarian mili-tia. In his early critiques of Egypt's Muslim Brothers, Hassan al Turabi noted that the organization's "Special Branch" had become a law unto itself and had ultimately hijacked the movement itself. Fearing that a security unit within the Islamist movement would do the same, Turabi at first insisted that the Islamic Charter Front be a strictly civilian party. After the May Revolution that brought Jaafar Nimeiri to power, and which resulted in military opera-tions against the *Ansar* and the Muslim Brothers, he changed his mind, and in due course his earlier fears came to pass. The Islamic movement eventually became dominated by its security organs and by a military mentality.

The dominant military mentality is bent on the demands of security, mostly organizational and political security. All security matters rank top among any internal agenda of the movement, with all other concerns deflected to the rear or even totally discarded. This resulted in a tendency to disregard most progressive and development-oriented projects and proposals, irrespective of their authorship within the movement. It also resulted in major structural developments, with security apparatuses being established in all corners of the hierarchy of the organization. Security reports and reporters alike ruled the day, although such reporters do not hold the highest party offices. It may suffice to cite the incidence of involvement of a handful of Sudanese security elements in the 1995 attempted assassination of the Egyptian president Mohamed Hosni Mubarak in the Ethiopian capital Addis Ababa. Until the shock of the assassination attempt had been felt the world over, neither Sudan's president nor the regime's mentor, Hassan al Turabi, knew of the involvement of their own security agents in the attack. The first official report filed by the suspects to their internal security organization was after evidence started to point towards them. The absolute power accorded to the security elements was also responsible for political ineffectiveness and corruption. Accordingly, developments in Darfur were ignored for many years, as long as they were not seen as of any security significance, while the current revolt was treated within a pure security perspective, with no or little attention to its significant political dimensions.

Central among the disastrous errors committed under the pressure of such mentality is when the current Sudan government decided to arm the Janjawiid in a proxy war against the armed movements. This came after a series of defeats inflicted on the army by the Darfur rebel movements on the ground, including the April 2003 battle in which al Fashir was captured for six long hours before the invaders decided to withdraw in the company of a significant prisoner, Sudan Air Force commander Lt. Gen. Ibrahim Bushra Ismail. On another front Musa Hilal, widely known as a chief Janjawiid, was in prison at the city of Wad Medani in central Sudan along with other local tribal chiefs, such as Abbas and Yousuf Abu Shouk (Fur), when he was called upon, freed, and equipped by the army for the unholy mission. The damage this security decision has done to Darfur and Sudan cannot be overemphasized. The wounds to the social sentiments and fabric in the region and nationwide could persist unhealed for years to come.

## Islamism and the Current Crisis in Darfur

THE SPLIT OF THE RULING Islamist party in 1999 had important implications for Darfur. Many in Khartoum have asserted that the Darfur revolt was the direct work of Turabi and his PCP, intent on revenge for their expulsion from power. However, this conjecture cannot be established. First, it is quite clear that the SLM was nurtured by the SPLM, which proffered to it much of its ideology, including the demand for the separation of religion from the state. The SLM leadership reluctantly compromised on this issue during the Abuja peace talks, by which time the SPLM had signed the Comprehensive Peace Agreement and entered the Government of National Unity, thereby compromising its own long-held demand for a complete separation of religion and politics throughout the entire Sudan. Secondly, the fact that most of the influential leaders of one of the two main rebel movements, JEM, came from the Islamic movement was the main reason behind the belief about the involvement of the PCP. However, while the PCP was created in 2000, three years before JEM, few of the JEM leaders had joined Turabi's PCP before their rebellion.

Third and most significantly, the real origin of the split in the Islamists was political in nature. Among the breaking points, as we have seen, were the proposed constitutional amendments by the National Assembly under Turabi, its speaker. Turabi then swiftly announced the creation of his new PCP. Disenchanted Darfurians had few if any options for taking an effective political stand. Little opportunity existed for political activism under the state of emergency imposed by the president. One course of action was to stay politically aloof—tantamount to withdrawal from any political engagement, surrendering the political sphere to the centrist groups. A second option was to take up arms.

President Bashir's crackdown on the PCP included imprisoning Turabi along with many of his followers. This repression was conducted despite the party's Islamist political orientation and its being led by Sudan's most veteran Islamist. If the government could take such action against the men who had been its closest allies, Darfurians were confident that any organized political opposition they mounted would meet the same fate, and their decades-old political demands would be wholly ignored.

Finally, the suppressive circumstances undergone by the PCP would not allow it to channel any significant material support to the Darfur movements. The government and its security organs were effective in freezing or confiscating most of the assets of PCP members, often using illegal means. As the rebellion grew, the main support for Darfur came from the international community, which provided humanitarian assistance to Darfurians and the logistics for the rebel movements to organize. Turabi could not be accused as working in concert with the international community which, for example, would not boost any of Turabi's projects in Darfur or anywhere else.

According to the analysis of the PCP, the basic reason behind Darfur's conflict was competition over scarce resources, which was then exacerbated by faulty policies by Khartoum, including centrist concentration of power and wealth, the lack of proper representation of regional people in central positions, underdevelopment, politicization of native administration, enabling tribesmen to carry arms, and a reversal in federal, decentralized policy, coupled with the armed conflicts in neighboring Chad. Naturally enough, the PCP also adds the government's political recipe for Darfur to be a major reason behind the worsening situation. The PCP's vision regarding the settlement of the Darfur conflict is based on considering it a national, political problem relating to issues of freedom, justice, political participation, and good governance. It calls for a regional self-government for Darfur, a special fund to finance the peace requirements, including compensation of civilians and major development projects, local social reconciliations to heal the damaged social fabric, representing Darfur in the institution of the presidency, parliament, central cabinet, and the civil service, proportionately to the percentage of Darfur population (Popular Congress Party 2005).

The policies of JEM have not always been in line with those of the PCP. For example, the two entities have been at variance in relation to their respective positions vis-à-vis the United Nations Security Council decisions, such as that detailed in UN Resolution 1706 of August 31, 2006, which decided upon a robust UN operation in Darfur to replace the current African Union Mission in the region. While JEM openly rejected the Security Council's policy on the matter, the PCP Leadership Council (*Hai'atul Qiyadah*) voted in its favor.[15] The benefits of the confusion between the PCP and JEM accrue to the Sudan government, which presents the Darfur case as one made up by Turabi's PCP. President Bashir is able to use this to ease western pressure on it and, even better, redirect such pressure onto its two enemies, the rebels and the PCP, by its third enemy, the western powers and the international community in general. Given how events have unfolded since the partial signing of the DPA in May 2006, which included increased international response to the crisis, and branding of JEM and the National Redemption Front as spoilers in the conflict, it appears that that the Sudan government has attained a measure of success from its shrewd evasive strategy.

On the part of the Sudan government, two major obstacles currently prevent any genuine readiness for a real solution to the Darfur problem. The first is its insistence on the CPA power-sharing formula which gives the NCP a majority of 52 percent of executive and political power in Sudan during the interim period until the 2009 elections. Any equitable power-sharing with Darfur would by necessity touch on the security of that NCP share.

A second obstacle lies in the government's worry about the consequences of the UN Security Council Resolution 1593 of March 31, 2005, referring the crimes committed in Darfur to the International Criminal Court, which may lead to the indictment, arrest, and prosecution of those suspected of responsibility. Some of the suspects are believed to be senior government officials, most probably those handling the Darfur file. These government fears formed an important component of its rejection of the resolution authorizing a UN operation in Darfur. Once inside the country, any purposeful shift in the mandate of the UN operation forces could mean serious consequences for government officials. Although there is no palpable peace in Darfur to keep by a UN force, it is sad enough that no other hope for the suffering civilians against armed militia and government attacks seems to loom on the horizon.

The impact of Islamism on the current crisis in Darfur has thus been twofold, because of the split of the Islamic movement into two organizationally and politically distinct entities, despite claiming the same ideology. But it is politics that matters when it comes to power-mongering and pragmatic rivalry.

The ruling faction of the old NCP, still operating under the same name, has used all its state might to silence its pre-1999 political and ideological partner, the current PCP. This resulted in the victimization of its members, both current and departing, most of whom came from western Sudan in general and Darfur in particular. This policy helped fuel the rebellion even further and facilitated recruitment of new cadres over time.

The few Darfurians who remained in the ruling party, the NCP, can be divided into three categories. The first is made up of elitist, urbanized government officials who chose to remain in power, because opposing the government would mean dismissal or worse. The second category is composed of local traditional figures with their followers, who happened to come from minority tribes or from tribes not significantly participating in the armed rebellion against the government. Some of these figures, although not Janjawiid themselves, tribally relate to that militia, resulting in a form of joint interest which the government would exploit to the maximum. The third are flagrantly conniving elements, including the Janjawiid.

## Conclusion

IT IS DIFFICULT to identify any unified Islamist policy towards Darfur. To the extent that the Islamists have influenced the conflict in Darfur, it is on account of the very divisive, socially disruptive, and politically disastrous twin-headed, power-oriented tactics that emanated from a divided Islamic regime. Nor has there been in the past any effective policy with regard to the major demands of the people of Darfur. This was due to several factors. While Sudan has always been governed by mostly centrist policies, Darfur's geographical remoteness added up to its victimization in terms of regional disparities, marginalization, and social and economic injustice. When the movement was united, before and after it came to power, there was still no distinct program or even a streamlined vision for Darfur, as admitted by Muslim Brotherhood veteran Yassin Omar al Imam (interviewed for this chapter). Among other things, this was due to the urbanist and elitist orientation of the movement, at least until their *Inqaz* coup d'état in June

1989, after which they made efforts to gain popularity in remote rural and other areas as compared to urban centers.

The ruling faction of Sudan Islamists is practicing its policies on Darfur mostly in the open, to the witnessing eyes of international media. Its latest declared position is to take the Darfur Peace Agreement as a final peace accord, fight against those who refused to sign (non-Minni Minawi SLM factions, the new National Redemption Front that includes the JEM and G-19), adamantly refusing to accept any blue-hatted international intervention by the United Nations forces in Darfur while accepting an extended role there by the current African Union forces, with only UN logistical and expertise assistance. This position is not expected to bring a lasting peace for the region.

The other Islamist faction, the PCP, has been out of power since the end of the 1990s and has been suffering immense suppression by its former partner in power, which renders its Darfur policies of little practical significance. However, we have seen their documented views and positions with regard to Darfur, which are generally in line with the claims by Darfur's armed movements which, despite their factionalism, have been united in their political demands. The Islamist division has been detrimental to Darfurians and Darfur, adding only to the compounding of an already complex and immensely tragic crisis.

# 5

# The Origins and Organization of the Janjawiid in Darfur

## ALI HAGGAR

THIS CHAPTER IS CONCERNED with the origin and composition of the armed Janjawiid in Darfur. It addresses how certain armed groups that formed during the civil wars in Chad between 1962 and 1991 contributed to the formation of armed militias in Darfur, specifically the Janjawiid. It notes that all the major conflicts in Darfur over the last twenty years have been associated with the presence of armed Chadian groups and that armed Chadians constitute a significant proportion of the Janjawiid. It then looks at how the original Janjawiid have become part of a wider phenomenon of "Janjawiidism" in Darfur, which now includes armed groups that were not previously identified as Janjawiid. There are six categories of pro-government armed groups in Darfur that are, in one way or another, associated with the Janjawiid: the "Peace Forces" (Quwat al Salaam), the nomad protection forces, the Um Bakha irregular forces, the Um Kwak attacker forces, the Popular Defense Force (Difaa al Sha'abi), and the Popular Police Force (Shorta al Sha'abi). Excluded from this list are the national army and the official police force, which are not directly related to the Janjawiid, although elements within the Sudanese armed forces, especially military intelligence, work closely with the Janjawiid.

The origins of the Janjawiid lie at the intersection of the local politics of Darfur and the military mobilization of Chadian Arabs under Libyan sponsorship during the 1970s and 1980s. The Darfurian Janjawiid became active between 2001 and 2003 as a direct result of the agreements reached between Arab tribal leaders. These agreements included both Sudanese residents and Chadian migrants, who were increasingly under the supervision and coordination of central and regional governments. Since 2003, and especially after the expansion of the war into eastern and southern Darfur in 2004, additional Arab and non-Arab groups have been armed as part of the Janjawiid phenomenon.

"Janjawiid" is the term given to the armed groups of Arab tribes by other parties. Many Janjawiid prefer to call themselves "horsemen" (*fursan*). They came initially from the Baggara cattle herders in the central-south region of Darfur and the adjoining region, which extends into Chad, especially the Wadai and Salamat regions. The latter formed an alliance with the northern Abbala Rizeigat armed groups and other camel herders, who also lived in both Darfur and Chad.

The Arabs and Arabized Nubians of the Nile Valley consider the Janjawiid to be members of the Juhayna group of Saharan and Sahelian Arabs due to the Janjawiid's ideology of Arab supremacy. This alliance has earned them the support of successive governments in Khartoum. The justification given for this support is the belief, held by members of Sudan's ruling elite, that the Arab tribes' involvement in controlling Darfur constitutes the only guarantee that Darfur will remain part of the Republic of the Sudan. The Janjawiid carry out a role similar to the Arab militia forces in South Darfur and South Kordofan, who prevented the Sudan People's Liberation Army (SPLA) from expanding its operations in those regions in the 1980s. Many suspect that the overall plan is to create an "Arab belt" across all of western Sudan, displacing the non-Arab population. At minimum, the aim is to stabilize the Arab presence in Darfur; at maximum the objective is to change the demography of Darfur. The militarization of Darfur's politics allowed the Arabs' ideology to become an overt and official program. The Janjawiid were officially recognized, provided with uniforms, and used as a part of the Popular Defense Forces from 1999 onward. The horsemen (*fursan*) that had crushed Daud Bolad's 1991 rebellion were mobilized, as were the nomadic forces used against the SPLA's "New

Sudan" project in South Sudan. The government exerted great efforts to provide weapons and other support.

Some prominent Arab tribal leaders, especially those with territories away from the areas of conflict, have criticized the government for using the Janjawiid, pointing out that it is very difficult for such militias to abide by any moral code or to exercise restraint during times of war. In addition, the mobilization of the Janjawiid hinders the potential for a political settlement to the current crisis.

Understanding the Janjawiid demands knowledge of the historical background of Chadian relations with Darfur. Research into the immigrants—their identities, leaders, and numbers—brings to light their political and demographic impact, their relations with local and central authorities, their geographic location, and their areas of movement. One of the implications is that solutions must be found regionally, in collaboration with neighboring countries including Chad, the Central African Republic, and Libya.

## Chadian Migration to Sudan

THERE IS A LONG HISTORY of migration from Chad to Sudan for religious, economic, and political reasons. Religious migration has occurred since the coming of Islam along with the Muslim obligation to make the pilgrimage to Mecca. As a result of this migration there are more than two million Sudanese of West African origin, known as *Fallata*. In the late nineteenth century, the Mahdists replaced the duty of *hajj* with a requirement to migrate to the Mahdist centers of power in Omdurman, and later to Abba Island on the Nile. There, the migrants served as soldiers in the Mahdist army and as workers on the irrigated estates along the river. Economic migration has occurred due to droughts in the Sahelian region and because of the large demand for labor by the agricultural schemes of the Nile Valley and the major Sudanese cities in that region.

Political migration is particularly important in terms of Chadian links to armed groups in Darfur. This started with the first preparations for an independent government of Chad as both the Sudanese and Libyan governments organized Chadian Arabs militarily and politically. Meanwhile, the repressive measures against the Arabs by most Chadian governments resulted in many Arabs fleeing to Libya and Sudan for safety. Sudanese governments have been hospitable to Chadian Arabs.

The immigration of Chadians has changed the demography of parts of Darfur. In the areas of Zalingei, Kas, west Jebel Marra, and Wadi Saleh especially, most villages have Chadian minorities or a Chadian majority. Every group that has migrated to Darfur has sought to establish its authority in order to have access to land and other natural resources, and to government services including the granting of citizenship. Competition for control of local executive authority and native administration has been a characteristic of the Chadian immigration and settlement process. Most of the tribes migrating from Chad to Sudan have been transhumant semi-nomads who have no permanent settlements since they remain on the move in search of water and pasture.

Most groups migrating from Chad do not remain with their former Chadian administrative leaders, but instead live under leaders from Sudanese tribes, usually ones related to the migrants. This makes it easier for them to obtain Sudanese nationality and enables them to join official paramilitary forces such as the nomadic security forces and the Popular Defense Force. At times of intense war, the government and its representatives have actively recruited youth from Chadian-origin tribes for the militia.

Most Chadian immigrants are Arabs, although some non-Arab tribes have also migrated to Darfur, where they then joined with the Arab tribes out of fear and self-interest. This is particularly the case for small tribes such as the Tama and Gimir, and migrants from West Africa. A recent Darfurian Arab song has the following words: "The Gimir and Tama feared the missiles and joined us. The Antonov taught the Zaghawa fear." The women who sing this song describe how the small border tribes of Gimir and Tama joined the Arabs in war out of fear when the Zaghawa—seen as the true enemies of the Arabs—were threatened by aerial attack.

An important way for the Chadian immigrants to gain power and access to land has been through reforms of the native administration system. The native administration system was not originally designed to accommodate the substantial inflow of people and has required considerable change. The approaches taken have been very different in West Darfur, where the Fur and Masalit dominate the administration, and in South Darfur, which is dominated by the Baggara Arab tribes. In all cases, jurisdiction over land is vested in the officeholder within the system who "owns" the *hakura* (or "landholding"). If, through administrative intervention or a change in the demography, the "owner" of the *hakura* changes, then political power shifts.

In West Darfur, the local government reform of March 1995 was the first and most dramatic example of an attempt to accommodate Chadian Arabs within Darfur's administrative structure at the expense of non-Arab groups. The reform introduced eight Arab *amirs*, all holding the same rank as the five existing Masalit *furshas*. The Arab amirs thereby formed a majority within the electoral college of middle-ranking administrative chiefs who would elect the sultan of Dar Masalit. The same reform limited the sultan's term in office to seven years. These changes would have turned Dar Masalit into an Arab *hakura*. This threat sparked a conflict between the Masalit and twenty-seven other groups, mostly Arab. The Masalit formed self-defense units under the name "Front for the Liberation of Dar Masalit." Several tribes tried to remain neutral but lost property, land, and lives during the conflict. Several peace agreements were negotiated, beginning in 1996, but they failed to address the root causes of the conflict—the agreement of 1996, for example, declared the equality of Arabs and Masalit in authority and land.

A contrasting approach was adopted in South Darfur during the 1997 Rizeigat-Zaghawa settlement conference, which acknowledged the right of the Rizeigat Arabs to their land—that is, it retained a status quo favorable to the Arabs. This, combined with the changes in West Darfur shaped the Masalit and non-Arab tribes' belief that the government was only supporting the Arab population. This contributed to an upsurge in resistance against the government. The resistance then took political shape and expanded to include the marginalized populations and those excluded from power.

An example of the native administration system being manipulated to change land ownership and demography can be provided by the case of al Malam, east and southeast of Jebel Marra. The Arab *omodiya* (a middle-ranking chieftainship) of Bin Mansur, located in al Malam, was historically small with few inhabitants, and its administration was under the authority of the *shartais* of Birgid Umroshung, a non-Arab tribe. In an administrative reform, al Malam was made into region's the senior administrative center and obtained authority over the surrounding areas. Eighteen village councils from Umroshung, and seventeen from Dobo, were added to al Malam. The *omda* of Bin Mansur then enjoyed far more power over a much larger area. This in turn attracted a number of different Arab immigrant groups who entered the area and the places immediately to the west, until they reached the valleys, fertile pastures, and vast agricultural land inside Jebel Marra itself. These immigrants began to force the Fur and other non-Arab tribes out of the area. New omdas were appointed from Arab groups including Chadian Arab immigrants. The plan was reportedly to augment al Malam by adding territories further east, thus providing an excuse for the ethnic cleansing of a wide area of eastern Jebel Marra.

The single largest tribal migration to Darfur has been that of the Salamat federation of tribes, originating in the Salamat region of Chad, including the Salamat capital, Um el Teiman, and the town of Goz Beida. Salamat migration stretches back many centuries and continued through the middle years of the twentieth century, causing the British administrators to complain to their French counterparts in Chad. The Salamat established their first *omodiya* in Sudan in 1974, and their number has since grown rapidly. Three Chadian *omdas* have taken office in Wadi Saleh, four have been appointed in Nyala-Kubbum, two in Buram, and still more in Geneina. However, despite repeated demands from Salamat leaders, they have never been awarded a *nazir* (paramount chief), their own administration, or land jurisdiction. One Salamat scholar argues forcibly that, "The Salamat deserve a *nazara* because they are courageous, revolutionary, wild, and generous. This will make a big difference in Sudan in terms of security in the area. They have seven omodiyas in South Darfur and six in West Darfur and every *omda* has thirty-three sheikhs. That is 13 x 33 = 429 sheikhs. Each sheikh has about twenty people, on average, and if a sheikh has to pay one million Sudanese pounds as tax per year this means they pay 429 million pounds. Those are the criteria the government gave Arab tribes' *amarat* in Masalit and Fur areas."

The Salamat scholar's arithmetic may not be completely accurate, but the sentiments expressed are a true reflection of the logic and aspiration of the Salamat leaders. The Salamat are similar to other Arab tribes in that they offer support when it is requested from other Arab tribes. As the Arab proverb goes: "Support never hurts."

The Salamat tribes began their military organization in the early 1970s. This included the faction of the Chadian leader Mohamed Abba Saeed. The militia was known as "Tandasa," and its aim was both to acquire land and authority in the Tissi and Abu Gradil areas of West Darfur and to take power in Chad. This militia clashed with the Ta'aisha (known in Chad as Himat) in the 1970s.

## Chadian Migration and Armed Groups in Darfur

SUDAN AS A WHOLE and Darfur in particular have a long history of the peaceful absorption of settlers. The number of peaceably settled West Africans is considerably greater than the number of Chadian Arabs. What made the Chadian immigration problematic was their connection with armed groups that initially had designs exclusively to take power in Chad, but who also began to turn their attention to carving out space for themselves in Darfur. This section traces an outline of the extremely complicated and fractious history of the Chadian armed-opposition movements, which have used Darfur as a rear base since 1966.

Political opposition to the Chadian regime of François Tombalbaye originated with the Chadian Muslims who were organized within Chad, Sudan, and Egypt. Clandestine opposition began in 1958, two years before Chad's independence. Initial civil mobilization was crushed and the Chadian Muslim movement was recreated as an armed liberation movement. The National Liberation Front for Chad (FROLINAT) was formally constituted on June 22, 1966, in the Darfurian town of Nyala, under the leadership of Chairperson Ibrahim Abatcha. Among FROLINAT's leaders was Mohamed el Bagillani, the most prominent leader of Chad's Arabs. FROLINAT described the Tombalbaye government as a Christian dictatorship. Modeling his leadership after Zaire's Mobutu Sese Seko, Tombalbaye adopted the ideology of "African authenticity," creating an "African"-"Arab" polarization in Chad that had obvious, if superficial, parallels with the politics of North versus South Sudan. Arabic and Islamic statements issued by FROLINAT and its successor movements stressed the common cause between Chadian Muslims and Sudanese Arabs. After the Libyan revolution of September 1969, FROLINAT's link with Libya was also stressed. FROLINAT's initial declaration and subsequent mobilization were widely appreciated by Chadian Muslims.

Darfur soon became the base for the Chadian militias, which were formed and trained under FROLINAT command. The first armed camps were in the Salamat centers of Tissi and Abu Gradil, and in Jebel Marra, where the exiled "Jebel Marra Government" was formed. That government included: Goukouni Oueddai, President; Hissène Habré, Defense Minister; Mohamed Abba Saeed, Interior Minister; Ahmat Acyl Agbash, Foreign Minister; and Abubaker Abdel Rahman, Minister of Agriculture. Most of these individuals were key figures in the organization of the Chadian militia and their Darfurian counterparts. All were Muslim, several from the Toubou-Goraan group of black Saharans (Goukoni Ouaddai and Hissène Habré), while others were Arabs (Mohamed Abba Saeed is Salamat, Ahmat Acyl Agbash was Arab Abbala).

FROLINAT disintegrated due to many factors including geography, Sudanese-Chadian relations, and the African Christian-Arab Muslim conflict. Many successor fronts were formed. A seemingly endless process of fragmentation and the partial recombination of groups characterized Chadian politics and the civil war. Some of the splits occurred along ethnic lines, while others were the outcome of pure political ambition. Problems were compounded by the fact that the same or similar names recur among different groups and that the same group may have different names. Particularly significant was the Burkan ("Volcano") Brigade/Front/Movement, from which emerged the Conseil Democratique Revolutionnaire (CDR—widely known as "Sidi Ayr"), which became the umbrella organization for Arab groups. No fewer than eleven groups emerged from FROLINAT, each with a different ethnic/racial base. The Arab armed groups were known by names such as Um Bagga, Tameen al Marahil, and al Fursan.

The militarized factionalization of Chadian Muslim politics has two important implications: One is that Chadian politics is focused on patronage and the buying off of individuals. The second is that the groups that are excluded from power are constantly seeking to establish a base in a friendly neighboring country, usually Sudan.

## Libya and the Islamic Legion

MOST FROLINAT SPLINTERS had some connection with Libya and its international brigades, including the Islamic Legion (Failaq al Islamiya) and the Arab Gathering (Tajamu al Arabi). Some of the leading FROLINAT figures, including Goukoni Ouaddai and Ahmat Acyl Agbash, were also commanders in the Islamic Legion. Mohamed al Bagillani, Acyl, and Abba Saeed were members of the Arab Gathering. Beit Waliid, the first armed camp in Libya for Chadians, was established in 1974. The vanguard for the Libyan-backed enterprise was the Burkan militia. It was through this that the Arab militias that constitute the Janjawiid began, as an alliance between the Salamat militia and the camel herders of the North, both in Chad and Darfur. Most of the camel herders are Rizeigat but they also include Khuzam, Misiriya (including Tarjam), Beni Halba, and others.

The sponsor of the Sudanese-Chadian role in the Islamic Legion was Abdalla Zakaria Idris, a Sudanese national who served for a long period as secretary-general of the Sudanese Popular Socialist Front and as the leader of its troops since it was established in 1981 in Libya. The Front was established on the ruins of the Sudanese National Front in Libya, which had been created in 1971 by Sudan's Islamist and sectarian opposition parties. After its failed invasion of Sudan to overthrow the Nimeiri government in 1976, the National Front broke apart, with most of its leaders reconciling with Jaafar Nimeiri and returning to Sudan.

At that time Muammar Gaddafi was a militant Arab nationalist aiming for the creation of an Arab homeland across the Sahara. Gaddafi used an expansive definition of "Arab," which allowed any Bedouins to aspire to become Arabs. He was willing to enlist any Muslims who were ready to fight, and the

Islamic Legion allowed for this. This explains the involvement of the Zaghawa and other non-Arab Bedouins including Toubou, Goraan, Meidob, and Tuareg. Although a number of Zaghawa leaders participated actively in the Islamic Legion, the Zaghawa as a tribe did not.

Gaddafi created the Islamic Legion in the early 1970s. At its peak it had six divisions, though they never reached their intended strength. The legion's aim was to change the ruling system in Chad, Sudan, Niger, Mali, and beyond to promote the Jamaheeri system—the theory of Gaddafi's *Green Book*. When the major Sudanese figures in the National Front returned to Sudan after 1977, Gaddafi supported any who were ready to continue pursuing the military option. He also used Sudanese fighters to support his political and territorial ambitions in Chad, including the annexation of the Aozou Strip, and used any means necessary to oppose the activities of France and the United States.

The Libyan leader's philosophy of "revolutionary necessity" was built upon the experience of Latin America's rebels in Bolivia, Cuba, Chile, and other countries where rebels had united to achieve their objectives by gathering their collective military and fighting efforts to liberate their countries one after another. They also used the doctrine of the foco-ist revolutionary Che Guevara, whereby a small armed group could spark a wider rebellion by starting a "people's war" in an otherwise hostile territory.

The Sudanese Popular Socialist Front opened the Mazda camp in the Libyan desert in 1981, the first of several camps. A total of 6,000 recruits were trained; many of them were deployed to Chad as part of the Libyan project of changing the regime. A force of 2,500 Islamic Legion troops entered Chad with the goal of toppling Hissène Habré. They set up camp near Um Shalopa, but were defeated in a surprise attack led by Colonel Idriss Déby of Habré's army. Some of the remaining troops withdrew into Sudan and others returned to Libya. In Libya, two Sudanese Zaghawa, Osman Mohamed al Bushra and Adam Abakar Khalil, who set up a new army called the Sudanese National Revolutionary Force, deposed Abdalla Zakaria in a "revolutionary putsch." This army was short-lived, due to defeats by Habré and the fact that as non-Arabs they were not fully trusted by the leaders of the Islamic Legion.

## From FROLINAT to Burkan to CDR: The Arab Agenda in Chad

FROLINAT WAS FOUNDED by a broad cross section of Chadian Muslims, which included both Arabs and black Saharan peoples of the Goraan-Toubou-Zaghawa group. A few years later, specifically Arab factions arose within FROLINAT. Their first leader was Mohamed al Bagillani who is hailed as the founder of Arab nationalism within FROLINAT, and who is still recalled as the founder of the "Arab Gathering" political project in the Qoreish manifestos. He created the Burkan militia within FROLINAT. This, too, fragmented over time, and later there was an attempt to reconstitute it as a unified movement, CDR. This section outlines this history.

Chad's "First Army," the Chadian National Liberation Front (FROLINAT)-First Army, nicknamed the "Burkan Forces," was established in 1971. Its leader, Mohamed al Bagillani, was killed in a road accident in the Libyan city of Benghazi in March 1977. After Bagillani's death, the Burkan Forces were riven by disagreements, and was replaced by the CDR. The CDR was formed at a conference in Libya in 1978, bringing together four ex-FROLINAT factions, including Mohamed Abba Saeed's "Popular Liberation Forces" and one part of the Burkan Front.

The CDR was a signatory to the 1979 Lagos Agreement, which created a government of national unity in N'djamena. Goukoni Ouaddai, representing the Popular Army of the North, became president. The government also included Hissène Habré, who by this time had become a fierce rival of Goukoni and nursed a deep hatred of Arabs. The rivalry between the two led to nine months of fighting within the capital city itself, prompting an intervention by the Organisation of African Unity, at that time chaired by the Nigerian president Olusegun Obasanjo.

The CDR founder and leader was Ahmat Acyl Aghbash. In July 1982 an airplane propeller struck him in the head, killing him. The Libyan government appointed his successor, Acheikh Ibn Omer Saeed. During Ibn Omer's leadership, CDR split into two factions. Ibn Omer joined the government of national unity, and after its rapid collapse he became head of the Chadian units of the Islamic Legion. Al Rakhees Manan headed the other CDR faction.

He instructed his commanders to sign an agreement with the newly-installed Habré government and return to Chad. This defection caused Goukoni Ouaddai, now in opposition and still backed by Libya, to arrest Ibn Omer and keep him in prison for six months.

The government of Libya actively and substantively supported the CDR with money and heavy weapons. Libya made the CDR responsible for implementing the program of Arab nationalism and the Islamic Legion in Chad. However, the CDR disappointed its Libyan sponsors. The death of Ahmat Acyl and the withdrawal of Libyan forces from N'djamena, at the request of Goukoni who was fighting Habré in the capital, led to the collapse of the Libyan project for controlling Chad. At the same time, several groups within the fragmenting CDR became hostile to Libya and began fighting against the Libyans. Additionally, there was much internal dissatisfaction within the Burkan Front-CDR about the mishandling of finance, politics, and leadership.

If Mohamed al Bagillani introduced militant Arab nationalism into Chadian politics, it was his successor Ahmat Acyl, known as "al Minesi," who developed it into a formidable military force with allies across Chad and into Sudan. Ahmat Acyl has become something of a mythical figure among Chadian and Darfurian Arabs. He was from the Ziodi, a subtribe of the Awlad Rashid tribe, itself part of the camel-herding Rizeigat. A son of the head of the tribe, Ahmat Acyl was born in Alhamidia. He had his primary education in the Atia-Albatha region and completed his education in France. He had two wives—one Chadian and one French—and two daughters—one is a pilot and the other is a personal guard to Colonel Gaddafi.

After Ahmat Acyl completed his education in France he returned to Chad and participated in the Tombalbaye government as governor of the Atia-Albatha region. Many stories are reported about him. They are difficult to verify, but illustrate his fearsome reputation. It was said that he used to have a strong tribal bias, to the extent that he issued as legislation local decrees supporting the taking of women and men as slaves. It was also said that he despised the black Africans and allowed their honor to be desecrated by the Arabs. It was even said that when Ahmat Acyl was married, after celebrating his wedding in an army helicopter—a wedding in the sky that prefigured his death by rotor blades—he ordered the slaughter of a black man to fulfill a wish from the bride's mother. Such are the myths attached to Ahmat Acyl.

As mentioned above, Ahmat Acyl participated in the 1970s' government. After he was ousted from this position, he became a rebel and joined FROL-INAT, becoming a leader of the Burkan Front and then founder of CDR. He participated in the establishment of the Jebel Marra government, which also included Goukoni Ouaddai, Hissène Habré, and Abba Saeed. Thereafter, the Libyans opened three military camps on his behalf. One, the April 7 Camp, was in Tripoli, and two were in the desert, at Beni Waliid and Godaim.

Shortly after the camps were created, the Libyans rounded up Chadian and Sudanese elements in Libya. In this "kasha"-style raid, everyone in the vicinity was swept up. These roundups were organized by the security services in cooperation with Abdalla Zakaria. During the roundups—between 1975 and 1987—hundreds of Chadians and Sudanese lost their lives, some of them on account of the fights that broke out inside the camps. Within six weeks, Ahmat Acyl succeeded in collecting 4,550 recruits.

Ahmat Acyl was Libya's most important tool for changing the Chadian regime, spreading the ideology of the Jamhuriya, and expanding the Arab land through Arab nationalism, while also using the Islamic Legion to spread Islam. During the 1970s, Gaddafi shifted his emphasis from socialism to Arab nationalism. When Arab nationalism also failed, during the period of support to Ahmat Acyl, Gaddafi changed his strategy again. His new emphasis was on the Islamic Legion, which was to be activated with the support of other forces, especially in the Salamat areas. Under Libyan direction, Ahmat Acyl divided his army into three factions. One group advanced on Tibesti, under the command of al Saleel Mukhtar, a former herder from the Ta'aisha. The second group was led by al Nour Ahmed, from the Awlad Rashid Arabs. This group entered Chad from the south, through Cameroon

The third group was led by Idris Kum Ragmat, a Misiriya Arab, and entered Chad from Darfur in 1976. It is with this group that we find the first evidence of the historical relationship between Ahmat Acyl and Sheikh Hilal Mohamed Abdalla, the chief of the Mahamid in Sudan. The former sultan of the Mahamid, Aboud wald Sharara, was killed in 1910 while fighting at the head of the Mahamid forces against the French. Since then, Mahamid leaders opposed what they saw as the French-domination of Chad, and extended that opposition to the Chadian African leaders including Tombalbaye, Félix Malloum, and Habré. Libya also found the Mahamid camels to be a convenient means of transporting arms to the Chadians in Darfur. In 1981, the Libyans provided the Mahamid with thirty boxes of weapons and ammunition, both for their own protection and for them to supply to the Burkan forces.

The military operations that Ahmat Acyl began in 1977 ultimately led to the FROLINAT coalition, with Libyan support, entering N'djamena and taking power in 1979. Once in power, President Goukouni and his defense minister, Habré, fought nine months of street battles, which resulted in Habré's defeat. Ahmat Acyl sided with Goukouni and Habré fled to Sudan where, with Sudanese and American backing, he reinvaded and took power. Habré's defense minister was Hassan Djamous, a Zaghawa whose deputy was Idriss Déby.

On becoming head of the CDR after Ahmat Acyl's death in July 1982, Ibn Omer made the Tibesti Mountains in the Chadian Sahara into his headquarters. Later he had a disagreement with his deputy, al Rakhees Manan, which became a tribal dispute—while Ibn Omer is from the Awlad Rashid, al Rakhees is from the Misseriya. The dispute led to a number of the military leaders from the Ibn Omer group deserting and joining the Habré government. This internal conflict was devastating for the CDR. More devastating still was the offensive by Habré's forces—commanded in the field by Djamous—which defeated the Libyan army and the Islamic Legion at Ouadi Doum in May 1987. With extensive support from both France and the U.S., Habré's army destroyed a huge Libyan army and effectively ended Gaddafi's ambitions in Chad.

### The Janjawiid in Darfur

IN 1987, IBN OMER was driven out of Chad and tried to open a new front in Darfur using bases at Anjikoti, close to the border near Foro Baranga. He was defeated there by cross-border raids and retreated to

Kutum. The CDR troops were well known for their violent and undisciplined conduct. This conduct inflamed the Arab-Fur conflict, which had until then been entirely political and not military. At the end of 1988, after French and Chadian troops had chased the CDR and defeated it near Kutum, Gaddafi decided to recognize the Habré government and abandon his ambitions to control Chad. Immediately after this decision, Ibn Omer decided to seek reconciliation with Habré. This meant that the CDR leadership passed to al Rakhees, due a deal he had previously made with Habré. It was Ibn Omer's abandonment of the armed struggle at the beginning of 1989 that made possible the peace agreement reached in Darfur between Arabs and Fur in July that year.

Ibn Omer chose to make his base near Kutum because of his prior contacts with the Mahamid tribe of Sheikh Hilal Mohamed Abdalla. In 1986, Sheikh Hilal was incapacitated and his son Musa took over leadership of the tribe soon after. Ibn Omer made a political and military alliance with the Mahamid. In addition to resisting Habré's troops, the CDR forces fought alongside the Mahamid and other Darfurian Arab tribes to seize control of land in Darfur. When Ibn Omer decided to return to Chad, his fighters distributed their weapons to the Mahamid and other local allies. It was during this war that Darfurians first began to hear the word "Janjawiid" to describe the Arab militias.

There is no agreement on the origin or definition of the word "Janjawiid." Those versed in the culture of Arab tribes in Darfur state that the word "Janjawiid" has been in use for a long time, perhaps since the 1960s, when it was used as a pejorative term to describe poor vagrants from Arab tribes. These individuals survived by taking menial jobs and were looked down upon. One Darfurian scholar, Abu al Bashar Abbaker Hasab al Nabi, says that non-Arabs use the word "Janjawiid" to describe the militia that the Arabs themselves call *fursan* or "horsemen." Yusuf al Bashar Musa, a scholar from the Salamat, prefers to define the Janjawiid as a military organization from the Arab tribes, created after negotiation among Arab leaders, which embraces a variety of different armed groups including Marahiil protection forces, Anbaa forces, Um Kwak militia, the Quwat al Salaam, and a number of paramilitary groups absorbed by the Sudanese government.

One of the major Arab groups involved in the war of 1987–1989, and also in fighting the incursion of SPLA in South Darfur in 1991, and since 2001 in West and South Darfur, has been the militia of the Beni Halba. The Beni Halba call their militia *fursan* but others call it "Janjawiid." The Sudanese government's military intelligence supported the militia during all these activities.

The Marahiil Protection Force is an intrinsic part of the Janjawiid. Despite the fact that there are non-Arab nomadic tribes in Darfur (such as the Zaghawa and Meidob), the Marahiil Protection Force is formed exclusively from Arabs. It was formed during the Sadiq el Mahdi government to protect the Arab nomads as they moved on their migration routes.

## The Regularization of the Janjawiid

THE TRANSFORMATION of the Janjawiid into semi-regularized or paramilitary forces began with the intensification of the rebellion in Darfur and the government's response. This transformation has gone farthest in North Darfur, where the rebellion first began. In other parts of Darfur, where no Arab militia that could be called "Janjawiid" existed, the government instead created or regularized other militia, from both Arab and non-Arab groups, which have since become part of the Janjawiid phenomenon in Darfur.

In North Darfur, the majority of the Janjawiid became part of the government's armed forces beginning in 2003. Shortly after the SLA attacked al Fashir in April 2003, the Sudan Armed Forces began a major recruitment drive for the Popular Defense Forces. Both Arab and non-Arab tribes were targeted, but the Arabs were favored, especially when non-Arab recruits began to defect to the SLA. Very quickly, the government's response to the insurgency turned into wholehearted support for the Janjawiid. The Janjawiid were then absorbed into the Popular Defense Forces, the Border Intelligence and Border Guard units, the Nomadic Police, and other state security organs. Much the same happened in West Darfur.

In the eastern part of North Darfur and across South Darfur, there were few original Janjawiid, apart from the Beni Halba *fursan* and the Arab tribes that migrated to al Malam. The *murahaliin* militia of the Rizeigat, which was formed in 1985 to fight against the SPLA in South Sudan, and which participated in the 1987 massacre of the displaced Dinka people in el Da'ien, did not participate in other internal conflicts until 2004. The government's response to the rebellion in the eastern part of North Darfur and in South Darfur was to organize the entire native administration system as one of military command, creating militia units up to the level of brigade. In cases where the native administrator himself resisted this, he was replaced, or, where the government was unable to do that, rebellious elements in his tribe were organized as Marahiil Protection Force militias or other Janjawiid militia.

Many of the cases of "intertribal reconciliation" in South Darfur are examples of how the government is organizing the native administration for military purposes. The reconciliation near Nyala of Fur, Daju, and Zaghawa with the Arab tribes of Tarjam, Hawtiya, and Ta'alba, and the reconciliation around Shi'ariya between Rizeigat, Misiriya, Birgid, Daju and Zaghawa are examples. The basis for reconciliation has been the government's provision of resources to the tribal leadership on both sides, including paying salaries to native administration leaders, and providing vehicles and weapons to those who are ready to organize a militia in support of the government's military effort.

Among the native administration leaders who have mobilized their tribes in political and military support for Khartoum are the chiefs of the Habbaniya, Misiriya, Hawtiya, and Tarjam, from among the Arabs, and the Fallata, Birgid, and Daju, from among the non-Arabs. Special efforts were made to mobilize the Um Kamalti Zaghawa Arab clans also. The Ta'aisha have not been militarily engaged as their territory does not adjoin any of the areas in which the SLA has been active, but the tribe's leaders have given moral support to the militia of other Arab tribes.

The main native administration leader to resist government efforts to organize a Janjawiid militia has been the Rizeigat *nazir,* Saeed Madibu, who has tried to keep his tribe neutral in the Darfur conflict. The government has tried, and partly succeeded, in undermining Nazir Madibu's authority, and in creating a Janjawiid force. This force is commanded directly by Abdala Ali Masar (who belongs to the Nuwaiba clan and is an advisor to the president of the Republic) and Abdel Hamid Musa Kasha (of the Mahariya clan, who was the minister of international trade before the formation of the present national unity government). Masar was one of the original signatories of the 1987 "Arab Letter" to Sadiq el Mahdi, which established Darfur's Arab Alliance. Masar and Kasha have used the power of the state authorities to subvert the Rizeigat tribal authority and bring the Rizeigat cattle herders into armed conflict with SLA-Minawi forces in southern and eastern Darfur.

## Analysis of Documents

THE FOLLOWING two documents illustrate different aspects of the Janjawiid agenda in Chad and Darfur. The first document is the "Qoreish 2" manifesto, which has been dated to approximately 1998 or 1999. The document refers to the "Qoreish 1" manifesto of ten years earlier, which was written and circulated shortly after the "Arab Letter" of 1987. "Qoreish 2" is the clearest exposition of the Janjawiid agenda of Arab supremacism in Chad and Darfur, and is explicit about the origins of that agenda in the politics and ideology of the leaders of Burkan and CDR.

The second document, a report of the Coordination Council of the Arab Congress dated November 2003, shows how the Janjawiid political agenda has become part of the wider political agenda of Darfur's Arabs, illustrating the spread of Janjawiidism under the sponsorship of the Sudanese state apparatus.

### Document 1: "Qoreish 2"

In the name of Allah, the Most Gracious, the Most Merciful
[verses from the Qur'an omitted]

*The subject: Qoreish 2*

We tackled in Qoreish 1 the birth of a new Qoreish with some programs. Now that the country is undergoing some developments, with recent political events that have internal and external dimensions, we need to remind ourselves of our goals and to review our plans, consolidating what has been achieved in order to fulfill our noble objectives. As is well known, for the past century the three tribes of Ja'aliyyin, Danagla, and Shaigiyya have been an obstacle for us to rule Sudan. Whatever pretext they undertake such as pretending to be Arabs when they are half-caste that became a race and culture, a part of the interwoven Nubian-Egyptian texture—the group that will cling to power forever—whereby we have recently heard that these three tribes took an oath that the power should continually be circulated among them.

Qoreish is passing through a crucial period, it is required that all, particularly the Turafians, "tribal clans," overcome ideological and sectarian associations for the sake of achieving our immortal cause and preserving the achievements that have been fulfilled. There is a need for continual works to achieve the goals we seek, through commitment to the following:

- A general deadline of 2020, at the latest
- Achieve Qoreish 2
- The present phase: the six regions of western Sudan
- Plans, programs, and means

Internally:

- Special emphasis on education quality and quantity, and on preparing highly skilled groups in different sectors—political, economic, information, security, and military.
- Establishing economic institutions.
- To join the army and security organs in great numbers with great consciousness.
- To continue pretending cooperation with the present authority as planned.
- To preserve present working relations with some major personalities from the three ruling tribes.

- To coordinate with related tribes in the east and center.
- To emphasize the importance of border tribes, and to incite the state to provide more supports, arms, and training.
- To incite able relatives to join the peace forces.
- To keep contacts with the Dinka tribe.
- Total commitment with articles of Shahin operation for South Kordofan.
- To contain the risk of sedition between Nahud and Fula, and to call on our people in countryside to avoid internal conflicts that consume energies.
- Never to raise the petroleum issue before extracting it.
- To contain events at Nyala and its consequences, and to work to release the riders.
- To secure enough pastures for nomads in Sudan, Chad, and Central African Republic.
- To fight customs related to possession of land by all means.
- To focus on our national role in fighting non-Arab tribes in the West as a natural extension for the rebellion.
- To increase the confidence gap between central government and non-Arab tribes, by pushing selected leaders of the blacks to be more extreme in expressing the injustice in the West, and to comply with them consciously in espousing racism and regionalism.
- To get more constitutional posts in the central and state governments.
- To preserve achievements of the Jamus program for West Darfur with its calculated consequences.
- Ali al Turafi and Turaiti to continue the work for empowerment of Qoreishians in Darfur.
- Preparation for state elections in the six states.
- To behave with great discipline and to avoid bad manners like talking about the state of Baggara.
- The leaders should take more care about positive information.

- Top leaders of Qoreish should stay in the National Congress, among Qoreish, for decision making, according to the situation.

Externally:

- To strengthen coordination and consultation with Qoreishians in neighboring countries.
- To develop strategic understanding with Libya according to the plans of Bagillani, Ahmat Acyl, and Acheikh Ibn Omer.
- To develop the camel race, and use it to strengthen relations with brothers in Gulf States.

With God, Success.

### Document 2: Coordination Council of Arab Congress, report, November 2003

Coordination Council of Arab Congress (Sudan) Political Committee

Date: November 15, 2003

Subject: Report of the above-mentioned committee trip to local councils of Buram, Tulus, Reheid al Birdi, and Idd al Fursan

The committee left to meet with the Buram Local Council on Monday November 10, 2003 at 5:00 p.m. and arrived at 10:30 p.m. The committee started immediately by holding a meeting with leaders, tribal administrators, politicians, executives, and notables.

At the meeting the following recommendations were discussed:

- The idea [of Arab unity] should be pursued with strength and clarity so as to convey a powerful message.
- To seek assistance from learned men, and people known to have good ideas, and economists.

- To insure the equitable sharing of resources, especially under the expected peace agreement at state and federal levels.
- To erase any intertribal conflicts among the Arabs.
- To put the [issue] in the context of religion, *shari'a*, and Islamic goodness.
- Spread the thought through Sudan.
- Change the name of the state Dar Fur to another suitable name.
- The importance of information and documentation research.
- Appointment of brother Omer Ali al Ghali, assistant of the nazir, as coordinator of Buram Local Council to liaise between the citizens of the council and the Coordination Council.
- Collect signatures of members of the consultative commission in the state (South Darfur) and send them to Nyala as soon as possible.

All present attested on oath to work together to make success of this unification concept.

The following day the committee visited Nazir Salah Ali al Ghali to explain the details of the concept, to which he fully agreed. Also, the committee visited the commissioner [Motamad] at headquarters in his house, and the commissioner of the Local Council who welcomed the concept and fully agreed to it.

The commissioner of the Local Council was asked to support and assist the secretary of the National Congress in collecting the signatures and to provide transport for members of the Consultative Commission as soon as they requested.

On November 11, 2003, the committee visited Tullus where they met with leaders of the tribal administration, politicians, and the executives.

The commissioner addressed the meeting, thanking the
Coordination Council—as represented by the committee—and
explained the dangerous state of affairs and the necessity for unification and then presented the committee members to the meeting. After an elaborate explanation of the issue, followed by
discussion, the following recommendations were made:

- All agreed on the idea of unification and its implementation.
- Setting up of an information committee.
- Necessity for an extended presence in the Republic of Chad.
- To spread the idea of unification among university students.
- Opening up of transhumance passages and resting areas.
- Comprehension and organization of executive and political
  work.
- Security of relations with the federal government.
- Formulation of interclan defense plan.
- Appropriate economic planning for security of unification.
- Activation and development of native administration.
- Preparation of a clear memorandum of association for
  this work.
- Strict secrecy.

Omda Yousif Omer Khatir was appointed as coordinator (of the
committee) for Tulus. The Local Council Secretary of the
National Congress asked to collect signatures of the members of
the Consultative Commission and send them to Nyala as soon as
possible, while the commission was asked to provide transport
for the Consultative Commission members whenever they asked.
All confirmed to implement and protect the unity. The committee then met Nazir Ahmed al Sammani al Bashar who agreed on
the idea of unity and added more recommendations to affect:

- There is a need to bring together Arab leaders to ensure
  security of the idea and to implement it.
- Urge Nazir [Saeed] Madibu to take the matter seriously
  with all the leaders of his area.

On November 12, 2003, the committee visited Reheid al Birdi
Locality where it met with tribal leaders, politicians, and notables, who unanimously agreed on the idea (Unity) and affirmed
their willingness to protect it and made the following recommendations:

- Advertise the unit to the public since it is a noble idea.
- Secrecy of information regarding internal [local plan].
- Give a clear name for the unity.
- Clear goal for this unity and its implementation.
- To switch from a defensive to an offensive position by argu-
  ments and initiatives to refute gossip, lies, and rumors.
- Careful study to insure safety of action.
- Cleanliness in dealing with others.
- Remove popular police force from the state as it is involved
  in a number of violations.
- A well-studied economic plan to support this action.
- Complete take over of authority in South Darfur using the
  [Arabs'] numerical majority.
- Change name to another one.
- Review the issue of national service with Khartoum in all
  aspects.
- Encourage the sons the clans for recruitment in the armed
  forces, police, and security.

After oath taking brother Yousif Mohamed Yousif was selected
as coordinator for the locality, while the secretary of the
Congress was asked to collect the signatures of the Consultative
Commission to send them to Nyala. It is worth nothing that the
meeting was attended by all families and clans, especially the
Salamat, that are resident in Reheid al Birdi.

On Thursday November 13, 2003, the committee held a meeting with tribal leaders, notables, and politicians at Idd al Fursan.
After an explanation of the objectives of its visit the committee

listened to the discussion, which finally put forward the following recommendations:

- Setting up the information and research committee.
- Preservation of the principles and their development.
- Protection of the politicians of all the clans by all means.
- Change the names of Dar Fur states into more logical ones.
- Strengthening the social fabric of the Arabs and exchange of visits.
- Lay strong and clear economic foundations and principles.
- Announcement of Arab action without reservations.
- Organize the Janjawiid for benevolent action and protection.
- Unreserved obedience for the Arab leaders, especially the Coordination Commission.
- Arbitration to solve the interstate problems between all races to attain harmony and gain cordialness from others.
- To pay attention to external trade.
- Secrecy of information
- Adoption of university student researchers.
- Employment of graduates in government institutions.
- Improvement of administrative and executive systems in the capital of the state [Nyala] and strengthening of native administration at all levels.
- Review planned settlement to Goz Dango and water projects approved in the name of Idd al Fursan that end up in other areas.
- Review of immigration to Nyala.

This was followed by attestation on oath and brother Dabaka Issa Dabaka was appointed coordinator for the locality. The secretary of the congress was asked to collect signatures of the members of the Consultative Commission for dispatch to Nyala.

## Conclusion

THERE IS A MISAPPREHENSION that tribal and racial conflicts in Darfur are due to competition over resources between farmers and herdsmen. This misconception has led to the use of traditional civil conflict-resolution mechanisms such as the old *ajawid* or *judiya* processes in which the concerned leaders and others assemble to solve issues, tribal-reconciliation conferences, or comprehensive-security conferences. There have been more than fifty conferences held in the three Darfur states in the last twenty-five years. More than one hundred research papers, including masters' and doctoral theses, have been written and presented seeking a solution for this problem. Since independence, governments in Khartoum have opted for different policies in order to address this issue. To date, all approaches have been insufficient because they have not properly taken into account the relationship of the conflicts in Darfur to the politics of Chad.

As this chapter has illustrated, most of the major wars in Darfur have involved Chadian armed groups: Acheikh Ibn Omer and the CDR began the 1987–1989 Arab-Fur war; the Arab-Masalit wars involved a large number of Chadian Arabs; and the Janjawiid wars since 2001 have also involved armed groups of Chadian origin on a large scale. Each of these wars have been particularly bloody and protracted because both sides are fighting for survival and land. By contrast, the 1991 war with the SPLA was briefer because the forces on both sides were entirely Sudanese and did not covet each other's territories.

The problem of Darfur cannot be settled without addressing Chad's internal politics. It is also necessary to address the long-term issue of migration across Sudan's western frontier. Civilian migration cannot and should not be halted. But it is important to design the appropriate policies to accommodate the immigrants so they can settle peacefully in Sudanese society without becoming a threat or a burden. It is also essential to police the border in such a way that armed groups cannot cross and take refuge in Sudan in order to destabilize neighboring countries. The entire field of regional economic and social integration in the subregion of Darfur, Chad, the Central African

Republic, and Libya needs detailed study, so that the countries can positively support one another's social and economic development and not destabilize one another.

In response to the rebellion of 2003, the Sudanese government has adopted, spread, and intensified Janjawiidism, so that in many instances the armed forces and security institutions of the state have become indistinguishable from the Janjawiid. In addition, the government's efforts to militarize both Arab and non-Arab tribes in different parts of Darfur, have led to a situation in which native administration is now often indistinguishable from militia command, and tribal organization is considered one and the same as military organization. In this context, it is impossible for the Sudanese government to comply with UN Security Council Resolution 1556—to immediately disarm the Janjawiid—without the government itself surrendering control over Darfur.

# 6

## *Darfur's Armed Movements*

### Julie Flint

O N AUGUST 7, 2006, Minni Arkoy Minawi was appointed senior assistant to the president of the Republic of Sudan, on paper the fourth highest-ranking executive position in the country. Minawi's arrival in Khartoum was a lackluster affair. Concerned by his growing unpopularity among Darfurians, the government refused to pay for buses to transport the usual rent-a-mob to welcome him and most of those who turned out on the airport road were there to demonstrate against him. Minawi arrived in Khartoum not as the conquering hero of Darfur, but as an isolated figure, regarded more as a sellout than a savior.

Minawi is a secondary school graduate—his critics in the Sudan Liberation Army (SLA) like to call him "semi-uneducated"—with no experience of either civil politics or combat. He was secretary to the SLA's first chief of staff, Abdalla Abaker, and when Abaker was killed in January 2004 took to calling himself "secretary general." (Some of those close to him say he thought this made him the "Kofi Annan" of the SLA, superior even to the chairman.) In November 2005 he convened a conference in the small town of Haskanita in eastern Darfur, where a non-representative group of Darfurian resistance members dominated by his own Zaghawa tribe elected him "chairman" of the SLA. Beyond insisting that he is a "revolutionary," Minawi rarely showed any political vision and ran his faction of the SLA through a kitchen cabinet of close family members. The story of how he rose from obscurity to a senior rank at the Palace at the age of just thirty-four is a remarkable one—a testament to the parlous condition of the

SLA as much as to his own ruthlessness and the international backing he enjoyed because of his military strength and his undoubted willingness to use it.

The post of senior assistant to the president had been designed by the African Union mediators at the Darfur peace talks in Abuja, Nigeria, with Abdel Wahid Mohamed al Nur in mind. The original chairman of the SLA and a member of the Fur tribe, Darfur's largest, Abdel Wahid was "ousted" from his position by thirty-two of his erstwhile colleagues, including two of his oldest and closest collaborators, just two weeks before Minawi's elevation. The announcement on July 28 was careful not to criticize Abdel Wahid, but was the first public expression of long-simmering irritation at his chaotic leadership and what many called his "Minniphobia." If Abdel Wahid had realized the increasing fragility of his position, he gave no sign of it. On the eve of the final week's peace negotiations, he had been busy awarding posts in Darfur's future government to his subordinates—so confident was he that the highest-ranking Darfurian post in Khartoum was his for the taking. Many in the movement that he launched in 2001 thought he had earned the position by virtue of his activism for Darfur's rights, first at Khartoum University and then from his law office in Zalingei. For all his failings, they acknowledged that he had had the courage to take up the burden of leadership at a time of great danger and had built a multi-tribal coalition. Although only thirty-four when the SLA announced its first military operation in 2003, Abdel Wahid was unquestionably its dominant figure, and the only Darfurian rebel leader whose name was known in every displaced camp and every remaining village. He was brought down by his own failures of political leadership, especially his disorganization and erratic, isolated approach to decision making. Creating a cohesive and well-organized Darfurian resistance movement was never going to be an easy task. With Abdel Wahid at the helm it was an impossible one.

Almost from the outset, the SLA was marked by division at the top and constantly shifting allegiances lower down. Organizational structures were never put in place and military command and control disintegrated as the SLA split along tribal lines. By 2005, in the words of an Arab intellectual sympathetic to the rebellion, "every commander (was) the president of the republic of his own area."[1] As individual commanders took the law into their own hands, and Minawi's Zaghawa-led faction especially suffered serious defections from its ranks, the personalities of Minawi and Abdel Wahid and their battle for leadership dictated the course, and the disintegration, of the rebellion.

Darfur's third resistance leader, Khalil Ibrahim, chairman of the Justice and Equality Movement (JEM), by contrast runs a disciplined organization. It has not been immune from splits and dissension and has been opportunistic in its alliances. But JEM has, at least, benefited from clarity in its leadership structures. While Minawi joined the Government of National Unity and Abdel Wahid continued to vacillate, Dr. Khalil took the gamble of escalating the war. With the backing of Chad and Eritrea, and the support of many of the SLA splinters that are critical of the peace agreement, he launched the National Redemption Front and a new military offensive.

### Abdel Wahid and the Origins of the Sudan Liberation Movement/Army

THE SLA HAS ITS NEAR ROOTS in the failed rebellion of Daud Yahya Bolad, a Fur activist and disillusioned Islamist who joined the Sudan People's Liberation Army (SPLA) and attempted to provoke an uprising in Darfur in December 1991. The 1980s had seen three critical developments in Darfur: drought and the famine of 1984–1985; a new ideology of Arab supremacism promoted by the openly racist Arab Gathering; and the Arab-Fur war of 1987–1989. Fur politicians had long predicted that Darfurians' patience with their marginal status would run out. Bolad, the first president of the Khartoum University Students' Union who did not come from Sudan's riverine elite, put this to the test when he invaded Darfur from southern Sudan at the head of a well-armed SPLA unit. He was political commissar of the invading force; Abdel Aziz Adam el Hilu, a half-Masalit SPLA officer, was its military leader. A combined force of regular army and a militia drawn from the Beni Halba Arabs decimated the attackers. Bolad was captured and killed, and his network of collaborators rolled up. Government and militia forces burned dozens of Fur villages in reprisal.

From this moment, the Fur became the main enemy of the ruling National Islamic Front (NIF). Security argued that they were secularists and, unlike the Zaghawa, had refused to support the Popular Defense Forces in the war against the SPLA in southern Sudan. The government increased its support for the Arab militias around Jebel Marra—and especially for a young Um Jalul leader called Musa Hilal.

In Khartoum, a group of students who believed that change in Darfur could only come through armed rebellion analyzed the causes of Bolad's defeat. Their conclusion was that he failed because his force was not Darfurian, making it easy for the government to mobilize Darfurians against it; because he had little or no intelligence on the ground; and because he had relied on traditional leaders for support—"friends of the strong, enemies of the weak." The group included Abdel Wahid and three of his closest friends and collaborators in the years that followed. Two were Fur—Babikir Mohamed Abdalla, a law student from Kabkabiya, and Ahmad Abdel Shafi, a young education student from Zalingei. The third, Hafiz Yousif, the oldest of the group and a specialist in *shari'a* law, was Arab. Yousif and Abdel Wahid had grown up together in Zalingei, and were convinced that rebellion would succeed only if it had the support of all Darfurians—Arab and non-Arab. For Abdel Wahid, the main lesson of Daud Bolad's catastrophic invasion was: "If we move without the Arabs, the government will move the Arabs against us."

Although born in Zalingei in 1968, one of ten children of a modest trader, Abdel Wahid Mohamed al Nur came from a family whose roots were in Turra, the Jebel Marra capital of the Fur sultanate, and as the SLA chairman he was often accused of favoring the *jebeliyiin*, the people of Jebel Marra, over the *surokwa*, the people of the plains. While still at school, he joined the Ansar al Sunna, a conservative Islamic order, following family tradition, and quickly became the order's youth leader in Zalingei. But he became disillusioned—by his own account, when money earmarked for a religious school went missing—and never again joined a political party. He was fired by the vision of a "New Sudan" propounded by SPLA Chair John Garang, but rejected all ideologies, believing that "a country must depend on the rights of citizenship—not on ideology."

In Khartoum in the 1990s, Darfurian student activists began a clandestine organization of remarkable effectiveness. They sought financial contributions from Fur in Sudan and in the diaspora, bought ammunition from the army in Darfur and distributed it among the self-defense groups that had existed in Jebel Marra since the first Fur-Arab war. Anticipating opposition from Fur sheikhs, who still remembered the reprisals that followed Bolad's rebellion, they went straight to the *aqa'id*, village military leaders, arguing that in time of war the orders of the *aqa'id* were paramount. Based on voluntary contributions—millet from farmers, cash raised in Khartoum—the activists managed to mobilize the whole of Jebel Marra by the end of 1997 and began to organize outside the mountains, in Zalingei and Wadi Saleh. They portrayed their activities as purely defensive, and only against the Arab militias—the Janjawiid. "I lied to the people," Abdel Wahid says. "I told them we needed area defense more than village defense. I paid two *shartais* four million pounds to keep silent [about the mobilization]. I threatened and cajoled. It was a very tough job. It was not acceptable to fight the government. The Fur were not like the Zaghawa: they had no experience of fighting a government."

The Zaghawa, who had overthrown the Chadian government in 1990, were also initially reluctant to take on Khartoum. Most wanted to fight the Awlad Zeid Arab nomads with whom they had had continuous clashes since the early 1980s—not a government many hundreds of miles away. But it was becoming increasingly clear that the government was supporting and even facilitating the Arab attacks. In 1997, the Awlad Zeid had killed a number of tribal leaders in Kornoi and Dar Kobe. Some Zaghawa believed they were acting on intelligence given to them by Khartoum. Unwittingly, they did the same as the Fur: they mobilized the people with the excuse of fighting the Arabs. By 2000, the Zaghawa had established four self-defense camps with a committee of twelve to support them. The leader was Khater Tor al Khalla, his deputy Abdalla Abaker.

The point of no return came in May 2001 when Awlad Zeid killed more than seventy Zaghawa at Bir Taweel in the Kornoi area, one of the most important water sources for both Zaghawa and Arabs. After the clash, the army deployed in the area and kept Zaghawa away from the wells. The massacre convinced many Zaghawa that fighting the Arabs would not resolve their problems. Weapons captured at Bir Taweel included some that were made in Sudan, in government factories in Khartoum. "After Bir Taweel we knew for sure that the government was against us," says one of the first Zaghawa to join the SLA. "All the people in the area knew they had to do something to respond." Influential Zaghawa in Libya and in Khartoum agreed that there was a need to form an organized resistance group to confront the government.

In July 2001, a Zaghawa activist with close ties to Chad, Daud Taher Hariga, met Abdel Wahid in Khartoum and suggested a joint effort against the government. Hariga was the representative in Sudan of Chadian President Idriss Déby's ruling party, le Mouvement Patriotique de Salut, and his involvement seemed to promise Chadian support. The two men went first to Geneina, the capital of West Darfur state, in hope of linking up with Masalit activists, but were unable to connect and continued on to Dar Zaghawa where, in the third week of July, Fur and Zaghawa activists met in Abu Gamra and swore on the Quran to work together to foil Arab supremacist policies in Darfur. A first group of Zaghawa, led by Khater Tor al Khalla, set out for Jebel Marra almost immediately to train recruits and help the Fur, whose mountain was surrounded by six Janjawiid camps. Within a month, a total of 150 Zaghawa were in Jebel Marra.

The honeymoon lasted barely six months. In February 2002, Hariga received a Thuraya satellite telephone call from Abdel Wahid, who told him, "We can't control the Zaghawa." They were, he complained, running amok in Jebel Marra, looting and abusing civilians. On February 25, the rebels attacked a garrison in the south of Jebel Marra, between Nyala and Tur.[2] But there was disagreement over military strategy too: the Zaghawa wanted to attack government forces to the north of Jebel Marra; the Fur wanted to attack government and Janjawiid forces in the south.

In an attempt to put their house in order, Fur and Zaghawa activists met in Boodkay, on the western slopes of Jebel Marra, in March 2002. Minawi claims he opened the meeting as "secretary-general" and dates his authority within the movement from this time.[3] It was decided that a Fur would be chairman of the movement, a Zaghawa chief of staff, and a Masalit deputy chairman. The Fur chose Abdel Wahid and the Zaghawa chose Abdalla Abaker, a hugely popular member of the Ohora, a small Zaghawa clan, who had served as an artillery officer in the Chad army after fighting alongside Idriss Déby against Hissène Habré in 1990. Like Abdel Wahid, Abaker believed that the enemy was the government—not the Arabs; like Abdel Wahid, he enjoyed good relations with local Arab leaders. The Masalit had been organizing self-defense units ever since 1996, when administrative reorganization in West Darfur empowered Arabs at the expense of the old tribal administration and led to the first stirrings of a conflict that would send one hundred thousand refugees fleeing into Chad by 1998. But the Masalit leader, Adam Bazooka, had travelled to Eritrea to seek support from the SPLA after the Masalit war of the late 1990s, and Abdel Wahid and Daud Hariga had failed to make contact with him. In the absence of Masalit, the post of deputy chair was left empty and was only filled, three years later, by Khamis Abdalla Abaker. One of the first self-defense leaders in Dar Masalit, Abaker had been arrested in May 1999 and sentenced to twenty years' imprisonment for rebellion. He escaped from prison in June 2003, four months after the rebels attacked a government outpost in Golo in Jebel Marra and declared themselves to the world as the Darfur Liberation Front.[4]

The Boodkay meeting resolved nothing. The Fur considered the Zaghawa undisciplined; the Zaghawa, for their part, felt disregarded by the Fur and accused them of hosting them in Jebel Marra only to fight the Janjawiid. By May 2002, the Zaghawa were organizing a hierarchy of their own in which Abaker was commander in chief and Minawi secretary general. Abdel Wahid did not figure in it.[5]

Arab attacks meanwhile escalated, and the government's security forces failed to react. A government-appointed committee for the "Restoration of State Authority and Security in Darfur" detained activists on both sides in hope of nipping the conflict in the bud. Some of the Fur were accused of belonging to the Darfur Liberation Front. One of these, detained in Zalingei on July 11, was Abdel Wahid. In a passionate appeal from prison the following month, Abdel Wahid used the word "genocide" to describe the conflict in

Darfur. "In the area of Jebel Marra, Zalingei and Kebkabiya," he wrote, "the security forces act with virtual immunity, terrorizing the Fur people, raiding houses randomly, arresting people including the elderly and children, and detaining them without charge or trial. Many Fur men have fled to the mountains, to find a safe haven, and have left their lands."

## Gaining Support

THE REBEL MOVEMENTS began to organize in Darfur in 2001 with little more than the weapons they had for personal defense, supplemented by the weapons that self-defense units were willing to surrender. And they were not always willing: the first Zaghawa activists who went to Jebel Marra asked self-defense commanders to provide them with weapons, but most refused. A majority of Zaghawa still wanted to fight the Arabs—not the government.[6]

Early in 2003, limited shipments of military supplies were provided by Eritrea and the SPLA.[7] But most of the weapons and all the vehicles used by the rebels were seized in attacks on police and army posts in Darfur itself, brought by deserters, or acquired through Chadian and Libyan networks. The Chadian Zaghawa who dominated Chad's army brass and the upper ranks of the presidential guard supplied much, and Zaghawa who had positions in the Libyan army or in local administrations in southern Libya were generous supporters. Diaspora Darfurians, and the Fur and Zaghawa business communities also provided significant support. On many occasions, briefcases stuffed with tens of thousands of dollars were carried by hand to Nairobi and N'djamena.

From the outset, JEM had access to better sources of external support than the SLA. Because many of JEM's leaders held positions in government, they had access to funds and time to move them out of the country before beginning military operations in 2003. There were also persistent reports, but no hard evidence, that JEM was supported financially by Ali al Haj, Popular Congress Party deputy to Hassan al Turabi, the architect of Sudan's Islamist revolution. Ali al Haj is himself a Darfurian.

For political and logistical support the SLA initially looked to the Sudan Federal Democratic Alliance of Ahmad Diraige, a former governor of Darfur residing in London, and his deputy, Dr. Sherif Harir, an anthropologist. They were disappointed: Harir, a Zaghawa, actively encouraged the rebellion and in 2001–2002 sent money to the Zaghawa in Jebel Marra;[8] Diraige, a Fur, thought it would be counterproductive and withheld his support. The SLA was therefore receptive to an overture made late in 2002 by John Garang, who sent two SPLA officers from the Nuba Mountains to Jebel Marra with a Thuraya hidden in a jerry can for Abdel Wahid.[9] Having gained assurances from Abdel Wahid that the embryonic SLA was a political move-ment, and not an anti-Arab militia, Garang promised to send logistical help including weapons. On New Year's Day 2003, Ahmad Abdel Shafi and Babikir Abdalla met Garang in a small Nairobi hotel. Garang stressed the secrecy of the contact, which should be limited, he said, to a handful of sen-ior SPLA officials including intelligence chief Edward Lino and spokesman Yasir Arman.

Abdel Shafi and Babikir made clear that the SLA believed in the New Sudan "as a concept" but said Darfur had its own specific problems that needed separate treatment. They told Garang: "If we declare we are SPLA, the Arabs will not join us. Let us have our own movement first, and then we can see."[10] Garang asked them to send field commanders from Darfur to be trained in the weapons the SPLA would provide. Abdel Wahid sent two Zaghawa—Abdalla Abaker and Minni Minawi. Some Fur criticized his deci-sion to send only Zaghawa, but Abdel Wahid argued that the Zaghawa needed to be given confidence that they were an integral part of the new movement. And, he said, it was the Zaghawa who knew most about weapons because of their experience in the Chadian wars. Since government attention was focused on Jebel Marra, and the Janjawiid had the mountain encircled, the weapons—which included anti-aircraft guns, heavy recoilless rifles and Goronovs[11]—were flown from Akot in Bahr el Ghazal to the far north of Darfur.

Eritrea, too, had long been hopeful of rebellion in Darfur and like the SPLA seized the moment. Under President Isseyas Afewerki, Eritrea had been both consistent and opportunistic. As early as January 1994, Afewerki declared that since Khartoum was backing jihadists from Eritrea's Muslim population, he would respond by supporting the Sudanese opposition. In 1995, as part of these efforts, Afewerki sent a secret mission to N'djamena to try to persuade President Déby to help open a "western front" against Khartoum. The mission failed: Déby did not want to anger the Sudanese security officers who had helped him to power and who were still present in force in Chad.

When Idriss Déby took power in Chad in 1990, he did so with Sudanese backing and a pact with President Omar al Bashir: neither government would host the other's opposition armed groups. This was an easy deal to keep in the early years. The key to Déby's coup had been the mobilization of the Zaghawa of Chad and Sudan, including, importantly, two groups that are demographically and economically more significant than Déby's own Bideyat: the Kobe, who are settled mostly in Chad and who control JEM; and the more numerous Wegi of Dar Galla and Dar Tuer in Darfur, who dominate SLA-Minawi. Once Déby took power, many Sudanese Zaghawa were initially given positions in his army. But under a demobilization plan funded by the French government, which put Déby under pressure to disband parts of the army, the first to be pushed out were the Arabic speakers from Sudan. Later, when rebellion broke out in Darfur, Khartoum gave the Zaghawa another cause for concern: it made clear that it expected Déby to curb his kinsfolk across its border.

In 2002, both the SLA and JEM attempted to get Déby's support for rebellion in Darfur. Déby refused and in 2003 committed himself to cooperate militarily with Sudan, sending five hundred troops to take part in joint army operations against the Darfur rebels. Khartoum claims that Chad also contributed three helicopters and seventeen vehicles.[12] In October 2003, Déby helped mediate the first ceasefire agreement signed in Abéché. In November 2003, he signed an agreement with Khartoum to establish a joint task force to curb cross-border attacks and smuggling and to allow for the extradition of armed groups from Chad.

Déby did not, however, have complete control over the government or the army and many influential Chadians chose to engage with the movements. Members of Déby's own presidential guard provided the movements with ammunition, military hardware, fuel, and food (sometimes at a price). Déby's brother, Dawsa, whose mother is from Sudan, was active in raising money, and perhaps more besides.[13]

After the failure of its early efforts at a "western front," Eritrea reverted to supporting SPLA and Beja guerrillas based on its own territory along Sudan's eastern border. But Afewerki persisted in believing that President Bashir should be overthrown by force, and gave arms to any group ready to do that. After the Darfur rebellion began, Eritrea welcomed the SLA and JEM to Asmara, and quickly became the main conduit for external support including fuel, food, and weapons.[14]

### The Emergence of the Justice and Equality Movement

WITHIN DAYS of the attack on Golo in February 2003 and the first use of the name "Sudan Liberation Army," a second Darfurian rebel group announced itself: the Justice and Equality Movement. JEM's origins are in the mid-1990s, when Darfurians were already disenchanted with Sudan's Islamist leaders, including Hassan al Turabi, and regime insiders formed a secret twenty five-man committee from the six states of Sudan to collect information about political and economic marginalization.[15] The resulting document, *The Black Book: Imbalance of Power and Wealth in Sudan*, was distributed secretly in Khartoum in May 2000 and gave a detailed breakdown of where political and economic power in Sudan lies and has lain ever since independence—in the hands of a small elite from three tribes who live along the Nile north of Khartoum: the Shaygiyya, Ja'aliyiin, and Danagla. The *Black Book* roundly criticized the NIF, which, it says, has "demonstrated its inability to depart from established patterns of injustice."

As the intelligence services in Khartoum began hunting the authors of the *Black Book*, the committee called a cross-party meeting in house of a former deputy governor of Darfur—Ahmad Abdel Qasr Arbab, a Rizeigat Arab and a member of the Umma party.[16] The group met for eight hours. They decided to work inside existing traditional parties, for the moment, in pursuit of a decentralized, federal state with religious and political freedom and an equitable division of wealth and power. They ruled out self-determination. At a second, larger meeting early in 2001, they decided to send Dr. Khalil Ibrahim abroad as spokesperson. It took several more meetings to decide on a name for the new organization he would lead—JEM.

JEM did not begin to organize militarily for another year.[17] In June 2002, delegations were sent to talk to the Masalit and Zaghawa, including Abdalla Abaker and Minni Minawi, and early in 2003 JEM announced a first attack on a government position near Kabkabiya in which it seized three cars.[18] (In the Darfur rebellion, the success of military operations is judged as much by how many vehicles are seized as by how many weapons are captured.) JEM was eager to work closely with the far larger SLA. Both Abdel Wahid and Minawi were in favor of cooperation and conducted joint military operations with JEM in the early months of the rebellion, but ruled out any wider coopera-tion because of JEM's Islamist past.

Most of JEM's senior officials had held positions in regional government under the NIF and joined the rebellion from Islamist parties. Dr. Khalil him-self had served as state minister for health in North Darfur in the mid-1990s, minister for social affairs in Blue Nile in 1997, and advisor to the governor of southern Sudan in Juba in 1998. Because of this, many analysts have disputed whether JEM marked a genuine split from NIF policies and thinking, or whether it was, in truth, nothing more than the military wing of Turabi's Popular Congress Party in the wake of his political defeat by President Bashir in 1999–2000. By 2006, even the most skeptical could no longer deny that JEM's tribal coloring, which was strengthened by the mil-itary mobilization of Kobe living in Chad, was at least as significant as its Islamist roots. In May 2006, growing unhappiness with Kobe domination of JEM burst into the open when some members published a "reformatory memo" regretting that JEM, which began life by exposing rule by elite, had itself become dominated by an elite and "imprisoned by tribalism." Without mentioning the Kobe by name, the signatories deplored "the appropriation of financial resources, weapons and the continual attempts to dominate the key senior positions." They listed twenty key positions that the Kobe controlled in addition to eight advisers to the chairman—"in other words, all the Advisers."

### War and Lack of Cohesion

THE SLA WAS NEVER more than a loose alliance between its two main tribal components. Many in the SLA believe that two fateful decisions by Abdel Wahid in 2003—to send only Zaghawa to supervise weapons shipments' from southern Sudan and then to have the weapons flown to Dar Zaghawa—marked the beginning of a Zaghawa attempt to "steal" the SLA. Under the pretext of building an airstrip at Um Grud, north of Furawiya, Zaghawa commanders collected weapons from the Fur in Jebel Marra, saying they were needed to protect the airstrip.[19] They then took many of the SLA forces from Jebel Marra to Dar Zaghawa, saying they were needed to prepare the airstrip. In February 2003, Garang sent twenty-two SPLA officers to North Darfur. The Fur claim the officers were meant to travel to Jebel Marra to train the recruits there. But they never got there: they were retained in Dar Zaghawa to advise on military operations (and, according to some sources, to participate in them) but left after only a few months, concerned by indiscipline and tribal tensions, and warning one of the older generation of Zaghawa activists: "You will have trouble with these boys."[20]

The raid on Golo and other attacks in North Darfur in February and March 2003 signaled a marked escalation of the conflict. Pivotal, however, was the April 25 raid on al Fashir air base in which five military planes and two helicopter gunships were destroyed on the ground and an air force general was taken captive. It was a humiliating defeat for the Sudan Armed Forces, whose senior generals became instantly determined to avenge the insult. At first they could not make headway. In the space of a few weeks, the SLA and JEM attacked Tine, Kutum, and Mellit. The SLA's mobile forces literally ran rings around conventional army units that were totally unused to this style of warfare.

By the end of the year, observers estimated that the SLA could field about six to seven thousand men and JEM rather fewer than one thousand. More important than troop strength, however, was the style of warfare. Modelled on the highly mobile desert-warfare tactics perfected in the Chadian civil war, and mostly commanded by Zaghawa officers who had gained experience in the Chadian wars, the Darfur movements organized their strike forces around Land Cruisers that could cover Darfur's semidesert and savanna terrain at high speed and strike with frightening surprise.

But the rebels' success in fighting the government carried a high internal price. As operations began against towns in North Darfur, more and more forces were moved from Jebel Marra to North Darfur, on the understanding they would be rotated back to Jebel Marra to protect the Fur heartland. But they never were. By the middle of 2003, communications between Dar Zaghawa and Jebel Marra had broken down completely. In February 2004, when Abdel Wahid found himself surrounded by government troops and Janjawiid in Jebel Marra, Minawi failed even to respond to a request for reinforcements.[21] From this moment, the forces in Jebel Marra and those outside it responded to different commands. As a commander critical of both factions said in 2005: "The troops in Jebel Marra don't get their orders from Jumaa Mohamed [Minawi's chief of staff] and Dar Zaghawa doesn't hear from Abdel Wahid."[22]

In response to the rebel attacks, the government began a massive and indiscriminate program of arming the Popular Defense Forces in Darfur. In the first months, General Ismat al Zain, head of the western command, armed Arabs and non-Arabs alike. Most non-Arabs lost no time in defecting to the SLA and JEM with their weapons. Others surrendered the moment they came under fire, along with regular army units. As the government increasingly used the Janjawiid and other Arab militias, adopting a pitiless scorched-earth strategy, the abuses drove more and more non-Arabs into the arms of the rebellion.

At the outset, the SLA and JEM forces were a mixture of village defense militias and commando-style mobile units. Many of the latter had learned their craft in Chad and are still labelled "Chadian" by their government adversaries. In the first year of full-scale rebellion, the movements' forces expanded rapidly. Logistics, supplies, and command and control systems were not developed to match. This was a recipe for poor discipline. Lacking an infrastructure for logistics and supplies, the rebels lived off the land—or more specifically, off the inhabitants. By the beginning of 2004, many hundred Zaghawa recruits had put down their weapons and crossed the border to

Chad to live with their families in refugee camps. For the Fur, further away from an international border, escape was harder and many had no choice but to suffer the abuses of undisciplined commanders.

The lack of control generated by the all-consuming nature of the leadership dispute led to the emergence of rogue commanders answerable to none but themselves. The SLA leaders made little attempt to enforce discipline, but, even if they had wanted to, they would have had difficulty as the movement divided and then subdivided: a dissenting commander always had the option of deserting to another faction, or setting up on his own. Alcohol compounded the problem: young men whose society had been violently sundered drank to excess. There was rape too—especially by Minawi's men, whose mobile units were active far outside their own areas.

At the beginning of 2004, government forces launched a massive offensive in North Darfur and the SLA forces there scattered to the four winds. Minawi took a water truck and fled north toward the Libyan border. Some of his forces took refuge in Jebel Meidob; others fled to Jebel Marra where Abdel Wahid's men gave them shelter. But trouble was not long in coming. The Zaghawa forces began imposing taxes on the local population and attempting to assert their authority over Fur areas where they were being hosted. In June 2004, commanded by Yahya Hassan el Nil, they attempted to seize control of the mountain. They were defeated—but not before scores of Fur women had been raped and many civilians killed.

Instead of building strong foundations for the movement, the SLA's leaders became ambassadors. An internal-external divide was added to the ethnic split. Within a year of launching the rebellion, Abdel Wahid and Minawi were spending all their time outside Darfur, setting up headquarters in Asmara and lobbying for international support and assistance. Fur leaders who had respected Abdel Wahid for taking on the difficult work of organizing the resistance grumbled that he had become a "hotel guerrilla." His failure to brief his men in the field alienated many of them, and he began to be accused by his own tribe of corruption, favoritism, and disregard for the well-being of his soldiers. Minawi, too, came under fire: early in 2004, a group of Zaghawa commanders issued a statement from Wadi Howar in the far north of Darfur denouncing command by remote control and calling for support for a rival leadership. The splinter movement fizzled after a respected Zaghawa reformer, Adam Ali Shogar, advised change from within rather than confrontation from without.

After visiting Jebel Marra in October 2005 for the first time in eighteen months, Abdel Wahid professed himself "deeply shocked" by what he found: "quarrelling commanders," with one of them "accused of killing many, many people"; abuse of power by commanders who had imprisoned more than a hundred people without charge or trial, often for no other reason than a personal grudge; poor troop control; and lastly, "thousands of underage soldiers." Abdel Wahid claimed he took steps to remedy these problems, issuing orders to limit soldiers' contact with civilians and setting up a committee under a Fur *shartai* to reconcile commanders. But the root of the problem was the leadership conflict that paralyzed the SLA and permitted indiscipline to flourish and be tolerated.

### The Rise of Minni Minawi

NOTHING IN Minni Minawi's past suggested that he would one day, still in his early thirties, become the highest-ranked Darfurian in Sudan. So disregarded was he even by other Zaghawa when the rebellion first began that many Fur felt pity for him. "He was a very, very good guy at the beginning," says Abdel Wahid. "Quiet, and humble. But because of clan divisions other Zaghawa treated him very badly."

Minawi was born in Furawiya in the far north of Darfur in 1972, a member of the Ila Digen (in Arabic, Awlad Digayn) clan of the Zaghawa tribe. In the seventeenth century, the Ila Digen were the "royal" family of the Dar Tuer chiefdom, but lost the title after four generations to the Agaba of Um Berro, who have held it for the last fifteen generations. There is a tendency among some Zaghawa, and especially among Agaba, to look down on the Ila Digen, who are relatively poor, live in very dry areas, and because they have kept some pre-Islamic traditions better than other Zaghawa, are sometimes considered Muslims of an inferior order. (In one violent argument during the Abuja peace talks, one of Minawi's critics went as far as to call him a *haddad*, or blacksmith, the greatest possible insult to a Zaghawa.) Even though the Ila Digen were given an administrative unit of their own in the mid-1990s and a *malik,* Daud Basi Salem Tegel, based in Muzbat, many believe that Minawi's ruthless struggle for domination reflected a desire to restore the Ila Digen to their historical supremacy among Zaghawa. It is in this light that many Zaghawa interpret the murder by Minawi's men of the Agaba *malik* of Dar Tuer, Abdel Rahman Ali Mohammadayn, in 2004.[23]

Despite his meteoric rise, Minawi never rose above the narrow Zaghawa environment that had contained him since birth. After attending secondary school in al Fashir, capital of North Darfur state, he taught in Furawiya elementary school before joining his uncle, Bahr al Arabi, doing casual work in Nigeria. While tensions with Arabs were rising in the late 1990s, and the Zaghawa were forming self-defense camps, Minawi, by his own account, was working as a trader in neighboring countries. He returned to Darfur only in April 2001, and then for only family reasons: his father, a diabetic, was seriously ill. The Bir Taweel massacre occurred a month after his return and Minawi, like many young Zaghawa, joined a self-defense camp—the same camp as Abdalla Abaker. Unlike many Zaghawa in the camps, Minawi could read and write and so became Abaker's secretary. He spoke good English as a result of his years in Nigeria and was entrusted with a Thuraya with which to communicate with the world's media. He began travelling abroad, and became a recipient of, and conduit for, funds for the rebellion. He responds to any mention of tribe with a flare of anger, indicating how sensitive this issue is to him. If he has a political vision, he has yet to declare it.

But Minawi had many of the character traits so lacking in Abdel Wahid. He was thoughtful, decisive, and knew how to play to an audience, reserving one tone for his friends in Washington and another for the African Union, which he despised. But more importantly he was utterly ruthless. He had no hesitation to use force and relied on a security apparatus built on his own Ila Digen to remove anyone he felt might threaten him—especially those who had what he lacked: higher education, political experience, and popular appeal. "These intellectuals want to steal our movement!" was a common complaint of his. "These politicians, we don't like them!"

"Minni is a belligerent person and has disciplined commanders under his leadership to believe that fighting solves everything," an SLA colleague says. "Minni, I believe, feels himself inferior—maybe because of his little education—and tries to cover that gap by using force. He believes only in his relatives and himself."

After Abaker's death in the wake of a gunship attack in January 2004, Minawi began promoting first Zaghawa and then Ila Digen to senior positions in the SLA. The split in the movement widened, but Minawi's close aides made light of it. John Garang had used his own small clan, the Bor Dinka, to keep control of a divided SPLA, they said. Why shouldn't Minawi do the same? The historical Ila Digen–Agaba rivalry left a lasting legacy. Commanders who subsequently defected from SLA-Minawi say Malik Abdel Rahman Mohammadayn was bound hand and foot, hanged from a tree in the village of Shigeig Caro and beaten to death by a group led by Mohamed Zakaria "Shula," one of the Ila Digen inner circle. Zaghawa reformists compiled a list of dozens of "spies" and perceived opponents they say have been killed by Minawi's men—among them, Ali Abdel Rahim Shendi, an Arab commander who became an SLA hero after attacking the Abu Gabra oil field in South Darfur and who died two months later in a "car accident" in which he was the only casualty.

"All enemies of Minni die [shot] in the back, when they are fighting," says Daud Taher. "He doesn't listen to people who have experience. He pushes them away and cooperates with small boys. But if all the tribes hate you, who will obey you? We cannot govern Darfur by force." A still-loyal commander says: "Either you bend—or you are killed!"

As Minawi's Zaghawa forces penetrated as far as Greida in South Darfur, more than 350 miles south of their homeland, their unrelenting use of force to address every challenger marginalized the Zaghawa among Darfurians as never before. Dar Zaghawa is the most inhospitable land in Darfur. Nine months of dry season are followed by a short rainy season of such irregularity that drought threatens in two out of every four years, bringing with it a constant need to migrate. Today the Zaghawa, more than any other Darfurians, live in the *dars* of other ethnic groups. Although they are thought to account for less than 10 percent of the population of Darfur, Zaghawa

have acquired wealth and influence disproportionate to their number, especially in the fields of trade and commerce, because of their energy, drive, and
capacity for strategic action. Their success had caused tensions with other
tribes even before the present conflict. But after the rebellion began, the abusive behavior of Minawi's forces awakened old fears that the tribe had a hidden agenda—the creation of a "Greater Zaghawa State" carved out of the
more fertile lands of others.

Minawi's rise was possible because of the disorganization and poor leadership of the SLA. Seeking international backing and funding, the need for
structures was the main reason he cited for the necessity of a "General
Convention" of the movement at Haskanita, in Dar Berti, in 2005. At first,
Abdel Wahid gave a green light for the conference, but then stalled, accusing Minawi of forging ahead with preparations without proper consultation. The conference organizers resisted appeals to delay the conference
until it had across-the-board support, and it was widely perceived as
another step in Minawi's efforts to wrest control of the SLA from Abdel
Wahid. "A coup by Minni," was the view of a senior UN official. The conference went ahead, funded by Libya, and on November 3, 2005, elected
Minawi as chairman. Some of those who objected, arguing that the
Zaghawa were a minority in Darfur and should not rule the majority, were
arrested by Minawi's security detail and roughed up. A few days later,
Minawi's delegates to a meeting in Nairobi organized by the U.S. State
Department stormed out when Abdel Wahid entered, claiming that they
were the sole legitimate representatives.

The Haskanita conference did not resolve the legitimacy question. Rather,
it confirmed the split. At the Abuja talks that convened at the end of that
month, the African Union accredited separate delegations from SLA-Minawi
and SLA-Abdel Wahid. The international players all hoped, at minimum, for
peaceful coexistence between the different rebel factions and, at maximum,
for a common platform. They got neither.

After Haskanita, Minawi sent forces to attack three northern commanders
who contested his leadership—Jar al Nebi Abdel Karim, Zaghawa; Saleh
Adam Izhaq, Berti; and Suleiman Marajan, Meidob. Jar al Nebi talked his
attackers down; Saleh Adam fought them off, despite being by far the weaker

party; Marajan was captured and held for a month—in shackles—until he succeeded in escaping.[24]

This was the continuation of a well-established pattern of violence, almost always initiated by Minawi's troops—first against JEM, and then against SLA-Abdel Wahid. SLA-JEM relations had been good in the early months of the rebellion, and cooperation continued as the rebels expanded the war into eastern and southern Darfur. In Muhajiriya, for a while, the SLA and JEM maintained a model coexistence, but relations cooled when civilians began complaining of the behavior of the SLA forces. In May 2005, Minawi sent a delegation from North Darfur to Muhajiriya with orders to close a political office opened by JEM. JEM refused, saying: "We liberated Muhajiriya together, we have the right to an office."[25] The dispute led to fighting in which SLA forces chased JEM hundreds of miles across Darfur in a Chadian-supported offensive that continued, sporadically, for several months.

The pattern continued right up to the signing of the Darfur Peace Agreement. In March 2006, remnants of Minawi's forces that government troops had defeated at Haskanita were allowed into the Abdel Wahid–controlled town of Korma to receive treatment for their wounds. Within days, they demanded that their hosts evacuate the town. Fighting in and around Korma sputtered on until July, when SLA-Minawi, supported by government and Janjawiid forces, killed more than seventy people, injured more than one hundred and raped thirty-nine women in just five days (Amnesty International 2006). Although Minawi denied there had been any abuses, local people were now calling his faction "Janjawiid 2." The nature of Minawi's regime, thus far ignored by the international community, was becoming impossible to ignore any longer. In August, the African Union, which had turned a blind eye to his initial attack on Korma during the final round of the Abuja talks, issued a statement expressing "shock and horror" over the "brutal" beating, over two days, of a middle-aged man in SLA quarters in al Fashir. The AU said the incident lent credence "to the previous incessant allegations" about the abuses of SLA-Minawi.

More seriously for Minawi, his ascendancy as the international face of the SLA was not matched by support among the Zaghawa. He had initially enjoyed the support of the most important Zaghawa clans including the

Dawa, Giligerge, Nikeri, and Kaliba—the royal house of Dar Galla. By the time of the last round of Abuja talks early in 2006, even members of his own Ila Digen clan were distancing themselves from him, telephoning the rival SLA faction in Abuja to stress that their famous son did not represent the clan. When Minawi signed the Darfur Peace Agreement, the trend continued with further defections.

## Ideology and Ethnicity

FOR THE SLA, resistance came first and ideology later. Preoccupied with its internal struggles, the SLA was slow in moving from the negative—opposing marginalization—to developing positive proposals for tackling it. No structures were put in place to debate and decide what direction the movement should take, and there was little attempt to explain to Darfurians what exactly the SLA was fighting for. Moreover, as the leadership divide deepened, tribal politics came to the fore.

The SLA's manifesto was drafted in southern Sudan in January 2003 by the SLA delegation from Darfur and senior SPLA officials who were in Rumbek at the same time for a meeting of their own National Liberation Council. If Abdel Wahid had a model, it was John Garang, and the SLA Manifesto, made public on March 16, 2003, was a clear echo of Garang's vision of a "New Sudan." It demands a secular, decentralized state with the right of self-determination as a basis for "viable" unity, and calls for the "restructuring of power and an equal and equitable distribution of both power and wealth in all their dimensions." The manifesto makes no specific mention of *shari'a*, but says: "Religion belongs to the individual and the state belongs to all of us." Great emphasis is put on inclusivity: "The Arab tribes and groups are an integral and indivisible component of Darfur social fabric who have been equally marginalized and deprived of their rights to development and genuine political participation... The real interests of the Arab tribes of Darfur are with the SLM/A and Darfur, not with the various oppressive and transient governments of Khartoum."

Minni Minawi's Haskanita conference produced a seventeen-page "SLA/M Basic Rules and Regulations" that does not differ from the original manifesto in any significant way, but goes into greater detail about power and wealth sharing, in line with the movements' position at in the Abuja peace talks. Indicating concern about future accountability, it grants the chair—Minawi—complete immunity from investigation or prosecution.

More important than ideological orientation, from the very beginning of the SLA, has been ethnic identity. Minawi's faction had a veneer—a very thin veneer—of multitribalism, but at its center was a group drawn from Minni's own Ila Digen clan, and within the clan from his own family. Abdel Wahid led the SLA as a power unto himself. He seldom asked for advice and more rarely took it. But despite widespread criticism of his leadership, he was not considered a tribalist. His nominees to the Abuja peace talks included commanders from a broad range of tribes and none of his commission heads was Fur. His chief negotiator, Abdel Rahman Musa, was Tunjur. From the beginning, Abdel Wahid put great emphasis on bringing Arabs into the movement, and he persevered despite strong opposition. "People were very afraid to bring Arabs," he says. "They said: 'The Arabs are burning our villages!' But the problem is not the people—Arab or non-Arab. The problem is the mentality."

Abdel Wahid even made overtures to the Janjawiid in line with his conviction that "if we make a movement without the Arabs, the government will move the Arabs against us." In mid-2003, Hafiz Yousif, then the SLA's secret representative in Khartoum, was in almost daily contact with Musa Hilal. Hilal had been jailed in an attempt to cool things down in Darfur. Newly released, he was raging at the government and claimed to be thinking of joining the rebels until Zaghawa attacked his Um Jalul kinsmen and stole thousands of camels.[26] Before this happened, Hilal sent two representatives to meet Abdel Wahid in Jebel Marra. The two were turned back by the SLA and Abdel Wahid only learned of the overture in 2005, when he was again opening channels of communication to Arab Janjawiid. He regretted the missed opportunity. "They took two very bad messages back to Hilal," he said. "The first: 'They refused to let us pass.' The second: 'These people do not like Arabs!'"

By contrast, for JEM, ideology initially came first, although even then with a stiff dose of tribalism. Reflecting the experience its leaders had acquired while serving under the NIF, JEM's politics were more sophisticated and its focus was on national, as opposed to Darfurian, themes. It called for a restructuring of the entire nation, with a return to Sudan's six regions (South, Darfur, Kordofan, East, North, and Central) and a presidency rotating among them.[27] Its manifesto demanded a federal and democratic system of governance, "based on political pluralism, the rule of law, independence of the judiciary and the principle of separation of powers."

Unlike the SLA, JEM does not talk about separation of state and religion. It believes that all rights and duties should be based on citizenship regardless of religion, politics, culture, or gender. Islamic law should not be imposed on non-Muslims, "and the believers of the other faiths must not oppose Muslims' attempts to apply the laws of their religion for themselves." [28] This wording treads a fine line between constitutional secularism and enshrining *shari'a* for Muslims. It is a subtle position—perhaps inconsistent, but entirely within the mainstream of northern Sudanese political thought. Sadiq al Mahdi attempts precisely the same balancing act when he insists that rights should be based on citizenship alone, not religious faith, but also argues that Muslims have the right to live in a society governed by Islamic principles.

As JEM turned to armed struggle, it became more sharply identified with the Zaghawa Kobe, who already formed the bulk of its political leadership and now formed the core of its small but not wholly insignificant fighting force. Initially, the Kobe base put JEM in opposition to President Déby, due to the estrangement between him and the Kobe following Déby's murder of the Kobe leader, Abbas Koty, in 1994. For this reason, Déby tried to split and undermine JEM in 2003–2004, notably encouraging the National Movement for Reform and Democracy (NMRD), a splinter consisting of JEM dissenters, and sponsoring Minawi's attacks on JEM forces. But Déby's own internal problems pushed him to try to win support from more Zaghawa clans, and in 2005 he entered discussions with the JEM leadership, resulting in reconciliation. After this, JEM's ethnic character became increasingly dominant as it was sucked into playing the role of a military proxy for the Chadian regime against Khartoum-backed opponents based in Darfur. In January 2006, JEM took the lead in creating the (short-lived) Alliance of Revolutionary Forces for Western Sudan, which marked a theoretical but short-lived reconciliation with Minawi. In April, JEM fighters actively engaged in defending N'djamena against a rebel attack. By June, Chad was (with Eritrea) a cosponsor of the National Redemption Front, which brought JEM together with various other Darfurian factions that were determined to continue fighting Khartoum.

## The Decline of Abdel Wahid Mohamed al Nur

IN 2004, ABDEL WAHID enjoyed enormous political capital. He had taken on the leadership of a small provincial movement, and gained a place not only in national politics, but also on the world stage. His rhetoric of ethnic inclusiveness, his talk of the "New Sudan," and the prospects of a grand coalition of marginalized Sudanese under the overall leadership of John Garang made him an appealing figure to many. He was also, for all his faults, a man with a common touch. Ahmad Abdel Shafi, who led a break-away movement in July 2006, criticized him for many things—"He doesn't come up with initiatives. He is not innovative. He seldom consults. And he is unpredictable"—but stuck with him for longer than he might otherwise have done because "he is committed and very open. He genuinely likes people. He can be friendly with anybody."

What Abdel Wahid failed to see was that almost all of his political assets were won by default. Sudanese backed him because he seemed civil and because there was no obvious alternative. Internationally, Abdel Wahid gained a profile because of the humanitarian crisis and atrocities in Darfur, not because of deep-rooted sympathy for his cause or his ability to build an international coalition to back him. A more astute and organized leader would have seized the chance to build the institutions necessary to turn this immense goodwill into a Darfurian movement and enact real political change in Sudan.

Abdel Wahid lost it all. Bit by bit, he squandered every ounce of political capital that he had until, in the months after he refused to sign the Darfur Peace Agreement in Abuja, even his closest and most loyal comrades turned against him. His basic flaw is his personality: he is disorganized, indecisive, and, although his door is always open, is ultimately the sole arbiter and decision maker. He does not read memos and rarely writes. No records are kept of decisions, and it is common for him to make a decision one day and reverse it the next. He has on occasion countermanded critical decisions within the hour. An old friend says: "He talks and laughs loudly but does not have any deep thinking. That is why he avoids anyone who questions his behavior. But the good thing in him is that even if he becomes very angry with you in a few minutes he will apologize and laugh with you."

Enjoying goodwill and the benefits of many doubts, Abdel Wahid could have recruited experienced political organizers to run his movement. He was, however, almost pathologically distrustful of everyone—especially after Minawi showed his hand. "Leadership is about creating opportunities," Ahmad Abdel Shafi said shortly before he split with his old friend. "My brother is only fighting Minni Minawi. When we first took up arms, everything favored Abdel Wahid. Everyone loved him. Minni was very brutal with his guys and ruled through his clan. So many Zaghawa don't like Minni. But Abdel Wahid was convinced that Minni was supported by all Zaghawa. He alienated the Zaghawa."

Slowly but surely, Abdel Wahid lost the support of the movement. In September and October 2005, as Minawi's abuses caused many northern commanders to align themselves with his opponent while waiting for a genuine unity conference, Abdel Wahid squandered the opportunity by insisting that he alone, as chairman, could nominate delegates to the Abuja talks. For a couple of months following the Haskanita conference he seemed chastened and more systematic, reaching out again to others. At the end of January 2006, as SLA-Minawi and JEM systematically blocked any movement at Abuja, he decided to negotiate separately with the government. A group of nineteen commanders disputed his decision to talk separately and split from his faction. The "Group of Nineteen," led by Jar al Nebi, held on-and-off reconciliation talks with him for two months without success. On the final day of the Abuja talks, faced with a majority of his delegation in favor of signing, Abdel Wahid insisted on making the decision alone, whereupon he lost his chief negotiator, Abdel Rahman Musa, and a number of others. Ibrahim Madibo, the influential power-sharing negotiator for the SLA and the brother of the *nazir* of the Rizeigat, abandoned him ten days later.

Abdel Wahid counted on the continuing loyalty of the Fur and, more importantly, the Fur leaders' insistence on unity. That loyalty was tested to the limit as the African Union provided additional deadlines for him to sign the agreement—first May 16, then May 31—and each time he found a new reason for not moving. On the final occasion, First Vice President Salva Kiir organized a meeting in Yei, in southern Sudan, at which he would try to bridge the remaining differences between Abdel Wahid, the government, and Minawi. After several procrastinations, and a personal assurance of his security by Salva Kiir on the phone, Abdel Wahid agreed to go. But he changed his mind within the hour and went into hiding "for security reasons." At that moment, his most senior lieutenants and longest-serving comrades decided that enough was enough.

### Ahmad Abdel Shafi and Attempted Reform of the Movement

WHEN THE FUR CHOSE Abdel Wahid as the first chairman of the SLA in 2002, the preferred candidate of many was Ahmad Abdel Shafi—not the earliest Fur militant, but one of the most energetic. It was Abdel Shafi, a graduate of Juba University College of Education, who led the fundraising and mobilization drive in Khartoum in the second half of the 1990s and who went to Chad with Babikir Abdalla in 1997, while still a student, to try to win President Déby's support for rebellion. In 2003, two years after he graduated with honors, it was Abdel Shafi who opened a new front in the south of Jebel Marra to try to balance the Zaghawa domination of North Darfur. In 2005, it was he who led a Fur delegation to Haskanita to try to convince Minawi to postpone a conference that he believed would divide the movement, irrevocably, along tribal lines.

But Abdel Shafi, born in 1973, was not yet thirty at the time of the Boodkay conference and refused to have his name put forward for the most senior Fur position in the movement. Thereafter he remained a loyal, but in private increasingly critical, supporter of Abdel Wahid. He wanted structures, organization, and most importantly, "to remix the troops with a shared vision" to overcome the tribal division bedevilling the movement. He accused both SLA leaders of wanting "to prove he is the leader and the only person."

On July 28, a group of Fur announcing themselves as the "Military Council and Field Command of the SLA" announced the "ousting" of Abdel Wahid and the appointment of Abdel Shafi as "new chairperson of SLM and Commander in Chief for SLA." The thirty-two signatories asked Abdel Shafi to appoint a provisional leadership within three days to run the SLA until a convention could be organized. But the manner of Abdel Wahid's dismissal, without consultation with the wider movement, contained the seeds of future division and three weeks later, on August 18, Abdel Shafi felt obliged to issue an explanatory statement of his own. He thanked Abdel Wahid for "his achievements and his efforts." But he criticized him for having failed to maintain the SLA's unity and improve its organizational performance, and said the resulting divisions had weakened the rebels politically and militarily. He promised an all-SLM/A conference within forty-five days and said the Darfur Peace Agreement would be rejected until it "properly addressed" the demands of the people of Darfur.

In the following weeks and months, as Fur commanders shifted allegiance and the Jebel Marra constituency itself divided into two camps, Abdel Shafi attempted to mend fences with Abdel Wahid, realizing that he retained support not only among some commanders but also among many Fur in the camps for the displaced. The all-SLA conference did not materialize. Instead, Abdel Wahid and Abdel Shafi separately toured foreign capitals seeking support in a depressing echo of the earlier rivalry between Abdel Wahid and Minawi. In August 2006, Babikir Abdalla and three of his close collaborators were arrested by Eritrean Security and imprisoned for more than two months—with beatings—in an underground cell. They pointed an accusing finger at Abdel Wahid, who they claimed had bribed the Eritreans to remove them from circulation. There was no more talk of reconciliation. The Fur themselves were divided.

### The Group of Nineteen: A Third Way?

IN THE MONTHS following the conclusion of the Darfur Peace Agreement, the center of gravity of the SLA shifted—unexpectedly—to the

Group of Nineteen, a disparate collection of commanders from North Darfur who were united by personal experience of the abusive behavior of SLA-Minawi, opposition to the peace agreement, and a determination to reunite the rebel movement under new leadership. By late 2006, the Group of Nineteen, also known as G-19, was the strongest force on the ground in Darfur in alliance with JEM and was liaising with a new rebel group—the Popular Forces Army, the first rebel group to be organized by Darfurian Arabs. The new group staged its first operation in December 2006 against a government garrison in South Darfur. It denounced the Janjawiid as "a minority of mercenaries and hired individuals" and pledged to fight the "injustice" of Khartoum and the "terrorizing" of civilians.[29]

The emergence of G-19 was prefigured in a week-long meeting of Zaghawa, Fur, Meidob, and Berti reformers in Bir Maza in North Darfur in December 2005. Anger with Minawi had been growing ever since he targeted Jar al Nebi, Saleh Adam, and Suleiman Marajan after they dared to attend the sixth round of the Abuja peace talks against his wishes. It was exacerbated by the Haskanita conference, which many commanders in North Darfur, including some Zaghawa, saw as a simple grab for power by his inner circle.

The Bir Maza conference brought reform-minded SLA commanders together with tribal leaders and signaled a new desire to build bridges to sectors of Darfurian society which had been sidelined in the SLA's "revolution." In a statement issued at the end of the meeting on December 9 and signed by Abdalla Yahya—a lawyer and Khartoum University graduate who was one of the first Zaghawa to join the SLA in Jebel Marra—the reformers called for unity within a multi-tribal movement, cancellation of the resolutions of Haskanita, and "comprehensive Darfurian participation" in the Abuja peace talks. Five days later, the commanders decided to tour the areas under their control to insist on a "complete change of ideas and behavior" by rebel forces. To help this process along, they determined to remove Minawi loyalists from posts in the SLA army and police.[30]

In Abuja, the reformers initially aligned themselves with Abdel Wahid's faction, critical of his paralyzing leadership style but unconvinced by Minawi's sudden conversion to the peace process—a tactical shift that they attributed to heavy U.S. pressure and a steady trickle of defections by his commanders. Early in 2006, however, a number of factors conspired to convince them that their chairman was planning to cut a cheap deal with the government. First there were secret talks between Abdel Wahid and the government delegation, encouraged by the African Union in hope of getting Abdel Wahid's signature on a peace agreement. Then contacts between Abdel Wahid's closest collaborators and Janjawiid-connected Arabs lobbying in Abuja. And finally a meeting with Nigerian president Olusegun Obasanjo at which Abdel Wahid asked for help in getting supplies into Jebel Marra—weapons for use against the Zaghawa, some of the reformers thought.

This was the tipping point. "If we take up arms against the Zaghawa," Marajan said, "we are no better than the Janjawiid."[31]

In a statement issued on March 6, nineteen SLM/A members including Marajan, Jar al Nebi, the Masalit leader Khamis Abdalla Abaker, Daud Taher, Adam Ali Shogar, and Saif el Tijani, nephew of the murdered Agaba *malik*, said they were "freezing" Abdel Wahid's chairmanship because of his "inflexibility, rigidity, grudge [and] division" and establishing a Transitional Revolutionary Council under Vice Chair Khamis Abdalla. They accused Abdel Wahid of being "determined to go it alone to consolidate his dictatorship and marginalize all the institutions of the movements in his drive to carry out his narrow-minded personal agenda, surrendering himself to the desires of his entourage, incapable of performing the functions of leadership, while arrogating to himself standards of perfection, because to him, the determinant of leadership is how much one is admired by the others." Calling for a single negotiating position at Abuja, the nineteen urged a Darfur-Darfur dialogue "to lay the foundation for stability and development in Darfur." They proposed "to resolve the issue of Janjawiid by reintegrating them into society."

In the months that followed, the Group of Nineteen failed to break the mold and establish clear political and military structures. No sooner had Minawi signed the Darfur Peace Agreement than he attempted to recapture those areas of North Darfur he had lost in the last year or so. G-19 commanders found themselves systematically targeted both by his forces and those of the government. After an initial defeat in Bir Maza by a joint Sudan Armed Forces–Minawi offensive, the reformers turned the tide thanks to widespread popular rejection of SLA-Minawi, low army morale, and an infusion of heavy weapons acquired from Chad by JEM, a partner in the National Redemption Front. Decisive victories followed in Bir Maza, Um Sidir, Kulkul, even Muzbat. Vast quantities of arms were seized from the army and from SLA-Minawi, which the government had supplied with all manner of weapons. As commanders from other factions joined G-19, the group changed its name to SLA-Unity.

But battlefield successes were marred by tensions over relations with the National Redemption Front, whose leadership in Asmara was quick to claim credit for the military successes in Darfur. One of the strongest military leaders of SLA-Unity, Adam Bakhit, a former Sudan Air Force pilot, insisted on the importance of membership in the NRF, arguing that it offered strategic depth. But many others opposed it, increasingly angry that "we are dying, and they are claiming victory!"[32] Anger boiled over in October 2006 after JEM leader Khalil Ibrahim claimed, from Asmara, an operation against government forces at Kariari, near the Chad border. Marajan and Jar al Nebi had to intervene to prevent fighting between SLA-Unity and JEM, whose fighters withdrew towards the Chad border.

Despite the intensity of the new government offensive, and the inevitable concentration on military operations, SLA-Unity attempted to convene a meeting of field commanders to begin to build a consensus on how to operate in the post-DPA environment. They acquired chairs and loudspeakers, and scheduled the conference for mid-November, near Bir Maza. Plans were aborted after the government got wind of the meeting and pounded Bir Maza from the air. With little or no international pressure on Khartoum to halt its attacks, it was difficult to see how the commanders could ever come together in Darfur itself. And on one thing they were already agreed: without first reaching a consensus, they would not participate in efforts to salvage the Darfur Peace Agreement by re-examining its most controversial provisions—compensation for war victims, mechanisms and guarantees for the disarmament of the militias, and political representation, especially at regional level.

Those who were now the power on the ground found little international acknowledgement of their influence or recognition of their genuine desire for a negotiated end to the war that would get civilians safely back to their homes. The African Union especially persisted in the error of Abuja and continued focusing on the titular heads of the movements—Abdel Wahid and Minawi—while ignoring those who controlled the field and had popular support.

### Minni Minawi, Senior Assistant to the President of the Republic

MANY TIMES during the Darfur war, observers predicted that Minawi would not survive. He had too many enemies and too bad a human rights record to be acceptable either to Darfurians or to the international community, it seemed. But he was tolerated, and even encouraged, by the international community not because he had popular support but because he was seen as the strongest rebel leader and therefore essential to peace. While Darfurians turned against him in ever-greater numbers, the U.S. government turned a blind eye and made him its only interlocutor in the fractured Zaghawa community. With U.S. connivance, Minawi navigated his way through the chaos of the Darfur resistance, relying on brute force and the ineptitude of his main rival.

In his battle for survival, and supremacy, Minawi struck first and struck hard. While he was impressing negotiators in the last months of the Abuja talks with his quick grasp of practical issues and clarity of mind, his forces were busy attacking Abdel Wahid's positions in Darfur. This approach was not penalized in the peace forum, but it cost him much of his remaining support in Darfur. His decision to sign the Darfur Peace Agreement caused a further hemorrhage.

As Minawi became a pariah among Darfurians, he formed a military alliance with the government and Janjawiid against his former comrades in the movement. He denied it, but any doubts were dispelled in July when SLA-Unity captured government trucks filled with ammunition in Orori, one of the last pockets where Minawi retained a toehold. His abuses could no longer be disregarded: Amnesty International accused his faction of killing and raping civilians, and the UN's humanitarian chief, Jan Egeland, said his men were causing a new wave of displacement. But not even the displaced were safe from SLA-Minawi: in al Fashir, Minawi's troops entered camps for the displaced, looted and threatened civilians. A local human rights activist said: "They are becoming bandits in the town. They are drunk and drugged and living in the prostitutes' area, driving the cars of AMIS." Their banditry soon spread all across government-controlled Darfur and reached a zenith in December 2006 with looting of aid compounds, murders, and rapes—including among aid workers—in South Darfur.

Unhappiness with Minawi's alliance with the government reached into the heart of his delegation in Khartoum. On the eve of his appointment as senior advisor, a source in Khartoum reported that "Minni's group is falling apart, his delegation in Khartoum is severely divided, with some of them already packing their bags and moving out of the hotel. All those critical of the way he is dealing with the government are ordered out of Khartoum with the excuse that they are wanted to build the SLA's political movement outside Khartoum."[33]

As the peace talks reached their climax, Minni Minawi had faced a stark choice. Asked on May 6 why he signed the peace agreement, his answer was clear and guile-free: "I calculated the balance of forces, and I realized I should sign" (de Waal 2006a, 17). The Zaghawa in general and his forces in particular had reached a position that could only be sustained by cutting a deal with the government, which he duly, if reluctantly, did. Because of the international insistence on rushing the Abuja negotiations to a precipitous conclusion, the peace agreement that was concluded in Abuja was little more than a power deal between an abusive government and a ruthless insurgent. Minawi's signature on the agreement threatened to make it stillborn. Because of him, the Zaghawa were isolated and unpopular—and he was the most unpopular of them all.

As 2007 opened, the two men who had dominated the SLA since it first took up arms—Minni Minawi and Abdel Wahid Mohamed al Nur—appeared increasingly irrelevant. Their place was taken by a new group of field commanders who wanted unity, reform of the SLA, and peace—although not the peace of Abuja. Under attack by the government,

Janjawiid, and the remnants of SLA-Minawi, violently criticized by the National Redemption Front for their refusal to come under Chadian patronage, and condemned by the U.S. as the refuseniks of Abuja, they faced an uphill battle. Rebel unity, for the foreseeable future, would remain elusive.

# 7

# The Unseen Regional Implications
# of the Crisis in Darfur[1]

ROLAND MARCHAL

SINCE EARLY 2003, the Darfur crisis has had a high profile in the Western press. Yet its regional dimension has scarcely been mentioned. Even though eastern Chad and northern Central African Republic (CAR) are increasingly the location of skirmishes, full-scale battles, and abuses against the civilian population, Darfur's war is still overwhelmingly seen as an internal Sudanese crisis.[2] When reports do consider Chad, then the insecurity affecting Wadai (eastern Chad) is usually described as a spillover from the conflict in Darfur. Very few analysts have tried to make sense of this merger of the two different crises in Chad and Sudan that has reconfigured the political setting on both sides of the border, while the CAR is ignored completely. Some analysts have discussed relatively marginal military supplies from the SPLA, Eritrea, and some informal yet efficient Chadian and Libyan networks in support of insurgent movements, including the two most important, the SLA and JEM.[3] However, the political implications of such facts have never been fully addressed, perhaps because they challenged the common stance of the international community or raised difficult questions about the mediation process led by the African Union.

These political, social, and military connections must be contextualized in order to discern whether they are fairly marginal phenomena or whether they frame a set of grievances and alliances that reshape the actions of those engaged militarily. The cross-border engagements in turn create more opportunity for war instead of peace in Darfur and worsen an already low level of governance in Chad. In early 2005, most observers expected Sudan's newly-appointed first vice president, Dr. John Garang, to work toward a complete settlement of this conflict. This hope did not materialize when Garang was killed in a helicopter crash on July 30, 2005. Yet such an expectation should have been questioned not only for the lack of attention to the manner in which armed movements on each side of the border had evolved, but also because the regional equation had changed since the conflict erupted.

A few months later, in autumn 2005, Chadian opposition fronts were given improved facilities in Darfur while the Chadian republican guard was collapsing. From December 2005, a proxy war between N'djamena and Khartoum took shape, in which the stakes on each side were profoundly internal. By supporting the Chadian armed opposition, the Sudanese rulers expected to curb the Darfur insurgency; Idriss Déby was using the latter to secure his border and keep his grip on power. The signature of the Darfur Peace Agreement in Abuja on May 5, a few days after Idriss Déby was re-elected as President, did not change the mood of the war; nor did an apparent reconciliation between the two presidents in early August 2006. Full-scale war, as opposed to simple incidents or skirmishes, became more likely when Khartoum started adamantly opposing the UN Resolution 1706 that called for a UN peacekeeping operation in Darfur. One reason for this was the Sudan government's expectation that Chad would be the base of operations for international forces intervening in Darfur.

There are two other countries that need to be considered in this analysis: Libya and CAR, which have both had substantial but indirect roles in the history of the region. Libya was a key element in the regional order before 1990, since it attempted to exert an "Arabist" influence across a wide sphere in the Sahel after Muammar Gaddafi took power in September 1969. With UN sanctions in 1992 and acceptance of the settlement of the Aouzou Strip dispute with Chad in February 1994 Tripoli adopted a lower regional profile. Informal transnational networks benefited from this new environment. Imports and exports from Libya became significant, a pattern that was reinforced through new flows of labor migrants across the Sahara and the emergence of a regional oil economy in the late 1990s. Yet Libya could not be edged out and used the crisis in Darfur and Chad to reassert itself as a key actor in the regional order. However, its role must be assessed in a careful way: its whimsical leader is not as irresponsible or Machiavellian as is all-too-often claimed by Western media.

On the other hand, CAR has had a more indirect influence in the two conflicts. For years CAR was a sanctuary for armed oppositions to Chadian rulers after the latter's first two presidents, François Tombalbaye (1960–1975) and Félix Malloum (1975–1978), were militarily overthrown. Most dissidents who took refuge in CAR were from southern Chad, but others from central Chad gradually joined them. Droughts and insecurity also affected migration pathways. General François Bozizé's coup (strongly supported by Chadian forces and Paris) in March 2003 dramatically challenged this situation since many former rebels escaped back to Sudan via Darfur, playing into the hands of the Sudanese military intelligence. The Janjawiid received reinforcements thanks to those fighters who had good skills and on whom responsibility for mass killings could conveniently be placed as "foreign bandits."

This chapter provides background on how Idriss Déby's ethnic group, the Zaghawa, became prominent in Chadian politics, on the linkages between the civil war in Chad and the Darfur crises, and on the crucial role of Libya. Lastly, it explains why the crises in Darfur and Chad are increasingly linked because of the nature of Déby's regime. It concludes by elaborating prospective scenarios of destabilization.

## The Zaghawa Equation in the Chadian Civil War

UNDERSTANDING ZAGHAWA politics is essential to explaining the linkages among Chad, Libya, CAR, and Darfur. Zaghawa is a confederation of a great number of highly individualized clans, with separate habitats connected by religion and language. This cultural, tribal, and geographical diversity is accompanied by multiple names. In Sudan and Chad, they are known as Zaghawa and Bideyat; the latter are a branch of Zaghawa. Mostly nomads, the land of the Bideyat usually lies far from the settled Zaghawa, who enjoy more stability. But the language, customs, and traditions of the two are the same, although the Zaghawa call themselves *Beri* (Tubiana and Tubiana 1977).

The Zaghawa are scattered among and migrate between and within these countries, a feature they share with other non-Arab and Arab tribes from Chad and Sudan, such as the Masalit, Tama, Salamat, and Mahamid-Rizeigat. This situation has been exacerbated by distress migrations, occurring for two main reasons. First, drought and desertification provided a push factor over the last century (and especially in the 1960s, 1970s, and 1980s) that created the conditions for massive displacements of people (de Waal 1989). A second reason for forced migration has been the conflicts and feuds that took place on both sides of the borders since the 1970s.

The Zaghawa today appear to be in a more powerful position than other groups that straddle the eastern Chad basin. They have easy access to the many Gorane who have positions in the Libyan army and in local administration in southern Libya. Likewise, Idriss Déby and his extended lineage and allies monopolize power in Chad, while other members of this extended network associated with him are key leaders in the insurgency in Darfur (Khalil Ibrahim Mohamed, Minni Arkoy Minawi, Nourene Minawi Bartcham, Jibril Abdelkarim "Tek") and constitute the backbone of its military apparatus. In the CAR, General Bozizé was able to undertake his coup in March 2003 thanks to Chadian mercenaries and his success was achieved with the armed support of Idriss Déby.

In order to gain a full sense of the Zaghawa position, a brief review of Chad's civil war is in order. The war was not a surprise: as Robert Buijtenhuijs (1978, 1987, 1988) has noted, the main surprise was not that the civil war broke out, but that it took so long to do so. The conflict brought forth a number of tensions that arose from the authoritarian rule of François Tombalbaye, including the exclusion of the Muslim population in 1962 from civil service (leading to riots in 1963 in the capital city), and the absence of any decent policy to ease the harsh living conditions of many of the people. To a certain extent, many grievances raised in the case of southern Sudan would be valid in the context of Chad, despite the different histories of colonization and the insertion of prevailing clichés ("Christians and animists" being replaced here by "Muslims").

The peasant revolt in Mangalme in October 1965 and its merciless repression can be considered as the start of the civil war in Chad, though the FROL-INAT (*Front national de liberation du Tchad*) was set up only a year later in Nyala, southern Darfur. For more than a decade the situation could be interpreted in terms of opposition between southerners and their allies against a broad alliance in which Gorane (whose leaders were Goukouni Oueddei and Hissène Habré), Zaghawa (Hassan Djamous, Abbas Koty) and Arabs (Abba Siddick, Ahmed Acyl, and Acheikh Ibn Omar) constituted the core groups. However, this binary picture is further complicated by the amazing factional politics that affected all groups (including the southerners) in the 1960s and 1970s. The FROLINAT had to cope with internal infighting from the beginning, which led to a *de facto* split in groups, whose leaders had different agendas. Chronicles of the civil war are basically narratives of coalitions doomed to failure, endless competitions and recurrent exclusions framed by violence, opportunistic alliances practiced by local and national leaders, and the varying influence of external actors who used Chad as a battleground to advance their influence in central Africa.

The first round of the civil war was supposed to end in November 1979, when a series of international conferences in Nigeria convened by the Organisation of African Unity produced an accord among warring factions, creating a transitional government, the GUNT (*Gouvernement d'union nationale du Tchad*), which included the main rebel leaders. In March 1980, Libyan troops intervened to support Goukouni Oueddei against Hissène Habré. The Chadian war had, by then, become a proxy for a major confrontation between Western states and Libya. Habré, hosted by President Jaafar Nimeiri in Sudan, was receiving military aid from Egypt, France, and the U.S. to regain N'djamena and expel Libya from Chad. On June 7, 1982, Habré eventually took over the capital thanks to direct French and Zairian support.

However, matters were far from settled. Over the next few years, Habré fought against Libyan forces in northern Chad, the remnants of the forces led by Goukouni and Acheikh Ibn Omar, as well as against southern armed groups (the famed but ineffective *Codos*) to whom CAR was providing support and sanctuary. These years witnessed the establishment of a very coercive regime. Factional politics did not end, although Libya was cornered

(*Opération Manta* in June 1983 that later became *Epervier* [Sparrow Hawk] from February 1986 until 2007). Supporters of Goukouni joined Habré in 1986; those of Acheikh also joined in 1988, following the latter's defeat inside Darfur. At the same time, the alliance that brought Habré to the forefront, weakened tensions between old allies—or between old and new ones—and provoked a series of splits, as well as real and imaginary attempted coups that were put down by fierce repression of the supposed plotters and their ethnic groups.

It was in such a context that on April 1, 1989 Ibrahim Mahamat Itno (minister of the interior from July 1986, Zaghawa/Bideyat and half brother of Idriss Déby), Hassan Djamous (commander in chief of the army from 1985, Zaghawa/Kobé) and Idriss Déby Itno (then presidential adviser on security and defense, Zaghawa/Bideyat) tried to overthrow Habré. Only Déby survived the foiled coup and escaped to Sudan through Libya to reorganize his forces and create a new small party, the MPS (*Mouvement patriotique de salut*). Déby, backed by Sudan and Libya, finally took power in December 1990 after defeating Habré's forces at the strategic battles of Tine and Iriba. Habré then fled to Cameroon and subsequently went into exile in Senegal. A national democracy conference (1993) and multiparty elections (1996) confirmed Déby's (and thus the Zaghawa's) hold on power in N'djamena.

## Libya's Continuing Role

LIBYA IN THE 1970s and 1980s was pursuing Arabism and an active Africa policy aimed at consolidating its influence against conservative Arab states and former colonial powers, promoting its international agenda (especially against the U.S. and Israel), and building an influential network in all African polities. Tripoli gave generous support to liberation movements, such as the South-West African People's Organisation (Namibia), the African National Congress, and Mozambique's FRELIMO. In its own neighborhood, its policy was generally to restore the sphere of influence that the Sanussiyya *tariqa* had held before western colonial powers destroyed it. This explains for instance, why CAR has always interested Libya beyond its rulers' quest for a lucrative client relationship; intervention in Chad was a way to cross the Sahara and develop its "natural" influence.

Libya was a sanctuary for many Chadian politicians (even after Déby took power in 1990) and many Chadians had positions within the Libyan state apparatus. The support Libya provided to the Chadian Arab faction was therefore not surprising though it was coupled for years with support for the Gorane of Goukouni and other southern armed movements at different points in time. Arabism was certainly more than rhetoric, but it could be adapted to political contingencies.

Despite being seen as a strategic threat by France and the U.S., Libya proved to be insufficiently strong to sustain a military occupation, as was demonstrated by the increasing weakness of its troops in Chad from March 1980 to early 1981. Giving support to Chadian allies who were refugees in Darfur thus became a key dimension of Tripoli's policy for the following decade. Chadian Arab tribes (and therefore their Sudanese counterparts) benefited from generous military supplies, which helped militarize land disputes and social contradictions in Darfur in the 1980s. When the Chadian Zaghawa subsequently began to shift their support away from Habré (since they felt that the Gorane or the Anakaza—the Habré's subclan among the Gorane—were monopolizing all key positions and / or giving positions to rival groups), it provided Déby with the opportunity to organize his movement, the MPS, from Darfur. This movement was made possible by his kinsmen settled in Libya (some of the informal networks that supplied him in 1989 and 1990 may still be active today, acting with the JEM and SLA) and by Gaddafi more directly.

Libya's Islamic Legion—a flashy name for crude African mercenaries—was built up as an attempt to increase the chances of victory for Habré's opponents. Despite the Libya-phobia, so widely diffused in those years, this group was not the threat often described. It was made up of migrants and sometimes prisoners released for that purpose. These people, who were for the most part untrained, did not really alter the balance of forces. They just made the messy situation in western and northern Darfur messier (Harir 1994; Burr and Collins 1999).

Besides military supplies, Gaddafi's most important achievement in the late 1980s was to convince Sudan's Sadiq al Mahdi to turn a blind eye to the situation in Darfur after he became prime minister in 1986. Both leaders were friends and the former assisted the latter when he tried to militarily oppose Nimeiri's rule in Sudan between 1970 and 1977 by opening camps, providing military training, and allocating funds. The two also had pretensions to be Islamic thinkers and reformers, signalling their intentions to develop Islamic projects for their respective countries while actually opposing Islamism. Both disliked Egypt. Although Sadiq is still criticized today for his compliance with Libyan interests in Darfur after 1986, Khartoum may not have been in a position to drastically alter Libyan policy. The economic situation in Sudan was deteriorating and Libya was one of the last supporters of Khartoum through aid, remittances sent by Sudanese migrants back home, and the flow of goods that allowed for the easing of shortages in Sudan (as demonstrated then by the growth of *Suq* Libya in Omdurman).

The take over of Chad by Déby, though Tripoli supported it, did not mean a radical long-run increase in the Libyan influence in the region. First, Tripoli had to deal with the international consequences of terrorist acts perpetrated by its security services, and UN sanctions against the regime after 1992 had a tremendous impact on its resources and leverage in Africa and the Arab world. Second, the new rulers in Sudan and Chad built a close relationship that reduced Gaddafi's ability to influence political processes in both countries. Yet this new political setting was not unfavorable to the transnational economy. International sanctions against Libya boosted the informal economy and many operators from Darfur (mostly but not only Zaghawa) had good connections in Khartoum with the leadership of the National Islamic Front: a triangular set of commercial networks emerged with nodes in Kufra, al Fashir, and Abéché, while supplying markets were located in Malta or in the Gulf (Saudi Arabia and Dubai).

While Khartoum's Islamists were never Libya's best friends, issues of common security on the border area constituted a deterrent. Tripoli also turned a blind eye to the Gorane-based insurgency movement in Chad's restive northern Borkou-Ennedi-Tibesti (BET) region, both because it is seen as weak and irrelevant, and because of the fairly structural corruption of the Libyan army and the support provided by its Gorane officers. It could also have been that Gaddafi wanted to keep all options open. To a large extent, the war in Darfur has provided a window of opportunity for Libya to reshape its policy towards Khartoum and N'djamena, and reassert itself as the indispensable broker.

## Fusion and Fission among the Zaghawa

THE ORIGINAL EXPORT of Chad's war to Darfur in the 1980s had an important impact on the Zaghawa's collective identity. In 1987–1989 conflict in Darfur was sparked by the presence of Arabs who had been against Habré for quite a while (Déby was chief of staff of the army and special security adviser in the presidency when major mass killings occurred in Chad against southerners and Arabs). When the Zaghawa began to oppose Habré, war was not only waged in Chad but also in Darfur. Habré armed ethnic groups against the Zaghawa, and he also allowed his troops to cross the border at different times to wage the only form of war they knew, which included burning of villages, raping, looting, and mass killing. Since there was hardly a difference between Sudanese and Chadian Zaghawa settlements, they all became targets in the conflict. The key element in Déby's victory was the mobilization of his whole tribe in Sudan and Chad—especially the Kobé who were settled mostly in Chad but also in Sudan, and the Wegi (including the Tuer, Gala, Oulagi, Artaj, and Suweini sub-clans) settled mostly in Sudan. Kobé and Wegi are two Zaghawa clans that are demographically and economically more significant than the Bideyat, to which Déby belongs. Those two clans joined the war, following Déby under the assumption that solidarity would be rewarded if Déby was able to rule Chad. Expectations were high because Habré was not looking as strong as he once was; he did not enjoy much international sympathy due to gross human rights violations committed by his DDS (*Direction de la documentation et de la sécurité*) and his shifting allegiance between Paris and Washington D. C.

Yet it would be wrong to assume that this Zaghawa unity was without differences. Idriss Déby was some sort of a charismatic leader; but he was young (born in 1952) and did not take part in key episodes of war, since he was being trained in France in the early 1970s and in the mid-1980s. In addition, he was not from a main clan among the Bideyat (his Bireyara clan is second to the Sigeira clan among the Bideyat). Moreover, there were already rumors that Hassan Djamous—a charismatic leader—was executed after being captured in a fight near the border, with Déby benefiting the most from his death (this point arose repeatedly in bitter arguments between the Kobé and Déby in 2003 when they accused him of being responsible not only for the death of Djamous, but also for their Kobé kinsmen at the hands of the Sudanese army and the Janjawiid). Déby managed these differences by building an alliance with French-speaking Zaghawa against Arabic-speaking ones led by Abbas Koty, a Zaghawa/Kobé (see Haggar 2003).

Déby's victory was certainly a turning point in the definition of Zaghawa identity. Nevertheless, this event also meant the emergence of new tensions within his tribal group. Many expected unrealistic rewards for their involvement in the war. Many Sudanese Zaghawa did indeed find positions in the Chadian army. However, when Déby was put under pressure to disband parts of his army, the first among Zaghawa to be pushed out were the Arabic speakers. The disarmament and demobilization plan funded by the French government was not successful, and many Wegi went back to Darfur and found new reasons to fight, since the situation there had dramatically deteriorated in the 1990s. Access to state power also implied drastic changes in the social reading of Zaghawa history and the creation of a new kind of hierarchy: Zaghawa suddenly had to compete among themselves for a complex booty.

To a large extent, Déby's success in Chad was accidental, owing more to the weakness of Habré than to his own might. Although Libya supported Déby's campaign, informal Zaghawa transnational networks might have been as efficient as the support provided by the Libyan state. Sadiq al Mahdi was overthrown in June 1989, but the geopolitical interests of the new Islamist regime were then focused on Ethiopia: a regime change in Addis-Ababa implied a clear weakening of the SPLA. The Sudanese endorsement of Déby was at that time more of a decision obtained from Omar al Beshir (by one of his friends within the military junta, General Tijani Adam Tahir), than of a strategic reassessment of the role of Chad.

## Chad under Déby

IN THE EARLY YEARS of Déby's rule, power was consolidated through brutalities, killings, and authoritarianism. Under French pressure, a national conference took place in 1993 (as had become the vogue in other Francophone African countries) though it was controlled by the MPS. In 1996, the country's first multiparty elections were held. There were few arguments with the overall patterns and results, although the elections were hardly free or fair in southern Chad. However, the subsequent presidential election in 2001 was so controversial that Déby was forced to promise that this mandate would be his last one. Notwithstanding this promise, the constitution was opportunely changed in June 2005 to allow Déby to be a candidate once again in the elections scheduled for 2006, which he duly won handsomely.

Déby's reign confronted a number of interrelated challenges. The first was the eradication of the armed opposition and the control of the political arena. The second, more recent one, was the constitution of a Zaghawa regime, which was put at risk by the fragile health of the president and the rival ambitions of his kinsmen. The third was the inability of his regime to extend support beyond its most direct clients.

In the aftermath of his victory over Habré, Déby had to cope with armed oppositions from all quarters—some emanating from close allies, others from long-time enemies associated with Habré. From the very beginning, opposition to the seizure of power by Déby's closest friends provoked tensions that translated from time to time into open fighting. This happened not only with other tribal militias (such as the Hadjarai of Maldom Abbas in 1991) but also within the Zaghawa (the upheaval of the Zaghawa/Kobé in N'djamena in April 1992 and the elimination of Abbas Koty in 1993 despite a settlement guaranteed by Khartoum and Tripoli). Although some serious incidents have occurred within Déby's alliance, most of the atrocities in these various waves of insurrection were committed in the 1990s against southerners due to the upheaval of movements such as the CNSPD (*Comité national du salut pour la paix et la démocratie*) chaired by Moise Kette Nodji (d. in

October 2000) and the FARF (*Forces armées pour une République fédérale*) led by Laokin Barde Frisson (d. early 1998), which operated in the proximity of oil fields in the Logone region with the unofficial support of the CAR President, Ange-Félix Patassé. A peace agreement was reached in May 1998 because oil production needed to be secure and Déby was keen to compromise after having weakened—and physically eliminated—his southern opponents.

The most recent challenge came in October 1998, before the Darfur crisis broke out, with the creation of the MDJT (*Mouvement pour la démocratie et la justice au Tchad*) led by Youssouf Togoimi (Toubou/Mahaniya, minister of defense in Déby's cabinet until his defection in late spring 1998). Today, MDJT activity has been limited to the BET and has been supported by Goukouni, with Libya playing a very ambiguous—to say the least—role: Libya has not tried to stop the logistical supply lines to this group, though Tripoli is friendly with Déby.

The very nature of the regime and the impunity of Zaghawa militias (from the republican guard, an elite corps, or from the rank and file of the army) provided opportunities for looting, revenge, and appropriation of lands and livestock in various parts of the country. Incidents in Wadai and Biltine were numerous and notably pushed Arab, Tama, and other tribes to cross the border and join those who settled in Darfur in the 1980s. It is important to note that the ANR (*Armée nationale de résistance*) set up in 1994 by Mahamat Garfa, Déby's former chief of staff, recruited mostly among the Tama people and operated near the borders of eastern Chad, CAR, and Sudan. Despite defections (Mahamat Garfa went into exile in Benin and came back to Chad in 2003) and various agreements (the latest in January 2003), in June 2003 remnants of the ANR allied with the MDJT. Starting mid-2004, ANR fighters who were based in Darfur after Bozizé's coup in CAR were reorganized and re-supplied by Sudanese military intelligence to fight against the SLA and JEM. They emerged in summer 2005 as the RDL (*Rassemblement pour les libertés*) led by Mahamat Nour that became the main component of the FUCD (*Front uni pour le changement démocratique*) in December 2005. These remnants of groups were going to crystallize into bigger armed opposition movements because of the inability of Idriss Déby to reform his regime and the war in Darfur.

In passing, in order to avoid superficial comparisons between Chad and Darfur, it is worth noting that Arab tribes in Chad are not seen as a major threat to the regime. They do not have the same history of contested lands as in Darfur and, more importantly, they are deeply divided with many potential leaders in exile (Acheikh is a refugee in Orléans, France; Ahmat Hassaballah Soubiane, a founding member of MPS and ambassador to the U.S. and Canada, is still in Washington). What matters more in Chad, to use the new Darfurian vocabulary, are "African" tribes such as the Tama, Gorane, and Hadjarai.

Déby certainly succeeded in consolidating his political system. Political parties were slowly authorized, though they have limited relevance and capacities beyond the capital city. In the mid-1990s, Déby gradually restored basic functions of government and entered into agreements with the World Bank and the International Monetary Fund to carry out economic reforms. Oil exploitation in the southern Doba region began in June 2000, with the U.S.-based Exxon-Mobil leading a consortium in a $3.7 billion project exporting oil from October 2003 via a 1,000 km buried pipeline through Cameroon to Kibri, in the Gulf of Guinea.[4] The project included unique mechanisms for collaboration among the World Bank, the private sector, government, and civil society so as to guarantee that future oil revenues benefit local populations, resulting in poverty alleviation. But oil revenue only began trickling into the country in July 2004. The success of this project was ultimately dependent on intensive international monitoring efforts to ensure that all parties kept their commitments. In December 2005, Chadian law was modified by parliament in order to relax the international monitoring. The World Bank, under instructions from its new president, Paul Wolfowitz, who was eager to endorse the U.S. policy in Darfur at any cost, reached an accommodating new agreement in June 2006. Many doubts could be raised on the effectiveness of this new deal after months of crisis between the World Bank and the Chadian presidency and the deepening crisis in Chad itself.

As in Somalia in the 1980s, the military and security apparatus was fully controlled by elements of the president's ethnic group: most high officials (around 80 percent) belonged to Déby's group, as is the case for more than 20 percent of the army. Most parastatals (Cotontchad, *Société textile du Tchad*

(STT), *Société sucrière du Tchad* (Sonasut), *Office national des postes et télécommunications* (Onpt), Air Tchad) were directly or indirectly controlled by Zaghawa. Impunity was the rule, punishment (even for an attempted coup) the exception. Early 2005, before the crisis broke out, the army chief of staff was Mahamat Saleh Kaya, a cousin of Déby; Abakar Yousouf Mahamat Itno (nephew of Déby) commanded the Republican Guard; Mahamat Saleh Ibrahim (Déby's nephew), was in charge of the nomadic guard; Abakar Abdelkerim led the gendarmerie; Ramadan Erdebou was the director general (DG) of the national police; Mahamat Ismael Chaibo was the DG of the national security agency; and Mahamat Saleh Adoum was deputy director of the private office of the president. Abbas Mahamat Tolli (nephew of Déby) was minister of state for finance and, last but not least, Daoussa Déby (half brother of Déby), former ambassador to Libya, was the presidential advisor in charge of security and intelligence until the foiled coup of May 2004. (Many more names could be added, such as Moussa Faki, nephew of Déby, prime minister after the reshuffle of June 2003 until February 2005, but with little real leverage on the state.)

However, such a list should be read with a clear understanding that solidarity is not systemic or automatic. The Zaghawa tribe is more a confederation of clans than an organic solidarity group. Of course, there is common claimed identity, but regional affiliation (Ennedi is different from Biltine), autochthony (as exemplified by the divisions among the Borogate subtribe[5]) and various clans also create divisions, which are exacerbated by the wish for the greatest access to state resources and privileges. Co-optation of elements of others groups signal compromises designed to secure the oil revenues and to keep armed or civilian opposition movements as weak and as fragmented as possible.

### Regional Stabilization under Déby?

HOW HAS SUCH A SYSTEM survived over the years? Beyond the brutality of its coercion or, at some points, its accommodation, Déby played his regional and international cards well. In November 1990, he only barely received French endorsement. At that time, Paris was quite unhappy with Habré's perceived shift in allegiance to the U.S. (he provided camps to train Libyan prisoners to overthrow Gaddafi) and his humiliations of the French army on various occasions. But this competition meant that France did not want to show dissent. The link between Déby and the French government was built at the eleventh hour through Paul Fontbonne, an intelligence (DGSE) officer attached to the French embassy in Khartoum and well acquainted with General Tijani Adam Tahir and the NIF. As a reward, Fontbonne became presidential adviser in N'djamena for four years after Déby's victory and, in 1991, Elf-Aquitaine (at that time a French parastatal) entered the oil consortium (the French company left the consortium in 1999, provoking the expulsion of the French ambassador, Alain du Bois Péan[6]).

Chad became crucial to France when the French military base in CAR was closed in 1998 and extended military facilities were instead provided by Libreville and N'djamena. Today, there are more than 1,100 soldiers based in Chad and their presence is paid for by the French ministry of finance, not the ministry of defense. Until the present crisis, this meant that the latter was campaigning in favor of Idriss Déby, despite his gross violations of human rights. Déby was trained as a military pilot in France in the 1970s and attended a two-year course in 1985–1987 at the war college in Paris where he cultivated ties to French officers, who are now generals. Beyond these factors, which are meaningful in the French decisionmaking system, other issues were relevant. Many observers in Paris were convinced that a northerner was a better ruler for Chad because a southerner would have created the conditions for an upheaval in the BET, as was the case in the 1960s. Déby, though hot-tempered, proved to be compliant with the frank advice provided by Paris at different points in time (with respect to its relationship to Libya, the national conference and multiparty system, and elections). Though enjoying a warm relationship with Washington, he did not try to play up the competition between the two Western capitals (at least not at the level Habré had). Lastly, it is important to note that he is a friend of the former French president Jacques Chirac.

Déby also carefully managed his relationship with Libya. In the 1990s, Gaddafi was facing difficult times and thus moved to temper his destabilization policy in Chad. He knew that antagonizing N'djamena would allow more room for his Western opponents to operate from there or for his Islamist opposition to gain some kind of international recognition. Under these conditions, the Aouzou Strip dispute suddenly found a legal settlement and, despite some ambiguities, Libya pushed for a new agenda through the boycott of the UN sanctions it was facing as well as through the establishment of the Community of Sahel-Saharan States (CEN-SAD), a new regional organization established in February 1998.

With respect to the CAR, Déby eased tensions through a 1998 peace agreement (anti-Déby rebel groups had been operating from sanctuaries in northern CAR). But the agreement was not enough and in 2003 Chad contributed ground forces for General Bozizé's coup against Ange-Félix Patassé. Patassé's downfall went unlamented in Western capitals (because he had brought his country to the brink of disaster); in Paris specifically (because of the connection between Patassé and Jean-Pierre Bemba, rebel leader in the Democratic Republic of Congo); in Khartoum (because of Patassé's supply of arms and support to the SPLA) and in N'djamena (because of the MDJT connection: Patassé and the MDJT were supported by Libya). N'djamena and Paris officially sent troops to Bangui as parts of the CEMAC (*Communauté économique et monétaire d'Afrique centrale*) observation force. General Bozizé, as is usual in such circumstances, first claimed that he had no political ambition apart from restoring his nation and state and was then elected president in May 2005.

Recently, two more issues have ranked high on the international agenda, for which Déby succeeded in obtaining endorsement. The first was the emergence of an oil economy and the unfolding radical experiment in internationally supervised transparency of oil revenue wealth sharing. The second is linked to post 9/11 priorities: the "war on terror" and the alleged existence of radical Islamist groups in the Sahara, as exemplified by the fighting in March 2004 between Chadian troops and the GSPC (*Groupe salafiste pour la predication et le combat*) near the border with Niger. The new U.S. Pan-Sahel Initiative on counter-terrorism provides Chad and Déby, as other authoritarian regimes in northern Africa, with increased leverage.

Relationships between Khartoum and N'djamena were excellent in the 1990s. One may wonder how such a situation prevailed, since Islamists were ruling Sudan while a known heavy drinker was leading Chad. There were three main reasons for Khartoum to support the new regime in N'djamena. The relative importance of these factors changed over the years, but all were affected by both the peace negotiations and the Darfur crisis. These factors are: the security issue, an alternative to the containment policy enforced by the U.S. in the 1990s against Islamist Sudan, and the attempt by the latter to achieve greater influence in west and north Africa through business and proselytism (*da'wa*). Chad had its own reasons for keeping these relationships as warm as possible. Darfur had been a sanctuary used at different times in the civil war to challenge the rulers in N'djamena; to a large extent, its neutralization meant a consolidation of the regime. Chad also could use this Sudanese connection to better manage its relationships with Libya. Gaddafi had no real sympathy for the NIF in Khartoum, but Tripoli, on the other hand, knew that Khartoum could help its Islamic opposition and thus played by the rules. Lastly, N'djamena could be used as a transit point for a number of dubious forms of trafficking (fake Bahraini banknotes, weapons, and so on), which involved other capitals of Sahelian countries. However, the mobilization of the Zaghawa in the Darfur crisis threw this whole set of cross-national interests into shambles.

In the immediate aftermath of Déby's victory, Khartoum had to cope with the upheaval caused by Daud Bolad's incursion into Darfur at the head of an SPLA unit (see Marchal 2004b). This badly-planned revolt was repressed very quickly but demonstrated the absolute necessity to contain any extension of the war beyond southern Sudan. In the NIF view, Déby should give guarantees that no sanctuaries of any sort could be provided for its opposition. Nor should the SPLA be able to build new supply lines (as was almost the case during 1995). As a corollary, Déby should be prudent concerning the Sudanese who had joined him in his war against Habré and make sure that their skills would not be used by any opposition in Sudan (he was not as successful as expected).

For Khartoum, a friendly regime in Chad was also a way to challenge the containment policy increasingly enforced by the U.S. against the NIF. Eritrea, Ethiopia, Uganda, and Egypt after 1997 (all countries for their own reasons) endorsed, at various times, this U.S. policy (at least until the Eritrea-Ethiopia war), but N'djamena never did. The fact that Chad was a Francophone country was also considered an asset by Khartoum with respect to Paris. Furthermore, the alliance with Déby meant that people and goods linked to the NIF "civilization project" for west and north Africa could transit through Chad without much concern. Islamist militants and weaponry allegedly reached Algeria in this manner at different moments in the 1990s. One may assume that other north African countries enjoyed the same privilege.

Khartoum did well either by mediating (with Abbas Koty) or simply by arresting opposition members who were refugees in Sudan (notably, in 1992, 1994, 1998, and 2003), especially CNR (*Conseil national pour le redressement*), ANR (*Alliance nationale pour le redressement*), FNT (*Front national du Tchad*), and FNTR (*Front national du Tchad rénové*) activists: all those armed factions are linked to failed coups or armed dissidence). Contrary to what had taken place in the eastern and southern flanks of Sudan, there was a clear refusal to support proxy wars in Chad. Déby (and his close associates) benefited from this alliance not only by securing their power, but also by getting involved in various profitable businesses, especially those linked to oil exploitation and the building of the Chadian-Cameroonian pipeline. In November 1999, Elf-Aquitaine decided to pull out from the oil consortium, which was then reconfigured, taking on board the Malaysian firm, Petronas (already a key operator in Sudan and the successful architect of the pipeline to Port Sudan). In the end, Exxon got 40 percent of the shares, Chevron 25 percent and Petronas 35 percent. It is in this context that the 2003 killing of a Sudanese "businessman" by people connected to the Chadian presidency should be analyzed (as the disgrace of Daoussa Déby): this murder was linked to contracts related to pipe supplies in which the contractors were Sudanese and Chadians and illustrates the increased regional links in oil exploitation.

### Déby and the Darfur Crisis

IT IS AN UNDERSTATEMENT to say that the Darfur crisis disrupted this whole architecture of collusion and shared interests. There is no need to explain here the conditions in which the conflict started and how it developed.[7] The following comments will be limited to some important factors that link the fighting in Darfur with the political situation in Chad.

Given the earlier amity between the two, when the threat from Darfur first emerged, Khartoum considered N'djamena capable of and responsible for curbing the threat. In particular, Déby was expected to be able to control his own kinsmen. The ruling elite in Khartoum did not react the same way with respect to the two initial insurgent movements, SLA and JEM. Politically speaking, the latter was seen as the most threatening: many in its leadership had been part of the NIF, knew well the security apparatus' modus operandi, had local leverage in some parts of Darfur, and were directly or indirectly working to get the Islamist leader Hassan al Turabi released and back at the heart of Sudanese politics. But while the SLA obtained its first consignments of weapons from the SPLA and Eritrea, the JEM was generously supplied by Zaghawa officers from the Chadian army and presidential guard. Khartoum did not understand why Déby was unable to put his house in order.[8] Sudanese military intelligence mobilized would-be militias in Darfur to oppose what was locally described as (and to a certain extent was in fact) a Zaghawa upheaval. Arab and other segments of Chadian tribes that relocated to Darfur for safety in the 1990s were not slow to take this opportunity for an unexpected revenge. Thus, the longer the conflict and the survival of the Darfur insurgency, the less trust Khartoum had in Déby and the more bitter discussions with him became.

Déby was certainly not indifferent to the preparations for war in Darfur, nor was he only acting for the sake of his Sudanese friends. He also had his own reasons to counter Khalil Ibrahim, the future JEM chairman (whom he tried to have arrested in 2002; at that time, Idriss Déby was still supporting Khartoum). As head of state, he considered himself to be at the top of the Zaghawa social and political hierarchy: others were supposed to rely on him. Khalil never did rely on him, for various reasons. Among them, three are linked to their common Zaghawa identity. First, whatever is said in Sudan about the marginalization of Darfurians (not baseless, of course), Sudanese Zaghawa always received better opportunities for education or access to business than their Chadian brethren. In their discourse, they often describe themselves as more sophisticated, entrepreneurial, and open-minded than their Chadian kinsmen. Secondly, the Kobé see themselves as the true king-makers in Chad and are in very influential positions. The Kobé look at the Bideyat with a certain sense of superiority. Thirdly, Déby tried to build legitimacy not only by framing a political system that put him on top, but also by reframing the Zaghawa chieftainships and creating a Bideyat sultanate, for which he appointed his half brother, Timan.[9] This decision was supported in some Zaghawa quarters and disdained by many others. Khalil Ibrahim could claim much greater legitimacy, based on his family's history. He belongs to the Kobé, a much more important Zaghawa clan in Chad than the Bideyat, who were mostly destitute until Déby took over in 1990. His mother's family is directly related to the great Sultan Abderahman, the most important Zaghawa sultan after the Second World War whose father, Sultan Haggar used French support between 1930 and 1936 to redraw the chieftainships, unifying all those from Wadai and obtaining a much stronger representation for the Zaghawa. Through his father, he also belongs to the ruling family of one of the two Sudanese Sultanates (in Tiné) that were built by opponents who lost to Sultan Haggar. To a certain extent, Khalil's family shows the reunification of these two branches. This represents social capital that Déby will never possess. Lastly, Déby is a military man whose private life is subject to numerous allegations, while Khalil Ibrahim is described as a very good Muslim (an Islamist), an educated person, a fighter (he was in the People's Defense Forces for some time), and a poet. One may add that Khalil's mother and Timan Déby's mother are first cousins.

One can trace these contradictions in the way Déby (and Khartoum) tried to split or destroy the JEM. The creation of the NMRD (National Movement for Reform and Democracy) in autumn 2004 was a gift for Khartoum, since negotiations in December with the JEM and the SLA were going nowhere. The NMRD took away the Zaghawa Kabka away from JEM and the split was possible thanks to Sudan's money and operatives directly linked to Déby. Key NMRD figures were already put forward by Déby in April 2004 as the "true JEM representatives"; but at that time, international observers' protests obliged him to back off. The two main NMRD figures are Nourène Minawi Bartcham, previously a MPS member and the author of a hagiography of Déby published in Arabic, and Colonel Djibrine Abdelkarim "Tek," who was a deputy of Abbas Koty in 1992–1993 in Darfur and returned to Chad to be appointed to the presidential guard. Most of the fighters come from the Bigui clan of Zaghawa, which in 1936 had come under the authority of Sultan Haggar.

More recently, in 2005, recurrent violent clashes occurred in Darfur between the JEM and the SLA-Minawi at the instigation of the latter. The JEM claimed that Minni Arkoy Minawi had struck a deal with Déby and Khartoum to eradicate the JEM's influence from Darfur with the support and expertise of Mahamat Ali Abdallah at a time when Minawi was also trying to remove the other SLA leader, Abdel Wahid Mohamed al Nur. The reward, the JEM explained, would be money, the top political position in Darfur when peace is reached, and a sultanate for his sub-clan among the Wegi. The creation of new factions might weaken the core insurgency movements, but these factions would sooner or later become more autonomous and develop activities opposed to their former patrons. The NMRD troops clashed against the Chadian army; others went to Sudan to contest the leadership of Bartcham. When the SLA-Minawi and Chadian soldiers attacked the JEM near Tiné, Chadian Kobé entered the war alongside the JEM.

Nevertheless, a deal between Déby and the JEM was eventually struck in the summer of 2005. Its reasons had little to do with Darfur and much to do with Chadian politics. After an attempted coup in May 2004, parts of the security apparatus, of the Republican Guard, and of the first circle of the regime—mostly all Bideyat—decided to defect and establish an armed opposition in Darfur: they set up the SCUD (*Socle pour le changement, l'unité et la démocratie*) that became in February 2006 the RaFD (*le Rassemblement des forces démocratiques*) chaired by Timan Erdimi, once the head of the private office at the presidency and close relative of the president. These desertions increased dramatically in October 2005 and continued a year after, though at a limited rate. The whole cohesion of the ruling elite was put at risk, because family bonds connect most of the Zaghawa elite to both sides. Trust is no longer a common feature of Zaghawa internal dealing.

The slow disintegration of Déby's regime did not go unnoticed in Khartoum. Beginning in early 2003, many in the Sudan armed forces, military intelligence, and at the presidency, were convinced that the Chadian president was playing a double game. Their doubts about his reliability increased as they witnessed how the SLM delegations were close to key Chadian officials during negotiations in Abéché and N'djamena. Suspecting that the key to the logistics of the rebellion lay in Chad, Khartoum responded by supporting Déby's adversaries. By the middle of 2005, Chadian opponents who had until then been mostly employed as surrogate forces to fight against the Darfur insurgency were given clearance to set up their camps in Darfur and obtain military hardware. They launched a badly-planned offensive against the town of Adré in December 2005. This failed due to French intelligence and logistical support provided to the Chadian troops. Yet by the end of December a new group, the FUCD, was set up as an umbrella to the Chadian armed opposition in Darfur.

Déby's reaction was to try to reunify the Zaghawa elements of the Darfur insurgency to protect his own regime. An agreement was signed in January 2006 in N'djamena, creating the Alliance of Revolutionary Forces of Western Sudan, including JEM, SLA-Minawi, and the Masalit forces of SLA-Abdel Wahid headed by Khamis Abbaker. Khalil Ibrahim was announced as leader. The alliance was rewarded with military supplies from Eritrea. The JEM and its Kobé supporters were not too sympathetic to the entreaties of the SCUD/RaFD, as the supply lines from N'djamena were easier and the quantities were bigger. Due to the defections, the Kobé actually became more influential in summer 2006 than they were in 1992 when Abbas Koty had attempted his coup. This change in the internal balance of forces may explain why after a superficial reconciliation between al Beshir and Déby in early August 2006, some Kobé from JEM were put under arrest: the message was that they should not aspire to too much inside Chad. The SLA wing led by Minawi had less ambition in Chad, but had been at that time more cornered with the talks taking place in Abuja. The Darfurian groups knew well enough that if Déby was overthrown by the allies of Khartoum, their movements would no longer have any sanctuary.

Yet there were differences between JEM and SLA. JEM fighters fought alongside Déby's supporters in April 2006 when FUCD rebels attacked the capital city and border towns. The SLA was not as active. First, despite the SLA use of Chad as a rear base and the presence of some Wegi in the

Chadian army and the presidential guard, only the JEM has a major stake in Chadian domestic politics. Some of JEM's key officials could have local ambitions and, at some future date, could destabilize Déby. Second, the JEM leadership is aware that if their movement were annihilated, the Darfur conflict could be managed in purely Sudanese terms since the Wegi, who dominate the SLA, do not have the same access to Chad. The SLA may have more manpower and more hardware, but by comparison with the JEM, it is a more traditional kind of opposition that limits itself to one region of Sudan.

After an FUCD rebel column attacked N'djamena in April 2006, Idriss Déby tried again to mobilize his supporters. When the JEM and parts of the SLA did not sign the peace agreement in Abuja on May 5, he provided them with military support. After Déby's successful "re-election" a few days before, surrogate forces were needed more than ever. The National Redemption Front (NRF) was established with the cooperation of Eritrea and facilities were provided to its leaders in N'djamena. Moreover, Déby made a diplomatic move to isolate his armed opposition: in August 2006 he expelled the Taiwanese ambassador[10] and recognized Beijing. At least, this could reduce the alleged support provided by the People's Republic of China to Khartoum and the Chadian insurgents.

Strong internal differences existed within the Sudan government on the nature of a settlement in Darfur and, by corollary, political changes in Chad. The army and the palace, after having been the Chadian president's main supporters, became adamant in their opposition to Déby and worked to build a more effective opposition, while some in the ruling National Congress Party were still advocating for rebuilding a good relationship with Chad in order to isolate the rebellion and get it to accept an agreement under Khartoum's terms. The first attempt at sponsoring armed opposition was the creation of the FUCD. This failed for many reasons, including the weak leadership capabilities of its chairman, Mahamat Nour, recurrent rivalries among Chadian Arab groups settled in Chad, and ego problems between the co-opted leaders. After months of hesitation in June 2006, Khartoum invited Mahamat Nouri, a former associate of Habré and then Chadian ambassador in Riyadh, to take the lead. This again was not successful but thanks to Khartoum support, he was able to build a new coalition, UFDD (*l'Union des forces pour la démocratie et le développement*) that organized a number of successful military operations in Wadai and Salamat in October 2006.

The rationale for these October clashes was rooted in the merging of the two crises in Chad and Darfur. The UFDD offensive followed a major defeat of the Sudanese army against the newly formed NRF on October 6 due to the reinforcement provided to the latter by Chadian soldiers. One reason for the intensification of the proxy war at this point was that, from Khartoum's viewpoint, it could pre-empt the possibility of the UN using eastern Chad as a base to launch an intervention in Darfur as proposed by UN Security Council Resolution 1706.

As a consequence of these crises, one can confidently expect that troubles will start again in CAR. There are different dynamics determining a crisis in that country. First, the CAR has been, willingly or not, the refuge of many defeated guerrillas groups from other countries of the region, and so possesses manpower and weapons available for any kind of rebellion. Second, the Chadian army from 2003, officially or not, has kept control of the most sensitive areas in north and northeastern CAR, against Chadian armed opposition, CAR insurgents, and highway bandits. Today, that army has to fight within its own borders and can no longer police outside its southern border. Third, Bozizé's rule is not as successful as many would have expected in 2003 and discontent is widespread across all sectors of the society. In CAR, stability has never lasted long because plundering is the norm. If the situation continues to deteriorate, Gaddafi might express his dissatisfaction with the exile of his long-time friend, Ange-Félix Patassé, and take action to restore him to power.

### Conclusion

A SUBREGIONAL SYSTEM of wars has developed in the Sudan, Chad, and CAR, as armed conflicts resulting from distinct national situations and involving different actors, methods, and issues, have become connected with each other, spilling over the geographical, social, and political borders that originally separated them. Such a subregional conflict nexus has been seen in other parts of the continent, for example, in the Mano River countries

(Liberia, Sierra Leone, and Guinea) and the Great Lakes. All the conditions exist for such a complex of internal and regional violence to develop encompassing Chad, CAR, and Darfur, and possibly spread further.

If this analysis is correct, various questions need to be answered. Why has the international community been so blind to the political crisis in Chad and in the CAR? (And why did Chad remain as a co-mediator of the Darfur peace talks until early 2006?) Why has so much time been lost in seeking a political solution because the situation is becoming more dangerous and intractable every month? This chapter cannot provide answers to these questions. Instead it seeks to convince readers that the Darfur crisis has evolved in a way that increasingly requires a regional analysis as well as a more localized understanding of the conflict. It is also evident that Idriss Déby will have to face the consequences of the collapse of his alliance with Khartoum and of the many ways that Chadians have been involved in the Darfur war. It should be also clear from this analysis that any resolution of the conflict in Darfur will have implications for Chad and vice-versa: no solution to either crisis will be possible without taking the other into account.

In Sudan, any fair settlement in Darfur will both put an end to a conflict that has been continuing since the 1980s and will also have implications for the structure and functioning of the Sudanese state. In Chad, a genuine solution will include dialogue with all groups, but will also have to go deeper, to reverse the long-standing foundation of Chadian politics which is that political-military organizations share the looting of Chadian assets and people among themselves.

As far as Chad is concerned, three scenarios are possible at the time of writing (November 2006). One not-improbable scenario is a coup within the Zaghawa and the Chadian ruling elite. Several attempts have failed (including May 2004 and March 2006) but it is certain that the Zaghawa opposition will not give up. Beyond the key question of the technical ability to manage the forces, there is the question of who should then lead given that Déby has eliminated many Zaghawa leaders who could have constituted an alternative to his personal rule. Another scenario would be the consolidation of new (or renewed) rebel movements in parts of Chad and/or CAR and a war of attrition. In 2005, it was clear that many Gorane leaders felt sidelined and were waiting for their opportunity. This they got with Mahamat Nouri and built a new military alliance with some Arab tribes currently armed by Khartoum. A third scenario might entail Déby's consolidation through continued coercion. France would be inclined to keep a close eye on increased violations of human rights because the presence of its military is seen as a strategic asset. Yet France cannot allow herself to get militarily involved in a crisis that raises too many questions about the failure of French policy towards Chad, connivance in abusive regimes in Africa, or the financing of political parties in France.

The transnational dimensions of the Darfur, Chad, and CAR crises could prove be an asset for peacemaking, if this interconnectedness proves the reason to undertake a fresh attempt to mediate the conflicts that have torn the three countries. This could provide incentives for peace. Nevertheless, to acknowledge this, the international community needs to analyze its own blindness and choices in the region until now.

# 8

# The Comprehensive Peace Agreement and Darfur

ADAM AZZAIN MOHAMED

S UDAN IS MARRED BY POLITICAL INSTABILITY. The military has overthrown its civilian rulers three times. Southern Sudan's civil war has been the longest in Africa's history, drawing the attention and concern of the international community, and repeatedly contributing to the overthrow of governments in Khartoum. In 1972 the Addis Ababa Accord was signed, bringing an end to the first civil war. Unfortunately, the agreement was not carefully nurtured and a new, more devastating civil war erupted in 1983. Both the South and the North have paid a heavy price for this war.

Thanks to efforts made by neighboring states and the international community, an agreement was signed, once again in a foreign country—Kenya—on January 9, 2005. Officially named the "Comprehensive Peace Agreement" (CPA), it is widely called the Naivasha Agreement, after the Kenyan town where much of it was negotiated. The provisions of the agreement are not limited to putting an end to the "southern problem"; they also address the problems of national governance in Sudan. The problems of the marginalized areas of the Nuba Mountains region of South Kordofan as well as Blue Nile were also part and parcel of the agreement. This chapter discusses the CPA in relation to the threats to good governance in Sudan.

### Threats to Stable Governance in Sudan

THE THREATS to governance and stability in Sudan are numerous. Prominent among them are the still-unresolved question of southern Sudan and the conflict in Darfur. As stated above, the civil war in southern Sudan was the longest in Africa's history. Thanks to efforts being made by the global community and the Intergovernmental Authority on Development (IGAD), that war has been brought to an end, hopefully once and for all. But the war has already done considerable damage to Sudan, which had been siphoning off its meager resources to finance the war and creating bad feelings among its population, particularly the feelings of the southerners towards the northerners. While the war in the South continued, democracy and development was impossible in Sudan as a whole. The CPA was aimed both at ending the war, and laying the foundation for future good governance for the entire Sudan.

Sudan's civil wars and its efforts to resolve them must be seen in the context of three other interrelated threats to stable governance: the persistence of "big government" in Khartoum; its corollary, uneven regional development; and the urban dissident groups whose existence and roles are closely intertwined with the other two factors.

### "Big Government" in Khartoum

The Americans have a motto, "small government is good government," which implies that it is the society and not the government that delivers goods and services to the community, and that the most that the government can do is to act as a facilitator, so that the community might be able to deliver goods and services to its members. Government power is, therefore, limited and dispersed so that the chances for tyranny are eliminated.

By contrast, in Sudan power is concentrated both horizontally and vertically, and popular participation in decisionmaking is an alien notion. For instance, Sudan has never adopted a sustained decentralized system of governance that allowed the grassroots communities to be responsible for their local affairs. The over-centralization of decision making helped to create a culture in which the Sudanese people are recipients of central decisions as a matter of course. The result, however, has been an abandonment of the criteria for good governance. Accountability of government institutions has been lacking. The top-down approach to decisionmaking prevails even in local matters, extending to the appointment of local leaders (e.g., native administrators), and the determining of boundaries and competencies of local administrative units (e.g., local councils).

Repeated reforms of government systems in Sudan have failed to achieve legitimacy for any form of governance. As a consequence, whenever the government was changed in Khartoum, local government was also automatically changed across the entire country. Corruption became institutionalized, and those within the system had every incentive to avoid transparency.

Two attempts have been made to devolve power to subnational administrative units: first the 1980 regional governance system (Regional Government Act), and then again under the current government's so-called federal system. Both systems intended to give the impression that regional autonomy had been granted to the regional populations. In reality, however, the two systems masked continuing central control. Both attempts occurred under one-party systems and a tightened security apparatus, and neither was accompanied by a sound system of financing. For most regions and/or states, competencies have existed only on paper due to a lack of adequate funding. This is one of the major ailments that the CPA can correct, if it is effectively implemented.

### Uneven Regional Development

Sudan is characterized by uneven regional development. Within three years of Sudan's independence, the Beja Congress voiced dissatisfaction with its share of the national wealth and power. After its October 1964 uprising, the Beja Congress was joined by the General Union of the Nuba Mountains and the Darfur Development Front. The already-established national political parties, the Umma Party, and the National Unionist Party, strenuously opposed these new movements. All central power blocs, including the military, have accused regional parties of being threats to national cohesion. Successive central governments have dismissed the complaints of the marginalized, stigmatizing them as racists and parochialists that may be aiming at secession.

All social and economic indicators in Sudan display these extreme regional imbalances. Resources flow in one direction, from the peripheries to the center, and they do not return. Unsurprisingly, people follow the resources, which means vast populations of labor migrants and displaced people from the marginalized areas have congregated around the national capital and other major towns. Despite the extraordinary inequality, and the social and political problems this has generated, no central government has taken any steps to address the root of the problem. Instead they have only tackled its symptoms, with programs of forcibly relocating squatters. The CPA, if wholeheartedly implemented, will be the first serious attempt to address the problem of uneven development.

### Urban Opposition

Twice in recent history, Sudan's government format has been changed by means of nonviolent popular uprising. On many other occasions, demonstrations have forced changes in government policy. In 1988, urban dissent and the threat of violence forced the government to backtrack on the lifting of bread subsidies and to begin taking seriously the conflict in Darfur. The National Islamic Front (NIF) government took every step to try to ensure that it would not face such serious urban opposition, but events such as the January 2005 demonstrations in Port Sudan indicate that opposition in the cities remained a potent force. As in other developing countries, the national capital and a handful of other urban centers serve as the nerve center for the entire nation (Palmer 1980, 116). The concentration of political and economic activities within the confines of the capital means that dissident groups are able to greatly disrupt the economic and political activity of the city. Moreover, the very concentration of power and wealth in the capital means that it is ringed by settlements of the poor and dispossessed, who can be mobilized to present a political or security threat to the regime in power. In April 1985, those displaced by the famine, and the urban dwellers that sympathized with them proved a potent political coalition that helped bring down Jaafar Nimeiri's dictatorship. Thus, the government was brought down by the contradictions of its own political and economic policies. The wars in the South, the Nuba Mountains, eastern Sudan, and Darfur have added another dimension to these dangerous contradictions. The government policy of distributing arms to rural militia has resulted in large numbers of firearms in private hands. As an inevitable result, urban residents, including displaced people and squatters, are now heavily armed. These are volatile groups that can be easily touched off into urban violence. Meanwhile, the conditions for an alliance with disaffected elites have been created because the social strata that normally produce urban dissidents have been impoverished by government policies. These groups include unemployed school leavers, university graduates, once-employed bureaucrats who have been laid off, the political actors who have been denied access to political leadership, and the salaried classes whose wages have been reduced to no real value because of inflation.

While the CPA does not directly address the discontents of the urban poor, peace, prosperity, and good governance should serve to reduce their dissatisfaction.

## The Comprehensive Peace Agreement

MOST OF THE attention given to the CPA has focused on the government of southern Sudan and the referendum on self-determination, which is to be held in the South in 2011. This discussion will focus on the CPA's implications for the North, and then turn its attention to Darfur.

The agreement to end the civil war in southern Sudan came at a time of international commitment to good governance, namely a government characterized by transparency, accountability, participation, and concern for human rights. If faithfully implemented, the CPA will not only establish a good government system for Sudan, but will also remove all threats to governance that Sudan has been facing. But not everybody in Sudan is welcoming the CPA or working effectively for its implementation. Threats to the sustainability of the accord come from both those that are party to it and those that oppose it.

In principle, the CPA is a charter for the transformation of governance in Sudan. Its goal is to put an end to Sudan's vicious cycle of coups d'etat. This can occur if the CPA is permitted to implement its three major goals. First, it aims to bring about genuine democratization by making appointment to office a result of free and fair elections. Secondly, genuine local autonomies will be created not only in the South but also in the North, with regions and/or states given the constitutional rights to control their power and wealth. Thirdly, a sound system of revenue sharing has been formulated by the CPA, which will allow the local autonomies to receive transfers of enough national money to finance their decentralized services. The constituent governments will be duly represented in the center to ensure that the national wealth is distributed equitably. This is the first time in Sudan's history that a genuine fiscal federalism will be created. If this is to work, far more than the current level of transfers to subnational units will be required. Sudan currently transfers only about 7 percent of its total allocations, compared to 40 percent in Nigeria and 65 percent in Ethiopia. Such transfers will not only make decentralization meaningful, but will also shift the gravity of power away from Khartoum.

Some of the most radical provisions of the CPA in northern Sudan concern the Nuba Mountains area of South Kordofan as well as the Blue Nile. Substantial numbers of people from these two areas fought as part of the SPLA to attain local autonomy and the equitable sharing of the national wealth and power. The CPA contains a protocol for the resolution of conflict in the Nuba Mountains (South Kordofan) and Blue Nile states. In a nutshell, the protocol aims to create real local autonomy for the two areas. It provides for a political entity that is powerful and competent, with a secure financial base that enables it to deliver services and embark on development. Some important provisions are embodied in the preamble and general principles of the protocol. First, it emphasizes that equality, fairness, economic development, social welfare, and stability are overriding goals of the Sudanese people in general. Moreover, that human rights and fundamental freedoms shall also be guaranteed to all individuals. Furthermore, the development of human resources and infrastructure shall be the main goal of the state. Secondly, during the interim period, the CPA shall be endorsed by a "popular consultation" (Provision 3.1).

This provision for popular consultation is one of the vague parts of the protocol, as it has not been spelled out adequately. For this reason, the people in the Nuba Mountains, in particular, have leveled criticisms against it. They argue, correctly, that it falls short of the referendum granted for South Sudan. While Provision 3.2 specifies that the CPA shall be subject to the will of the people in the two states, through their respective democratically elected legislatures, the problem is with the popular consultation prior to the formation of the respective legislative councils. The protocol then proceeds to delineate the structure of governance, state's shares of the national wealth, the state land disposition, security arrangements, and pre-election governance arrangements, without clearly defining the concept of "popular consultation."

The CPA provides a strong wealth-sharing model for the South Kordofan and Blue Nile states, which could also serve as a framework for other marginalized areas. Provision 8.1 stipulates that the national wealth shall be shared equitably among different levels of government, so as to allow enough resources for each level of government to exercise its constitutional competencies. The transfer of centrally collected revenue to the states and regions should not lead to a regional dependency on the central treasury. On the one hand, Provision 8.2 stipulates that each state shall raise and collect its home-produced revenue as listed in Schedule D, which is amended to the protocol. On the other hand, a tax-collection effort is an important component of the criteria that determines a region's share of the national allocations. Important among expected sources of wealth coming to the states and regions is a 2 percent share of the oil they produce.

There are two types of money transferred to the states and regions: development funds and current-budget funds. Regarding development transfers, a National Reconstruction and Development Fund (NRDF) was founded, and the money is earmarked for reconstruction efforts (Provision 8.5). A Fiscal and Financial Allocation and Monitoring Commission (FFAMC) is to be established to allocate transfers to the two areas and "other war-affected areas and least developed areas," according to criteria that take into account regional differentials in population, current expenditure responsibility, level of development, geographical area, financial effort, and the effects of war (Provision 8.8). By properly allocating transfers, these areas can be brought up to the national average standards and level of development (Provision 8.8).

Comprehensive equalization criteria have yet to be developed. States will be duly represented in the FFAMC.

The Darfur Peace Agreement (DPA) builds directly on this development, providing more details on the functioning of the FFAMC, and on the financing and operation of a Darfur Reconstruction and Development Fund.

The main doubts about the CPA's provisions for democratic transformation and decentralized governance are not based on what is provided in the text signed by the Sudanese government and the Sudan People's Liberation Movement (SPLM), but whether it will actually be implemented. To begin with, there are important decision makers in the incumbent government who do not wish to see Sudan become a political democracy if that means a regime of "civilian rule through representative institutions and public liberties" (Shils 1965, 51). The National Congress Party's preferred political model is not based on free competition among parties which might lead to "disharmony," but rather on mechanisms of "consultation" whereby political elites sort matters out internally in a form of "oligarchic governance" or, at best, a "tutelary" democracy (Shils 1965, 60–61).

Sudan's traditional sectarian parties, including the Umma Party, the National Democratic Alliance (NDA), and Hassan al Turabi's Popular Congress Party are not in agreement with the incumbent government or with the at best limited role assigned to them the by the CPA's power-sharing arrangements. Leading members of all these parties are threatening that if they are denied access to real political democracy, they will be ready to take to the streets.

The CPA is an agreement between two belligerent parties, the ruling National Congress Party (NCP) and the SPLM. These two parties have established institutions to effect a transfer to democracy, while ensuring that they retain control of those key institutions and others. The speed and soundness of Sudan's democratization will be dictated by commissions that regulate elections and the conduct of political parties, and which oversee the preparations for the referendum in the South. Other commissions deal with the Abyei region and the North-South boundary. At the time of writing, the Abyei Boundary Commission's recommendations have been frozen by the NCP, which is unwilling to accept its findings. It seems likely that either the work of the commissions will be paralyzed by the failure of the NCP and SPLM to agree on basic steps, or the two parties will come to an informal agreement that tilts the outcome in favor of the incumbent government in the North and the SPLM in the South.

Similarly, the provisions of the CPA that are meant to ensure an effective transfer of the national wealth to the states and regions are not being implemented. At the time of writing, the FFAMC has not been established and there is no proper specification regarding the amount of transfers to the regions from the centrally collected revenue. The allocation of development funds according to region has not been clarified or implemented. Nor is the sharing of oil revenues between North and South being implemented in a transparent and efficacious manner.

The Commission on Wealth Sharing at the African Union-mediated Darfur peace talks conducted its discussions against the backdrop of the lack of implementation of key provisions of the CPA. This put the movements' negotiators in a dilemma. They recognized that the CPA provided in-principle solutions to many of their demands, or at least templates for such solutions; therefore they did not want to undermine or overrule institutions such as the FFAMC. But these institutions were still nonfunctional when the text of the DPA was being finalized. Additionally, the DPA provides only partial solutions to these quandaries. It provides more detail on how fiscal federalism should work, but ultimately it relies on the faithful implementation of the CPA if it is to work at all.

## The Case of Darfur

DARFUR'S VIOLENT conflicts began between the Fur ethnic group, on the one hand, and the nomadic, livestock-herding Arabs, on the other. The early conflict was limited to the area around Jebel Marra, the Fur's central and historical homeland. Competition over the rich natural resources of that area is what brought the two groups into conflict. Ownership of the land and the right to access its resources underlie the present conflict.

It is not clear who started the fighting: the nomads, in a bid to drive the Fur out of the land, or the Fur, who wanted to drive these newcomers out of it. The fact of the matter, however, is that the nomads had many advantages that tilted the war in their favor; important among these advantages is the support of the Sudanese government. It has become clearly evident that the government had an undeclared alliance with the nomads, who happened to be Arabs. Perceiving the government as either unable or unwilling to protect the Fur's villagers against raids by the nomads, the Fur accused the government of complicity and therefore regarded it as their true enemy. Consequently, some of the Fur climbed Jebel Marra and established training camps, not only to fight back against the assaulting nomads, but also to attack nearby government garrisons. A Zaghawa faction that also had grievances against the government joined this Fur group, as did the Masalit, whose land to the west of the Fur's was also being encroached upon by the livestock herders.

Realizing that their enemy had become the government rather than the livestock herders' militia ("Janjawiid"), the Fur, Zaghawa, and Masalit militias decided to broaden their base of political support by appealing to a wider spectrum of the Darfurian people. They declared that they were struggling against the marginalization of the region. Darfur is indeed the most marginalized among all northern regions and the regional elites have been bitter about this situation since as early as 1964. The call for an equitable share of the national wealth and power drew a large number of sympathizers. Although the government media repeatedly described the movement leaders as bandits and armed robbers, this did not succeed in isolating them.

Resolving the conflict in Darfur will require taking into consideration both the internal Darfurian and the national dimensions of Darfur's plight. As mentioned above, formulae for handling the latter can be derived from the CPA, and the DPA also goes some way toward addressing Darfurians' grievances against the center, especially in the areas of wealth sharing and fiscal federalism. The main challenge is ensuring goodwill during implementation, which is unfortunately lacking for both the CPA and the DPA.

Addressing the root causes of the intergroup conflicts is more intricate and calls for four measures to be taken: the settlement of disputes over land and rights to natural resources; the handling of the return of internally displaced persons (IDPs) and refugees; compensation for lives and property lost in the war; and accountability. Additionally, the global community is now concerned with bringing to justice those who committed war crimes or crimes against humanity in the region.

There is no simple formula for equitable power sharing within Darfur. At the Abuja peace talks, the armed movements unsurprisingly called for the application of the North-South principles to Darfur, which would have awarded near-total control of Darfur to them. They rejected the comparison with South Kordofan and Blue Nile. But the trickier question is: who is to fill the positions allocated to the NCP and the movements? The DPA awards a bare majority of the posts in Darfur's state legislative and executive bodies to the NCP, but should these posts be allocated to Janjawiid representatives, who are the clear supporters of the government, to the pro-government Darfur elites in general, or to members of the NCP from outside the region? Even more vexing problems arise with the allocation of the posts to the movements. Had the two SLM factions and the Justice and Equality Movement (JEM) all signed the DPA, they would not have readily agreed on who was to get what. With only the SLM-Minawi signing, the position of the fragments from the SLM-Abdel Wahid and JEM that want to be associated with the DPA is unclear.

Issues about Darfur's governance during and after the interim period cannot be resolved without Darfurian elites, armed and unarmed, agreeing on how to divide regional and central power among themselves. Presently, the regional elites are divided into three main categories. One grouping is the armed opposition, which is internally divided into the two main groupings of the SLM and its numerous fragments, and JEM, which also has its splinter groups. A second grouping is the unarmed Darfurian political platform headed by retired General Ibrahim Suleiman, and a third is the grouping headed by retired General Adam Hamid Musa (who is more closely aligned with the NCP). These groupings also remain in flux as alliances and circumstances shift.

A survey of 236 members of the Darfur elite revealed some important patterns (Mohamed 2005). The majority of elite members refuse to be identified by ethnic labels and instead call themselves "regional patriots." They discern the root cause of the conflict to be disputes over natural resources, and consider equitable development programs that address the problems of both farmers and nomads as a long-term solution. They have confidence in the native administration as mediators for the conflict. Perhaps most strikingly, the Darfurian elites have little confidence in the capability of either the NCP or the armed movements to govern Darfur during the interim. Forty-five percent of respondents would prefer Darfur's technocratic elites to govern the region and a further 13 percent suggested Sudan's national technocratic elite. Only 15 percent wanted power sharing between the NCP, the movements, and the SPLM. Fewer than 5 percent wanted the current arrangement, the armed movements alone, or power sharing between the NCP and the movements. While almost 70 percent of the elites accepted the CPA as a "framework" for resolving the Darfurian conflict, they did not want the outcome of the peace process to keep the NCP in power in Darfur, whether on its own or in partnership with the armed movements.

The structure of negotiations at the Abuja peace talks predetermined the most important issues in the DPA's power-sharing formulae. The parties represented at the talks, namely the government (predominantly the NCP) and the armed movements, obtained the lion's share of the positions of power. The government, on the twin rationales that it was militarily undefeated and that the CPA had already decided the NCP should hold a majority throughout the North until the elections. The movements received a minority—much less than they had hoped, and below the minimum that Abdel Wahid and JEM considered acceptable. "Other parties," including the NDA and the SPLM received less. The Darfur elites not aligned with any of these parties received nothing. A proposal to allow the recently formed Darfur-Darfur Dialogue and Consultation to allocate a handful of seats in each state legislature was removed by the mediation after objections by the government's chief delegate, Dr. Majzoub al Khalifa Ahmed. This meant that the Darfur elites that were not aligned with either party—notably the group headed by General Ibrahim Suleiman—were entirely shut out from representation in Darfur's interim structures. Nonetheless, independent groups are the strongest supporters of the DPA because they see it as the best chance for peace, and believe that even a flawed peace deal is better than continuing the war.

Resolving the underlying local causes of the conflict is more difficult still. The government's attempt to militarily quell the armed opposition complicated the situation and compounded the existing problems. The use of the Janjawiid, which seized the opportunity to settle scores against their enemies, brought the war to an entirely new level. Janjawiid attacks were directed against the ethnic groups to which the rebels belong rather than against the rebels themselves. With the help of the government, the Janjawiid succeeded in forcing the Fur and Masalit out of their homelands (dars) and driving many Zaghawa into refugee camps. This strategy created more problems for the government and the Janjawiid. It created a humanitarian crisis and brought charges of crimes against humanity. Amid mounting concerns from human right organizations, the U.S., and the global community—represented by the UN—the government was forced to negotiate with the rebels rather than continuing its attempts to crush them. But while the government was reluctantly sitting down for peace talks, the armed forces and Janjawiid continued their military assaults.

The peace talks could only deal with the land rights issue at a general level rather than with the specificity that is needed to create lasting peace. A legal solution to Darfur's land question is needed. Currently, two legal systems govern land usage in Darfur. The first is customary law, which recognizes communal ownership of land, locally manifested in what are known as tribal dars and individual *hawakir* (singular: *hakura*). The Fur, Masalit, Zaghawa, and others all have their customary-recognized dars. The second system is the Land Registration Act of 1970, which states that all unregistered lands are to be regarded as government owned (*de jure*). Tribal dars are not registered and therefore could be regarded as *de jure*. If so, identity groups would have equal access to lands. This would, understandably, be strongly resisted by dar owners wishing to protect their customary rights. The legal position of hawakir, which were granted by sultanic land charters to individuals, remains unclear. Documents were drawn up and registered by the Fur's sultans, but not by the government of Sudan. In addition, many hakura documents have been lost or destroyed, and some deliberately burned by the Janjawiid.

The government manipulates the land-rights situation expediently. It will turn a blind eye to the tribal ownership of land when it serves its purpose, but it can use the provisions of the Land Registration Act if that better serves its purpose. In the current conflicts over land, the government tends to interpret land ownership in line with the provisions of the Land Registration Act, further alienating the Fur, Masalit, and other non-Arab groups. But the government also finds ways to respect the dars of the Arab tribes of South Darfur, which are mostly allied to the government. The Zaghawa are in a complicated position: They want to retain their historical dar in North Darfur against claims from Arab camel herders, many of whom are Janjawiid, but they also want to claim land rights in other parts of Darfur where Zaghawa farmers and shopkeepers have settled since the droughts of the 1970s.

The government seems to maintain a double standard when it considers the repatriation of the IDPs and refugees. Currently, it is not talking about letting them return to where they once were. Rather, it talks about leaving them where they are so that they eventually become urban dwellers. The government is encouraging their voluntary movements back home, without providing them the security that they ask for, or the government will consider taking them to selected areas that are not necessarily their original homelands. In all cases, Janjawiid groups, which now occupy the lands of the displaced, would be in control of the historical dars of the Fur, Masalit, Tunjur, Daju, and others.

### Conclusion

THE POWER-SHARING provisions contained in the CPA cannot solve all of Darfur's problems. They do not address identity-group conflicts within the region, nor do the power-sharing provisions of the DPA satisfy both the demands of the armed movements and the expectations of the Darfurian elites.

Resolving the crisis in Darfur appears to depend on the government and the movements taking measures that they both presently find unacceptable. The consensus among Darfurian elites is that the best mechanism for an interim government is an administration consisting of technocrats who are true believers in democratic governance, but are not themselves office seekers or political activists. Their mission would be to implement the various provisions of the DPA for rehabilitation, reconstruction, and security, and to prepare political activists to agree on succession to power by peaceful means through free and fair elections. This caretaker government should work closely with the current government and international forces to see to it that the agreed upon peace will prevail.

An equally important measure to be taken by the government is to pursue reconciliation among identity groups. This includes assessing war losses and compensation for war-affected individuals. If the victimized are adequately compensated, they will be more apt to cooperate with calls for peaceful coexistence, thus making the task of reconciliation possible, and easier.

At the heart of the matter, however, is the dispute over land. Resolving this must be made the responsibility of the regional tribal leaders (i.e., native administrators) because they know how to use the customary law to resolve disputes among all contenders to land. They will not restrict the problem to its present territory of conflict. Rather, they will be able to work out a solution that meets the demands of all conflicting parties, taking into consideration that the size of the current regional territorial areas are enough for their populations. They only need to be better utilized. This utilization may include the settlement of the nomads in areas that are not necessarily the ones they are now occupying.

For the native administrators to be effective, it is imperative that they go back to their tradition of political neutrality. One of the more serious blows that the system has received was its politicization. The native administrators cannot have political affiliations while acting as mediators, especially when the region, and entire country, are moving toward a multiparty system. Following a comprehensive reconciliation, the repatriation of the displaced will become easier and more manageable. On the other hand, with a wholehearted reconciliation, even pardoning perpetrators becomes possible. Darfur will then be well placed to go back to peaceful coexistence among its identity groups.

# 9

## The African Union Mediation
## and the Abuja Peace Talks

DAWIT TOGA

F OR SEVERAL DECADES, the Darfur region of Sudan was ravaged with intermittent conflicts due in part to competition
between sedentary groups and pastoralists over water and grazing land. Lack
of good governance, the inadequate representation of the people of Darfur
in the running of the state, as well as the increasing circulation of small arms,
which was a result of the ongoing wars in the region (such as Eritrea and
Chad), greatly exacerbated the conflict.

The catalyst for the current conflict was when the Sudan Liberation
Movement/Army (SLM/A), initially called the Darfur Liberation Front,
attacked and captured Gulu, the capital of Jebel Marra province, in February
2003. At the time, the SLM/A's demands included that the government of
Sudan (GoS) bring an end to the socioeconomic marginalization of the
region and, most importantly, a halt to the activities of Janjawiid tribal militias. Subsequently, a number of attacks took place, particularly on al Fashir,
the capital of North Darfur, and Mellit, the second largest city in North
Darfur. In response to the attacks, the GoS forces launched major land and
air offensives against the SLM/A. Later that year, the Justice and Equality
Movement (JEM) joined with the SLM/A to wage a military offensive against
the GoS and the militia groups.

Chad—as the country sharing a one thousand kilometer–long border with
Sudan, and with identical ethnic groups living on both sides of the Sudanese
and Chadian borders—was the country most adversely affected by the erup-

tion of the conflict. Over 100,000 refugees crossed into its territory from Darfur.

## The Abéché Agreement

UNDER THE MEDIATION of the president of Chad, Idriss Déby, on September 3, 2003, in Abéché, Chad, the GoS and the SLM/A signed a ceasefire agreement. The agreement called for the cessation of hostilities for forty-five days, the control of irregular groups, and the cantonment of SLM/A forces at locations to be agreed upon. In addition, the parties agreed to start comprehensive political talks to address the political and socioeconomic undercurrents of the conflict within fifteen days of the signing of the agreement.

At their second meeting, on November 4, 2003, the parties agreed to extend the ceasefire for a month, committed themselves to facilitate humanitarian assistance, and agreed to meet in N'djamena on December 16, 2003. However, this meeting never took place. Although the September ceasefire agreement contributed to the lessening of fighting between the GoS and the SLM/A, violence intensified against the civilian population. The Janjawiid continued to deliberately target the groups they viewed as providing the bulk of the support for the SLM/A and JEM.

On the part of the African Union (AU), the containment of the conflict was viewed as essential. To that end, diplomatic missions were launched. Arresting the spread of Darfur conflict was also considered essential, in part to insulate the ongoing Naivasha peace process concerning southern Sudan from its adverse effects. In early March 2004, senior AU officials held consultations with GoS officials in Khartoum to firm up the AU's role in the conflict. Sudanese authorities expressed their view that although they considered the Darfur issue to be an internal one, they had no objection to the AU's participation in the N'djamena talks. On March 26, 2004, once the green light was given by the GoS, AU Chairperson Alpha Konaré dispatched a senior AU team to N'djamena. The team, led by the director of the Department of Peace and Security, Ambassador Sam Ibok, was to assist the

Chadian authorities with the Inter-Sudanese Peace Talks on the conflict in Darfur.

## The N'djamena Ceasefire Agreement

THE INITIAL ROUND of the Inter-Sudanese talks on Darfur started on March 31, 2004, in N'djamena, under the auspices of President Déby. The GoS, however, objecting to the presence of the international community, did not attend the official opening of the talks. The GoS also refused to have face-to-face negotiations with the SLM/A and JEM. As a result, the initial articulation and presentation of the positions of the parties were made through proxy negotiations.

Concerned by the slow movement of the talks in N'djamena, Chairperson Konaré consulted with President Omar Hassan Bashir on April 6, in Khartoum. Chairperson Konaré reiterated his concern about the humanitarian situation in Darfur and the need for an early and successful conclusion of the talks that were going on in N'djamena. To this, President Bashir replied that the situation in Darfur was, in fact, under control. Just two days later, on April 8, in the presence of Chairperson Konaré, as well as international observers and facilitators, the two parties signed a Humanitarian Ceasefire Agreement on the Darfur conflict and a protocol on the establishment of humanitarian assistance in Darfur. The parties agreed to:

- Cease hostilities, and specifically to proclaim a ceasefire for a period of forty-five days, automatically renewable except if opposed by one of the parties;
- Establish a Joint Commission and a Ceasefire Commission, with the participation of the international community, including the African Union;
- Release all prisoners of war and all other persons detained because of the armed conflict in Darfur;

- Facilitate the delivery of humanitarian assistance and the creation of conditions conducive to the delivery of emergency relief to the displaced persons and other civilian victims of war, in accordance with the protocol on the establishment of humanitarian assistance in Darfur, referred to above;
- Create a team of military observers for the ceasefire, protected by an armed force jointly called the African Union Mission in Sudan (AMIS).

The N'djamena agreement contained a major flaw: it existed in two versions. After the parties had agreed to the text of the Humanitarian Ceasefire Agreement, the GoS delegation insisted that the agreement should also include a provision for the assembly of the movements' forces in selected sites, to be conducted in parallel with the disarmament of the Janjawiid. In the presence of the Chadian Foreign Minister, an additional sentence was handwritten on one copy of the agreement, which had already been signed. The GoS took this copy and insisted thereafter that it was the correct version. The SLM/A and JEM delegates' version, however, did not include this clause, and they insisted that the N'djamena agreement never included any mention of assembly of forces.

After the N'djamena agreement, senior AU officials felt the need to broaden the scope of the talks and work for a comprehensive peace agreement. To that end, on April 10, 2004, the AU Commissioner for Peace and Security, Ambassador Said Djinnit traveled to Khartoum and N'djamena and held discussions with both President Bashir and President Déby, respectively.

The issue of Darfur, again, was on the agenda of the third ordinary session of the Assembly of Heads of State and Government (commonly called the "AU Summit"), which was held July 6–8, 2004, in Addis Ababa. On that occasion the assembly, having reiterated its serious concern over the prevailing situation in Darfur, underlined the centrality of a political solution and agreed that the political dialogue between the parties should resume in Addis Ababa on the scheduled date of July 15, 2004, with a view toward reaching a political agreement. The assembly also urged all the parties to participate in the meeting at the highest level.

### The Operationalization of the Ceasefire Commission

IN ITS MEETING of May 25, 2004, the AU's Peace and Security Council requested that the AU Commission take all necessary steps to ensure the effective monitoring of the Humanitarian Ceasefire Agreement of April 8. The council referred in particular to the deployment of an "observer mission" with the required civilian component and, if necessary, a protection force, to support the work of the Ceasefire Commission (CFC). To that end, the AU Commission convened in Addis Ababa May 27–28 in a meeting that brought together the GoS, the SLM/A, and JEM, as well as the Chadian mediation group and members of the international community. The meeting culminated with the signing, by the Sudanese parties, of an agreement on the modalities for the establishment of the CFC, and the deployment of observers in Darfur. The AU and its partners, namely the UN, the EU, and the U.S., witnessed the signing of the agreement.

As stipulated in the agreement, the CFC is made up of the AU, as chair; the international community, as deputy chair (the international community was represented by the EU, through France); the Chadian Mediation, the GoS, JEM, and the SLM/A. The UN and the U.S. were invited to participate as observers. The operational arm of the CFC is the African Union Monitoring Mission, composed of observers from the parties, the Chadian mediation, AU member states, and other representatives of the international community.

The CFC reports to the Joint Commission, which consists of two senior members from each of the parties, the Chadian mediation, the AU, the U.S., and the EU. The chairperson of the Joint Commission is selected by the AU from an African Union member state. Other international representatives from the UN and major contributors are invited to attend the meetings of the Joint Commission as observers. At the time, Chairperson Konaré asked President Déby, as the mediator, to provide the Joint Commission with a chairperson.

The CFC's headquarters is located in al Fashir and, according to the Humanitarian Ceasefire Agreement and the Implementation Modalities, headquarters is responsible for coordinating investigations and verifications, and monitoring and reporting compliance.

Initially, the AU Observer Mission was composed of the twelve members of the CFC and 132 observers, sixty of which were from African Union member states, thirty-six from the Sudanese parties, eighteen from the Chadian mediation and the rest from the international community (the EU and the U.S. had eighteen observers). The support staff, consisting of translators and interpreters, was made up of twenty-four people. Taking into account the volatile situation in some parts of Darfur and as a confidence-building measure for the population of Darfur, the agreement made provisions for a 270-person protection force for the Mission.

On June 2, 2004, an AU "advance mission" composed of AU officials and six military observers from Ghana, Namibia, Nigeria, and Senegal went to Sudan with a mandate to secure and establish the headquarters of the CFC in al Fashir. During its visit in Khartoum, the advance team negotiated and signed the Status of Mission Agreement (SOMA) with the Sudanese government and took steps to make the Liaison Office in Khartoum operational. On June 9, the first six military observers were deployed to the CFC's headquarters, and other military observers—from Kenya, Mozambique, and Nigeria—were also deployed to al Fashir. That same day, the chairperson of the CFC, Brigadier General Festus Okonkwo from Nigeria, reported for duty at the AU Commission. From there he traveled to N'djamena and Khartoum for consultations before assuming his duties on June 19 in al Fashir. Also on June 19, the representatives of the parties and an acting representative of the EU, as deputy chair, arrived, thereby making the CFC fully operational on June 19, just two months and eleven days after the signing of the Humanitarian Ceasefire Agreement. By the end of June, there were eleven representatives at the CFC headquarters; twenty-two military observers (MILOBs), from five member states (Nigeria, Namibia, Ghana, Kenya, and Mozambique); two MILOBs each from the SLM/A and JEM; three MILOBs from the U.S., and one from the EU.

## The First Round of the Inter-Sudanese Peace Talks on the Conflict in Darfur

WHEN THE Inter-Sudanese Peace Talks on the conflict in Darfur resumed in Addis Ababa on July 15, the senior leadership of JEM and the

SLM/A refused to attend the talks, choosing instead to send junior representatives. The GoS sent a senior delegation led by Dr. Majzoub al Khalifa Ahmed, minister of agriculture, who remained as leader of his delegation until the signing of the Darfur Peace Agreement in May 2006.

In presenting its initial position at the talks, the GoS highlighted the efforts it was making to implement the Humanitarian Ceasefire Agreement, while accusing the rebel movements of violating that instrument. The GoS delegation specifically stressed several points: the need to neutralize the armed groups; the cantonment of the rebel groups; the need for an increase in humanitarian assistance, as well as the repatriation and return of refugees and internally displaced persons (IDPs); and the launching of the political dialogue.

On their part, the representatives of JEM and the SLM/A accused the GoS of violating the Humanitarian Ceasefire Agreement, including its failure to disarm the Janjawiid militia. They also expressed outrage at the continuing government attacks against the civilian population by Antonov warplanes and helicopter gunships. The two movements further insisted on the following as necessarily conditions to be fulfilled before beginning a comprehensive political dialogue: the need to disarm the Janjawiid militia; the launching of an international inquiry to investigate the charges of genocide and bring the perpetrators to justice; the cessation of attacks on the two rebel groups and the civilian villages; the removal of all obstacles to the delivery of humanitarian aid; the release of political prisoners; and the need to find a new venue for the next round of talks.

In retrospect, it can be stated that although the parties were unable to agree on an agenda and on a concrete framework on how to proceed, the Addis Ababa meeting sensitized the mediators and allowed them to better understand the issues at stake. At the conclusion of the talks, an agreement was reached on the need to have further consultations in order to determine the next steps to be taken before the resumption of the political dialogue. Subsequently, the newly appointed AU special envoy, Hamid al Gabid, the former prime minister of Niger, traveled to Geneva to meet with the representatives of the rebel movements and then traveled to Khartoum to consult with the GoS.

· As the international community's concern about the widening conflict in Darfur increased, so did their desire for action-oriented policies. Indeed, the crisis in Darfur was discussed on July 24 by the U.S. Congress, which adopted a resolution characterizing the human rights abuses in Darfur as "genocide." The resolution further called on the U.S. to lead an international effort to resolve the conflict and consider multilateral—or even unilateral—intervention, and to impose targeted sanctions on the government. The UN Security Council also tabled a draft resolution on Darfur, outlining specific timelines for actions to be taken by the government and raising the possibility of sanctions if they were not carried out. On July 21, the UN Secretary-General warned that "the Sudanese Government doesn't have forever" to meet its obligations.

Predictably, the GoS criticized the ongoing initiatives called for by the UN Security Council, arguing the resolution would exacerbate the situation in Darfur. The GoS stressed that it was exerting efforts to implement the joint communiqué that it signed with the UN on July 3, and requested more time to do so.

The AU also accelerated the timetable for restarting the political dialogue. To that end, throughout July, high-level consultation by the then-chairperson of the AU, President Olusegun Obasanjo, and the chairperson of the AU Commission, with the parties and other stakeholders continued. Subsequently, on August 7, after President Obasanjo traveled to Khartoum and Tripoli in early August to meet with the two countries' leaders, the Commission announced that the second round of the Inter-Sudanese Peace Talks would convene in Abuja, Nigeria, on August 23.

### The Second Round of the Abuja Talks

THE SECOND ROUND of the Inter-Sudanese Peace Talks on the conflict in Darfur (hereafter referred to as the "Abuja talks") formally opened in Abuja, Nigeria on August 23, 2004, by President Obasanjo and the AU chairperson. Both parties were represented by high-level delegations. The parties met in a closed session, under the chairmanship of President

Obasanjo, and agreed the following day to a four-point agenda: humanitarian issues, security issues, political questions, and economic and social affairs. The discussion on these substantive issues began immediately, and was chaired by Special Envoy al Gabid, with the support of Chad as co-mediator, and a mediation team comprising representatives from Nigeria and Libya as facilitators, as well as observers from the UN, the EU, the League of Arab States, the U.S., the UK, and France. Norway and Canada attended as invited guests.

On September 1, the parties concluded the discussions on humanitarian issues, agreeing on a protocol on the improvement of the humanitarian situation in Darfur. The protocol addressed the issues of free movement and access for humanitarian workers (removal of all restrictions and procedures that may hinder free movement and access, authorization of cross-border humanitarian activities, etc.), and the assistance and protection of civilians (prevention of all attacks, threats, intimidation, or any other form of violence against civilians; reaffirmation of the principle of voluntary return; respect for the rights of IDPs and refugees to return to their areas of origin; respect for the civilian character of IDP and refugee camps, etc.).

Under the protocol the parties requested that the AU take the necessary steps to strengthen AMIS on the ground and to ensure a more effective monitoring of the agreed commitments. In this regard, the protocol also provided for the establishment of a Joint Humanitarian Facilitation and Monitoring Unit based in al Fashir under the leadership of AMIS, to ensure such compliance.

During this round, extensive discussions were held on a draft protocol on the enhancement of the security situation in Darfur, in accordance with the N'djamena Humanitarian Ceasefire Agreement of April 8, 2004. However, despite serious efforts, the gulf between the parties was irresolvable and the talks were adjourned. Nonetheless, the parties reached agreement on a number of provisions of the draft protocol, including the reaffirmation of their commitment to respect the ceasefire, the release of all persons detained in relation to the hostilities in Darfur, and the strengthening of the AU presence on the ground. The contentious issues in the provision included; the development, by the CFC/AMIS, of a plan for the separation and relocation of forces to ensure that no exchange of fire would take place, and to facilitate the monitoring functions of the CFC/AMIS; the modalities for the neutralization and disarmament of the Janjawiid and other militias; specific measures aimed at building confidence between the parties and restoring trust among the local communities; and the detailed modalities, including the required mechanisms, for the effective implementation of the protocol.

In addition to those mentioned above, the parties also requested the inclusion of additional issues in the last version of the draft prepared by the mediation team. In response the GoS delegation proposed that: the armed elements of the movements be assembled in clearly identified locations, to be agreed upon with the CFC and within the framework of the separation plan; that they refrain from any action that may undermine the fulfillment of the government's obligations toward the UN; and they initiate a process of self-disarmament under the supervision and assistance of CFC/AMIS. For their part, the movements requested: the establishment of a no-fly zone for military and civilian aircraft used for military purposes over the Darfur region; the withdrawal of Sudanese military and police forces to their administrative positions or original garrisons, and their replacement by AU forces; and an international investigation into the charges of genocide and crimes against humanity in Darfur.

The mediation felt that although the remaining gaps in the respective positions of the parties on the security protocol would not allow for the signing of an agreement, it would still be possible for the parties to formally sign the Protocol on Humanitarian Issues. However, while the government expressed its readiness to sign immediately, the two movements declined, but reaffirmed their commitment to the provisions of the protocol. The Abuja talks were formally adjourned on September 17.

## The Third Round of the Abuja Talks

THE THIRD ROUND of the Inter-Sudanese Peace Talks on the conflict in Darfur convened in Abuja, from October 21 to November 10, 2004. The objective of this round was to continue deliberating on the remaining items on the agenda adopted during the second round. In the meantime, the UN Security Council had met twice on Darfur and passed resolutions 1556 and 1564. The first resolution demanded that the GoS take "substantial, irreversible and verifiable" actions to improve security for civilians in Darfur. This included taking immediate action on its commitment to disarm the Janjawiid,and to apprehend and bring to justice those who had committed human rights violations and other atrocities. If the GoS failed to do this, the UN Security Council would consider action that included sanctions. The second resolution established the International Commission of Inquiry into Darfur, to investigate the grievous human rights abuses perpetrated during the conflict. This was one step toward meeting the movements' demand for accountability for crimes against humanity, and their demand that the GoS cooperate with the expansion of the mandate of AMIS.

The opening meeting of the third round was held on October 21, and a seminar organized by the AU mediation team followed from October 23-24. The seminars dealt with the Naivasha process and negotiation techniques; the nature, purpose, and mandate of the UN Advance Mission in the Sudan (UNAMIS); and the role of AMIS. Prior to the resumption of the substantive talks, a consultative meeting was also held between the mediation team and the international partners to develop a strategy to restart the Abuja talks. During this meeting the following approach was agreed upon:

- Pressure should be exerted on the two movements to sign the Humanitarian Protocol, as called upon by the UN Security Council, the Tripoli Summit of the AU, and the AU Peace and Security Council (PSC).
- The discussions should start with the political issues since most of the security and human rights concerns that generated the previous round's deadlock had been addressed by the UN Security Council resolutions 1556 and 1564. However, should the parties insist on continuing with the security issues, a committee would be established, comprising the mediation team and representatives of the parties, to finalize the draft security protocol in light of recent Security Council and PSC decisions, while political discussions continued in a plenary session.

- Concerning the previous draft protocols, the same procedure should
  be followed by the mediation team in conducting the political talks,
  that is, the parties would be requested to submit their positions in
  writing and the AU drafting team would prepare a working document
  based on these submissions.

The first plenary session of the third round of the Abuja talks was convened on October 25. The head of delegation of the government of Sudan, Dr. Majzoub al Khalifa, outlined what he described as the global vision of his government for the comprehensive settlement of the conflict in Darfur. He noted that a federal system of government, anchored on decentralization of power, would be the most suitable for the political resolution of the conflict. Equitable distribution of wealth, he further argued, would be key for the development of the country, as it would impact social and economic development.

The representatives from the two movements informed the meeting that they would also be submitting documents to the mediation team detailing their visions for a comprehensive political settlement. But they outlined the main elements that should be included in a Political Declaration of Principles, namely:

- A recognition of the ethnic, cultural, and religious diversity of Sudan;
- The necessity to put an end to marginalization and to alter the power
  relationship between the central government and the provinces;
- A guarantee of the equitable distribution of wealth and power;
- The preservation of the unity of Sudan, based on the sovereignty of
  law, human rights, and ethnic and cultural diversity;
- An affirmation of the political nature of the conflict and the necessity
  to arrive at a comprehensive political solution for its settlement;
- A reaffirmation of the principle of positive discrimination for Darfur's
  people;
- A right of compensation for accumulated damages and the reconstruc-
  tion of Darfur.

Separate consultations between the mediation and the parties continued, and on October 31 the GoS, SLM/A and JEM submitted in writing, as requested, their views on the draft Declaration of Principles (DoP). Soon after, the AU secretariat and partners held a meeting to map out a strategy on the preparation of the DoP, and a small committee, led by the AU secretariat, was requested to draft a preliminary DoP based on the parties' submissions. On November 2 the AU mediation team presented the draft DoP to the parties.

The aim of the DoP was to provide a framework on the basis of which the issues of power and wealth sharing, as well the broader security issues, would be addressed in a detailed manner. The mediation was also influenced by the importance of the DoP signed between the GoS and Sudan People's Liberation Movement (SPLM), which had provided the framework for the Naivasha talks that were, at that moment, poised to be concluded with the signature of Sudan's Comprehensive Peace Agreement.

Subsequently, a plenary session to finalize the security protocol was held on November 2. The GoS delegation reiterated the two clarifications they sought from the mediation team during the separate consultations they held with the AU secretariat. These two issues related to the replacement of the term "Janjawiid" with "armed militias" as stipulated in the N'djamena Humanitarian Ceasefire Agreement, and to the provision calling for the parties to refrain from conducting hostile military flights in and over Darfur. In the opinion of the mediation and the observers, accepting these modifications from the GoS would have seriously set back the process, and as such, the GoS was urged to accept the language as proposed in the draft document. The AU mediation team argued that, first, the word "Janjawiid" was used in UN Security Council resolutions, as well as in the Joint Communiqué signed in early July between the GoS and the UN Secretary-General. Second, the provision on hostile military flights was a reiteration of the relevant provisions of the N'djamena Agreement. Indeed, the mediation pointed out that the provision in the UN Security Council Resolution 1564, which urged the GoS to refrain from military flights in and over Darfur, was stronger in language than the one contained in the draft security protocol since it applied to all military flights, be they hostile or not. The movements, for their part, requested additional time to consult on the revised draft protocol on security issues.

On November 3, separate consultations were held with the parties to seek their views on the revised draft security protocol, during which both parties made additional amendments. Based on those proposals, the mediation team made an attempt to bridge the gap between the parties. However, after exhaustive discussions about the parties' amendments that afternoon, the mediation team came to the conclusion that the differences were so great they could not be reconciled. It was strongly felt that any attempt to accommodate one side would set back the process. At the same time, it was agreed to formulate compromise language on some of the differences to forward to the parties in the event of a continued deadlock.

That day, the mediators reported to the parties that it could not reconcile the respective amendments. The mediators, along with all the international partners, made a strong plea to the parties to reconsider their respective positions and sign the revised security protocol as proposed by the mediation team. The following day, President Obasanjo met with the parties' representatives, in the presence of the AU mediators, and urged them to show flexibility and to accept the draft protocol. Notwithstanding his appeal, both the GoS and the movements reiterated their positions as stated above. Therefore, in an attempt to reach a solution, President Obasanjo suggested using the language contained in UN Security Council Resolution 1564. He also proposed a formulation on the issue of military flights to the parties as a way out. Again, both parties failed to accept the proposed amendments.

In a plenary session held on the same evening, the mediation team and the international partners made another unanimous plea for the parties to accept the draft protocol as it stood. Both parties again refused to consider the draft unless their specific amendments were incorporated into a new revised draft. The GoS felt that the issue of military flights was non-negotiable, and the movements insisted on its inclusion. The movements insisted that, in light of the aerial bombings that had taken place in the course of the conflict, and their traumatizing effect on the civilian population, a no-fly zone should be imposed as part of the confidence-building measures and the efforts to facilitate the return of IDPs and refugees. The mediators made it clear that these demands were unacceptable. The mediators wanted to take into account the expressed concerns by finding a formulation based on the commitments that were already entered into. It should also be added that a number of other demands by the rebels had been rejected by the mediation, notably the request for the redeployment of the Sudanese forces to their original garrisons, and the establishment of an AU-led mechanism to disarm the Janjawiid. Instead, following the UN Security Council's decision, the disarmament of the Janjawiid remained the responsibility of the GoS.

However, in a dramatic turn of events, on the evening of November 4 the SLM/A and JEM accepted the draft security protocol at the start of the plenary session, and expressed their readiness to sign it. They indicated that the draft was not fully satisfactory, but they had no other option than to respond positively to the plea made by the international community. In a separate consultation with the GoS, and in hope of the acceptance of the security protocol by the movements, the mediators further appealed to the government to reconsider its position. The international partners concurred and pressed the GoS to accept. Every effort was made to explain to the GoS that its concerns could be addressed on the basis of the current formulation on military flights and to convince it to accept the document as is. The mediators stressed that the provision prohibiting hostile military flights could not be seen as imposing a no-fly zone in Darfur, as the GoS delegation was implying. It was no more than a restatement of obligations already enshrined in the N'djamena Agreement, which, *inter alia*, committed the parties to a ceasefire on land and air, and requested them to refrain from any military action, reconnaissance operation, or any form of hostile act.

In the meantime, a revised DoP based on the parties' written submissions was circulated on November 5. In its reaction to the draft DoP, the GoS argued that the Darfur crisis was essentially a political issue, and as such, it should be viewed within the broader context of the conflicts in Sudan. In this regard, the GoS delegation emphasized the importance of having a federal system of government where Darfur could play an important role. The relevance of the Machakos Protocol, the framework agreement for the imminent Comprehensive Peace Agreement and the ongoing Naivasha process were also stressed. After outlining its position, the GoS, in a surprise move, and partly as a defensive strategy to react to the movements' acceptance of the security protocol the previous evening, accepted the draft DoP and expressed its readiness to sign it. The movements, while surprised by the government's readiness to accept and sign the draft DoP, were of the opinion that the revised DoP represented a good beginning, but that further discussions should be undertaken before its finalization.

Subsequently, the movements hardened their positions. Indeed, in a separate consultation held with the AU mediators three days later, they argued that the humanitarian and security protocols should be signed before they started discussions on the draft DoP. Despite the pleas of the mediators and the international partners, the movements submitted additional amendments to the draft DoP on November 9. Given the divergent positions of the parties on the DoP and the movements' attempt to delay the consideration of the DoP, the mediators felt it was necessary to end the third round of Abuja talks that day.

## The Fourth Round of the Abuja Talks

THE FOURTH ROUND of the Inter-Sudanese Peace Talks on the conflict in Darfur was held in Abuja from December 11 to 21, 2004, and it turned out to be the least productive. It was essentially aimed at finalizing the draft of the DoP discussed during the third round. However, the talks were complicated from the outset as the GoS, more by design than coincidence, launched a military operation on December 8, ostensibly to clear roadblocks mounted by the SLM/A. The two movements then decided to suspend their participation until the government stopped its offensive and withdrew its forces. More alarmingly, the SLM/A leadership that had participated at previous talks failed to turn up for this round.

Therefore, despite the efforts of the AU leadership and the international community, the fourth round was adjourned with very little progress: the parties issued a joint statement in which they reaffirmed their commitment to seek a peaceful and negotiated solution to the conflict in Darfur, and they made a number of security and military commitments to create an environment conducive to the resumption of the talks. The GoS reaffirmed its commitment to completely stop its military operations in Darfur and to withdraw its forces to previous positions, while the SLM/A and JEM undertook to cease all attacks against humanitarian and commercial activities, to restrain their forces from making attacks on government infrastructure, and to withdraw their forces to previous positions. No party adhered to its commitments.

On February 16, 2005, a Summit of Heads of State was held in N'djamena to consider working modalities to reinforce the implementation of the Humanitarian Ceasefire Agreement and the Abuja Protocols of November 9, 2004, as well as to facilitate the early resumption of the Abuja talks. At the end of the summit, the heads of state agreed to pursue a two-track strategy: First, they requested the chair of the Joint Commission to send, on the ground in Darfur, a team to verify the positions occupied by the forces of the parties so as to work out a separation plan between those forces. Second, they requested that the mediation prepare a framework agreement to be submitted to the parties at the next round of the Abuja talks. In late February and March, the AU mediation team visited Khartoum, Asmara, N'djamena, and Abuja, and undertook extensive consultations with the Sudanese parties.

In Khartoum, the mediation team held a series of meetings with the senior government officials in charge of the Darfur dossier, namely Majzoub al Khalifa, Najib al Khair, and al Tijani Fidail. They discussed a draft framework protocol for the resolution of the conflict in Darfur, jointly prepared by the co-mediators, the AU, and Chad. After visiting Khartoum the mediation team held similar consultations with the leaders of the SLM/A and JEM in Asmara, March 3–6. During those consultations, the movements stressed that the improvement of the security situation on the ground, and the withdrawal of the GoS forces from areas they occupied after December 8, 2004, were major concerns that needed to be properly addressed prior to the resumption of the Abuja talks. The movements also requested that the Joint Commission be strengthened to enable it to enforce the implementation of its decisions and ensure the parties' full compliance with their commitments. The draft Framework Protocol was also submitted to the two movements during these consultations.

### The Fifth Round of the Abuja Talks

DR. SALIM AHMED SALIM, former secretary-general of the OAU, was appointed as the Chairperson's Special Envoy and Chief Mediator for the

Abuja talks. The fifth round of the Inter-Sudanese Peace Talks resumed under his watch on June 10 and lasted until July 5, 2005. This round was devoted to finalizing the Declaration of Principles, which was initially discussed during the previous two rounds.

This round of talks had been delayed for much longer than anticipated, partly due to the deteriorating security situation on the ground as well as the split within the SLM/A leadership. During several consultations during the interim, the SLM/A leadership had repeatedly requested more time, wanting to organize a general congress of the movement before designating new leadership and negotiators.

After extensive negotiations, the DoP was signed on July 5, 2005. In the DoP, the parties reiterated their commitment to all previous agreements. The SLM/A continued to object to the DoP until the last moment, but after JEM indicated its readiness to sign, SLM/A too came forward. Key provisions in the DoP included: the establishment of a federal system of government with an effective devolution of powers, and a clear distribution of responsibilities between the national and other levels of governance (this was considered essential to ensure effective local participation and the fair administration of Sudan in general, and Darfur in particular); the equitable distribution of national wealth, to ensure the effectiveness of the devolution of power in Darfur within the framework of a federal system of government, and to ensure that due consideration will be given to the socioeconomic needs of Darfur; and finally, that power sharing and wealth sharing shall be addressed in accordance with a fair criteria to be agreed upon by the parties. The DoP also included a provision for establishing the Darfur-Darfur Dialogue and Consultation, a process intended to include in the peace process all the armed groups and stakeholders not represented in Abuja, so as to ensure inclusivity and full Darfurian ownership.

It should be noted that the adoption of the DoP during the fifth round of talks was extremely difficult due to the complexity of issues being discussed, including land ownership rights, issues of impunity, the separation of state and religion, wealth sharing and power sharing, and security arrangements. After lengthy deliberations, procrastination, and deadlocks, the compromise text that was finally agreed upon was made possible by high-level interventions from African leaders and the international community. Progress at this round was also marred by side issues such as the presence of Eritrea and the role of Chad as co-mediator, which prevented, for days, the beginning of the discussions on the agenda items.

## The Sixth Round of the Abuja Peace Talks

THE SIXTH ROUND of the Inter-Sudanese Peace Talks on the conflict in Darfur opened in Abuja on September 15, 2005. The objective of the talks was to commence and, if possible, conclude the negotiations on the substantive issues of power sharing, wealth sharing, and security arrangements, with a view of arriving at a broad political framework that would pave the way for a settlement of the conflict in Darfur. Prior to resuming the talks, a workshop was organized to assist the parties in gaining clarity on many of the substantive issues that would be the subject of detailed negotiations.

The first plenary session opened on October 3, during which the special envoy reminded the parties that there would be strict accreditation mechanisms in place for the negotiators representing the three parties in the various committees. This was a result of the movements' insistence on having every member of their delegations present for all discussions in the previous rounds. This greatly slowed down proceedings as most of those present demanded the right to speak and no single delegate was authorized to lead the negotiations.

By October 10, after extensive consultations, the mediators finalized and provided to the two parties for their consideration a harmonized text that included the parties' respective positions on the criteria and guidelines for power sharing. This compromise text covered general criteria for power sharing as well as representations in the various competencies including the legislature, the judiciary, the executive, Council of States, Council of Ministers, federal civil service, state executive, state legislature, and all institutions of government in the states.

While progress on the power sharing negotiation was notably slow, the discussions on wealth sharing had not even started as late as October 12 because the movements were unable to meet simultaneously in the two committees. Indeed, the unresolved issue of leadership in the ranks of the SLM/A remained the single obstacle hindering progress in the talks. The delegation led by Abdel Wahid Nur contained only few of the SLM/A members affiliated with Minni Minawi, who rarely, if ever, attended any of these talks. However, a group of military commanders belonging to Minawi arrived in Abuja on October 5, transported from the field. After their arrival the special envoy, as well as the international partners, engaged them with intensive consultations to minimize the differences between Abdel Wahid and Minawi, so that their combined delegations could fruitfully represent the SLM/A, and whichever decisions and agreements were reached in Abuja would be binding on the organization. However, these attempts failed, as Abdel Wahid insisted that he alone could choose the members of the SLM/A delegation. The military commanders left Abuja without resolving the outstanding leadership issues. Several of them later became prominent members of the G-19/SLM-Unity group.

On October 20, the sixth round was adjourned.

## Preparations for Convening the Seventh Round of the Abuja Talks

PRIOR TO beginning the seventh and final round of the Abuja talks, Minawi informed the AU of his desire to unilaterally convene the movement's congress. The AU cautioned him of the need for an all-inclusive conference that would reflect the wide diversity of its membership. He was also advised that the leaders of the SLM should afford its membership an opportunity to freely choose its leadership in order to ensure that both the reorganization and programs of the SLM would reflect the different tendencies within the movement. When it became apparent that Minawi would proceed with the conference, the AU and its partners also advised him against the plan to conduct elections for a new leadership under the divided backdrop from which the conference was held, especially given that not all the leaders, most notably the chair and vice chair of the movement, would attend.

Notwithstanding this advice, the conference was held in Haskanita, from October 29 to 31, 2005, and the movement elected a new "leadership" for the SLM. Subsequently, the chair and vice chair, as well as some other members of the SLM, rejected the outcome of the conference as "illegal" and therefore "null and void." The conference and the "elections" deepened the division within the SLM, creating serious implications for the peace process and other efforts to end the conflict in Darfur.

These developments alarmed both the AU and the international community, and efforts were made to find ways to reconcile the two wings of the SLM. Indeed, November 8–9, the U.S., with the support of the AU, organized a meeting in Nairobi, Kenya, to help unite the SLM. U.S. Deputy Secretary of State Robert Zoellick presided over the deliberations, which were also attended by the AU's special envoy and chief mediator, special envoys, and other representatives. This meeting failed to realize its most important objectives, namely uniting the leadership of the SLM/A around one delegation to the talks and adopting a common negotiating position. Minawi, newly elected as chair of the SLM/A in Haskanita, failed to attend the Nairobi meeting, and his designated representatives refused to accept the proposal made by the deputy secretary of state with the support of the AU and the international partners. Minawi's representatives initially refused to sit in the same room as Abdel Wahid and his delegates. Another U.S. attempt to engage the two SLM/A groups, this time led by Assistant Secretary of State Jendayi Frazer, visited al Fashir on November 19 and also failed.

Even after the efforts in Nairobi and Darfur faltered, efforts by the AU and international partners continued to engage the leaders of the SLM/A with a view attempting to encourage them to adopt a united and inclusive approach to the negotiations. Through the efforts exerted by the government of Chad, with the support of the AU, Eritrea, and Libya, a meeting of the SLM/A leaders was convened in N'djamena on November 26. Both Abdel Wahid and Minawi attended this meeting and committed themselves to harmonizing their negotiating positions and establishing a commission to work for reconciliation within the SLM/A. This agreement was never implemented. For the AU, it became evident that the upcoming seventh round would be the critical phase of the Abuja talks and the consolidation and unity of the movement's leadership would be absolutely critical to making progress and arriving at a lasting solution.

## The Seventh Round of the Abuja Talks

THE SEVENTH ROUND of the Inter-Sudanese Peace Talks on the conflict in Darfur opened in Abuja, on November 29, 2005, and ended, after more than five months of long, difficult, and frustrating negotiations, on May 5, 2006. The negotiations took place within three categories: power sharing, wealth sharing, and security arrangements. For over four months the parties, with the assistance of the mediation team and international partners, participated in a torturous negotiation process, often in bilateral consultations and, at times, in plenary sessions.

In a series of incremental steps, the Abuja talks had shifted from being chaired by the Chadian government, to being co-chaired by the AU and the Chadians, to being chaired exclusively by the AU. This final shift occurred during the seventh round, by which time relations between Sudan and Chad had deteriorated to the point at which President Déby declared that his country was in a state of war with Sudan. During the early months of 2006, N'djamena hosted a series of meetings in which Chad provided political and military support to elements of the Darfur movements, while the GoS supported Chadian insurgents.

By the beginning of April 2006, the discussions in power sharing and wealth sharing had come to a conclusion. In the case of power sharing, the parties had aired their views on all the key questions but there was no move toward compromise. Regarding wealth sharing, most of the issues had been resolved although the critical question of compensation remained a focus of disagreement. In April, the mediation team started deliberating on what it considered to be a fair and judicious compromise document, which would then be submitted to the parties for their consideration. For the mediation team, preparing such a compromise document was a Herculean task, given the fact that the positions of the parties in the power-sharing commission remained far apart, especially on issues such as the presidency, the future status of Darfur, and the representation of Darfurians in the executive, the legislature, and the civil service. For example, on the future status of Darfur, the movements' demanded the establishment of a "Region for Darfur" immediately after the signing of an agreement, without a referendum and prior to consultation of the people of Darfur. The GoS, for its part, while agreeing to the creation of mechanisms to enhance interstate coordination, pending a final decision, continued to reject any changing of the status quo without securing the full consent of the people of Darfur.

Regarding representation at the national-executive level, the demand by the movements for the post of a second vice president continued to be rejected by the GoS. Nor was there consensus between the parties on the appropriate level of representation for the movements at the Council of Ministers, the national legislature, the Council of States, national judicial organs, the civil service, the armed forces, law enforcement agencies, national institutions, educational institutions, and the administration of the national capital. The parties also failed to agree on the percentages of power sharing within Darfur: while the GoS demanded that the National Congress Party retain a 70 percent share of positions (as stipulated in the CPA) the movements demanded that they take up to 90 percent of the posts. This applied to both the legislative and the executive. They also failed to agree on Darfur's entitlement to quotas in national institutions, with the movements insisting that Darfurians represented as much as 40 percent of the Sudanese population, and the GoS objecting to any quota systems at all and even arguing that Darfurians were overrepresented in many institutions.

On the topic of wealth sharing, the respective positions of the parties were more manageable, although by the end of March 2006, there were still four unresolved issues, including the needs for the resettlement of IDPs and refugees, and most contentious of all, compensation. The movements were insisting on initial financial support to be provided to the returnees in addition to other basic services, to enable them to restart their livelihood. The government maintained its position of no cash payments to individuals.

Regarding the money to be paid by the government to the Darfur Reconstruction and Development Fund (DRDF) through transfers from the Fiscal and Financial Allocation and Monitoring Commission (FFAMC), both parties were sticking to their previous positions. The movements were insisting that 6.5 percent of the annual revenue of Sudan be paid to the DRDF for a period of ten years. The government, on the other hand, wanted to deposit seed money into the DRDF for 2006, and make payments for the next two years, which would be adjusted against its contribution as determined at the end of the Joint Assessment Mission exercise, to be led by the World Bank. There was also little significant movement in the area of vertical allocation from the central government to the states. The issue at stake was the inclusion of a provision for the eventuality that the FFAMC would not be operational in 2006. Specifically, what rate should be applied for the vertical allocation from the central government to the states? The movements wanted 35 percent of the national revenue to be applied as a formula. The government argued that fixing a formula in Abuja was not acceptable because it was not based on a scientific economic study; furthermore, the movements were not mandated to negotiate a formula on behalf of other states.

Concerning compensation, the parties agreed to the idea of establishing a Compensation Commission but there were disagreements related to the creation of a Compensation Fund, and the amount of money that should be placed into the fund as an initial installment. The GoS, conscious of the lack of any compensation payments to the southern Sudanese at the end of the North-South war, wanted to minimize compensation and instead provide funds through rehabilitation and development, while the movements insisted on individual cash payments to all families affected by the war.

Discussions at the security arrangements commission remained the most problematic. Given the extremely divergent positions of the parties, on March 12 the mediation team proposed an Enhanced Humanitarian Ceasefire Agreement (EHCA) as a bridging attempt to stabilize the security situation on the ground.. The reason for the designation was the GoS's insistence that the N'djamena Humanitarian Ceasefire Agreement should not be jettisoned although it was apparent to all that it was not being honored. The EHCA was created to:

- Stop the violence;
- Alleviate the suffering of the people of Darfur;

- Create a climate conducive to the conclusion of the Abuja talks; and
- Make it possible to more effectively implement the N'djamena Ceasefire Agreement of April 8, 2004.

The EHCA also contained provisions for:

- The strengthening of the Ceasefire Monitoring and Verification Mechanisms;
- The protection of IDPs and humanitarian supply routes; and
- The disengagement and redeployment of forces, and limited arms control.

Most importantly, the EHCA had a bridging provision committing the parties to the finalization of a Comprehensive Security Agreement by concluding their discussions on issues such as the speedy disarmament of the Janjawiid, the establishment of assembly areas for the movements' combatants, the demobilization and reintegration of the movements' combatants, and a detailed roadmap indicating the sequencing and timing of the final security arrangements.

The EHCA was neither a new nor a stand-alone agreement. As noted above, it was necessitated by the fact that the parties had repeatedly, and with impunity, violated the N'djamena Ceasefire Agreement. The proposal for beginning with the EHCA prior to moving to a comprehensive peace agreement for Darfur was based on the assumption that the parties would be able to reach agreement on these relatively limited issues more quickly than they would be able to agree on power sharing, wealth sharing, and final status issues within the security arrangements brief, such as the integration of former movements' combatants into the national army. However, progress on reaching consensus on the key issues in the EHCA proved so slow that this rationale began to appear questionable. In addition, the GoS, the SLM-Minawi, and JEM insisted that they would only sign an enhanced ceasefire agreement when they had a clear indication of the progress of final-status security issues.

In mid-March the parties started an exercise to chart the positions of their forces on secret maps to be kept solely in the possession of the mediators team, in order to identify their exact locations on the ground as demanded by the N'djamena Agreement and the joint commission. This exercise also allowed a team comprising the AMIS force commander, his staff officers, and senior military officers seconded from UNAMIS to prepare a detailed implementation plan for the security arrangements, subsequent to the signing of an agreement. The mapping exercise had the beneficial side effect that it raised a host of practical issues concerning demilitarized zones, Janjawiid camps, redeployment phasing, and the administration of IDP camps. This allowed areas of potential compromise to be sketched out by the mediators.

Pending the outcome of this process, as well as agreement on the sequencing of disengagement, redeployment, and limited arms control, the mediators started to draft a compromise document for all aspects of security arrangements. Members of the security arrangements commission were able to consult with all the parties on most aspects of final-status security issues, but the question of the absorption or integration of movement combatants remained especially divisive. The GoS position was that no integration of former rebels would be allowed, but that possibly some individuals could be "included." The position of the SLM-Minawi and JEM was that they should retain significant separate forces under their own command throughout the interim period. The draft mediation document adopted the position that movement combatants should be integrated into the army and other security forces, but put X's instead of indicating the actual numbers to be integrated.

At no time in the security discussions was the question of a transition from AMIS to a UN force raised. The position of the mediators was that this issue would be resolved elsewhere and references in the agreement to "AMIS" and "AU" would automatically be replaced by "UN." The mediation team was given to understand that during March meetings in Brussels and Paris, Vice President Ali Osman Mohamed Taha had given an assurance to U.S. Deputy Secretary of State Zoellick that once a peace agreement had been signed, the GoS would permit the dispatch of a UN force. The standard rules and operating modalities for a UN peacekeeping force, operating under either a Chapter VI or Chapter VII mandate, allow for the force to enforce a peace agreement, not to enforce peace. Meanwhile, AMIS struggled to obtain the funds needed to maintain even its small and insufficient seven thousand–strong force. As the security situation in Darfur remained dire due to repeated ceasefire violations, the pressure for a transition from AMIS to the UN mounted, and with that, so did the demands for a rapid agreement among the parties in Abuja.

In the meantime, Special Envoy and Chief Mediator Salim continued to engage in consultations about the Abuja Talks with President Obasanjo. During their last meeting, which took place on March 22, Dr. Salim briefed the president on the progress and the outstanding issues, as well as the way forward. In a meeting on April 11, the UN Security Council insisted that the talks reach a conclusion by the end of April, and the presidential statement of that day issued a deadline of the end of the month. Dr. Salim returned from New York to Abuja ready to accelerate the mediation's efforts to meet the deadline.

## The Final Phase of the Abuja Peace Talks

ON APRIL 25, the chief mediator submitted to the parties a comprehensive set of proposals for a Darfur Peace Agreement, affirming that the draft DPA was the culmination of intensive deliberations and negotiations conducted by the AU mediation team, with the support of the facilitators and international partners, and that it represented a fair, comprehensive, and workable solution to the conflict in Darfur. These proposals covered aspects of power sharing, wealth sharing, security arrangements, and the Darfur-Darfur Dialogue and Consultation (DDDC), as well as implementation mechanisms and modalities.

The mediation team made use of the presence of Vice President Taha in Abuja, along with other senior officials of the Government of National Unity (GoNU), including leading members of the SPLM, to facilitate direct negotiations between the government's delegation and the leaders of the movements. Expectations were high that the vice president's meetings with the SLM/A and JEM leaders would enable a breakthrough to occur. During the event, however, these hopes were disappointed, and Taha left Abuja on the morning of April 27, pessimistic that any deal would be reached.

Before the deadline of April 30, the government of Sudan, while expressing reservations on some aspects of the document submitted by the chief mediator, formally informed the mediation team that it accepted the draft as a good basis for an agreement to end the conflict in Darfur. For their part, the movements continued to express concerns over some aspects of the document, which, according to them, did not fully address their original demands and aspirations in some of the fundamental areas, even though they had consistently raised them throughout the negotiations.

In light of the government's acceptance of the mediation's proposals, and the belief that extra efforts were required to get the movements to adopt and sign the agreement, the chairperson of the AU and the president of Nigeria appealed to the parties to continue with the negotiations until an agreement was reached. Consequently, the special envoy, following consultations with the facilitators, observers, and international partners, extended the deadline for the Abuja talks by forty-eight hours.

In the meantime, on May 2, U.S. Deputy Secretary of State Zoellick, U.S. Assistant Secretary of State for African Affairs Frazer, and UK Secretary of State for International Development Hilary Benn joined the mediation. Mr. Zoellick and Mr. Benn, together with representatives from Canada and the European Union, and in close coordination with the chief mediator, consulted with the parties and proposed amendments to the draft DPA. These amendments were subsequently presented to the parties for their consideration. The proposed amendments mainly covered security arrangements (notably specifying numbers of movement combatants to be integrated into the army), but also sought to address some of the concerns expressed by the movements on power sharing and wealth sharing. As the new deadline drew near, there was still no agreement, and the host of the talks, President Obasanjo, at a meeting with the chief mediator, requested another forty-eight-hour extension to enable the presentation of a final enhanced text of the DPA to the parties.

At 9 p.m. on May 4, at the state house in Abuja, President Obasanjo hosted the final stretch of negotiations, which were attended by the current chairperson of the AU, President Denis Sassou-Nguesso, the representative of the leader of the Libyan Arab Jamahiriya, Ali Treki, and the chairperson of the commission, along with the chief mediator, the commissioner for peace and security, the special representative in Sudan, representatives of the parties, the facilitators, and the international partners. The meeting lasted until 4:30 a.m. the next day, and after a short break, resumed at 9:00 a.m.

On the second day of the meeting, Minawi and his SLM group, after sustained engagement by the leaders and the international partners, confirmed their acceptance of the DPA as amended and expressed their readiness to sign it. For their part, Abdel Wahid and his SLM group, and Khalil Ibrahim Mohamed of JEM felt that the draft agreement did not address most of their fundamental areas of concern. They, therefore, announced that they were unable to sign the agreement unless substantial modifications were made to address those concerns.

Following intensive consultations at the highest level, and despite the negative response from the leadership of the SLM-Abdel Wahid and JEM, the DPA was signed at 5:55 p.m. on May 5, 2006, by Majzoub al Khalifa, on behalf of the GoS, and by SLM/A Chairperson Minawi. Immediately after the signing ceremony, fourteen members of SLM-Abdel Wahid, led by Abdel Rahman Musa, who was until then the chief negotiator of that group, handed in a letter that expressed their wish to join the peace process and to be included in the implementation mechanisms, so that they could be part and parcel of the efforts to bring peace to their people in Darfur.

Although the DPA was signed by the GoS and the SLM-Minawi, because two of the parties involved in the negotiations declined to sign it, President Obasanjo announced that efforts should continue to bring those two movements on board. Consequently, the AU announced that the agreement should remain open for signatures until the meeting of the Peace and Security Council on May 15. Several members of the AU mediation team remained behind in Abuja and facilitated continuing discussions between the SLM-Abdel Wahid and the GoS. While these ongoing negotiations succeeded in narrowing the areas of disagreement between the parties, no agreement was reached. The outstanding areas of difference were:

- In security arrangements, the SLM-Abdel Wahid demanded that SLM/A forces be allowed a greater role in guaranteeing the security of returning IDPs and refugees, and monitoring the disarmament of the Janjawiid. In a letter to Abdel Wahid on May 14, Majzoub al Khalifa accepted these demands as consistent with the DPA.

- Concerning wealth sharing, the SLM/A demanded a substantial increase in the GoS's initial payment into the Compensation Fund, from $30 million to $200 million. The GoS responded that it had put no ceiling on the amount of compensation to be paid, but did not specify any additional amount to be provided.
- Regarding power sharing, the SLM/A demanded greater representation in the legislature and executive bodies of the Darfur state and local governments. The exact demands were not spelled out. The GoS replied that consideration could be given to greater representation when the SLM/A had signed the DPA.

Efforts to bring the SLM/A and JEM into the DPA continued into June but did not succeed, leaving the DPA with only the signatures of Majzoub al Khalifa and Minni Minawi. The supporters of Abdel Wahid and JEM condemned the DPA and vowed to oppose it.

## Conclusion

THE INTER-SUDANESE Peace Talks on the conflict in Darfur suffered from a number of significant shortcomings that made the process frustrating and flawed. The most important of these shortcomings were internal to the conflict itself, and the structure and strategies of the belligerent parties. The peace negotiations were launched when the conflict between the SLM/A and JEM on the one side, and the GoS on the other, was itself less than six months old—at a time when both parties believed they could advance their positions on the battlefield. Therefore, each was a reluctant negotiator from the outset. Until the very end of the talks in May 2006, the parties tended to see the Abuja talks as a tactical forum, rather than the central stage on which a solution to Darfur's conflict would be found. Throughout the entire negotiating process, fighting continued on the ground in Darfur, both between GoS and the movements and among the movements themselves. This not only indicated the poor faith of the parties but also showed their relative lack of concern for the integrity of the mediation process compared to that of the battlefield.

The movements in particular suffered a chronic and systematic problem of cohesion and representation. This was unsurprising for the young insurgent groups, which had been precipitously thrust into the world's spotlight without having had the opportunity to establish political organization in the field, and which were led by relatively young and inexperienced political leaders. They were not only ill-prepared for negotiating with an experienced and skilled adversary, but also suffered problems of disunity that only increased with each passing month. However, the GoS was not innocent of inconstancy. It repeatedly reneged on its commitments and presented hard-line negotiating positions as its bottom line without indicating where flexibility was possible or necessary. Rarely did any of the parties work constructively with the mediation in search of solutions. Under these circumstances, a negotiated settlement was always going to be very slow, and ultimate success was improbable. The AU mediation team's strategy of developing a compromise text and presenting it to the parties as the basis for a final expedited negotiation was the product of these frustrating circumstances, coupled with the urgency for finding a settlement in the light of the continuing humanitarian emergency.

The April 30 deadline and the concerted attempt to press the parties to sign the DPA over the following six days was a calculated risk. It came very close to succeeding, as the relatively minor issues raised by Abdel Wahid and his group over the following days, as preconditions for their signing, indicate. That this approach did not succeed has been a tragedy for the people of Darfur.

# 10

# The Making and Unmaking of
# the Darfur Peace Agreement[1]

LAURIE NATHAN

IN LATE 2005, the seventh round of the Inter-Sudanese Peace
Talks on the conflict in Darfur commenced in Abuja,
Nigeria, under the auspices of an African Union (AU) mediation team. The
mediation was led by Salim Ahmed Salim, the former secretary-general of
the Organisation of African Unity, and supported by the UN, the UK, the
U.S., and other international partners. The aim of the talks was to broker a
comprehensive peace agreement between the government of Sudan and
the main rebel movements in Darfur—the Sudan Liberation
Movement/Army (SLM) and the Justice and Equality Movement (JEM). On
May 5, 2006, the Darfur Peace Agreement (DPA) was signed by the government and Minni Minawi, the leader of one of the two SLM factions, but it
was rejected by JEM and Abdel Wahid al Nur, the leader of the other SLM
faction.

The agreement did not achieve peace, and in certain respects it heightened conflict. Immediately after the signing ceremony there were violent
protests in Darfur against the DPA. More ominously, the government and
Minawi formed an offensive military alliance and attacked communities
that supported Abdel Wahid (Flint 2006b; *Sudan Tribune* 2006o; ICG 2006).
There was widespread opposition to this deal within the Minawi group,
with some commanders announcing a suspension of the DPA (*Sudan
Tribune* 2006l, 2006n). Conversely, four senior officials from JEM and the

Abdel Wahid faction signed a declaration of support for the agreement. No sooner had the SLM leaders left Abuja than the organization began to splinter into different blocs. A group of nineteen prominent dissenters from Abdel Wahid's faction set themselves up in northern Darfur under the name "SLM-Unity." A group of thirty commanders led by Ahmed Abdel Shafi Bassey then announced the ouster of Abdel Wahid and split the movement further. Several other commanders, including some of Minawi's, also broke away. In an attempt to unify the non-signatories, JEM formed the National Redemption Front with support from Eritrea and Chad.

At the end of June 2006, Jan Pronk, the UN secretary-general's special representative in Sudan, warned that there was a significant risk that the DPA would collapse. He argued that it was a good text and an honest compromise between the extreme positions taken by the parties in Abuja, but it did not resonate with the people of Darfur and was meeting growing resistance from internally displaced persons (IDPs) in particular who believed that the agreement "ha[d] been forced upon them and, rather than meeting the interests of all parties somewhere halfway, only strengthen[ed] the position of the government and [Minawi's] minority tribe, the Zaghawa" (2006). Pronk concluded that the DPA, though not yet dead, was severely paralyzed.

In September, the government mounted the first of three major offensives aimed at crushing the rebellion. It bombed villages, attacked them with helicopter gunships, terrorized IDP camps, slaughtered women and children, and rearmed and deployed the Janjawiid. By this time, hopes that the non-signatories could be pressured or persuaded to sign on to an unamended DPA had vanished. On November 16, UN Secretary-General Kofi Annan and AU Commission Chairperson Alpha Oumar Konaré convened a high-level meeting in Addis Ababa, where they called for a new round of talks with the non-signatories. Minawi, appointed as a special advisor to the Sudanese president under the DPA's power-sharing provisions, had by then been completely marginalized in Khartoum's decisionmaking. In early December, as fighting between Janjawiid and rebels broke out in the North Darfur city of al Fashir, Minawi threatened to abandon the government and resume fighting.

Intended to address the causes of the conflict, the DPA contains provisions on power sharing and political representation, wealth sharing and compensation for the victims of the conflict, ceasefire arrangements and long-term security issues, and a Darfur-Darfur Dialogue and Consultation designed to facilitate local dialogue and reconciliation (de Waal 2006). The content of the DPA has been criticized by a number of analysts (Africa Confidential 2006; Flint 2006c), including the ICG, whose commentary sparked a heated exchange with the AU (ICG 2006; *Sudan Tribune* 2006m; Evans 2006). This chapter does not cover that ground. It focuses instead on the process of negotiations and mediation in Abuja between November 2005 and May 2006, and seeks to show that the manner in which peace agreements are prepared and concluded is as important as their content.

In summary, the Abuja talks had three primary dynamics: the negotiating parties were unwilling to engage in negotiations and failed to forge agreements; the AU and its international partners, desperate for a quick accord, pursued a counterproductive strategy of "deadline diplomacy" that inhibited progress; and the mediators were consequently unable to undertake effective mediation. As a result of these dynamics, the DPA was not a negotiated settlement and its implementation was bound to experience severe difficulties.

The Abuja process reinforced two general lessons regarding mediation in civil wars. First, these wars are not conducive to a viable quick accord. They have multiple historical, structural, political, social, and economic causes that are complex, deep-rooted, and intractable. The difficulty of resolution is compounded greatly by the protagonists' mutual hatred and suspicion. However grave the situation, mediators have no option but to be patient. Second, an enduring peace agreement cannot be forced on the parties. It has to be shaped and owned by them because it cannot be implemented without their consent and cooperation and its sustainability requires their adherence to its provisions in the long term. These lessons are frequently ignored by states and multinational organizations that seek to end civil wars through power-based diplomacy rather than confidence-building mediation (Nathan 1999).

This chapter is based on the author's participation in the Darfur mediation process, although the author has tried as much as possible to substantiate his personal observations and claims with reference to published material.[2] The chapter is organized as follows: section one examines "deadline diplomacy" and the failure of the AU and its international partners to distinguish between getting the parties to sign a peace agreement and obtaining their genuine consent to its terms and execution; section two considers the psycho-political dynamics, balance of power, and other factors that gave rise to the parties' reluctance to enter into real negotiations; and section three explores the ways in which the deadline diplomacy prevented the mediators from doing a proper job.

## A Diplomacy of Deadlines

THE SEVENTH ROUND of the Darfur peace talks began at the end of November 2005, the previous rounds having produced nothing more than a declaration of principles and a series of ceasefire accords that were violated regularly by the parties (AU 2005; Dawit Toga in this volume). Nevertheless, on a visit to Abuja in early 2006, Jack Straw, the British foreign secretary, admonished the parties for having failed to meet the December 31, 2005, deadline set by the UN Security Council for a comprehensive peace agreement (2006). In January 2006, Pronk proposed a new cut-off date in February (*Sudan Tribune* 2006a). In early February, the AU commissioner for peace and security, Said Djinnit, told the mediators and the parties to wrap up by the end of the month. In March, the AU Peace and Security Council called for the conclusion of a comprehensive agreement by the end of April (AU 2006b). The UN Security Council endorsed this date as the final deadline (UN 2006a).

As they hopped from one monthly deadline to the next, top officials from the UN, the AU, the EU, and donor governments complained that the negotiations were proceeding too slowly. Their constant refrain was that the "patience of the international community is running out."[3] They threatened the parties with sanctions and warned that funding for the mediation could dry up in the absence of a quick accord. For example, Jack Straw, whose government was one of the major funders of the Abuja process, told the parties in January that "the international community has poured a lot of money, time, and effort into the talks" but "our patience is not unlimited. If the parties do not reach an agreement here soon, we, with the AU, will need to start looking at the alternatives" (Straw 2006). On an earlier visit to Abuja, the Dutch prime minister had issued a similar warning (AFP 2005).

The posturing over deadlines was ignored by the Sudanese parties because it was not backed up by action. It was meant to apply pressure on the parties and convey the international community's seriousness about ending the conflict, but the deadlines came and went without any negative repercussions. They were consequently not an effective form of pressure and suggested a lack of seriousness on the part of the international community, which talked loudly about Darfur but carried a small stick. In July, 2006 a senior Sudanese government official was quoted as saying that "the United Nations Security Council has threatened us so many times, we no longer take it seriously" (Prendergast 2006).

Moreover, the monthly deadlines for a comprehensive peace agreement would have been fantastically unrealistic even if the Sudanese parties had been negotiating in earnest, which they assuredly were not. By comparison, in the early 1990s, negotiations aimed at reaching a settlement took over two years in the case of the Mozambican civil war and over three years in South Africa. Whereas these processes experienced steady progress punctuated by blockages and breakthroughs, the Abuja talks and preceding rounds were characterized by deadlock and an absence of negotiations. This did not deter the political leaders who were driving the deadlines. For example, in mid-April the chairperson of the AU, President Sassou-Nguesso of the Republic of Congo, failed to make headway in high-level discussions with the parties and promptly asked the mediators to quicken their preparation of a comprehensive agreement (*Sudan Tribune* 2006c).

An informed commentator has noted that "the best of the AU's experts in Abuja believed [that the target of] April was unrealistic, off by a couple of months at least" (Flint 2006a). Nevertheless, five days before the April 30 deadline, the mediation team presented the DPA to the parties on a take-it-or-leave-it basis, giving them less than a week to read, comprehend, debate within their ranks, and then endorse an eighty-six-page English-language document aimed at achieving a ceasefire and addressing the causes of a civil war through a set of complicated security, political, economic, and administrative arrangements.

The five-day timeframe for the approval of the agreement would have been wholly unreasonable and impractical in any negotiations to end a civil war. It was especially so in the context of Abuja: the parties disagreed profoundly on virtually every one of the critical issues covered by the DPA; they were confronted in the document by mechanisms and arrangements they had not considered previously; they loathed each other and doubted their opponents would implement their undertakings in good faith, if at all; the rebels had no opportunity to inform and consult their members and constituents in Darfur; and many of them had great difficulty understanding complex documents. Exacerbating this difficulty, the version of the DPA in Arabic, the language of choice for most of the rebel negotiators, was only completed on April 28, and contained some significant mistranslations and ambiguities.

The rebels asked the mediators to give them three weeks to study and comment on the document (Abuelbashar 2006). When they were turned down, they rejected the DPA. They complained that it watered down proposals made earlier by the mediation team, favored the government, and did not address adequately the political, economic, and security rights and demands of Darfurians (*Sudan Tribune* 2006g, 2006h). They also objected to the imposition of a deadline and to the AU having "fixed a time that was never realistic or reasonable for studying the Project, given that the translated (Arabic) version was made available only one day before the deadline stipulated by the Mediation" (*Sudan Tribune* 2006h). The government, on the other hand, stated that it was prepared to endorse the agreement despite its reservations.

At the request of the international partners and President Olusegun Obasanjo of Nigeria, Salim extended the deadline by forty-eight hours and then a further forty-eight hours (*Sudan Tribune* 2006i). In this brief period the lethargic pace of the talks changed dramatically. There was a frenzy of behind-the-scenes deals, counter-deals, offers, and threats as various leaders and officials—including Obasanjo, U.S. Deputy Secretary of State Robert Zoellick, and British Secretary for International Development Hilary Benn—endeavored to stave off collapse. They offered the rebel movements guarantees regarding the implementation of the DPA, tabled a list of non-negotiable amendments aimed at meeting the rebels' concerns, and threatened them with collective and individual sanctions (*Washington Post* 2006).

Minawi, who was regarded by the African and foreign dignitaries as the most important of the rebel leaders because he had the largest fighting force in Darfur, came under particularly strong pressure (ICG 2006). He was warned that his failure to sign the agreement might lead to his name being added to the list of Sudanese individuals on whom the UN Security Council had imposed sanctions (*Africa Confidential* 2006). At literally the last minute he relented. He appealed for more time to bring the other rebel movements on board but the "patience of the international community" had finally run out, and there would be no waiting for Abdel Wahid and JEM. On May 5, Minawi and the government's chief negotiator signed the agreement at a ceremony hosted by Obasanjo. A group of Abdel Wahid's colleagues, believing his stance to be unreasonable, joined the ceremony to declare their support.

After the ceremony, the AU set a deadline of May 15 for Abdel Wahid and the JEM leaders to add their signatures. Abdel Wahid beseeched the mediators to help him resolve his outstanding concerns.[4] Two members of the mediation team remained in Abuja to do this and the AU extended the cut-off date to the end of May and then to the beginning of July. The decisive deadline had passed, however, since the DPA could not be amended after it had been approved by the government and Minawi. Even the relatively modest demands of Abdel Wahid were rejected by the international partners on the grounds that the DPA could not be "renegotiated" (Alex de Waal, pers. comm.). The process ended in the first week of June when Abdel Wahid reneged on a commitment to attend a meeting with Minawi and the first vice president of Sudan, Salva Kiir.[5] He thereafter called in vain for the UN to take over the mediation (*Sudan Tribune* 2006k).

Salim had previously told the parties that "the only page [of the DPA] that really matters is the last page, which has the space for the signatures of the Parties" (AU 2006e). His point was that the document was worthless without those signatures, but the more important point was surely that the DPA was worthless without the parties' genuine endorsement. At the climatic showdown in Abuja, as with the preceding deadline diplomacy, the AU and its partners appeared to have lost sight of the distinction between getting the parties to sign an agreement and obtaining their real commitment to its terms and implementation. The import of this distinction was already starkly evident: previous rounds of talks had produced several ceasefire accords that the parties had signed and then breached systematically and brazenly. So it was with the DPA. In the months following their formal approval of the agreement, the government and Minawi repeatedly contravened its security provisions (*Sudan Tribune* 2006p; UN 2006b).

According to the assessment of one of the members of the mediation team, the manipulation and threats of the international partners in the final days of the Abuja process undermined the AU's authority in the eyes of the parties, compromised Minawi, and created general suspicion of the DPA in Darfur.[6] In addition to these problems, a peace agreement that did not include Abdel Wahid, whose faction represented the largest ethnic group in Darfur and the majority of the IDPs, was never likely to achieve its goals. At the end of the Abuja showdown, Abdelbagi Jibril, executive director of the Darfur Relief and Documentation Center, argued that more time should have been taken to achieve an inclusive deal:

> Signing a document for just the sake of signing is not helpful at
> all because at the end of the day, our objective is to have some
> kind of sustainable peace in Darfur, and that cannot be really
> reached unless all the parties, all the parties, I mean all of them,
> come to terms with the kind of agreement that would be helpful
> (VOA News 2006).

As far as Abdel Wahid and JEM were concerned, the AU's insistence on the April 30 deadline and the take-it-or-leave-it status of the DPA were as much the cause of their rejecting the document as was their unhappiness with its content (*Sudan Tribune* 2006h). According to Tadjadine Bechir Niame, one of JEM's delegates at the talks, the essence of the problem was that the agreement "does not address the root causes of the conflict and was not the result of a negotiation between the parties"; upon receiving the DPA, he notes, JEM and the SLM proposed amendments to tackle the causes but "the AU insisted that this is a take it or leave it document. They said they are not going to add even a comma" (*Satya* 2006). Abaker Mohamed Abuelbashar, one of Abdel Wahid's negotiators, puts the case as follows:

> Above all the [rebel] Movements have been given an ultimatum of five days to sign the document or leave it and this is clearly against the prevail[ing] understanding of negotiation norms world-wide which allow the parties to negotiate every issue and reach a compromise position, where everybody is a winner (2006).

This comment sums up the procedural and commensurate political weakness of the DPA, which was a product of externally imposed deadlines, international pressure, and the mediators' drafting efforts rather than a product of negotiated compromises and agreements reached by the parties themselves. Yet the comment is also disingenuous in that it ignores the context in which all of this occurred. As discussed in the following section, the parties were not only unable to forge collectively acceptable compromise positions but scarcely made any attempt to engage in negotiations.

### The Posture of the Parties

PRIOR TO the end of April the parties in Abuja paid no attention to the deadlines demanded by the AU and its partners. For weeks on end they attended meetings without entering into negotiations. They made no attempt to accommodate each other's concerns and showed no interest in trying to find common ground. None of them was willing to make concessions to its opponents. There was no bargaining, let alone collaborative problem solving. Instead, the parties merely reiterated their demands *ad nauseum*; rejected the claims of their adversaries; traded accusations, recriminations, and insults; indulged in grandstanding for the benefit of the international observers; and endeavored to win support for their positions from the mediators.[7]

In January 2006, Salim told the UN Security Council that the negotiations had thus far been wracked by frustratingly slow progress, deep distrust, and an unacceptable level of inflexibility (AU 2006a, 3, 5). In March the head of the AU mediation team, Sam Ibok, captured the key features of the conflict with the following lament:

> While we have been attempting to negotiate a peace agreement,
> the Parties have continued to fight it out on the ground in Darfur
> [and] have violated the 2004 Ceasefire Agreement repeatedly and
> with impunity. . . . Our experience over the past sixteen months
> has led us to conclude that there is neither good faith nor com-
> mitment on the part of any of the Parties. (AU 2006c)

In the second week of April, President Obasanjo and President Sassou-Nguesso failed to budge the parties in high-level talks and the latter urged them to move away from their "fixed and maximalist positions" (*Sudan Tribune* 2006b). Shortly thereafter the government and rebels began talking directly to each other for the first time since January, having spent the previous months meeting separately with the mediators (*Sudan Tribune* 2006c). In light of the direct talks, Salim told the UN Security Council that the conflict "seems at last to be ripe for resolution" although "further frustrating hesitation" was expected from the parties (Reuters 2006; Mail & Guardian 2006). Little progress ensued. On April 15 the rebels denounced the government's "rigid political position that does not allow for any compromise" (*Sudan Tribune* 2006d), and on April 23, Minawi threatened to suspend negotiations if the government did not abandon its hard-line stance (*Sudan Tribune* 2006f). On April 24, the day before the DPA was tabled, Ibok again expressed doubts about the parties' interest in peace (*Sudan Tribune* 2006e); nor was he optimistic two weeks later when interviewed the day before the DPA was signed by the government and Minawi (AFP 2006).

William Zartman's concept of "ripe for resolution," invoked by Salim, provides a useful analytical lens for understanding these dynamics (2001, 8–18; 1989). Zartman's premise is that conflicts are resolvable at certain moments but not others. "Ripe moments" arise when the disputant parties believe both that there is a mutually hurting stalemate—being a situation in which victory is out of reach and the deadlock is painful to all sides—and that negotiations have the potential to resolve the conflict. These are subjective considerations, reflecting the parties' assessment of objective conditions, the balance of power, and the likely trajectory of the struggle. It is therefore quite possible that different conclusions are reached by independent observers and the parties' leaders, and also by different factions within a party.

Zartman notes that the identification of a ripe moment in a given conflict requires research and intelligence to identify the objective and subjective elements (2001, 9–10). While the conflict is still under way, however, the subjective component can be elusive. The parties are likely to downplay the extent to which they are hurting, for fear of exposing their vulnerabilities and appearing weak; they may also be inclined to play up their professed commitment to negotiations lest they be perceived as opposed to peace. Because the stakes are so high, the protagonists' strategic calculations are intensely private affairs. In Abuja the parties' delegates frequently took the mediators and foreign diplomats into their confidence and shared "sensitive" information, but this was invariably a form of public relations and manipulation. Throughout the process the mediators struggled to discern the parties' real calculations, uncertain how much of their intransigence was due to an unwillingness to negotiate and how much was due to an inability to negotiate.

There appeared to be four major reasons for the non-negotiating posture of the parties. First, as in all deadly conflicts, the parties viewed each other with hatred, suspicion, and contempt. These psycho-political dynamics are an intrinsic feature of deep-rooted violent conflict. They are a powerful barrier to dialogue and negotiations, which require at least a small level of trust between the adversaries and a willingness to cooperate with the enemy. One of the primary functions of the mediator is thus to build the parties' confidence in each other and in the process of negotiations (Nathan 1999). This did not happen in Abuja, where there was no thawing of suspicion and enmity. The mediators later identified the mistrust between the parties as one of the foremost constraints on the talks (*Sudan Tribune* 2006m).

More specifically, the government regarded the rebels as unworthy military, political, and negotiating opponents: it believed that they did not pose a serious military threat, were not representative of the people of Darfur, were too divided to ever achieve a unified negotiating stance, and did not have legitimate grievances. Dismissing the SLM and JEM as "rebels without a cause," the government saw no need to make substantial concessions to them. It was also concerned that meeting the rebels' political and economic demands might intensify similar demands from marginalized communities elsewhere in Sudan. Most galling to the government negotiators was their conviction that the Abuja talks did not reflect, and were not a consequence of, the balance of power—the talks were underway only because international intervention had prevented Khartoum from redeploying its military forces from southern Sudan to crush the Darfurian insurgency when it broke out in 2003.

The rebels regarded the government as an evil regime that reneged on peace agreements. It had come to power through a coup; it had a notorious human rights record; it had repeatedly undertaken to disarm the Janjawiid militia and failed to honor that commitment; and it was not implementing faithfully the Comprehensive Peace Agreement concluded in 2005, which had ended the civil war between the government and the Sudan People's Liberation Army/Movement in southern Sudan.[8] In addition, the government had enormous wealth and power. The rebels had neither wealth nor power, and the extreme marginalization of Darfur was one of the fundamental causes of the rebellion. Therefore, according to the rebels, the government could, and should, make extensive concessions, whereas the rebel movements had nothing to give up.

Second, the divisions among the rebels contributed greatly to their non-negotiating posture: there was significant disagreement and mistrust between and within the SLM and JEM, the former being wary of the latter's Islamist agenda; the SLM was split into two factions that were attacking each other in the battlefields of Darfur while the talks were underway; the two factions were themselves loose and tenuous alliances of local leaders; and there were constant quarrels within the Abdel Wahid faction, some of whose members attempted to oust him as their leader during the Abuja process.[9] Salim identified the splits and fragmentation of the movements as another of the major constraints on the talks (*Sudan Tribune* 2006i).

The divisions inhibited progress in several ways. They were an unwelcome distraction as the rebels focused on internal disputes and intrigue at the expense of the official talks. They also heightened the climate of suspicion, making the rebels afraid that the government or the mediators might use divide-and-rule tactics against them. Most importantly, the divisions made it virtually impossible for the movements to adopt a flexible negotiating stance. In light of the difficulty the rebels experienced in formulating common positions, and their fear of divide and rule, the most viable and prudent course of action was to hold fast to maximalist bottom lines. In the middle of February, the Abdel Wahid faction refused to meet in the same room as the Minawi faction and the mediators were thereafter unable to convene plenary negotiating sessions. While this condition prevailed there was little hope of building trust and common ground with the government.

Third, the balance of power was such that it reinforced intransigence on all sides. The rebel movements had little military leverage; many of their representatives at the talks were inexperienced and unconfident negotiators; they were confronted in the field and in Abuja by a strong and sophisticated adversary; and they were unfamiliar with the concepts and practicalities of ceasefire arrangements. They were consequently frightened of being outwitted in the negotiations and especially scared of agreeing to anything that might weaken them militarily or expose them to government attack. Intransigence can be the natural refuge of weak parties in negotiations. Perversely, as in this case, it is also sometimes a negotiating option chosen by strong parties that are not threatened and see no necessity to make concessions.

Fourth, most of the parties in Abuja appeared to view the battlefield as the strategic arena of conflict and the negotiations as simply a tactical arena. Given the international outcry over the humanitarian crisis in Darfur, the parties had to be seen as engaging in peace talks, but this was not the principal means of defending and advancing their interests. As Zartman points out, participation in negotiations does not in itself indicate the existence of a ripe moment; it may be merely a tactical interlude or a sop to external pressure, without any serious intent by the parties to look for a joint solution (2001).

Minawi seemed to believe that his interests were best served through a war of maneuver against the militarily weaker grouping of Abdel Wahid. In the midst of the negotiations, his forces in Darfur seized strategic locations from Abdel Wahid with little public protest other than from Abdel Wahid. The government, on the other hand, seemed to believe that its interests would be served through a war of attrition. It was not overly troubled by the weak international pressure on it; it did not have a strong sense of responsibility to protect civilians in Darfur; it was not under any great military threat from the rebels; it was not incurring onerous military costs since it relied on the Janjawiid as a proxy force; and the rebels were busy fighting each other. For its part, JEM had a national political agenda that would not be met by a peace agreement for Darfur and, although the organization lacked a sizable fighting force, its military activities in western (and eastern) Sudan helped to maintain its profile and status as a liberation movement.

Abdel Wahid, whose community and forces were being hammered by the Janjawiid, the government, and Minawi, was the only leader who keenly wanted a settlement. He was therefore well placed to seize the initiative in the talks and occupy the high ground internationally as a leader desirous of peace. He did not exploit this potential and ended up being seen by the AU and its partners as the main spoiler. In his discussions with the mediators he was erratic and indecisive, projecting confusion and backtracking on promises (*Sudan Tribune* 2006i); in January and February 2006 he entered into secret talks with the government and then pulled out just as an agreement looked imminent (ICG 2006, 2). His formal demands, on the other hand, remained the same from the start to the end of the Abuja process. This was not a tenable negotiating posture; the demands reflected legitimate grievances but the rigidity amounted to a "win-lose" approach in relation to the government and had no prospect of success. For all his weaknesses, though, Abdel Wahid was not an opportunist. He sought an agreement that satisfied the needs of his constituency and he was convinced that the DPA did not do this.[10]

As a result of the four sets of factors outlined above, the parties were not ready for a negotiated settlement. None of them was willing to meet the essential requirements for successful negotiations in a civil war, namely cooperation with the enemy, reciprocal concessions, and mutual accommodation of each other's needs and interests.

## The Pressure on the Mediators

FOR ALL THE FUSS made by the international partners about the violence in Darfur, they did not provide guaranteed funding for the peace talks. Instead, a small number of donors provided grants retrospectively to cover expenses already incurred and warned repeatedly that funding could dry up in the absence of a quick accord. Aside from the anxiety this caused the mediators, the reliance on uncertain deficit funding was not sustainable. In January 2006, Salim complained to the UN Security Council that the funding situation was extremely precarious (AU 2006a, 9); when Djinnit told the mediators to wrap up by the end of February, he cited the lack of funds as the main reason; and when the Peace and Security Council announced in March that the DPA had to be concluded by the end of April, the mediators were informed that the talks would not be funded thereafter.[11]

Whereas the deadline diplomacy was ignored by the parties until the climax of the Abuja process in April, it was taken very seriously by the mediators who were obliged to adhere to the targets set by their donors and political masters. Reinforced by the acute funding pressure, the deadline diplomacy had several negative consequences for the mediation.

First, the ever-looming deadlines made it pointless to develop a comprehensive mediation strategy and plan. If the talks were always due to shut down in a matter of weeks, then there was no need to prepare a plan of action for the following six months. The deadlines inhibited a programmatic effort to build momentum gradually over time and led instead to an ad hoc approach that proceeded in fits and starts. The deadline diplomacy *was* the strategy and the plan, and it was far too simplistic, vacuous, and rigid for this purpose. Given the nature of the conflict in Darfur, what was required was a multifaceted plan with objectives, strategies, taskings, and resource allocations not only in relation to the parties in Abuja, but also in relation to Sudan's neighboring states, the people of Darfur, AU and UN headquarters, key AU member states, and the power blocs that comprise the Sudanese state.

Second, the deadlines and the imperative of producing the DPA by a certain date severely reduced the mediators' control of the process and constrained their flexibility, options, and ability to make strategic decisions on the basis of their best judgment. For example, in late February and early March, confronted by the deadlock in Abuja and the fierce fighting in Darfur, the mediation team debated at length whether it was more likely to make progress by putting forward a comprehensive peace agreement aimed at addressing the root causes of the conflict or by tabling an enhanced human-itarian ceasefire agreement aimed at reducing the level of violence and improving the climate for negotiations. The debate was rendered moot by the Peace and Security Council's decree that the comprehensive agreement had to be concluded by the end of April.

By way of further example, the mediators believed that the rebels' intransigence was due partly to a lack of expertise with and confidence in negotiations, and in the modalities of a permanent ceasefire and other issues. The mediators consequently provided training to the rebels, at their request, but were unable to do this properly; in light of the deadlines, the requisite training was considered a waste of time. Nor were the mediators able to explore procedural alternatives to the ineffective plenary sessions with large delegations in Abuja, such as relocating to Darfur and making the dialogue more inclusive, or moving to the AU's headquarters in Addis Ababa and limiting the talks to party leaders. In short, the external pressure fixed in place a process and trajectory in which neither the mediators nor the parties had any confidence, but from which little deviation was possible.

Third, the deadline diplomacy contributed indirectly to the absence of negotiations between the parties. In order to comply with the calls to speed up and meet unrealistic deadlines, the mediation team prepared position papers that moved far ahead of the parties as it tried to bridge the yawning gaps between them. This reinforced the parties' misconception that the mediators were arbitrators rather than facilitators of dialogue and negotiations. In response to the mediators' papers, the parties applauded what they liked, rejected the rest, and devoted much time and energy to lobbying the mediators. To the great frustration of the mediation team, the parties' most strenuous negotiating efforts were directed at the mediators and not at each other.

Fourth, the tight deadlines made it impossible for the mediators to communicate in a meaningful way with the people of Darfur and with important groups that were not represented at the talks. Similarly, the rebel negotiators were unable to brief and consult properly with their constituencies. Darfurian civil society had no opportunity to shape, or even view, the content of the draft DPA and could not conceivably have acquired a sense of ownership of it. As Pronk observed, the perception of many Darfurians was that the agreement had been forced on them (2006). So great was the geographical and political distance between Abuja and Darfur, that when violent protests against the DPA broke out after the signing ceremony, the mediators were convinced that much of the opposition was based on an incomplete and inaccurate reading of the document.

The AU believed that the envisaged the Darfur-Darfur Dialogue and Consultation (DDDC) would ensure popular ownership of the agreement and secure the support of stakeholders who were not present at the negotiations (AU 2006d; *Sudan Tribune* 2006m; DPA 2006, ch. 4). This perspective was badly flawed. The DDDC was only due to start after the agreement's entry into force, at which point the document would have been set in stone. Groups that felt aggrieved by their exclusion from Abuja were unlikely to have been assuaged by consultations at that stage. Indeed, the agreement states explicitly that the DDDC cannot "reopen [the DPA] for further negotiation" (paragraph 461[a]). This limitation reduces considerably the scope, utility, and credibility of the DDDC process. It creates the risk that the process will fail to meet popular expectations, generating resentment and conflict. At the time of writing, the DDDC was not yet properly underway.

Fifth, the haste induced by the deadline diplomacy precluded effective mediation and the parties' ownership of the DPA. Barring a decisive military victory, the only sustainable solution to a civil war is a settlement shaped and embraced by the protagonists. A settlement cannot be forced down their throats since their consent and cooperation are required to implement the agreement and adhere to its terms thereafter. Consequently, the mediator's job is to help the parties overcome their enmity and mistrust, build their confidence in negotiations, and facilitate dialogue, bargaining, and collaborative problem solving (Nathan 1999). This always requires protracted efforts and immense patience. It cannot be done in fits and starts between externally imposed short-term deadlines.

In lieu of mediation, the deadline diplomacy led to the production, by the mediators, of a peace agreement covering cardinal issues on which the parties disagreed bitterly; an unreasonably brief period for the parties' consideration and approval of the document; and a burst of intense pressure on the parties in the dying moments of the process. Each of these elements was antithetical to the parties' ownership of the agreement.

Politically and psychologically, the question of ownership is most sensitive and important in relation to the compromises contained in a peace settlement. Compromises entail concessions to a hated adversary and give rise to perceptions of weakness and defeat. They have to be sold to militants in each party, and make negotiators and leaders vulnerable to accusations of betraying the struggle. Responding to criticism from the rebels and analysts that the DPA favored the government, the AU was at pains to insist that the compromises in the text were unavoidable because of the balance of power:

> Throughout the entire process of negotiations at Abuja, the African Union Mediation was constrained by several important factors. An elementary reality, that sometimes appears to be lost on some commentators, is that the Movements did not win a military victory and were therefore not in a position to impose their terms on the Government of Sudan. Any deal reached involved the SLM/A and JEM making compromises on dearly-held political objectives. (*Sudan Tribune* 2006m)

This argument reflects the broader truth that compromise is an intrinsic feature of negotiated settlements in civil wars, but it misses the equally fundamental point that the DPA and its compromises were crafted by the mediators and not the parties, enabling the mediators, but not the parties, to claim ownership of the agreement. Salim was thus able to refer to provisions in the DPA as the "mediators' proposals," "our proposals," and the "mediation's compromise" (AU 2006e). Abdel Wahid's faction, on the other hand, was able to insist that "the legitimate question is on what basis the Movement have to sign an agreement, [for] which it did not participate in its discussion?" (Abuelbashar 2006, 5). According to a JEM official, "we have rejected the proposed peace accord because we do not think that the document is a product of a negotiated settlement. In fact, we think that this document is a product of intimidation, bullying, and diplomatic terrorism."[12]

On May 7, six members of the mediation team, including its head, Sam Ibok, issued a 3,000-word "Open Letter to Those Members of the

Movements Who Are Still Reluctant to Sign." They sought to ease the rebels' objections and fears by explaining aspects of the DPA and suggested that "many of the suspicions about this Agreement are based on misunderstanding and the fact that many of you have not had time to study the text in detail, and understand what it provides."[13] This statement, made after the DPA had been signed by the government and Minawi, is a telling indictment of the inappropriate deadlines and haste. The AU ended the formal talks and closed the agreement to negotiation and amendment before many of the rebel negotiators were able to comprehend the document, never mind embrace it.

## Conclusion

THE DEADLINE diplomacy for Darfur, which aimed to produce a quick accord, was motivated chiefly by the appalling level of death and destruction in western Sudan. It was also driven by a range of geopolitical factors. The other major strategies for tackling the crisis—tough sanctions and the deployment of a UN force with a robust mandate—were not attractive or even feasible in the short- to medium-term. These strategies are always difficult to implement, their impact is not predictable, their efficacy is uncertain, they are no substitute for a genuine peace agreement, and, in the case of Darfur, they were opposed within the UN Security Council by Russia and China. In addition to the humanitarian benefits, a quick accord would end the political struggles around these issues. It would also meet the U.S. desire for reduced tension with Khartoum, regarded by Washington as an ally in the "war on terror,"[14] and enable the U.S. to concentrate its attention on the Comprehensive Peace Agreement, which had led to a new Interim National Constitution for Sudan and encompassed an arena of conflict deemed more important than Darfur.

Underlying the deadline diplomacy, moreover, was a growing frustration among the funders of the negotiations, who were covering not only the costs of the mediation but also the accommodation and subsistence costs of the sizable rebel delegations in Abuja. These costs might have been bearable had the parties been making steady progress, but no material advancement had been recorded between the first and the seventh rounds of talks. The donor governments had nothing positive to report to their parliaments and the future looked bleak. They were not willing to continue funding unproductive talks whose successful conclusion seemed improbable. On the other hand, jettisoning the talks without a peace accord would have been hugely unpopular with the Western constituencies agitating for strong action on Darfur. From the donors' perspective, the talks had to be brought to a close with an agreement on the table and, if at all possible, with the parties' signatures on that agreement.

Notwithstanding these various rational motivations, the deadline diplomacy reflected a deeply flawed understanding of peacemaking in civil wars. There are numerous failed mediation initiatives in Africa that similarly, and as mistakenly, sought a quick settlement and relied on strong-arm tactics, underestimating the complexity of the conflict and neglecting the imperative of ownership (Nathan 1999). A comparative study of some of these cases, published in 2004, led to the following general observation that describes almost perfectly what happened in Abuja in 2006:

> Mediators deployed by states and multinational organisations frequently focus more on the solutions to a conflict than on the process of peacemaking. They formulate solutions, endeavour to win the parties' consent thereto, and press for rapid results through a combination of persuasion and leverage. They might adopt this approach because they regard the solution as fairly obvious and consider the demands of one or more of the parties to be completely unreasonable. They might also be concerned about the high level of fatalities and the financial cost of a drawn-out engagement. Whatever their motivation, however, a mediator's confidence that he or she can quickly bring the parties to their senses is both naïve and arrogant. (Nathan 2004, 71)

In the case of Darfur, the deadline diplomacy inhibited effective mediation, resulted in a peace agreement that did not achieve peace, and sowed divisions that exacerbated the conflict. As with all civil wars, the humanitarian need for a quick accord was indisputable, but there is never a quick fix.

These wars are social phenomena whose causes, dynamics, and contested issues are multiple, complex, and intractable, and the difficulty of resolution is heightened immeasurably by the protagonists' mutual hatred and suspicion. In these circumstances, shortcuts, and quick fixes are invariably cul-de-sacs.

For a combination of political, psychological, and pragmatic reasons, a peace agreement has to be owned by the disputant parties. They have to sell the agreement to their constituents; they have to come to terms, in particular, with its compromises; they have to implement it; and they have to adhere to its provisions in the long run. The Abuja experience demonstrates that there is no benefit to be gained from pressuring the parties to sign an accord to which they are not committed; and the process by which an accord is prepared and concluded determines its acceptability and legitimacy, and is therefore no less critical than the content.

Finally, it is necessary to comment briefly on certain inferences that might be implied by the preceding discussion, but would not in fact be justified. The claim that the deadline diplomacy had many negative consequences does not imply that a more patient and supportive approach by international actors would definitely have yielded a positive outcome. Given the parties' intransigence, the talks might simply have dragged on interminably and inconclusively. For this reason too, it cannot be claimed that a different mediation strategy or style would necessarily have borne fruit. Mediators can stimulate and exploit opportunities for progress but there is little they can do if the disputant parties refuse to engage in negotiations.

The suggestion that the Sudanese parties were not ready for a negotiated settlement does not imply that international actors should have stood by idly in the face of the mass killing and displacement of people in Darfur. If a conflict is not ripe for resolution, then the challenge is precisely to determine how best to alter the strategic calculations of the belligerents and generate a ripe moment through a mixture of incentives and pressure (Zartman 2001, 14–15). Although the impact of punitive action in high intensity conflict is unpredictable, it seems clear that the approach adopted in relation to Darfur, where the international community issued threats and then failed consistently to act on them, emboldened the belligerents.[15]

There is sufficient evidence to argue that the DPA heightened the conflict and made its resolution more difficult. Yet it is overstating the case to maintain that "much of the violence [in Darfur] is a direct result of the shortcomings in the Abuja agreement, particularly the failure to provide meaningful international guarantees and guarantors" (Reeves 2006b). The international community's failure to provide adequate support to the AU peacekeeping force in Darfur, which cried in vain for resources to oversee a tenuous ceasefire and protect civilians, has been especially shameful, but the responsibility for the violence lies squarely with the perpetrators of the violence. The heaviest burden falls on Khartoum, whose marginalization of Darfur provoked the rebellion and whose wanton destruction of communities thereafter invoked the charge of genocide (Leitenberg 2006, 34–60; Kristof 2006).

Similarly, the deadline diplomacy was counterproductive, but the failure to produce a viable peace agreement in Abuja is attributable to the parties. In a major address on April 30, Salim stated that the mediators had agonized over every detail in the DPA before presenting it to the delegations, had considered the pros and cons of every article and paragraph, and had always been guided by concern for the people of Darfur and responsibility for ending their suffering (AU 2006e). None of the parties could have made any of these claims. This was greatly to their discredit and to the detriment of the agreement.

# II

## Darfur's Deadline:
## The Final Days of the Abuja Peace Process

ALEX DE WAAL

THE DARFUR PEACE AGREEMENT (DPA) is controversial. Representatives of many governments were present during the final negotiating session in the grounds of the presidential villa in Abuja on May 4–5, 2006, most of whom subsequently argued that the agreement was the only basis for achieving peace in Darfur.[1] Dr. Majzoub al Khalifa, who signed the DPA on behalf of the government of Sudan, has argued strongly that it is a legitimate agreement and that those who oppose it are "outlaws" or even "terrorists." On this basis, the Sudan government insisted that the groups that had refused to sign the DPA—the Sudan Liberation Movement (SLM) headed by Abdel Wahid al Nur and the Justice and Equality Movement (JEM)—be expelled from the Ceasefire Commission and its political oversight body, the Joint Commission. The African Union and the United States agreed with this proposal at the time.

There has also been strident condemnation of both the substance of the DPA and the procedure whereby it was finalized. Some of these criticisms are cited in Laurie Nathan's contribution to this volume. Foreign activists have also criticized the substance of the DPA (International Crisis Group 2006b) or written it off as "a meaningless piece of paper" (Reeves 2006a). Minni Arkoy Minawi and his supporters have been caught in the middle and their public views on the DPA have vacillated.

This chapter has the modest aim of documenting some aspects of the final days of the mediation effort under the auspices of the African Union in

Abuja, based primarily on the author's notes from his own involvement in the mediation as an advisor to the chief mediator, Dr. Salim Ahmed Salim. These were the critical weeks in the search for peace in Darfur and much of what happened has not been adequately reported. The account focuses on May 2–5, when the "quartet" of the U.S., Great Britain, Canada, and the European Union negotiated "enhancements" to the DPA proposals and presented them to the parties, and the subsequent week when individual members of the AU mediation made last-gasp efforts to bring Abdel Wahid al Nur into the agreement.

The events prior to the formulation of the draft DPA are detailed in the chapters by Dawit Toga and Laurie Nathan. One further explanatory detail is in order, namely how a mediation paper became an almost-final set of proposals. At an internal meeting on March 3, the AU mediation team discussed how to take the negotiation process forward in the face of the very slow progress in the talks thus far. Some members of the team argued that progress would be expedited if the mediation presented a comprehensive paper covering the three areas of power sharing, wealth sharing, and security arrangements which would then be the basis for further discussions between the parties. Those negotiations would be conducted on the principle of give-and-take based on the proposals on the table, so that if one side demanded a concession on one point, it would need to be prepared to give a concession in another area. Others argued that this "big bang" approach risked derailing the peace process and it was preferable to focus on obtaining agreement on a ceasefire first. The "ceasefire first" argument won the day. However, Salim requested the heads of the different commissions to prepare compromise proposals in their respective areas, to be ready should the need arise.[2] Until the "mini-summit" of April 8–9, convened by President Olusegun Obasanjo of Nigeria and President Denis Sassou-Nguesso of the Republic of Congo, the "ceasefire first" strategy remained in place. Following this meeting and the UN Security Council discussion on April 11, Salim instructed the mediation team, under its team leader ambassador Sam Ibok, to finalize a document containing a set of comprehensive proposals, so that negotiations on a comprehensive peace agreement for Darfur could be underway during April.

The mediation presented its draft proposals to the parties on April 25. They comprised 510 paragraphs in 87 pages. Majzoub al Khalifa expressed satisfaction. Official Sudanese media cameramen photographed him holding the Darfur Peace Agreement. The movements' representatives expressed shock and rejection, and Abdel Wahid did not turn up to the session in which the document was presented. The Arabic version was given to the delegates on April 28. Also on that day it became clear to the parties and the members of the mediation team that the April 30 deadline was qualitatively different to all previous deadlines. Conducting negotiations on a comprehensive text would not be considered sufficient to satisfy the UN Security Council demand. But as the evening of April 30 approached, it was clear that the movements' leaders had only just begun to digest the contents of the document. In particular, they professed shock at the power-sharing proposals, which came as a surprise to them.

## April 30–May 4

IN AN INTERNAL mediation meeting before a plenary session on the evening of April 30, Salim proposed that he would "stop the clock" pending the arrival of African heads of state and high-level representatives of the international community to try to unlock the impasse. In the subsequent plenary, the U.S. ambassador to Khartoum, Cameron Hume, formally requested a 48-hour extension of the deadline, which Salim duly granted. In that session, Majzoub al Khalifa announced that the Sudan government intended to initial the agreement as it stood.

During the day of May 2, an array of politicians and diplomats descended upon Abuja. U.S. Deputy Secretary of State Robert Zoellick had arrived with a team. British Secretary of State for International Development Hilary Benn also arrived. They met with the mediation and divided up their tasks: Zoellick would "enhance" the security arrangements text while Benn worked on the power sharing. This duo became a quartet with the addition of Canada (represented by its ambassador to the UN, John Rock) and the European Union (represented by its special envoy for Sudan, Pekka

Haavisto). During the last four days, the members of the AU mediation team were almost entirely spectators.

Zoellick focused on two aspects of the security arrangements. The first was the number of rebel troops to be integrated into the Sudan armed forces and the conditions of that integration. In the April 30 plenary, ambassador Hume had announced that he had obtained an agreement with Khartoum to integrate 5,000 rebel combatants into the army. Minni insisted that his fighters regarded going through a disarmament and demobilization program as tantamount to death. In response, Zoellick proposed the higher figure of 8,000 including a number of senior posts and that integrated units should comprise one-third or one-half former rebels. General Ismat al Zain on behalf of the government insisted that 8,000 was larger than the total number of rebel forces.

The second aspect was the disarmament of the Janjawiid. The security commission discussions on this had been cut short on April 4 by the requirement to present a ceasefire document to the parties before the "mini-summit" of April 8–9. The text's provisions for disarming the Janjawiid were unacceptable to both sides. The government objected to Paragraph 415, which gave a five-month timetable for disarming the Janjawiid as a precondition for the rebel forces moving to assembly zones. General Ismat said that disarming the militia in this timeframe was simply impossible and would therefore stall the implementation of the agreement.[3] Abdel Wahid agreed that it could not be done, but Minni wanted tougher provisions. Zoellick proposed tightening the requirements but also tried to keep within what his own military advisers said was realistic.

Throughout the evening of May 2, Zoellick pressed the government negotiators on every point. This was the session in which the U.S. put its maximum pressure on Khartoum. Majzoub and General Ismat argued each point, extracting some concessions from Zoellick. The number of rebel fighters to be integrated was kept at 5,000, with a further 3,000 provided with special training. More detailed provisions on the Janjawiid were written in. Negotiations between the U.S. and Sudan government continued late into the night of May 2. At midnight, a second 48-hour extension of the deadline was announced.

The following day, the U.S. team revised the security text and Zoellick presented the new points to Minni and Abdel Wahid. The U.S. team had expected Minni to focus exclusively on security issues, at this point were surprised that he raised objections to the power-sharing text as well.

Hilary Benn was tasked with enhancing the power-sharing provisions to make them more acceptable to the movements. On May 2, the British team closely examined the text and began work. They closed one obvious loophole, which was that the draft made no mention of local commissioners and their deputies. They increased the powers of the senior assistant to the president, the most senior position awarded to the Darfurian movements, giving him greater direct authority over the Transitional Darfur Regional Authority. Their greatest headache was the division of positions at the state level. The mediation had sought to follow the principle of parity of representation between government and opposition in its proposals, but the need to include members of parties other than the ruling National Congress Party and the SLM and JEM created an arithmetic fix. Despite many discussions throughout the seventh round, members of the mediation had not reached a robust consensus on how to interpret "parity" and the April 25 proposals were based on a 50/50 split between the NCP and all other parties combined. The British enhancements increased the movements' representation in the Darfur state legislatures from eighteen to twenty-one and provided more ministerial posts.

On the evening of May 3, the members of the quartet met with Salim and Ibok and presented their proposals for enhancements. These were discussed and agreed, and the U.S. and British teams went to their respective offices to finalize the wording. A final round of bilateral meetings was conducted during the day of May 4, during which the enhancements were presented to the parties. Zoellick obtained a commitment from Minni that he was satisfied. Majzoub refused to give his final word on behalf of the government. Abdel Wahid and Khalil Ibrahim continued to express their discontent.

Working to fill the "X" in the wealth-sharing text, members of the quartet obtained a promise from the government that it would make an initial payment of $30 million into the compensation fund.

In the evening of May 4, the Americans' closing strategy became clear. A final meeting would be convened at Aguda House in the grounds of the presidential villa. Obasanjo would chair and invite in the leaders of the movements, one by one, and ask if they agreed with the enhanced text. Minni would be first, then Abdel Wahid, then Khalil. Minni was considered the deal breaker: if he failed to agree, there could be no DPA. If he agreed, the assent of the others was desirable but not essential. On the basis of a yes from Minni and hopefully at least one of the others, Majzoub would be invited in to give a response on behalf of Khartoum. His "yes" was not assured as he had raised numerous objections to the enhancements. If he then agreed, there would be a deal. The leaders of the two sides would not actually meet until they had separately agreed on the text. Uncertain as to the outcome, the mediation prepared two public statements, known internally as the "wedding announcement" and the "obituary." In the event, neither was used.

### May 4–5

THE FINAL mediation session of the Abuja peace process began at 10:15 p.m. on the evening of May 4. Four tables were laid out in a square in a hall of Aguda House. At the head of the table were places for President Obasanjo and President Sassou-Nguesso. Next to them were Professor Alpha Oumar Konaré, Chairperson of the African Union Commission, Salim Ahmed Salim, and the Libyan envoy Ali Treki. Opposite them were Zoellick, Assistant Secretary of State Jendayi Frazer and their team, Hilary Benn and his team, Allan Rock and his team, and Pekka Haavisto. Along one side were ambassadors and envoys from Egypt, the Arab League, the Netherlands, Norway, France, and Italy. The final side of the square comprised representatives of the AU.

Obasanjo opened the meeting with some formalities and Zoellick explained his negotiations over the previous three days, including the new language on Janjawiid disarmament and a new figure of 8,000 movements' combatants to be integrated into the army or given special training. Zoellick reported that Minni had indicated that he was favorable. Zoellick said that Abdel Wahid was positive on the security issues, but was still raising political issues. "Does he have the courage to say yes?" he wondered. He described JEM as "non-committal." Lastly, he said that Khartoum had accepted the non-security items but had voiced five concerns over the security issues—that is, it had not fully indicated acceptance of the final text. Benn then briefed the group on the enhancements to the power-sharing text and Khartoum's offer on compensation.

At 11:15 Obasanjo called for Minni. A few minutes before Minni entered, ambassador Hume led Zoellick out of the room. In Zoellick's absence, Benn took the floor to summarize the non-security issues. At 11:30 Obasanjo turned to Minni: "This is the moment of decision. What decision we make here tonight—or fail to make—will have monumental implications for Darfur and for Sudan. This opportunity will not come again. . . A grave responsibility falls on you." Speaking quietly, Minni gave a long preamble, and then concluded, "We have just consulted. We have been receiving phone calls from Darfur. . . We have reached our conviction that the security arrangements are acceptable, but in power and wealth areas, there is more needing to be done. The Darfur authorities do not have the necessary representation for the movements. We want parity of representation in Darfur." Having expected Minni's assent, the room fell silent. Obasanjo pressed for clarification, and Minni explained that this was a common position of the movements and that the matters in question were minor. Benn responded, "If these changes are not momentous, as you say, then we can also ask, 'do they matter?'"

Meanwhile, Zoellick had re-entered. At three minutes before the midnight deadline he took the floor and spoke coldly. "Mr. Minawi, I am disappointed. I expect people to keep their word to me. I won't support any change in this document . . . If you want to choose whoever, like JEM, you can do it—or you can choose the United States." Zoellick explained that Minni had given him his word that he would sign, and was not keeping it now. He reminded Minni that the proposal included democratic elections. "I cannot believe that are dropping peace for a few more seats." Then at precisely midnight, he said, "Have no doubt where I stand. I am a good friend and I am a fearsome enemy."

After a further twenty-five minutes of discussion, Obasanjo declared a recess to give Minni the opportunity to consult and return later in the night. Meanwhile the meeting broke for food, reconvening at 1:00 a.m. A few minutes later, Abdel Wahid entered with four colleagues. He gave a long speech about Darfur's history and how he had compromised on his initial demands.

He stressed the need for security and for control over executive authority in Darfur. Moving to security arrangements, he said, "The documents submitted are acceptable. We have accepted that part." Then he came to his central demand. "But we have a historic responsibility in the SLM, and the root of the problem is political. We have a humanitarian problem, but to solve the root causes we should address the political problem at its root. This is the minimum right of our people. The power-sharing document did not reach this minimum." He called for stronger guarantees and more time to negotiate.

Zoellick responded first. "This is not a time for speeches. I suggest you look to the future. If you pass up this historic opportunity, to whom do you intend to turn? If you pass this up you will remain victims forever." He then turned to the issue of guarantees and produced a letter from President George W. Bush which he read out. The letter included the words, "I assure you that the United States will strongly support the implementation of the Darfur Peace Accord. I will insist on holding accountable all those who are not supporting the implementation of the Accord." After him, many other international representatives spoke. Obasanjo stressed, "If there is no agreement tonight it may all be lost. There is a very thin line between victory and defeat." Benn asked Abdel Wahid, "Will you remembered for achieving nothing, or for getting a fine compromise?" Obasanjo concluded, "We stand for the victimized. You go and decide." Abdel Wahid asked to return to the hotel to consult his team. Obasanjo blazed: "Who the hell do you think you are?" Then Abdel Wahid's chief negotiator, Abdel Rahman Musa intervened, explaining, "The plan for tonight was not clear to us. The negotiating delegation here in the hall is not yet fully authorized. We ask your indulgence to consult our colleagues." Obasanjo gave leave to Abdel Wahid and his team to hold a meeting of their negotiating council in Aguda House.

At 2:15 a.m. the JEM delegation entered, and Obasanjo introduced the topic of the night. Khalil then spoke at length. "I am keen for a comprehensive and lasting peace . . . the AU could have produced a text and crowned the seventh round, but we were disappointed. . . We were keen to see the new draft produced by the U.S. and UK, but this draft has not met our core demands. . . . This doesn't address the demand for compensation. There are demonstrations around the world and in Sudan pressuring us. . . . The document has no reference to budgets for rebuilding Darfur, or for development...There is no region for Darfur.... The Darfurians must govern themselves...There is no representation [of Darfurians in national institutions] accounting for population size in the civil service or the judiciary. There are three million Darfurians in Khartoum but we are given no representation there. The people of Darfur are 40 percent of Sudan's population ... The senior assistant to the president has no powers.... The security arrangements are generally okay, but there are some shortcomings. JEM has more than 8,000 troops, who should be integrated into the army at the end of the transition period. The government should pay all the costs of the movement forces including salaries during the transition.... The draft gives the Janjawiid to the government with no timeframe for disarming them." Khalil concluded, "I express my deep regret that the AU has not dealt with the situation in an objective and just manner. I cannot sign. The document needs radical modifications."

Obasanjo was abrupt. "You must take responsibility for what happens in Darfur. Go. Leave." Khalil interrupted him: "The AU will be responsible too." Obasanjo became angry and sarcastic. "The AU started this war? Are you saying the AU started this war? What nonsense. You are utterly irresponsible. What the hell are you saying?" He thumped the table. "An African of good family who is well brought up does not treat his elders like that. I can see that you are not from a good family or well brought up."[4] He paused. "See what will happen!" Obasanjo gestured dismissively, "The floor is open."

International representatives lined up to condemn Khalil. He was accused of not having read the document and of being disrespectful. The Libyan representative Ali Treki called him "mad." Zoellick remained silent until called upon by Obasanjo and then said: "I was not intending to speak as I prefer not to waste any more time with this man." Obasanjo concluded: "You insulted us." Khalil replied: "I didn't mean any offence that might have been taken. We need knowledge and patience. I represent the people, the will of the people." He turned to address the mediation, "Reconsider how to manage our cause and don't blame us." Obasanjo said curtly: "JEM you can go." At 3:15 Khalil and his team walked away.

Five minutes later, Minni was ushered back in. He came straight to the point, "We appreciate the document. However we want one small point—we want to enhance one small point, which is power in Darfur. If you can help us, we can bring the others and bring this to agreement in the next few hours." Obasanjo spoke slowly, clearly masking his impatience by emphasizing each word: "What specifically do you want? What specifically do you want?" Minni specified: "We want parity in Darfur legislative councils." Obsanjo and Zoellick were conciliatory, explaining the government's objections to giving more seats to the movements. Zoellick said, "I recognize you are trying to represent the movements. But it is inconceivable to throw away peace for a few seats. If we could give you more we would." Zoellick then read out Bush's personal letter to Minni. This was identical to the letter to Abdel Wahid, except that it emphasized security arrangements, whereas the one to Abdel Wahid had stressed power sharing. Minni expressed his appreciation and continued, "However we would like you to appreciate what we are saying. I appreciate you all. But the seats are necessary. We cannot convince our people except with some things." He asked for a few more hours to convince his colleagues. For twenty minutes, the international representatives pressed Minni but he held firm, insisting that he needed more time. Obasanjo proposed that he return at 9:00 a.m. Zoellick intervened: "I was told once today that Mr. Minawi could agree. I will only agree to come back at 9 a.m. if I can be certain of agreement." Minni replied, "God willing there is no deception and we shall come at the time agreed upon with all blessing." Obasanjo commented, this answer is "partly political and partly divine, half carnal and half spiritual. Minni, we take that."

Immediately, Abdel Wahid entered with a delegation of 22, who lined up to stand behind him. Unlike the earlier session in which he was relaxed, this time he was visibly anxious. His position had hardened. "We consulted with our team, field commanders, IDP [internally displaced persons] camp representatives. They insist we must include our negotiating platform, our just negotiating platform." He asked for American and British guarantees for implementation "like in Bosnia." Zoellick riposted, "I don't know what more you want than a statement by the President of the United States that I will strongly support the implementation of the peace accord." Zoellick offered additional support for making the SLM into a political party to help it win the elections. "What more can I give?" Abdel Wahid clarified: "The document must be developed, in the fields of power sharing and compensation."

Obasanjo: "If there can be no more enhancement you won't sign?" Abdel Wahid: "Yes that's what I said." Zoellick's voice was tired. "I clarified compensation and I answered each one of your concerns... I conclude that you are not serious about an agreement. Going forward, we are parting ways for good. If you think there is an alternative, you are dead wrong. And I mean, dead wrong." He paused and repeated, with emphasis on "dead." Then he continued, "I will not accept bad faith... You will not see me again until there is accountability for actions at the UN Security Council. You are making a decision, you will live with it and you will die with it." Obasanjo had also had enough. He warned that Darfur would be neglected, would become a forgotten war. "The decision you are taking today is a decision that cannot be undone. You are throwing away your chance for compensation, for power sharing... If you win the elections you will be in charge. You want to throw that overboard? That I cannot regard as responsibility. The story can be told one day and you cannot hide it." Obasanjo concluded: "We shall be here at nine if you want to see us we will see you, otherwise au revoir." It was 4:55 and the meeting broke up.

The session reconvened promptly at 9:00 a.m. At 9:15 Minni entered, looking tired and expressionless, somber. Obasanjo welcomed him, "What have you got for us?" Minni said, "We have accepted the document with important reservations concerning power." "Objections" had become "reservations"—he had indicated that he would sign. He continued, asking for international help for Darfur to escape from its predicament. He said, "We consulted but at the end of the day the decision is mine as chairman of the movement." There was a long pause before Obasanjo asked for applause. Obasanjo explained that the task was not concluded—next he would invite the government delegation for its response. Meanwhile, the heads of delegations congratulated Minni. Zoellick added, "Those who don't sign are outlaws to the process." Minni repeated quietly, "Indeed this is a historic moment. It is sad that our allies in peace are not here." He asked for discussions with both Abdel Wahid and Khalil. Obasanjo refused, "No. What we have we keep, then we try to get more."

At 10:20 a.m. Majzoub led his delegation to the table. Obasanjo apologized for keeping them waiting the whole night. He explained the story. "As a government the initiative is essentially yours . . . you have more to keep than to receive. We called you for your reaction to minor modifications. Anything acceptable to the Sudanese parties is acceptable to us." Majzoub gave a long introduction and numerous greetings. He told the story of the conflict as beginning among tribes and getting out of hand, and how Sudan accepted international mediation. He congratulated the AU. Then Majzoub spelled out his main reservations over the agreement. "One, we want the President to nominate the head of the Darfur security arrangements implementation commission, with the deputy to the movements." His second problem concerned foreign combatants in Darfur (i.e., Chadians). "It is only the government of Sudan that can disarm them, but insofar as the movements become part of the government then that is okay." His final reservation was on the numbers of combatants to be integrated, saying that the figure of 5,000 was too high. Majzoub concluded, "These are technical remarks for the sake of implementation which I wish to place on the record, you are my witnesses. If you feel that the amended document should remain as it is, there is no reason for us to object. We shall accept and cooperate in the implementation. Discrepancies will be remedied. It is acceptable."

Obasanjo thanked the Sudan government for its "responsible and proper reaction." He explained that "one rebel group has indicated that it will sign and wants to talk. I hope it is not reopening negotiations. It is not totally satisfied. It has offered to work with the other two groups." He suggested that "the government and this group should sign and we believe it will create some impression on the others." Obasanjo overruled a request from Majzoub that they delay the signing until President Bashir could fly to Abuja. He set the time of 1:00 p.m. for signing—just ninety minutes thence.

However, back at the Chida Hotel, the text of the DPA was not ready to be signed. The facilities for printing and photocopying had reached their limits. Computers had broken down and fuses had blown. It would take several hours for copies of the DPA to be made ready for signature. Shortly after midday, Abdel Wahid arrived back at Aguda House with his delegation. He was in combative mood. Obasanjo confronted Abdel Wahid, springing into the posture of a boxer. "You let me down!" he said, his fist in Abdel Wahid's face. Abdel Wahid began to explain, "You are our Baba, not just the Baba of Nigeria

but the Baba of Darfur, but I am demanding the rights for our people..."
Before he could continue, Obasanjo seized him by the collar and pulled him
into a side room, "I need to talk to you, boy." For more than two hours, a shut-
tle followed with Obasanjo, Zoellick, and Benn pressing Abdel Wahid to sign.
Abdel Wahid's key demand was stronger guarantees.

Minni had meanwhile disappeared. Obasanjo had instructed that he should
not leave the presidential compound and that if he needed to consult with his
commanders, they should come to meet him here. The commanders arrived
about 2:50 and went into long and tense meetings. At that time the news
arrived that Minni's brother had been killed that morning. Rumors circulated, that he was killed by the government and this would make Minni bitter, or that he was shot by his own troops to stop Minni from signing. While
Minni grieved and discussed with his commanders, Majzoub and his delegation sat in their places in the hall and did not move.

Abdel Wahid came out from his room and retired to a spot in the garden
with his delegation to consult. He turned away anyone sent to intervene. The
guarantees offered by Obasanjo, Zoellick, and Benn had not been enough.
Abdel Wahid and his group went back to the Chida Hotel for one last con-
clave. The majority was for signing, but Abdel Wahid refused to put the question to a vote. "I, Abdel Wahid Mohamed al Nur, will never sign!" He stood
up and left the meeting.

Finally, just after 5:30, Minni entered the hall looking ravaged. His chief of
staff, Juma Haggar, sat next to him expressionless in his camouflage.
Obasanjo gave a long oration and concluded, "Will you attach your signature?" He paused. "Unless the right spirit is there this document is not worth
the paper it is written on." Minni sat silently throughout, his face registering
no expression. At 5:55, Obasanjo called upon on Majzoub and Minni to sign.
The two men came forward, shook hands and sat down at the table specially
prepared in the center of the square. Minni signed first and then Majzoub—
even at this final hour Majzoub wanted to be certain he had Minni's signature
first. The room broke into applause and the speeches began. Majzoub was
gracious. Minni had not prepared his speech and reiterated the points he had
made earlier. Others spoke at length. It was a joyless climax. An hour later,
Abdel Rahman Musa and a group of thirteen delegates from the Abdel

Wahid group turned up at the ceremony and demanded that they should be allowed to join. Each one was individually embraced by Obasanjo and for the first time in the day, Majzoub smiled.

## Postscript

OVER THE FOLLOWING days, as the Chida Hotel emptied, Abdel Wahid sat in his room, insisting that he was still determined to make peace. The mediation discussed how to handle the unforeseen circumstance that he had not signed. Should the AU continue to engage him? The decision was that the DPA would be held open for signature until the meeting of the AU Peace and Security Council in Addis Ababa on May 16. What would happen to the Ceasefire Commission and the Joint Commission, both institutions on which SLA-Abdel Wahid and JEM were represented? No decision was made, but the general view was that the representatives of the non-signatories should stay, but not be party to discussions about implementing the DPA's security arrangements.

Two members of the mediation team—Sam Ibok and Alex de Waal— stayed behind in Abuja to continue discussions with Abdel Wahid. They met with him several times each day and encouraged him to be specify his objections to the DPA in writing. On May 10, Abdel Wahid wrote a letter to Salim (who was by this time in Addis Ababa). The letter said:

> I am writing to you to seek the support and assistance of the African Union to close the final gap between the SLM/A and the Government of Sudan. In that respect I am making two requests. The first is that you will register certain specific clarifications on the text of the Darfur Peace Agreement, and thereby ensure that our concerns are addressed during the implementation of the Agreement. These clarifications are detailed in this letter, below.
>
> The second is that, subsequent to our signing of the Agreement, you will facilitate discussions between the SLM/A and the GoS to reach political agreement on some outstanding

issues concerning power-sharing. These discussions will lead to a Supplement to the Agreement.

Abdel Wahid's clarifications included ensuring that the $30 million in the compensation fund was only the first payment and not a ceiling and that the SLA would be involved in monitoring the disarmament of the Janjawiid and in providing security to returning refugees and displaced people. He asked for further discussions to produce a supplement to the agreement on power-sharing issues. Abdel Wahid concluded,[5]

> I respectfully request that the African Union facilitate such discussions.
>
> Once you have indicated that you will register our clarifications, undertaken work to ensure that the Agreement is implemented fully and faithfully, and undertaken to facilitate further discussions with the Government of Sudan on the issues mentioned above, I shall be ready to attach my signature to the Darfur Peace Agreement.

Salim consulted with senior members of the AU and UN before sending his reply, which was received on the morning of May 13.[6] He had no difficulty with Abdel Wahid's clarifications. But the sentence that Abdel Wahid demanded, which was that the AU would witness any agreement reached between the signatory parties and attach it as a supplement to the DPA, was not included. Instead, Salim wrote, "the African Union is ready, at any time, to facilitate discussions between the Parties, if they would promote the peace process and the implementation of the Darfur Peace Agreement." The letter said that the AU could not re-open the DPA but was willing to provide support to any steps agreed among the parties for the implementation of the agreement. On reading the letter, Ibok and de Waal both knew it fell short.

Abdel Wahid's mood had been volatile over the days since May 6. In the 24 hours after he wrote his letter he was ebullient and impatient to sign. His mood darkened thereafter, especially after he was removed from the Chida Hotel after the AU stopped paying his bill—an action that he took as a calculated insult. Abdel Wahid moved into a small down-market hotel called the Capitol Hotel. Ibok made an appointment to deliver Salim's letter to him at that hotel at 1:00 p.m. that day. Ibok arrived late because there are three Capitol hotels in Abuja and the driver, having assured him that he knew exactly which one it was, went first to the other two. Ibok did his best to present the letter in the most favorable light. He said,[7]

> No agreement can be taken as a Koran or a Bible. It must be open
> for interpretation and adjustment during the implementation
> phase. The implementation is in many respects the real agree-
> ment, the translation of the document into a reality on the
> ground. It is inevitable that the parties will need to sit together to
> agree many things as they proceed with the implementation. If
> there are adjustments to be made, and the three signatory parties,
> the African Union is obliged to respect the wishes of the parties.

But Abdel Wahid knew that his pivotal demand was not being met: the AU would not support additional negotiations to produce a supplement to the agreement. He rejected the letter. The following day, Ibok flew to Addis Ababa along with the copies of the DPA. The AU mediation had closed down.

But many in Abdel Wahid's delegation had not given up hope. The following morning, his power-sharing negotiator, Ibrahim Madibu, called de Waal out of the check-in queue at Abuja airport, saying there was still a chance—for direct negotiations with the government. De Waal returned and that morning, Madibu and other members of the team crafted a four-point memo to submit to Majzoub, who was in Khartoum.[8] The most tricky point was the last: "The National Congress Party shall provide at least one additional ministerial position in Darfur and one in the central government to a nominee of the SLM/A as a gesture of goodwill pending further discussions in this respect." This was sent through the Sudan ambassador in Abuja. In the evening, Majzoub replied.[9] On the first point (more funds for compensation), he said that the government had already begun distributing compensation. This was correct but misleading: it had set up its own party-based compensation fund with $70 million. On points two and three (SLA participation in monitoring the disarmament of the Janjawiid and the safe return home of refugees and displaced persons), he wrote that "such objective is absolutely, seriously and uncompromisingly agreed upon." On the final point (power sharing) Majzoub simply referred back to the DPA. Mohamed Yousif, minister of youth and sports in the government, called ahead to alert the team to what they described as a "soft no."

That evening, Abdel Wahid composed a letter to the AU Peace and Security Council. He included a positive reference to cooperation with Minni—who had been kept abreast of the efforts to bring Abdel Wahid into the agreement—and offered to be part of the comprehensive ceasefire. He signed the letter and went to bed. The following morning Abdel Wahid's aides "polished" the letter, woke him for him to sign the new version, and sent it off. This version omitted the reference to Minni and was less conciliatory about a ceasefire. That day, demonstrators in the displaced camps were demanding that Darfur become an autonomous region and Abdel Wahid be appointed as vice president. However, Abdel Wahid's own demands remained much more modest and focused on the four issues he had raised in his memo. He was insistent on a supplement to the agreement, but flexible on what that might include. When news came that the AU Peace and Security Council had extended the deadline for him and JEM to sign the DPA for an additional two weeks, Abdel Wahid was jubilant, and assured de Waal that he would sign before the month was out. But the next afternoon, citing "security reasons," Abdel Wahid abruptly packed his bags and went into hiding, cutting contact with the last mediator in Abuja (this writer). He traveled to Nairobi to join his wife and five-month-old baby.

A final effort was made to bring Abdel Wahid into a negotiating process at the end of May, by Pekka Haavisto of the EU, Kjell Hødnebo (representing Norway), and de Waal. The focus of this was an offer by the SPLM chairman and first vice president, Salva Kiir, to convene talks in Yei, southern Sudan, to help bridge the final gaps. During the last week of May, Abdel Wahid dithered on whether he would attend or not. He demanded and received a personal guarantee of his safety from Kiir. But despite this, on June 3, he finally decided not to go and instead flew to Asmara, Eritrea, at the invitation of Khalil Ibrahim to discuss the founding of the National Redemption Front. The DPA negotiations were over.

# 12

# Darfur after Abuja: A View from the Ground

ABDUL-JABBAR FADUL AND VICTOR TANNER

THE DARFUR PEACE AGREEMENT (DPA), signed in Abuja in May 2006, was stillborn. Yet it triggered striking dynamics inside Darfur. On the one hand many Darfurians sensed that the crisis was entering a new phase. The region's main ethnic groups recognized both their need to live together and the role played by the government in the violence between them. On the other hand, it was quickly clear that the very conditions of the accord—the fact that two of the three rebel factions did not sign and the manifest lack of goodwill on the part of the government—left Darfur facing spiraling violence and increased ethnic tensions. The way Darfurians perceived issues of unity, responsibility, and security reflected this tension between promise and gloom.

This chapter tracks the impact of the Abuja accord on the ground in Darfur during the six months after the DPA was concluded. It examines how Darfurians viewed the accord, how it impacted the rebel movements and government forces, and how people in Darfur viewed the conflict and issues of violence and security. Local perceptions are sometimes overlooked outside Sudan—and indeed outside Darfur. Based on about 120 interviews conducted jointly by the authors in May–June and September–October with Darfurians from many walks of life, including local inhabitants, displaced people, traditional leaders, and educated professionals, as well as on the long experience of the Darfurian author, this chapter aims to provide this local perspective.

## How Abuja Was Perceived on the Ground

IN MAY 2006, after seven rounds of negotiations facilitated by the African Union and under intense pressure from the U.S., the Sudan Liberation Army (SLA) faction headed by Minni Arkoy Minawi signed the DPA with the government of Sudan. The faction of the SLA led by Abdel Wahid Mohamed al Nur and the Justice and Equality Movement, headed by Dr. Khalil Ibrahim, refused to sign. For many, the Abuja accord represented Darfur's last and best chance, especially since it carried the understanding that the Sudan government would allow the deployment of United Nations peacekeeping forces in Darfur. The U.S. in particular, having invested prestige in the process and strong-armed it to a close, was committed to seeing the DPA succeed.

Very quickly, however, it became clear that the DPA would not prove a viable option to bring peace to Darfur. From the beginning, the fact that Abdel Wahid did not sign the agreement boded ill. The DPA may have been sound in terms of its contents, but to many Darfurians this was irrelevant, as violence increased after it was signed. Security was the primary concern for people in Darfur. In conversation after conversation across the region, security emerged as the number one concern, to the near exclusion of all other issues. This was especially true of Darfurians who had been victims of violence. Shortly after the Abuja agreement was signed, violence, insecurity, and forced displacement rose in Darfur. Some of this was the result of fighting between the groups that refused to sign the DPA—the "non-signatory factions"—and the governmental "coalition" which now included SLA-Minni. But the great majority of violence was been due to renewed attacks by Janjawiid and government of Sudan forces on both rebel forces and civilians.

The result was more suffering for Darfurians. The UN stated that "200,000 people [were] displaced by intensified fighting and increased insecurity between July and September [2006]" (UNOCHA 2006b, 3). After May, new displaced people from rural areas in South and West Darfur arrived in Nyala, Geneina and other displacement centers on a daily basis.[1] People were displaced by government forces around Saiyah, northeast of al Fashir, and in Korma, west of al Fashir, the latter after especially brutal attacks by SLA-Minni (Amnesty International 2006). In Gereida, an area supposedly under SLA-Minni control, the number of displaced increased from 90,000 to 130,000 between June and September (OCHA 2006a, b). Everyday insecurity also deteriorated, especially in towns and in and around the camps for the internally displaced, often at the hands of governmental militias, for example the looting al Fashir's Mawashei market on October 11 by Janjawiid.[2] One aid agency documented 200 cases of rape in Kalma camp (near Nyala) in a five-week period over July and August, "a massive spike in figures" (International Rescue Committee 2006).

In the face of such abuses, many non-Arabs in Darfur said the agreement in Abuja meant little to them. They could not return home. They often hesitated to venture beyond their camps because of the risk of attack. One sheikh said,

> We have no freedom, no freedom at all. We cannot move. We
> cannot meet. I think twice about going to the market [a few hun-
> dred yards away]. I can say nothing. So what reconciliation?
> What peace? I cannot go beyond the gate of the camp. They can
> take me anytime.[3]

Other issues also emerged in conversations—compensation, the rehabilitation of infrastructure, basic services, and reconciliation—but people always stressed these were secondary to security. In contrast, Darfurians in Khartoum—individuals in leading positions as well as ordinary people—were far more adamant about demanding compensation than displaced Darfurians in Darfur.

Who signed the DPA (or not) was more relevant to people than the contents of the agreement. Another striking point was that people were, by and large, not interested in the details contained in the Abuja agreement. As long as security remained bad and Abdel Wahid had not signed, they considered the rest moot, including the actual provisions of the agreement. This was true of both ordinary citizens and traditional leaders. The lack of attention to the nuts-and-bolts of the agreement was widespread. In May and June 2006, many Fur, Masalit, and other non-Arabs in government-held areas stated that the Abuja agreement was "bad." When asked whether they had read the agreement, they often replied that they hadn't, but had heard about it from peers or from radio news programs. When asked why they thought it a poor agreement, the answer often came that it must be bad, since Abdel Wahid did not sign it. Conversely, during this period many also said, that if Abdel Wahid signed, it meant that Abuja was a good agreement, and that peace would follow.

This was an interesting departure from a common perception among foreigners that the globe-trotting Abdel Wahid did not possess a strong popular base in Darfur, a perception possibly rooted in the very real disconnect between him and Fur rebel commanders on the ground. In fact, Abdel Wahid had a strong following among many Fur, especially in the displaced camps. They heard of him in the international media, he represented them in negotiations in faraway capitals, he was "their guy." Without him on board, the prospects of a peace agreement taking hold were slim—at least then.

Three months later, in September and October, it was therefore striking to hear people, especially Fur (both displaced and non-displaced), say that even if Abdel Wahid signed, they would not support the peace agreement. This was the result of the months of violence that followed the signing in Abuja. By October, people in Darfur were saying that peace was impossible because the government clearly had no intention of honoring any agreement. They said there could be no peace unless it was forced on the government militarily. In other words, peace depended on one of two things, a non-consensual deployment of Western troops or a rebel military victory—or both.

Indeed, as 2006 progressed there was a noticeable hardening in popular opinion. Early in the rebellion, it was hard to gauge popular support for the SLA and the JEM. On the one hand, the SLA's demands for an end to the neglect of Darfur enjoyed overwhelming popular support, including among many of Darfur's Arabs. Communities supported the rebels and young men joined them. At the same time, however, it was not hard, in those years, to detect ambivalence about the idea of armed rebellion. Field research, conducted in North and West Darfur in June 2004, concluded that,

> most of the Darfur people interviewed [for the research], rich
> and poor, Arab and African, victimised and not—and most of
> them supportive of the rebels' agenda for change—stated both
> their opposition to armed rebellion, and their belief that the current
> violence escalated in response to the insurgency (which is
> not, of course, to say that they excused the violence). (Tanner
> 2005a, 13)

Two years later, following the agreement in Abuja, the situation was very different. People were desperate for security and a chance to return to their homes. But they believed that only force could achieve that for them. Popular support for the non-signatory groups appeared stronger even while people expressed widespread fatigue with the violence and dismay over the lack of unity of the rebellion. (It should be pointed out that the great majority, though not all, of the interviews described above were with men. Experienced researchers who have spent more time with women report they heard immense weariness and a desire for the violence to stop.[4]) A similar pattern existed among educated Darfurians. As late as 2004, many Darfurian intellectuals criticized the decision to take up arms against the government. The brutality of Khartoum's reaction was predictable, they argued, and the violence had cast the region back many decades. By late 2006, it was striking to hear many of those same individuals say they believed armed rebellion was the only solution to Darfur's problems, despite disenchantment with the shortcomings and human rights abuses by rebel groups on the ground.[5]

## The Warring Factions after Abuja

THE ABUJA ACCORD has affected the warring groups in different ways. In the second half of 2006, after signing the DPA, Minni Minawi lost most of what he had going into the final round of negotiations in Abuja, including fighters and vehicles in the field, territory, and what popularity he still had within Darfur. Reports abounded of local-level SLA-Minni forces, including Zaghawa, peeling off and joining the non-signatories with their vehicles (four-wheel drive vehicles are the basic component of rebel units and the main gauge of the importance of a commander is the number he possesses). The following examples, which arose in conversations in September and October, are illustrative of broader losses. In September, in the government-held town of Kutum in North Darfur, a group of three or four SLA-Minni vehicles simply slipped town and drove north to rebel lines. In Wada'a, in eastern Darfur, in early October seven SLA-Minni vehicles reportedly defected to non-signatory rebels. In Gereida, in South Darfur, a local SLA-Minni commander, a Masalit, grew disenchanted with his movement's unwillingness to protect local Masalit from increasing Janjawiid attacks and left with several vehicles for an area west of Buram where he was said to have led small-scale attacks on government forces. In Nyala, in September and October, a top SLA-Minni leader said his fighters were leaving town on a nightly basis, either to join other rebels in the bush or to return home.[6]

Minni also lost men and materiel in consecutive defeats at the hands of non-signatory groups around Korma, Kafod, and Saiyah (North Darfur) in June and July 2006. SLA sources in Chad (both for and against Minni) interviewed in October agreed that, between June and September 2006, as many as three-quarters of Minni's troops had joined non-signatory groups. Others simply went home.[7] By early 2007, Minni had lost most of the territory his forces once held. He only retained partial control of a few enclaves around al Fashir, some isolated Zaghawa territories east of Jebel Marra including Tabit, Shangal Tobay, Dar es Salaam, and Muhajiriya, and the Masalit towns of Gereida and Jughana, south of Nyala. These areas were insecure as they were contested among numerous, increasingly autonomous groups. Local communities had suffered repeated and brutal attacks at the hands of Janjawiid as well as of rival signatory rebel groups even while some had joined the non-signatory factions or were in the process of doing so.

Minni's credibility among Darfurians also waned. The fact that SLA-Minni forces fought alongside government forces, including Janjawiid in Korma and Tabit where they received Sudanese air support, further alienated Minni from many Darfurians.[8] So did the widespread reports of atrocities (rape, murder, displacement) his troops committed in Korma and other places (Amnesty International 2006). The rise in Janjawiid violence following the signing of the DPA is a clear indicator of the Sudan government's enduring contempt, not only for Darfurians, but for its DPA partner. Minni possessed little if any power and the National Congress Party clearly did not take him seriously. As a consequence, SLA-Minni representatives began to distance themselves from the DPA and from Minni, speaking openly of the possibility of returning to rebellion.

Following the Abuja accord, the various non-signatory groups sought to regroup in a more united fashion. Complicating the effort was the strong disconnect between field commanders and the diaspora politicians. In June 2006, most of the main opposition groups came together in a new, loosely knit group, the National Redemption Front (NRF, *jebhat al khalas*). The NRF is made up of JEM, the leaders of the Sudan Federal Democratic Alliance, and assorted other commanders. The "Group of Nineteen" (G-19) commanders who had split from Abdel Wahid in February were also associated with the NRF and formed its military backbone. The G-19 comprises a group of mostly (but not only) Zaghawa commanders who had first rejected Minni as too authoritarian and then Abdel Wahid as ineffective. While their leaders have expressed their political differences with the NRF, in Darfur they are widely identified as the same group. The non-signatory Fur groups in Jebel Marra, headed by Abdel Wahid and Ahmed Abdel Shafi Yagub Bassi, did not formally join the NRF but made it clear that they supported the group's opposition to the government.

What followed, over the summer of 2006, was a string of surprising military victories on the part of the non-signatories, taking over large territories in North Darfur from SLA-Minni and the government. In early October, non-signatory forces destroyed a large government force in Kariyari, near Tine on the Chadian border. Each victory yielded vehicles, weapons, and large amounts of fuel and ammunition. Finally, in late November, rebel forces attacked oil installations near Abu Jabra, in the Misiriya area of southwestern Kordofan, on the border with South Darfur. These victories were important on several levels. First, they allowed the non-signatories to build a military force at the expense of the Sudanese military, deeply demoralizing the latter.

Second, the different groups cooperated militarily, including the non-NRF Fur groups of Jebel Marra (Tanner and Tubiana 2007). The reaction to government and SLA-Minni offensives helped bind the groups together: "Under duress, facing a common threat, those on the ground really did not have much time for the political splits . . . I would talk to all different leaders and they would say as much—'we are all in this together.'"[9] But disunity swiftly reappeared. There was resentment within the non-signatories at the political prominence assumed by the JEM and its leader Khalil Ibrahim, especially following his claim that the NRF was responsible for the defeat of the government forces at Kariyari. The G-19, which had borne the brunt of the fighting, was angered by Khalil's claims and took on a new name, SLA-NSF (Non-Signatory Factions) and its leaders sought to re-unify the rebel commanders. On the ground, however, many local commanders remain highly opportunistic in their calculus. The unity the Darfur rebels so desperately needed to counter Khartoum's political and military remained elusive.

The military victories by the non-signatory groups—after expectations that the government offensive in August would wipe out the rebels—deeply disheartened the Sudan armed forces. Sudanese army officers who escaped a military debacle at the hands of the non-signatories at Um Sidir were reportedly charged with desertion. One of them told a close associate that many of his soldiers had fled without fighting and that others had joined the rebels.[10] Another former officer told that the rebels had captured a high-ranking officer at Kariyari, a former comrade of his.[11] Interviews with Sudanese military survivors of Kariyari who escaped to Chad revealed soldiers wholly unprepared for combat.[12] In October, after Kariyari, a young Sudanese army officer bitterly quipped that the military was doing a wonderful job at handling rebel logistics.[13]

Government-supported Arab militias were also reported to be demoralized, especially in North Darfur. Many Janjawiid leaders felt betrayed by the DPA: they were not consulted and the agreement did little to represent their interests. The conventional wisdom among citizens in al Fashir was that the various government forces—the military, the Popular Defense Forces (PDF), the *haras al huduud* ("Border Guards"), the so-called *quwat as salam* ("Peace Forces") and others—had little no desire to fight, and that the government had trouble controlling them. According to local residents, the Peace Forces were mostly former *murahiliin* of the Baggara Rizeigat militias, since disbanded, whom the government recruited as a post-Abuja force. They apparently did not expect to have any fighting to do, and were unhappy with their conditions. The outbreak of looting in Mawashei market in al Fashir in October, allegedly by Peace Forces, was seen as proof of that. One al Fashir resident described how he bought gravel that soldiers, desperate for an income, made by breaking up tarmac at the airport and selling through the enclosure.[14]

### Changing Perceptions of Violence and Security in Darfur

AFTER ABUJA, people in Darfur clearly felt the crisis had entered a new phase. In May and June, it seemed that the acute phase of widespread catastrophic violence—massive landgrabs, direct challenges to the traditional political order—was behind them. Groups and leaders were positioning themselves for survival in a different context. A number of factors were at play, often driven as much by perception as by reality—and sometimes more so.

One new factor was the fact of the Abuja agreement. The DPA's very existence made it the de facto backdrop for all future political calculations. The agreement provided the framework for agreements and potential conflict between groups. It defined how groups presented themselves and how they were in turn defined by others. Rebels who signed, for example, found they had to explain why they had done so to communities in Darfur, while at the same time trying to make sure the Sudan government and the international community made it worth their while to have signed. Non-signatory groups, on the other hand, found it easier to explain their stance to their constituents in Darfur. But they also had to face strong pressure from the U.S. government to sign up to the DPA, and at the same time endure military attacks by both the government and signatory forces.

Darfurians perceived a shift in international opinion. Many people in Darfur said they perceived a clear shift in international—and especially U.S.—

opinion on Darfur. Darfurians are assiduous listeners of Arabic-language news on Western radio broadcast services such as the BBC, Radio Monte-Carlo, and Voice of America. Listening to these, they said they felt a growing international impatience with the violence in Darfur, which translated into impatience with what is described in the West as rebel intransigence. Many saw the Abuja process—the deadlines and arm-twisting, the agreement itself and its aftermath—as proof of international determination to put an end to the violence, regardless of whether the resulting "peace" was just or not.

The hardening of opinions in Darfur with regards to the West was palpable. People did not seem to believe, for instance, that Western efforts to halt the violence and achieve a peace agreement were at all motivated by a desire to protect Darfurians. They explained what they perceived as the change in international heart with reasons mostly exogenous to Darfur. These included the U.S.-UK war in Iraq, Washington's counter-terrorism alliance with Khartoum, the 2006 elections in the U.S. and prime minister Tony Blair's domestic problems, French designs in Chad, and Western pandering to Russia and China over Iran. The only Darfur-based reason put forward was oil—the belief that Western powers were somehow cutting a deal with Khartoum based on Darfur's oil reserves.

The agreement in Abuja initially offered the prospect of a deployment of UN troops which added to the perception that the crisis was entering a new phase. Darfurians firmly believed that UN troops could and would bring an end to the violence This was based on the premises that U.S. and other Western troops would make up the bulk of peacekeepers deployed, and that a Chapter VII mandate would mean that the troops would be proactive in protecting civilians against the depredations of the Janjawiid. At a minimum they believed that the presence of UN troops would fundamentally change political dynamics, both locally and nationally.

The final reason for the perception of a new phase in the crisis after Abuja was the fluid political scene in Sudan as a whole. As 2006 progressed, most Sudanese were convinced that the country's current political situation was untenable. A fundamental tension existed between the opening-up of political space that came as a result of the North-South peace process and the enduring violence of a highly repressive military regime, in Darfur and elsewhere.

Sudanese did not in expect radical political change such as the fall of the regime but they expected intensified power struggles within the regime in coming years, and perhaps lurches toward either liberalization or greater repression—or both—as national elections scheduled for 2008 or 2009 approached.

Also changed were perceptions, among the victims, of who was responsible for the violence. Early in the conflict, conversations with groups who had borne the brunt of the violence left no doubt that the focus of anger and fear were the Janjawiid militias in particular and "Arabs" in general.[15] Two years later, feelings had changed. For sure, there was no understating the anger against Arab groups for the violence. But victims focused less on the actual perpetrators—named Arab clans or militia groups, or the individual gunmen themselves—and more on those who had encouraged the violence, organized it and supported it, namely the Khartoum government. Darfurians, both ordinary displaced citizens and traditional leaders at various levels, stressed that the *government* was their enemy, not the "Arabs."

For example, a displaced Fur *omda*, originally from an area southwest of Nyala, described how Arabs, both local and not, had attacked his village in March 2004, forcing him and most of his people, including many non-Fur, to flee. But he immediately stressed that "it was not a tribe fighting us, it was the government." He said the National Islamic Front government had, since the early 1990s, "fanned the flames, used the Arabs against the Africans."[16] In Kas (South Darfur), a place where bitterness runs deep, a displaced Fur leader, surrounded by men from the camp, drew the same difference between the Arabs in his home area and the Sudanese government. "Our problem is not with the Arabs, it is with the government. The government destroyed our area. Even if Arabs did take part, they are just poor people like us. The government is behind it."[17] Also in South Darfur, a Mararit *omda* explained that his people had lived with the *abbala* (camel-herding Arabs), and that they knew them. They had suffered so much from them, but knew they would still a have to live with them in the future.[18] Even in West Darfur, where anti-Arab feelings remained particularly high among local Masalit, people emphasized the responsibility of the government. The Masalit suffered vicious Arab militia attacks in the mid-1990s and again in 2003–2004—

a time when there was very little rebel activity in the area. In Geneina, a powerful Masalit traditional leader railed that the Arabs "got arms from the government, they got uniforms from the government, they got cars from the government, they got Thurayas [satellite phones] from the government. They got, they got, they got..."[19]

Part of the issue was that the Arab militias have been integrated, officially or de facto, into the Sudanese armed forces and wore uniforms. People could no longer distinguish between militiamen and soldiers. "You can't know who is who. You don't know who is in charge. They are all armed, they all wear khaki, and they all intimidate and rob the people."[20] It was becoming clear to Darfurians that the ubiquitous lawlessness was the result of government policies rather than just intertribal tensions. This distinction was echoed by Hausa displaced people in South Darfur: "the problem is not tribal, it is anarchy [*fawdha*]."[21] *Fawdha* is a word loaded with meaning in Arabic. *Fawdha* is what happens when there is no government—at all. It is a state far worse than being under a repressive government (*zulm*). In other words, for people in Darfur, the government had brought the worst kind of governance to Darfur: the absence of government. In 2004, by contrast, it was not uncommon to hear Darfurians say that all they wanted was *heibat ad dawla*, literally the reverence of the state. In other words, they expressed the hope of once again living under the protection of the state (Tanner 2005, 40). In 2006, that expression, *heibat ad dawla*, was not heard once.

One of the factors driving the perception of the violence as increasingly political was Khartoum's very efforts to tribalize the violence. Official government explanations, addressed at both national and international audiences, presented the violence as inherent to a historically unruly region (Hoile 2005). The government also aggressively pushed tribal reconciliation (*musalaha*) meetings in all three Darfurian states as a panacea to the conflict[22]—thereby indicating its firm belief that the violence was tribal in nature, not political. Darfurians resented this. "The government says the problem is tribal. I say the problem is the government," said a Masalit leader in Geneina.[23] Even a high South Darfur state official, involved in these reconciliation meetings, recognized the central issue at state: security. "Some situations will need time...Because of the instability and the insecurity, people cannot negotiate fairly."[24] When the African Union held its first public consultation on the Darfur-Darfur Dialogue and Consultation[25] the government tried to turn it into an endorsement of its own view that Darfur's political problems had been entirely resolved and that all that remained was tribal disputes and criminality.

In the months after the DPA, Darfurians did not see reconciliation meetings as an immediate need. Why reconcile when there is no security? How to reconcile when the government continued to manipulate relations between groups and foment violence? People dismissed "reconciliation" efforts as an effort by the government to buy off non-Arab leaders. "Reconciliation is nonsense [kalam fadhi]... There can be no reconciliation before people go home," said a senior Fur traditional leader, echoing feelings expressed widely by other people across Darfur.[26] A Masalit leader in Geneina expressed another common theme: "There is no need for reconciliation [among] tribes. It is the government that attacked us. We need reconciliation with the government. End of story."[27]

Conversely, the discourse of groups implicated in the violence was often far less belligerent in late 2006 than it had been in the early years of the crisis. The Abuja accord left many Arab groups associated with the Janjawiid in an awkward position. Their leaders had, for the most part, very little say in the negotiations, and the agreement itself indicated Khartoum's willingness to sacrifice their interests in a bid to reach a deal with the rebels, and especially to placate the international community. The provisions on the disarmament of Arab militias were especially troubling to these Arab groups—though it was clear early on that the government had neither the will nor the ability to enforce the ambitious provisions for disarming the Janjawiid in the DPA. As a result, many hard-line Arab leaders started sounding more conciliatory than they had in the past. This was not uniformly true across all parts of Darfur and was especially not the case in Dar Masalit, where Arab leaders remained intransigent. But it was striking that individuals who, when interviewed in 2004, had denied, downplayed, or justified the violence, two years later were ready to acknowledge that atrocities did indeed occur, that members of their group took part in them (though they usually stressed that they participated as individuals, not as groups), that the displaced needed to return to their land, and that the land would be theirs when they did go home.

For instance, an Arab *nazir* from the Kebkabiya area sounded far more conciliatory in 2006 than he had in 2004. Then, he was surly in answering a visitor's questions, denying that any widespread violence had taken place in Kebkabiya and, incredibly, in Jebel Si, where Fur communities had in fact suffered vicious and sustained attack. In an interview in June 2006, the same gentleman acknowledged the violence and displacement, stressing that Jebel Si was quite empty of its inhabitants. He also acknowledged that some of his people had been involved, though he was careful to emphasize they did so as individuals, not as representatives of his group. He stated his belief that it was clear the displaced had the right to return to their land and that some form of compensation would have to occur. Finally, he said that, had there been better coordination between the tribes, the rebellion could have united all Darfurians, Arab and non-Arabs, in claiming their rights. "The demands of the rebels are the right ones," he added.[28] Similarly, a Tama *omda* from the Kebkabiya area also sounded far more conciliatory than he had in 2004. Many Tama, a non-Arab group centered in northwestern Darfur, had taken part in attacks alongside Arab militias, mostly out of a longstanding animosity for their Zaghawa neighbors and out of fear of retribution from camel-herding Arab groups. In an interview in 2004, the *omda* expressed rather hard-line ideas on the violence. Two years later he showed a visitor a written directive to his sheikhs, instructing them to enforce a ban on local Tama cultivating farms belonging to displaced, unless they were able to secure the displaced farmer's express agreement to cultivate his land.[29]

What these opinions indicate is the possible re-emergence of the historic "Darfur consensus." Darfur's central majority bloc brings together the main ethnic groups of the region: the Fur, the *baggara* Arabs, the Masalit, the Zaghawa, the Tunjur, and the many smaller "African" tribes that normally and naturally gravitate towards Fur positions. This central political consensus group has been the historic bedrock of Darfur society and is the foundation of the region's stability. It comprises the traditional political order that made Darfur viable, first as a Fur-dominated yet multi-ethnic sultanate until 1916, and then as a region that, while prone to local conflict over resources, remained quite stable until the late 1980s. Over the last twenty years, external forces have undermined the viability of the Darfur consensus and pushed the region over the edge. These extraneous factors have included the blow-back from the Chadian wars, Libyan trouble-making, willful disruption on the part of the central government, and severe drought.

Land is the lynchpin of the Darfur consensus. The groups that make up this majority bloc come together in enjoying access to land under the *dar* and *hakura* systems.[30] They share a common view on the legitimately land ownership and management system, in turn based on the native administration system of local government.[31] The consensus also holds that these conjoined land tenure and administration systems provide the blueprint for future coexistence between groups in Darfur. Most Darfurians contend that the current conflict constituted an assault on the Darfur consensus. Khartoum has targeted two key groups of the majority bloc, the Fur and the Masalit, as part of its counter-insurgency against the rebels. The main Arab groups that form the basis for the militia attacks are motivated by access to pasture, water, and fertile land. The current crisis is itself a continuation of governmental efforts in the 1990s to weaken Fur and especially Masalit communities in western Jebel Marra and Dar Masalit.

In this context, it was striking to hear al Hadi Issa Debaka, *nazir* of the Bani Halba who is well-known as a hard-line Arab leader, stress that the Baggara Arabs and the Fur share not only a common claim to the land but also a common vision of how the land should be managed. In May 2006, he went so far as to say that he agreed with Abdel Wahid that only the traditional tenure system could guarantee a peaceful future for Darfur.[32] This put him in clear opposition to the political ambitions of the landless Arab groups, which claim that the *hakura* and dar systems should be abolished and Sudanese land laws enforced. This is remarkable because Debaka is considered to be close to Janjawiid elements, certainly by many Fur leaders.[33] He had also led the Bani Halba in the anti-Fur wars of 1987–1989 (Flint and de Waal 2005, 55).

The problem with the majority consensus over land is that it leaves unaddressed a number of difficult problems. One is the issue of landless Arab groups in Darfur, such as the northern camel-herding Arab nomads and Chadian Arab pastoralists who have settled in various parts of Darfur in the past thirty years (and more). Their grievances—manipulated and politicized by Khartoum—are one of the root causes of the conflict (de Waal and Young 2005, 2–4). The more conciliatory tone described above notwithstanding, there are still parts of Darfur such as Dar Masalit, Wadi Barei, and Wadi Salih, that remain "occupied" by mostly *abbala* Arab pastoralists who are unlikely to want to leave.

A second and related issue is competition for land between and within landed groups. In the course of the 1990s, the absence of any policy framework for agricultural development or land use led to the exponential use of land and especially water, notably with the development of dry season crops along Darfur's *wadis* (seasonal water courses).[34] Permanent cultivation leads of course to conflict with herders, but can also raise tensions among settled farmers as newcomers come to the area and traditional resource-allocation mechanisms are no longer able to manage local demands for land and water. Displacement and violence has destabilized these mechanisms and the traditional leaders who manage them, and such tensions could be further exacerbated in a post-return environment.

Historically, the Fur historically constitute Darfur's pre-eminent group. During the conflict and the peace talks, the Fur's role had been partly eclipsed by the strong representation of Zaghawa leaders and fighters in the rebel groups. Following the Abuja agreement and the refusal of Abdel Wahid, seen as representing the Fur in the talks, they began reclaiming this central place. This was especially clear in the public discourse of other groups, including powerful Baggara leaders such as *nazir* al Hadi Issa Dabaka or members of the Madibu family of the al Da'ien Rizeigat. After Abuja, ordinary non-Fur Darfurians across the board concurred that it was the Fur who would lead the way to peace or further conflict. Many expressed their belief that no peace agreement was possible without the Fur. A displaced Hausa in South Darfur stated clearly, to the agreement of a large groups around him, that his people would only return home when the displaced Fur communities they lived with went home, and when the Fur traditional leaders, whom their own traditional leaders answer to, were back in place.[35]

It is very significant that the large Baggara Arab groups of South Darfur also expressed support for the majority bloc and professed allegiance to an intertribal consensus on land. The main Baggara groups—the southern Rizeigat, the Ma'alia, the Bani Halba, the Habbaniya and the Ta'aisha—have had a complex role in the conflict. As groups, these tribes mostly managed to stay out of the Janjawiid movement. However, the senior leaders of the these groups had to navigate a turbulent political environment, which included strong governmental pressure on them to come out in support of the counterinsurgency and efforts by party officials and military intelligence officers to undermine them by co-opting their followers to join the militia. Jérôme Tubiana (2005, 176) contends that the Baggara of South Darfur were involved in the Arab militias, more so than has been generally thought, and that their leaders turned a blind eye to this. The public rhetoric of Baggara leaders was often bellicose and violently pro-government and many individual Baggara, including local leaders, joined the Arab militias. *Nazir* Madibu of the southern Rizeigat is a notable exception to this, having consistently and publicly avoided taking sides in the war. The investigations of Tubiana and this author suggest that Baggara participation was often a local affair, driven in part by rivalries within Baggara groups.

The majority bloc also includes some of the relative newcomers who have arrived at various points in the past century, for instance Fallata from West Africa, and Tama, Mararit, Erenga, Dajo, and others from Chad. Many take their cues from the Fur, whose senior traditional leaders they often live under (especially in South Darfur).

The Abuja accord left the Zaghawa in a difficult position. Arabs and non-Arabs alike voiced deep resentment and distrust towards the Zaghawa. Darfurian interlocutors invoked a host of reasons, both historical and current, for their anti-Zaghawa prejudice. The Zaghawa comprise only about 8 to 10 percent of the population but have a disproportionate influence on the politics of Darfur and Chad.[36] In the 1990s, the Zaghawa were seen as close to the Islamist regime and many Darfurians resented them for that. But bad blood grew between the Zaghawa and Khartoum over the latter's support to Arab groups with whom the Zaghawa were feuding in northwestern Darfur. In the early 2000s, many Zaghawa joined the nascent rebel groups. Their reputation as livestock rustlers, successful traders, settlers on the lands of others and, more recently, rebels has led many non-Zaghawa to view them as an aggressive, expansionist group. In recent years, Khartoum has fueled this perception with warnings of Zaghawa plans for a "greater Dar Zaghawa" (*dar zaghawa al kubra*) that would stretch from N'djamena to Omdurman. None of these suspicions was new, but in 2006 they were exacerbated by the fact the sole rebel leader to sign the DPA was Minni who was regarded as a Zaghawa tribalist. This sparked fears among other Darfurians that the Zaghawa had struck a side-deal with Khartoum. The fact that there was vehement dissent against Minni's decision among many Zaghawa commanders did not diminish the ethnic character of this resentment. Some Darfurian interlocutors even pointed out that the original SLA rebellion was to a large extent Zaghawa-led. This anti-Zaghawa prejudice played out in intra-SLA clashes and in tension between Zaghawa settler communities and their Baggara hosts in various parts of South Darfur including Dar Rizeigat, Dar Habbaniya, and south Buram that resulted in heavy Zaghawa displacement.[37]

In many ways, the re-emergence of Darfur's central bloc was a hopeful development indicating the existence of a regional coalition for peace and stability. Without these groups coming together, there can be no peace in Darfur. But serious problems remain. First, as noted, the central bloc does not address the needs of landless groups which have been responsible for much of the violence in recent years. Second, the spiraling violence after the Abuja agreement led to a situation of heightened ethnic tension as communities turned to ethnic militias to protect themselves. The tension was stoked by the government and fueled by competition over land, and was masked by the conflict between the government and rebels. In these circumstances, the re-emergence of Darfur's central bloc may prove to be short-lived.

### From Community Self-Defense Groups to Tribal Militia?

IN 2005 AND 2006, a number of non-Arab groups felt they had no choice but to organize their self-defense on a tribal basis, as opposed to based on local communities. This was a radical change for Darfur, one that the post-Abuja violence exacerbated.

From the 1980s onwards, in Darfur and elsewhere, successive governments in Khartoum mobilized and armed Arab groups to do their bidding, mostly to attack and subdue populations considered hostile. The NIF government furthered the tribal militia policy with the passage of the Popular Defense Act of 1989, making the PDF official. The government entrenched the policy in local government by elevating Arab traditional administrators above non-Arabs in the native administration, and sometimes giving them typically Arab or even jihadist titles, such as *nazir* or *amir*. The Arab groups of western Sudan, Darfur, and Kordofan have been militarized for over two decades.[38] By contrast, non-Arab communities mobilized along far more local lines, resorting to community-level strategies to try to ensure their protection. One such response was the establishment of self-defense committees. In the late 1980s and early 1990s, as Arab violence against non-Arab communities mounted, especially in western Darfur, and the state did not intervene, some of these communities started arming themselves. They re-energized traditional village mobilization structures, *warnang* for the Fur and *ornang* for the Masalit, which were historically used to organize hunting parties, communal work in the fields, and feasts. These groups were poorly equipped and ill-coordinated, despite isolated attempts in the late 1980s and early 1990s to organize them. They relied on occasional help from a handful of small-town traders and local officials. They sold government sugar rations and livestock, and bought light weapons and ammunition from the Chadian military on the border. A Sudanese political activist who spent nine months in 1990 along the Sudan-Chad border working with Fur and Masalit self-defense groups, recalled bartering sugar for ammunition with the soldiers of Chadian leader Hissène Habré's soldiers using a *kora*, a small bucket that measures volume (around two liters) in local markets—the ratio was five *kora* of sugar for one of bullets. He said Masalit communities tended to be better organized than the Fur, because of their past experience with Arab groups.[39]

The important point here is that the locus of these groups was the village and its outlying homesteads. There was little if any tactical cooperation among the self-defense groups: if Arab militias attacked one village, the self-defense force in the next village would most often just stay put until it in turn was attacked. The activist quoted above explained how these groups resisted his efforts to establish procedures whereby the villages could communicate and assist each other. The Fur-Arab war of 1987–1990—a coalition of 27 Arab groups, mobilized and armed by Libya with the tacit agreement of the Sudanese government, against Fur self-defense committees at the village level—was a case in point of the disparity between the tribal mobilization of Arab groups and the community-level mobilization of non-Arabs. The failure in 1990–1991 of the incursion by an SPLA unit headed by Daud Bolad (*hamlat Bolad*) to win over Fur communities in Jebel Marra also indicates that non-Arab groups resisted thinking beyond the local. In the latter half of the 1990s, Zaghawa groups in North Darfur, embroiled in a escalating feud with the camel-herding Awlad Zeid, an Arab group, and feeling that the authorities were supporting their foe, also started organizing, and turned out to be more effective.

In 2003 and 2004, the virulence of the government's attacks on civilian targets swept many of the Fur, Masalit, and Zaghawa self-defense committees, especially in West Darfur and the western areas of North Darfur, areas that were virtually emptied of their inhabitants. In other parts of Darfur, areas that had not witnessed as much violence in the 1980s and the 1990s, self-defense committees had not formed. Again, people focused on local and even individual solutions. Communities fled to nearby towns or to the state capitals, often led by local-level, low-ranking traditional leaders, sheikhs, and sometimes *omdas*, because these were the ones whom Khartoum had not bought off and who remained close to their people. Many young men joined the rebel groups, attracted by their initial string of military victories.

Another local response was, in some instances, to rely on the police. This was an understandable reaction. First the Condominium and then post-independence governments placed a high priority on local stability. Central authorities would swiftly deploy constabulary forces to tamp down communal tensions. A former district official recently recalled how, in the 1970s, under the Nimeiri regime, he was dispatched to southeastern Darfur with a detachment of several dozen policemen because of brewing trouble between Ta'aisha and Salamat Arabs—before real violence even broke out. He contrasted that with the practice of the Sadiq al Mahdi and NIF governments which have actively fueled local tensions.[40] As late as 2004, many Darfurians retained the hope that the Sudanese police could offer some protection if local conditions allowed them to operate. People drew a distinction between the regime on the one hand, and institutions of the Sudanese state, like the police, for whose services they yearned. Local police in fact managed to protect people in a number of occasions. In Tawila, a town west of al Fashir, the governor of North Darfur responded to a devastating government and militia attack in February 2004 by deploying a police force made up of both Darfurians and men from elsewhere in Sudan. This police force managed to ensure a minimum of security between March and September 2004, keeping marauding Janjawiid at bay, and this despite the presence of a hostile PDF contingent. In another example, in Sese, southeast of Geneina, villagers fleeing attacks found security near a simple police checkpoint on the Geneina-Mornei road. In late June 2004, 6,500 Masalit displaced had gathered under the protection of thirteen policemen, led by a sergeant, who on at least one occasion fired back at encroaching Janjawiid.[41] It is likely that there were other such instances elsewhere in Darfur.

But these respites were mostly short-lived. Conditions in Tawila deteriorated from September 2004 on, proving just how difficult it is to maintain good relations between police and residents, even in a locale where there seems to have been mutual good will, when the general law and order situation is out of control. In places like Kabkabiya, Geneina, and Kutum, local residents described in 2004 how the military, PDF, and militias threatened and even attacked local police forces. Without support from the authorities, the police were sidelined and could not protect citizens.[42] Finally, in many cases, the police operated alongside the military and its militia proxies, abusing the population. In 2004, when asked by a visitor how so many neighboring villages had been burned, the young police commander in Mornei, an Arab from central Sudan, replied "Really, it is not known [*wallahi, ma ma'rouf*]."[43] At that time, Mornei, some eighty kilometers east-southeast of Geneina, with an original population of about 6,000, hosted some 80,000 displaced from 111 destroyed villages (MSF 2004, 1).

But as the violence of the past four years raged on, people began to assume that nothing good would come from national or state authorities, and that any positive police action at the local level would be met with state-sponsored violence. The spike in violence that followed the Abuja accord left many non-Arab leaders saying they would never again trust an accord with the government. There was also widespread anger at the rebel groups for not offering better protection—an old grief as the rebels had triggered the acute phase of the crisis in the first place. More and more, non-Arab and Arab leaders and citizens said they had no choice but to organize the defense of their communities on an ethnic basis, rather than based on the local communities themselves. The rebel groups themselves are one of the main expressions of "militarized tribalism," to echo the words of Ali Haggar in this volume. Many rebel units and even some entire groups are based on a given sub-group, clan, or "tribe." The JEM's base, for instance, is a narrow Zaghawa sub-group, the Kobé, which straddles the Chad-Sudan border in the Tine area.

Ethnic groups have also organized militias in order to try and keep the violence at bay. The clearest example of that is the Meidob "police" force. The Meidob are non-Arab camel-herders who live in the arid hills around Malha, in northeastern Darfur. Their relations with the Zaghawa are strained, yet Meidob fighters and commanders, including Suleiman Marejan, were important in the SLA. In late 2003, as the SLA came under intense pressure from air and land attacks by the Sudanese military and Arab militias, the Meidob sought a solution to ensure that violence would not engulf their area. In early 2004, government forces attacked and bombed Malha. As recounted by two influential Meidob leaders, the Meidob turned to the rebel groups for protection. Abdel Wahid was isolated in Jebel Marra and could do nothing. Minni Minawi reportedly answered that the SLA's policy was to let tribes protect their own areas, and that he could not spare any weapons. Meidob leaders then negotiated a deal with senior government officials whereby the central government would fund and arm a reserve police (*ihtiyat al markazi*) unit of several hundred Meidob men in Malha. In return, the Meidob promised to prevent rebel groups from operating in their territory. The commander of the force, a Meidob, was commissioned as an officer in the police. Many of his men had fought with the SLA. The force was in fact a tribal force in official garb, and it has for the most part kept Arab militias out. The Meidob Police successfully repelled a 2005 incursion by a Border Guard unit (many Arab militias had converted into Border Guards). "For the Meidob, this [has been] very positive . . . It made the Meidob area one of the safest in Darfur," said one of the Meidob leaders in late 2006.[44] He also stressed that the force did not in fact answer to Sudanese authorities, but to the Meidob king, and that links with the non-signatory rebels remained strong.

This example was in many ways unique, made possible by a number of factors specific to the Meidob: the warrior tradition of the Meidob, their high level of group cohesion, the respect that the Meidob king commands among his people, the fact that they hold undisputed sway over their territory with few other groups living there, and last but not least the fact that their territory is of little interest to others because it is so arid. If anything, the long-term non-Meidob interest in Dar Meidob is that it remain stable so that trucks can ply the road from Darfur to Kufra in Libya (the border has been mostly closed since May 2003).

Other groups also sought to organize along tribal lines in order to stay out of the violence. The Bani Hussein, an Arab group west of Kabkabiya, had their own tribal police and managed to keep both rebels and Janjawiid at bay. They are one of the few Arab groups in Darfur to have stayed out of Janjawiid violence (Tubiana 2005, 177). In 2006, travelers entering or leaving the Bani Hussein center, Sereif al Zawiya encountered Bani Hussein militia, in reserve police uniforms, manning checkpoints—though it is unclear to the authors whether they are, like the Meidob, paid and armed by the government. In South Darfur, the Fallata of Tulus and the Gimir of Katila managed to avoid being attacked by Arab militias by obtaining arms. It is commonly accepted that the Tulus Fallata, a group of West African origin who view themselves as Arab, received weapons from the government to counter the SLA who attacked them in the past. In 2006, there were tensions with Masalit from Gereida and Jughana, and Tulus residents said their *omdas* told them not to retaliate against Masalit in order to avoid SLA reprisals.[45] But local non-Arabs say that Fallata militias were raiding the Masalit, as well as Fur, Dajo, Birgid, and other non-Arab communities around Tulus—a clear example of how the creation of tribalized militias leads to more aggressive behavior. The position of the South Darfur Gimir in Katila was somewhat different. Unlike the Gimir of Kulbus (North Darfur), the Katila Gimir did not participate in Janjawiid violence. Rather, Gimir traditional leaders said their people faced increased robbery and rape at the hands of camel-herding Arabs who became more present and more aggressive as the conflict unfolded. They said they did not get weapons from the government.[46] But Gimir leaders also acknowledged that Janjawiid had not targeted them as much as other groups because "we have weapons."[47] Another example of how tribalized militias can lead to instability was the SLA-Free Will (*irada hurra*), a militarily inconsequential splinter faction of SLA-Minni.[48] The SLA-Free Will, essentially a Birgid militia, received support from the government in return for its support for the DPA. Because of Birgid-Zaghawa tensions over land in eastern Darfur, it ended up fighting SLA-Minni forces in the Muhajiriya area in late 2006. There were even rumors, hard to substantiate, that the government was empowering the Birgid in order to counter the influence of *Nazir* Madibu and the southern Rizeigat (Tanner and Tubiana 2007).

It was no surprise that tribal militias are on the rise in Darfur. Historically, the military power of outlying groups in Sudan has followed the rise and fall of central authorities, depending on the relationship, positive or negative, of those groups to the center. This was true under Funj, Turkish, Mahdist, and even Condominium rule (Ahmed 2002, 74–76). The current Darfur crisis put the government on the defensive. It remained the primary player, but it could no longer control the situation: it could neither put down the rebellion nor probably rein in Janjawiid violence. It could only ride through by playing local groups off each other—namely through the creation of tribal militias. Khartoum could thus ensure that, while it was weak, others groups were weaker yet. But the consequences were dangerous. Ethnic tension mounted behind the veil of the conflict. The wider war provided the necessary ingredients—weapons, lawlessness, impunity. Tribal militias provided the mechanism. Starting in late summer 2006, fighting broke out between Birgid and Zaghawa in eastern Darfur, between Fur and Zaghawa on the northern slopes of Jebel Marra, between Fallata and non-Arabs in South Darfur, between Rizeigat Baggara and Habbaniya in southeastern Darfur, between Abbala Arabs (Hotiya and Nawaiba) near Zalingei, among Zaghawa (the tensions between Ila Digen, Minni's clan, and both Tuer and Bideyat are both political and clan-based[49]), as well as countless incidents of localized violence. The government thrived on the instability because it was that much harder for groups opposed to its policies to organize. This explained why Khartoum supported certain militias that were initially set up to protect populations from the violence of government proxies.

## International Forces

IN 2006, the strong consensus among non-Arab Darfurians was that the African Union mission, AMIS, was unable to protect people from violence—though some contingents did receive praise from local people, for instance the Rwandan forces in Kabkabiya. Not only was AMIS weak but it was increasingly seen as partisan. The AU's role in imposing the DPA on the non-signatories compromised its neutrality in the eyes of those groups. In August, when the AU expelled the non-signatories from the AU-chaired Ceasefire Commission and AMIS was seen providing logistics to the forces of SLA-Minni amid escalating violence, many Darfurians concluded that the AU had taken sides.

Another strong consensus in Darfur was that the violence would only stop with the deployment of international (i.e., UN) troops. Strikingly, Sudanese of all political colors—Darfurian and not, pro-UN deployment and rabidly opposed, educated and not, displaced and not—assumed that United Nations troops meant a Western force, most likely a U.S.-led NATO force. It was unclear why this belief was so widespread. Perhaps it was because UN operations in Sudan in general and in Darfur in particular are expatriate-driven, or perhaps because the U.S. government led the charge for UN deployment. Or perhaps it was because the expression *quwat duwaliya* ("international forces") is an oft-used expression in the Arab media for Coalition forces in Iraq and Afghanistan. Perhaps it was just a result of wishful thinking on one side and paranoia on the other.

Opponents to the government's policies in Darfur—a group that included not only the non-signatory rebel groups but most non-Arab Darfurians, including many members of SLA-Minni, as well as many Darfurian Arabs—expected that the arrival of UN troops would have led to a decrease in the violence. They anticipated that the "international troops" would comprise a stronger force:

more numerous, better equipped and better armed, notably with air power, with a stronger mandate and, more pointedly, with a fiercer commitment to ending the violence. People felt that even if such a force deployed with the consent of the government, once on the ground it would do what had to be done.

On the other hand, Darfurians opposed to an international force were swift to fall back on old arguments that often contradicted their current analysis of the conflict. Arab leaders who had just explained that the government was the main driver of the crisis promptly declared that an international force would not solve the region's "tribal" problems, and possibly exacerbate them. They said a UN force would be tantamount to an invasion and that it would be resisted the way Sunni insurgents resist the U.S. presence in Iraq. What seemed to be behind this, however, was fear of what actions an expanded international force would take, notably in the area of war crimes. Local Arab leaders who had done Khartoum's brutal bidding had no trust that senior echelons in the government would not turn on them in order to curry favor with the International Criminal Court.

Both views failed to recognize the twofold reality about UN forces. First, the Sudan government was successfully resisting any such deployment. It reneged on a number of clear pledges to allow UN troops in—first in Brussels and Paris in March 2006, when vice president Ali Osman Taha indicated that it would agree subsequent to the conclusion of the DPA, and then in November 2006 in Addis Ababa, when it first accepted a "hybrid" AU-UN force and then went back on that commitment. There was little likelihood of Khartoum changing its stance. Second, past experience with UN peacekeeping operations indicates they are not often successful in protecting civilians. Assuming that a UN force could do so in Darfur was unrealistic—on the part of both proponents and opponents of such a deployment.

With a UN force unlikely to be effective, why then was the Sudan government so uncompromising in holding its position? Conventional wisdom in Sudan in 2006 was that the government was afraid that UN troops would execute arrest warrants on behalf of the ICC. But conversations and informed speculation with Sudanese in Khartoum and Darfur revealed more intricate motives. One, the government may have feared that an expanded UN mission could lead to the collection of more evidence of war-crimes—documents, testimony, and physical evidence such as mass graves. Second, leading government figures may have feared that a powerful UN force would have opened up endless possibilities for deal-cutting and double-crossing within the leadership, ushering in even more uncertainty and instability. Last, many Sudanese pointed out that, with the elections only a couple of years away, President Bashir did not have the popular constituency that other NCP leaders had built among the population or within the security forces. Positioning himself as an Islamo-nationalist leader defending Sudan's Islamic and national identity (promising jihad against "foreign forces") could prove effective electoral politics, especially with the militant wing of the NCP, many of whose members could threaten at any time to defect to Hassan al Turabi's more radical Popular Congress Party.

## Concluding Thoughts

IN A REMARKABLE essay published in 1988, Paul Doornbos described a wave of momentous social change rolling through Darfur over the previous decade. Using case studies of two villages on Darfur's western border, he described how peoples of the Sudanese periphery were "becoming Sudanese." In village elementary schools and local markets, rural people were abandoning their traditional cultures and converting (his expression) to the lifestyle of the urban centers of central Sudan—the associated market economy and the social and economic mores of the more orthodox Islamic vision that was taking hold, not only in Khartoum, but in cities around the Muslim world. The process was driven by government services, trade, and preachers of Islamic orthodoxy. Writing in the wake of the killing famine of 1984–1985 but before the visitation of widespread violence, Doornbos was at pains to stress the radical nature of the process underway. "Sudanisation," as he called it, was "a revolutionary ideology and praxis, most of all because it constitutes a comprehensive assault on traditional social organization and culture" (Doornbos 1988, 101–102).

Nearly twenty years later, and four years into a conflict which may yet last many years more, that process of modernization is accelerating, driven by violence on a vast scale. And the changes afoot are even more radical than the peacetime transformations described by Doornbos. The violence has displaced a third of Darfur's population, as refugees in Chad or internally within Darfur—and no-one is counting the Darfurians who have fled the conflict to seek refuge elsewhere in Sudan. This immense dislocation will have irreversible impacts on Darfurian society.

Darfur has undergone the most rapid urbanization in its history. Millions of people are living in camps and still more within towns. Nyala is Sudan's second largest city, spreading by the week and swallowing up villages. Many Darfurians have not farmed in two, three, and four years, and live off precarious peri-urban livelihoods and emergency relief. Even if there is peace, many will not return to village life. At the same time, many displaced rural Darfurians have access to a level of services they never knew before: health services, schools, clean water. This new life has led many Darfurians to acquire new habits and new expectations. But meeting these expectations depends on international charity, which is by definition fickle.

In the camps, the displaced have started listening to new leaders. They find that the skills of old leaders, sheikhs and *omdas* who know customary land law and how to resolve local conflicts, are no longer useful to people who have no land to farm. The new leaders are often younger, with some education: teachers, technicians, local government employees, small merchants. These emerging leaders have new skills that are necessary to surviving displacement. They understand the workings of both Sudanese officialdom and the humanitarian system. They are also more political—and often more radical in their views. Many of these leaders have ties to the rebel groups. Darfurians live in new surroundings, with new livelihoods, new social and cultural habits, and new leaders. Displaced Darfurians are both more integrated into the modern world then they were at the turn of the millennium, but also far more vulnerable. They remain exposed to violence and are dependent economically. For many, the prospect of return to life as it was before is illusory.

This chapter has documented the unfolding of Darfurians' reactions to their new predicament. There are two parallel and contradictory responses— the resurgence of Darfur's central consensus bloc and its associated "Darfur consensus," alongside the formation of ethnic militias among non-Arab groups. The central bloc, predicated on a common vision of how to manage Darfur's land and resources, could become the foundation for a form of majority rule. But it is not politically consolidated around any party, movement, or leader, and is at risk of destabilization by those groups whom the bloc excludes, especially the landless Arabs who have wrought much of the violence of the past years. The ruling NCP fears a united Darfur bloc because it represents a large electoral constituency, not only in Darfur but also in central Sudan and the national capital, where so many Darfurians live. In the past, Darfurian votes have decided the outcomes of general elections in Sudan, and may do so again. The other trend is fragmentation and militarization. Ethnic militias allow certain groups to ensure their own protection, but they encourage aggressive behavior and are easy for the government to manipulate, both of which lead to instability and further violence. This trend may yet overwhelm the re-emergence of the historic "Darfur consensus."

Superficially, these two processes are contradictory. But they also have common points. Both represent a hardening of Darfurian opinion, especially regarding the role of the Sudanese state. Both proceed from the notion that the current government in Khartoum is unwilling to provide security for local communities. The "Sudanisation" process that Doornbos described was driven by the spread of government services and trade in the 1970s and early 1980s. Today the situation is diametrically different: there are no government services, only government violence. Services had started collapsing around the time Doornbos's paper was published and in many parts of Darfur, the violence has dislocated local markets and disrupted trade patterns. Farmers and herders alike can no longer rely on their livelihoods to survive. People suffer and blame both the Khartoum and the rebel groups, but they say it is the Sudan government that is at the root of their region's problems. This view that hardened with the violence that followed the Abuja agreement.

The question for the future is whether this hardening of opinion will translate into a revived common regional identity. The re-emergence of the Darfurian majority bloc would suggest so, as does the increasing number of Arabs aligning themselves with the non-signatory rebel groups (as of early 2007). Arabs and non-Arabs are becoming conscious (again) of the fact that they are Darfurian, that past government policies have discriminated against them all, that they are all affected by the violence, and that they have common interests for the future. The promise of regional identity is there. But too much disunity endures in Darfur. The rebel groups remain divided and fractious. The effort that began in Abuja towards an intra-Darfur dialogue—the Darfur-Darfur Dialogue and Consultation—has so far failed to hand Darfurian leaders a genuine opportunity to discuss issues and grievances. Darfurians who are affiliated with neither the government nor the rebels have little or no voice. Rather than stifle the violence, the trend towards tribal militias runs the risk of further bloodshed. Darfur's renewed regional sentiment has promise but stops well short of the politically organized unity required to counter the sway of the government, which remains determined to see Darfur weak and divided.

# 13

## Narrating Darfur: Darfur in the U.S. Press, March–September 2004

### Deborah Murphy

O N MARCH 24, 2004, in a column titled "Ethnic Cleansing, Again," on the *New York Times'* op-ed page, Nicholas D. Kristof wrote:

> The most vicious ethnic cleansing you've never heard of is . . .
> a campaign of murder, rape and pillage by Sudan's Arab rulers
> that has forced 700,000 black African Sudanese to flee their
> villages . . . The culprit is the Sudanese government, one of the
> world's nastiest. Its Arab leaders have been fighting a civil war
> for more than 20 years against its rebellious black African south.
> Lately, it has armed lighter-skinned Arab raiders, the Janjaweed,
> who are killing or driving out blacks in the Darfur region
> near Chad.

This was Kristof's first column on the subject, as well as the *Times'* first op-ed on Darfur, but it was far from the last. Beginning in March 2004, the conflict in Darfur began to attract an unusual degree of attention in the U.S. press for a catastrophe in Africa. How was the conflict presented, what were the proposed solutions, and what arguments were used to convince the public of the need for action? This chapter is a review of the eighty-three editorials and op-eds on Darfur appearing in the *New York Times*, the *Washington Post*, the *Wall Street Journal*, and the *Washington Times* from March to

September 2004. The selected articles display near unanimity in the descriptions of the conflict and the recommendation for outside intervention.

While most of the articles acknowledged Darfur's complexity, there was little deviation from Kristof's first description of the conflict on March 24. This narrative, which assigned polarized Arab and African identities to the perpetrators and victims, usually labeled it a genocide, and assumed the government controlled the violence, probably accounts for a great deal of the success had by human rights advocates in attracting attention to Darfur. Almost half the reviewed articles described the violence as genocide or potential genocide. Taken together, the ethnic targeting of the victims, the plight of the displaced, and the culpability of the Sudanese government proved to be a powerful formula for demonstrating the need for intervention.

In urging intervention, extensive parallels were made to the shame of U.S. and UN inaction in Rwanda. However, when specific policies were proposed, the current realities of Iraq loomed larger than the memory of Rwanda. Liberals and conservatives debated the merits of multilateralism versus unilateralism, expressed growing frustration at the failure of EU members and other powers to take the situation as seriously as the U.S. did, and derided the effectiveness of the UN. In doing so, they demonstrated the extent to which the aftermath of the Iraq invasion colored the debate over Darfur.

### Description of the Conflict

DARFUR BEGAN to attract attention in the U.S. press in late March and early April 2004. Twelve editorials on Darfur appeared in April in the selected newspapers—with eight of them appearing in the first half of the month, clustered around the tenth anniversary of the Rwandan genocide on April 7—eight editorials appeared in May, nine in June, sixteen in July, fifteen in August, and nineteen in September. Fourteen of the eighty-three articles described a visit that the authors had made to refugee camps in Chad, or in two cases, to Darfur itself.

The articles appearing in April, May, and June were primarily concerned with explaining the background of the crisis and urging the U.S. and UN to "take action." Later in the summer there was much less emphasis on providing background or even focusing on what was going on in Darfur; instead, the focus shifted to the developments on the international scene that were driving the response.

Over April, May, and June, a common description of the conflict quickly emerged: the Arab-dominated Sudanese government had armed local Arab militias (usually called "Janjawiid") to attack civilians (identified either as "African" or "non-Arab"), causing thousands to flee to neighboring Chad and hundreds of thousands more to remain internally displaced in Darfur beyond the reach of relief agencies. Twenty-three of the eighty-three articles also stated that the violence was a response to a local rebellion, which was itself a response to, variously, the government's favoring of the Arab population, the historical neglect of the Darfur region, or the exclusion of Darfurian groups from the North-South peace process. However, little attention was paid to the role of the rebels.[1]

Of the eighty-three articles reviewed, forty-one identified the conflict as one between Arabs and Africans. Several writers used the term "non-Arab" rather than "African" to refer to the victims, but the perpetrators were almost uniformly identified as Arab. Kristof and Jerry Fowler (of the U.S. Holocaust Memorial Museum's Committee on Conscience) both identified the victims as primarily members of the Fur, Masalit, and Zaghawa tribes,[2] but no other articles described the role of different ethnic groups in the conflict.

Eleven articles also mentioned how the historical competition between Arab pastoralists and African farmers over scarce land and water resources contributed to the conflict. Environmental degradation was blamed for causing the rise of these tensions, and the Arab militias were said to be motivated by a desire for the farmers' land.

The Sudanese government was held to be ultimately responsible for the violence because it had armed the Janjawiid and also conducted bombing campaigns. It was also assumed to be capable of stopping the violence, if it so desired, by disarming and disbanding the Janjawiid.[3]

Besides depictions of the violence, most descriptions of the crisis emphasized the humanitarian plight of the refugees and the internally displaced people (IDPs), and the criminality of the Sudanese government's refusal to allow adequate access to IDPs in Darfur. Frequent mention was made of the UN's Sudan Coordinator's March description of the conflict as "the world's most severe humanitarian crisis" and of USAID Administrator Andrew Natsios's estimate, in early June, that 300,000 to 1 million people would die in the region before the year's end depending on the international response. The need to stop this imminent mass starvation was at least as urgent a basis for action as the need to stop the violence.[4]

## Rwanda, the War on Terror, and the Call for Intervention

DARFUR WAS completely unknown to most Americans before it began to receive coverage in the spring of 2004. (From 1994 to 2003, according to the *Washington Post*, the *Post* had mentioned Darfur four times and the *New York Times* had mentioned it twice.)[5] Journalists reached for analogies readers were more familiar with to act as shorthand for the severity of the crisis and the need for intervention. By far the most common analogy was Rwanda. Twenty-eight of the eighty-three articles referenced the Rwandan genocide, as did eleven of the sixteen appearing in March and April. The conflict was commonly described as "the new Rwanda," "the worst humanitarian crisis since Rwanda," "another Rwanda," and so on.

The Rwanda comparison associated Darfur with genocide in the reader's mind. However, other than stating the fact that both were genocides, few efforts were made to illuminate the similarities and differences between the conflicts. Instead, the focus was on the West's failure to stop the Rwandan genocide in 1994, and the risk of repeating that mistake in Darfur. The comparisons to Rwanda were aided by the tenth anniversary of the Rwandan genocide in early April; many of the editorials commemorating Rwanda urged the West to take action in Darfur to expiate its previous sins.[6] The *New York Times* summed up the prevailing ethos with, "The worsening humanitarian disaster in western Sudan, where thousands of people have been killed and almost a million people driven from there homes by government-backed forces, will test whether the world has learned anything from the failure to stop the genocide in Rwanda 10 years ago."[7]

The crisis in Darfur revived the debate over humanitarian intervention that had dominated U.S. foreign policy in the late 1990s, but that had been nearly absent from the debates over intervention in Afghanistan and Iraq, in which its relevance to the war on terror was considered paramount. While observers recognized that analogies could only be taken so far ("The horrors in the Darfur region of Sudan are not 'like' Rwanda, any more than those in Rwanda were 'like' those ordered by Hitler," Samantha Power wrote in the *New York Times*[8]), the specifics of how they were alike or different were set aside. The important thing was the international community's response, which was always (with the partial exceptions of Kosovo and East Timor) shamefully inadequate. As columnist Fred Hiatt wrote in a column in the *Washington Post* criticizing the lack of attention to Darfur in the U.S. presidential election, "Darfur should be debated precisely because it raises difficult questions—and because these questions aren't so different from the challenges that were posed by Iraq and Kosovo and that may arise again in Iran, or Burma, or Zimbabwe, or in many other spots. When is it legitimate to infringe on a nation's sovereignty to ensure global security or rescue an imperiled population? Who should perform these jobs? What if the United Nations says no?"[9]

Darfur was expected to be included in the "canon of historical tragedy" (de Waal and Conley-Zilkic 2007) it was assumed that barring outside intervention, the victims in Darfur were as surely doomed as victims of other genocides had been. According to the *Washington Post*:

> The early preparation for the genocide in Darfur, Sudan's vast
> western province, played out behind a veil of ignorance. Almost
> no foreign aid workers operated in the region, and the world
> failed to realize what was happening. Stage two of the genocide,
> the one we are now in, is more acutely shameful: A succession of
> reports from relief agencies, human rights groups, and journal-
> ists informs us that hundreds of thousands of people are likely to
> perish, yet outsiders still cannot muster the will to save them.

Unless that changes, we are fated to live through the genocide's third stage. There will be speeches, commissions of inquiry, and sundry retrospectives, just as there were after Cambodia and Rwanda. Never again, we will be told.[10]

The United States, as the world's most powerful nation, was considered to have a particular responsibility. On April 7, Samantha Power wrote, "Even when the United States decides not to respond militarily, American leadership is indispensable . . . And it remains true despite the Bush administration's unpopularity abroad."[11] U.S. policy makers who had served in the Clinton administration expressed regret for the administration's failure to act in Rwanda and urged the U.S. to take action in Darfur. After delivering a speech in Kigali, Richard Holbrooke wrote: "The lesson of each genocide is the same: The killings really take off only after the murderers see that the world, and especially the United States, is not going to care or react."[12] On May 30, Susan E. Rice and Gayle E. Smith (formerly senior officials in the Clinton administration) wrote:

> Ten years ago CNN ran footage of bloated corpses floating down
> Rwanda's rivers, while Washington debated whether to call it
> 'genocide'. As U.S. officials who were later responsible for U.S.
> policy toward Africa, we helped plan several subsequent military
> interventions in Africa. But, like many others, we remain
> haunted by the Rwandan genocide. So it is with some humility
> and a full appreciation of the complexity of decisions to deploy
> U.S. forces that we hazard to recommend how to deal with a new
> Rwanda now unfolding in the Darfur region of western Sudan.[13]

UN Secretary-General Kofi Annan was also regularly singled out as having a moral responsibility to act on Darfur, because he had been head of peace-keeping when the UN force was evacuated during the Rwandan genocide, though the criticism seemed muted by Annan's early outspokenness and his personal popularity. "I hate to say it," Nicholas Kristof wrote of "a man I like and respect," "but the way things are going, when he dies the obituary will begin: Kofi Annan, the former UN secretary general who at various points in his career presided ineffectually over the failure to stop genocide, first in Rwanda and then in Sudan, died today."[14]

Occasionally other humanitarian crises—such as the Holocaust, Cambodia, Bosnia, and Kosovo—were used as points of comparison to urge U.S. intervention. Kosovo was invoked as the only example of Western intervention stopping a government from committing genocide.[15] Michael Soussan, editor of *Africa Geopolitics*, advocated establishing a no-fly zone for Darfur from Chad, similar to the one used to protect Iraqi Kurds in the 1990s: "Just as the UN cannot afford 'another Rwanda,' the U.S. can hardly afford 'another Somalia.'... In Iraqi Kurdistan, it wasn't even necessary to put troops on the ground. A no-fly zone was enough to dissuade Saddam Hussein from unleashing his tanks and helicopters against the Kurds."[16]

One compelling analogy was largely overlooked: The war in southern Sudan, which had been ongoing for the most of the forty-nine years since Sudan's independence then seemed to be drawing to a close, due in no small part to U.S. diplomatic efforts. The vicious counterinsurgent tactics seen in Darfur had first been employed against rebels in the South, as described by John Ryle:

> Darfur has been described as "Rwanda in slow motion." But more significantly, it is southern Sudan speeded up. For two decades in the south successive Khartoum governments have employed the same counterinsurgency techniques as in Darfur today, with similar results. During the 1980s and 1990s Arab militias from Darfur and neighboring Kordofan, similar to the Janjawiid but known to the southerners by the derogatory term "Murahaliin" (nomads), were deployed against communities in SPLM-controlled areas of Bahr-el-Ghazal, the province to the south of Darfur. The famines that afflicted Bahr-el-Ghazal in 1987–1988 and 1998–1999 were the result of these attacks.... These attacks were coordinated by military intelligence and sometimes accompanied by aerial bombardment, as in Darfur. And an ideology of Muslim religious and Arab racial superiority was used to justify them. (Ryle 2004)

These precedents were largely ignored, however; only fifteen of the reviewed articles mentioned the North-South war, with seven articles making explicit comparisons between the causes and conduct of the wars in the South and Darfur. There was also little attention paid to the imminent end of the war in the South, except for concern that the U.S. diplomatic investment in Naivasha would hamper strong action on Darfur. In general, Darfur was removed from the Sudanese context and was instead incorporated into the history of genocide.

As a result, the specter of Rwanda dominated the call for intervention. Criticizing the lack of leadership on Darfur, the *Post* wrote, "It is as though, in the wake of the West's failure to prevent Rwanda's genocide, the gods of history are asking, okay, if we give you a second chance and months of warning, will you do better?"[17] Nicholas Kristof profiled Carl Wilkens, a Seventh-Day Adventist missionary who was the only American to stay in Rwanda during the genocide, and wrote, "We don't have to wonder idly how we would respond to such an African genocide—one is unfolding, right now, in the Darfur region of Sudan, and once again we're doing next to nothing."[18]

But those who argued that the shame of U.S. inaction in 1994 compelled a humanitarian intervention in Darfur could not ignore all that had changed in the intervening decade. The 9/11 attacks, the war on terror, and the war in Iraq were blamed for U.S. unwillingness to take robust action. "It's hard to remember now," journalist James Traub wrote in the *New York Times*, "but the question of when states were obliged to prevent or limit catastrophic harm was a burning question in the 1990's . . . The crusade against terrorism also seemed to have erased the distinction between 'interests' and 'values,' since the wars in both Afghanistan and Iraq, whatever their original motives, had the effect of liberating a people from tyranny."[19]

While the arguments for taking stronger action in Darfur were overwhelmingly humanitarian, a few writers, particularly conservative ones, used the war on terror as justification for intervention in Sudan. Neoconservatives William Kristol and Vance Serchuk summarized this view:

> After all, in addition to the humanitarian imperative, the United
> States has a strategic interest in Sudan. Khartoum is one of seven

regimes on the U.S. government's list of state sponsors of terrorism, and Sudan's dictatorship has had ties with almost every significant terrorist organization in the broader Middle East. Al
Qaeda was based in Sudan during the 1990's, and other terrorist
groups continue to operate there freely. This month [German
newspaper] *Die Welt* reported that Syria and Sudan have been collaborating in developing chemical weapons and may have used
them against civilians in Darfur. Thus, in moving against
Khartoum for its human rights abuses, we will also be striking a
blow in the war on terror.[20]

Sudan's deportation of Osama bin Laden in 1996 as a result of Western
pressure was cited as evidence that the U.S. had leverage to press Khartoum
to act differently in Darfur. Neoconservative columnist Frank Gaffney gave
Darfur as a reason why U.S. citizens should divest from Sudan,[21] as well as
four other terror-sponsoring states (Iran, North Korea, Syria, and Libya).[22]

There was some concern over whether an intervention in Darfur would
provoke a backlash in the Muslim world. "Lately, fliers have appeared in
Khartoum mosques urging jihad," Sam Dealey wrote.[23] But this was generally dismissed as a reason not to intervene. "There is the fear that a foreign
intervention in Sudan . . . could trigger a popular backlash throughout the
Muslim world," the *Washington Post* wrote. "If this were correct, it would be
extremely serious: The war against terrorism is a battle for Islamic hearts and
minds. . . . But the key to winning hearts and minds throughout the region is
not to defer to the autocratic government of Egypt [which opposed interven-
tion], still less to Sudan's rulers, whose victims in Darfur are after all Muslims.
In contemplating intervention in Sudan, Arab opinion must be considered.
But it's not clear that this means intervention should be ruled out."[24]

Some writers seized on the Bush administration's depiction of its war on
terror as a battle between good and evil to urge the administration to take on
the evil in Darfur. "Mr. Bush seems proud of his 'moral clarity,'" Nicholas
Kristof wrote, "his willingness to recognize evil and bluntly describe it as
such. Well, Darfur reeks of evil, and we are allowing it to continue."[25]
Columnist Nat Hentoff wrote, "Of course this is genocide. It is also pure evil.

Mr. Bush is not afraid of that word. Let him, right now—unlike Bill Clinton turning away from Rwanda—save lives in Darfur."[26]

Some commentators felt that the post-9/11 world would be more a more permissive environment for humanitarian intervention. In an editorial critiquing the realist school of foreign policy and the principle of noninterference in sovereign states, the *Post* wrote:

> This "realism" has always had a tenuous hold on American for-
> eign policy for the good reason that this nation was founded
> upon universalist principles. But it seems particularly misplaced
> in the age of international terror, when respecting the sover-
> eignty of failed states such as Afghanistan is not a viable option.
> The attacks of Sept. 11, 2001, demonstrated that what states do
> within their borders can affect international security... Refusing
> to save hundreds of thousands of lives in Darfur out of deference
> to an already tattered doctrine seems unwarranted.[27]

But others saw intervention in conflicts where America's national interests were not at stake as less likely after 9/11. Reflecting on the Bush administration's failure to intervene in Liberia in 2003, Holbrooke wrote, "Will it always take a 9/11 to mobilize our nation? Perhaps 9/11 will be a wake-up call for actions that go beyond the war on terrorism. But our failure to act in Liberia last year was a depressing reminder that 'never again' is more a slogan than a policy for our nation."[28]

Most articles avoided any mention of Iraq. Many conservatives had embraced the Bush administration's reframing of the Iraq war as a humanitarian intervention. But when conservatives wrote about Darfur, they were usually more interested in pillorying the UN than in urging the U.S. to play a stronger role (further discussed below). The liberal press, which argued more strenuously for intervention in Sudan, nonetheless wanted Europe or Africa to provide any necessary troops. Though both had liberal editorial boards, the *Washington Post*, which had supported the Iraq invasion, took a much stronger stand for intervention in Darfur than the *New York Times*, which had not. The two facts may be unrelated; the *Times* left most of its writing on Darfur to Nicholas Kristof, who was more focused on raising awareness than proposing specific policies. But the *Post* was concerned that fallout from Iraq accounted for the reluctance to take action in Sudan: "One generation ago, after another much-criticized war, the United States was for a long time unwilling to project force. But if the nation is to avoid succumbing to an Iraq syndrome to match the Vietnam syndrome of the past, it must prove its continuing readiness to lead in the world. There could scarcely be a more compelling cause than Darfur."[29]

## Policy Options

"IRAQ SYNDROME" or no, the debate over which policies the U.S. and UN should pursue in Darfur was informed at every stage by the still-unfolding aftermath of the Iraq war. Three major themes emerged at different times.

### 1. Public Pressure

Initially the emphasis was on persuading the government of Sudan to change its behavior. Nicholas Kristof summarized a common point of view in the early months of the crisis when he wrote, "One of the lessons of history is that very modest efforts can save large numbers of lives. Nothing is so effective in curbing ethnic cleansing as calling attention to it."[30] Early articles were focused on raising awareness of the atrocities, and urged the U.S., as well as the UN, EU, and African and Arab states, to condemn the violence. Liberals took the declaration of a cease-fire in early April following negotiations in N'djamena, and a phone call from President Bush to President Bashir as evidence that U.S. leadership could help resolve the crisis (even as they realized the cease-fire was immediately violated.)[31] The U.S. was called upon to use diplomacy and threats to persuade Khartoum to disband the Janjawiid and lift restrictions on humanitarian access. It was presumed that the U.S. and its allies had the leverage to do this, and that the primary problem was whether the U.S. would have the political will to do so, particularly given its investment in the North-South peace process.[32]

Calls for public awareness and diplomatic pressure dominated the discussion of policy options from April through June. Of the thirty-three articles published during that period, only four called for sanctions to be imposed (as opposed to merely threatened) on the government or on specific individuals, and only three called for international peacekeepers. However, during June and July, as the government broke its promises to rein in its militias and substantially improve humanitarian access, there was a growing realization that Khartoum could not be trusted to keep its word and provide security.

## 2. Multilateralism versus Unilateralism

At the same time the U.S. press realized that there was a need to impose harsher penalties on Khartoum, however, it realized that the international community lacked the will to impose them. Initially, the liberal journalists and human rights advocates who called for action considered the UN to be the appropriate forum for handling the crisis. However, discontent with the effectiveness of UN institutions and with the behavior of UN Security Council members was registered almost immediately. This launched a debate about the proper role of the U.S., its allies, and the UN in responding to a rogue member state, which revisited the similar debates about Iraq.

In June and July, editorialists became increasingly disgusted with the politics of the Security Council, which had hampered U.S. efforts to pass even a weak resolution. Facing particular criticism were veto-wielding China, Russia's oil and arms interests in Sudan, Pakistan and Algeria's support for Sudan as a fellow Muslim country, and the efforts of the African bloc to protect one of its own. On April 26, a *Washington Post* editorial castigated the UN Human Rights Commission for postponing the release of its own report on Darfur, and therefore a vote on the appointment of a rapporteur.[33] The fact that Sudan was itself a member of the Human Rights Commission, and that the U.S. ambassador had been alone in walking out in protest at its reappointment, was also a source of disgust.[34]

The ineffectiveness of the UN was mourned by the liberal commentators who had pressed for a multilateral solution, and trumpeted by conservative newspapers as vindication of the unilateral route the U.S. had pursued in Iraq. With the exception of the UK, which was second only to the U.S. in donating to the relief effort and at one point offered to send five thousand troops, the rest of the world was not doing enough. Many liberal editorial writers argued that by failing to join the effort to act on Darfur, Europe was undermining the multilateral ideal it claimed to be protecting by resisting U.S. unilateralism. The *Washington Post*, in response to the minimal relief contributions by France, Germany, and Japan, wrote, "The tightfistedness of these allies is outrageous, as is the reluctance of France and other members of the U.N. Security Council to support a tough resolution on Darfur. To excuse their failure to contribute to Iraq's reconstruction, these nations complain that the Bush administration's Iraq policy was insufficiently deferential to the United Nations. But none other than the UN secretary general has just visited Darfur to demonstrate the urgency of humanitarian action. What excuse can there be now?"[35]

France, owing perhaps to its particularly strong resistance to the Iraq war, was singled out for the majority of criticism. In a June 20 editorial, the *Post* alleged that France's interest in Sudanese oil concessions was the reason it resisted a strong Security Council resolution.[36] On September 11, Kristof wrote, "France and Germany, I sympathized with your opposition to the war in Iraq. But are you really now so petty and anti-Bush that you refuse to stand with the U.S. against the slaughter in Darfur, or even to contribute significant sums to ease the suffering? Does the Chirac government really want to show the moral blindness to Sudan's genocide that the Vichy regime did to Hitler's?"[37]

After the Security Council passed a resolution on July 30 giving the government of Sudan thirty days to disband the militias and improve humanitarian access, criticism of the UN increased dramatically as observers realized that failure to comply would carry no repercussions. On August 24, the *Post* warned, "Darfur already has become a synonym for dithering by outside powers in the face of genocide. Soon it may also deliver another grim verdict on the ability of the Security Council to back up its own resolutions."[38] On September 13, after months of UN inaction, Morton Abramowitz and Samantha Power wrote in the *Washington Post*, "Countries do not want to do what is necessary to prevent large-scale loss of life in messy, complex Africa. Crises such as Darfur require urgent action, and states are well aware that the Security Council cannot act urgently. It is not by accident that they throw the problem into the labyrinth of UN deliberations . . . The international system is broken, at least when it comes to Africa."[39]

Discontent with the UN grew so great that some liberal commentators were willing to consider the possibility of the U.S. acting unilaterally or in concert with a few allies, without UN approval, although this was also regarded as fundamentally unfair to the U.S. On June 20, a *Washington Post* editorial criticized the Security Council's failure to pass a tough resolution and urged the U.S. government to use other routes to resolve the crisis. Specifically, it recommended travel bans and asset freezes for members of the government deemed responsible, announcing the intent to prosecute Sudanese war criminals if the violence did not stop, and supporting an AU force.[40] On July 22, it returned to the idea of unilateral intervention: "This would add to the unfairness with which the world's burdens are shared—American taxpayers already pay most of the bills for global security. But if nobody else will act to save up to 1 million civilians, questions about sharing the burden must be set aside."[41]

Susan Rice and Gayle Smith wrote in the *Post* that the U.S. should encourage the EU, and Arab and African states to bear the military burden of an intervention and provide financial support, and that "Given the demands on U.S. forces in Iraq, Afghanistan, and Haiti, it is reasonable to ask Europe and Africa to play a key role." However, "the United States should begin urgent military planning and preparation for the contingency that no other country will act to stop the dying in Darfur."[42]

In the conservative press, on the other hand, there was no expectation that the UN or any other country would aid Darfur. Rather, it was anticipated that the burden of stopping the violence would fall on the U.S. In its first editorial on Darfur, on May 18, the *Wall Street Journal* omitted the U.S. when it wrote, "the United Nations, the Arab world, and Europe are failing to speak up, much less to act."[43] On July 2 it stated, "While the world's moralists are in full cry about the threat of 'another Rwanda,' no one sees fit to actually do something. No one, that is, except the U.S."[44] It went on to state, "The lesson of Sudan is that the world is a Hobbesian place outside the U.S. sphere of influence . . . It is fashionable these days to express distaste for American 'unilateralism' and 'hegemony.' The unfolding catastrophe in Darfur offers a chilling view of what the alternative really looks like."

On September 22, conservative commentators William Kristol and Vance Serchuk advocated a unilateral U.S. intervention in the *Post*: "The failure of world nations to force Sudan to change its behavior is merely the latest reminder of a fact we should have learned since the end of the Cold War—in the Balkans, in Rwanda and in Iraq. The United Nations is slow and weak, and the United States, especially when waiting on the United Nations, is itself often too slow to act."[45] After the UN Security Council failed to act on the U.S.'s genocide determination, conservative *New York Times* columnist David Brooks wrote a scathing response:

> Every time there is an ongoing atrocity, we watch the world community go through the same series of stages: 1) shock and concern, 2) gathering resolve, 3) fruitless negotiation, 4) pathetic inaction, 5) shame and humiliation, 6) steadfast vows never to let this happen again. The "never again" always comes. But still, we have all agreed, this sad cycle is better than having some impromptu coalition of nations actually go in "unilaterally" and do something. That would lack legitimacy! Strain alliances! Menace international law! Threaten the multilateral ideal![46]

### 3. Support for the African Union

As it became clear that the UN and Western governments were not prepared to take meaningful action, an unlikely alternative vehicle emerged in the African Union. The AU was viewed with a certain level of distrust as "a mutual protection group of governments good, bad, and indifferent"[47] that had failed to deal with other outlaw states such as Zimbabwe. But it garnered praise for its offer to send more troops to Darfur and for its monitors' honesty in reporting cease-fire violations. On August 1, the Security Council gave the Government of Sudan thirty days to stop the violence or face the threat of sanctions. A consensus emerged among the editorial writers that since Khartoum would certainly fail to meet the Security Council's demands and could not be trusted to supply security anyway, and because the Security Council would certainly be unable to muster the political will to impose punitive measures, the Security Council should authorize a larger force of AU monitors and peacekeeping troops at the end of the thirty days.[48] The AU was still criticized for being reluctant to deploy the additional troops without

Khartoum's consent, however. The three thousand troops it had offered were also seen to be a grossly inadequate number, but at this point the editorialists seemed to be willing to settle for what they could get.[49]

What was missing from the policy discussions is almost as notable as what was said. There was next to no discussion of regime change, though the limited discussion that did take place was shadowed by the Iraq war. Nicholas Kristof explicitly stated several times that he was *not* advocating an invasion, once in response to readers who asked him, "Haven't we invaded enough Muslim countries?"[50] Some conservatives felt that regime change was the only solution but was not politically feasible: "The real problem, as everyone knows and no one will admit, is Sudan's murderous regime. But Mr. Annan and company can't abide regime change, and in any case the U.S. military is too preoccupied to make that happen. That means we're left with diplomatic pressure and visits like Mr. Powell's, which are better than nothing but don't solve the long term problem."[51]

Only two editorials, from opposite ends of the political spectrum, advocated regime change. On August 23, Smith College professor Eric Reeves wrote in the *Washington Post*, "In the distorting shadow of the Iraq war, this is an exceedingly difficult moment to argue for 'regime change' in Khartoum. But regime change alone can end genocide as the domestic security policy of choice in Sudan. And it is the only thing that can avert the deaths of hundreds of thousands in Darfur."[52] Regarding Iraq, "one consequence of the Iraq war (though of course not a justification in itself) is that public discussion of regime change by the United States will resonate much more deeply in Khartoum's despotic thinking." (Others disagreed, arguing that Khartoum knew the U.S. was militarily overstretched and so felt that it could act with impunity.)[53] He favored a multilateral approach: "If regime change is not to be chaotic, it must be organized by a consortium if international actors, including regional governments; efforts must be made to reach out to all opposition parties throughout the country and in exile."

On September 22, William Kristol and Vance Serchuk predicted that the U.S., as a global defender of human rights, would undertake an Iraq-style military intervention in Sudan: "For months it has been obvious that stopping Sudan's campaign in Darfur will require putting several thousand foreign troops on the ground. It has also been obvious that some of these troops will have to be American."[54] The UN would not support such an effort, and African troops would not be sufficient: "If the regime in Khartoum is going to be forced to accept foreign intervention on its territory, or if that regime is going to be changed, Washington must be a leader in the effort. So, as is so often the case, the coalition of the willing that goes into Sudan is going to have to be largely organized, sustained and financed by the United States, most likely without a UN mandate."

There was also little emphasis on peace talks, and the few mentions were divided as to their utility. Europe's unwillingness to support a strong resolution on Darfur was attributed in part to its desire to push the government into peace talks with the rebels, but the *Post* urged "the humanitarian crisis is so appalling—at least 300,000 may die, according to an official U.S. estimate—that peace talks cannot be allowed to delay action."[55] Urging stronger sanctions on Sudan, the International Crisis Group's John Prendergast wrote, "Human rights should no longer be traded off against endless peace processes that never quite come to fruition . . . For 15 years, the international community has negotiated with this regime, soft-pedaling human rights concerns in order to keep it at the negotiating table. This has played directly into the hands of the government's strategy, which has been to maintain endless negotiations as a means to deflect international pressure."[56] However, Senator Jon Corzine and Richard Holbrooke praised AU head Olusegun Obasanjo's commitment to peace talks in Nigeria, and urged the U.S. and UN to give the talks more support.[57] On August 8, journalist Sam Dealey warned, "As despicable as Sudan's regime is, the international community may wish to restrain from setting early deadlines for intervention. Such deadlines only encourage rebel intransigence in pursuing peace deals."[58]

## The Role of Arab and African States

THE UN AND EU were not the only entities to face criticism for their inattention to Darfur. Arab and African states were routinely criticized for not speaking out against the violence and, in the case of oil-rich Arab states, contributing more to the relief effort. Arab governments, and their citizens in particular, were lambasted for hypocrisy. On April 4, the *Washington Post* began its first editorial on Darfur, "According to the UN, one of the world's worst humanitarian crises now afflicts a Muslim people who face a horrific campaign of ethnic cleansing driven by massacre, rape and looting. These horrors are unfolding not, as Arab governments and satellite channels might have it, in Iraq or the Palestinian territories, but in Sudan, a member of the Arab League. Maybe because there are no Westerners or Israelis to be blamed, the crisis in Darfur, in northwestern Sudan, has commanded hardly any international attention."[59] The *Wall Street Journal* castigated Security Council members Pakistan and Algeria, "which feel their 'Muslim solidarity' must be with the regime in Khartoum and not with their fellow Muslims starving to death."[60]

The only article written by an Arab among those reviewed was by Tunisian journalist Kamel Labidi, who joined in the criticism of Arab governments and civil society for not speaking out: "It is not the first time the state-run Arab media and even civil-society advocates have remained tight-lipped as death, devastation, and human-rights abuses unfold in a 'brotherly' Arab country. . . Such atrocious campaigns of ethnic cleansing in Iraq at the end of the last century and in Sudan today would have prompted deafening official and popular protests in Arab capitals had the victims been of Arab descent and the perpetrators non-Arab." He stressed the need for human rights education in the Arab world, but concluded, "The majority of Arabs will be inclined to continue to turn a blind eye to crimes against humanity and gross human-rights abuses against their non-Arab neighbors or other minority groups in the region as long as they live in police states where freedom of association, assembly and expression are still severely curtailed."[61]

Initially, African leaders and civil society were also criticized for not speaking out, though this faded as the AU mobilized to play a peacekeeping role. On April 6, novelist Emmanuel Dongala—the only African to write on Darfur in the reviewed articles—recalled the Rwandan genocide: "I still think the genocide in Rwanda has not been the electroshock that should have jolted me and other African scholars from our 'Africanly' correct way of thinking. Some of our outdated ideological ideas must be challenged. With the backing of the government, Arabs are carrying out a massacre of genocidal scale against black Africans in Sudan, yet many academics and leaders in Africa are reluctant to speak out because of a misplaced sense of solidarity."[62]

Some writers made connections between Darfur and the problems of Africa as a whole. Rather than focusing on intervention, Dongala emphasized the need for domestic political reform:

> In Africa, the genocide happened in Rwanda, but it could have
> taken place in any of the many pseudo-nation-states that are the
> legacy of colonialism—states in which the people are more loyal
> to their ethnic communities than to a faraway central govern-
> ment. The manipulation of ethnicity by politicians has given eth-
> nicity an importance it does not intrinsically have . . . States must
> be rebuilt by taking the different ethnic groups into account so
> no group feels ostracized and all share the country's resources.
> Transforming the state along these lines will bring security to all
> citizens.

"So why is Africa such a mess?" Nicholas Kristof asked on March 31. "Africa's biggest problem is still security. The end of the cold war has seen a surge in civil conflict . . . African and Western leaders should try much harder to stop civil wars as they start. The world is now facing a critical test of that principle in the Darfur region of Sudan . . . This is not just a moral test of whether the world will tolerate another genocide. It's also a practical test of the ability of African and Western governments alike to respond to incipient civil wars while they can still be suppressed. Africa's future depends on the outcome, and for now it's a test we're all failing."[63]

On August 19, *Washington Post* columnist Jim Hoagland, while deploring the violence in Darfur, wrote, "the Darfur moment in global consciousness also raises troubling questions about Africa's tenuous relationship with the outside world. That relationship is now dominated by the politics of misery, a poor base on which to build a partnership or a future . . . The pattern is unlikely to change until Africans themselves take the lead in preventing or resolving the continent's potential or festering Darfurs. Africa has for too long relied on the uncertain kindness and intentions of outside powers."[64]

Hoagland had supported the war in Iraq on humanitarian grounds, but said, "historical and strategic circumstances argue against the United States leading a humanitarian and military intervention in Sudan . . . Sudan possesses neither that history [of U.S. support for Saddam Hussein and betrayal of the Kurds' aspirations to overthrow him] nor the strategic position of Iraq." This was the only article reviewed that argued that the U.S. did not have a moral obligation to act in Sudan.

### The Genocide Determination

THE DARFUR CRISIS was labeled "genocide" almost from the moment it first attracted attention. On March 27, Kristof wrote, "In my last column, I called these actions 'ethnic cleansing.' But let's be blunt: Sudan's behavior also easily meets the definition of genocide in Article 2 of the 1948 convention against genocide. That convention not only authorizes but obligates the nations ratifying it—including the U.S.—to stand up to genocide."[65] Forty-one of the eighty-three articles reviewed call the conflict "genocide" or "possible genocide." So did fourteen of the twenty-four articles appearing between March and early June, when the Bush administration announced it was undertaking a legal analysis to see if the killings in Darfur met the convention's definition. This announcement attracted interest, but it was not seen as a substitute for immediate action.

It was anticipated that a finding of genocide would spur some kind of further action under the Genocide Convention, particularly since the desire to avoid such obligations accounted for the Clinton administration's refusal to use the word "genocide" to describe Rwanda in 1994. On June 20, the *Washington Post* wrote that a genocide determination "would impose moral, political and arguably also legal obligations to intervene in Darfur."[66] Several of the editorials appearing between June and September argue for a determination of genocide. "The Darfur killings do look very much like genocide," the *Post* continued, describing the "physical destruction" of "a group defined by its black skin." Kristof wrote several columns about a group of refugee women whose families were "all killed because of the color of their skin, part of an officially sanctioned drive by Sudan's Arab government to purge the western Sudanese countryside of black-skinned non-Arabs."[67] Jerry Fowler returned from a visit to refugee camps in Chad to write, "I fear the specter of genocide... When asked why their villages were attacked and burned, most of the refugees said it was because of their black skin. They believed that the Khartoum-based government of President Omar Hassan Bashir wants to give their land to his Janjaweed allies who, like him, are Arab... Racism undoubtedly does play a part in Bashir's support of the Janjaweed, as the blacks are seen as inferior."[68]

However, experts felt that the emphasis on a genocide determination was a misreading of the Convention. Fowler continued:

> In cases like Darfur, there is always a great deal of handwringing about what is and is not genocide. But such discussion misses the point: A key element of the Genocide Convention is prevention. It calls for action once it is apparent that genocide is threatened. There is no need for an absolute determination, which is inevitably elusive, that genocide is underway... There is more than enough going on in Darfur to justify preventive action.

"Whatever label one attaches to these killings, there is a moral obligation to do everything possible to stop them," the *Post*'s June 20 editorial agreed. "Bush administration lawyers are busily studying whether this meets the legal definition of genocide, but that misses the point. Whatever you call it, the rising death toll could soon evoke memories of the tragedy in Rwanda a decade ago... That shameful failure must not be repeated," the *New York Times* wrote.[69] As early as April 6, Samantha Power warned, "Outside powers cannot wait for confirmation of genocide before they act... American officials need not focus on whether the killings meet the definition of genocide set by the 1948 Genocide Convention; they should focus instead on trying to stop them."[70]

The liberal press was stunned when, in early September, Secretary Powell announced that while genocide was determined to have taken place in Darfur, the U.S. would take no new action to stop it. "The moral order we inhabit fell into focus on Thursday, and it was an awful moment," the *Post* wrote on September 12. "In an act without precedence since the UN Genocide Convention was adopted in 1948, a government accused a sitting counterpart of genocide—a genocide, moreover, that even now is continuing. And yet the accused government may not pay a price for committing this worst of all humanitarian crimes, because there is a limit to how much powerful nations care."[71]

The conservative press, however, hailed Powell's honesty in making the declaration, ignored the fact that he said U.S. policy would not change, and blamed the UN for the world's inaction. The *Washington Times* wrote, "If Mr. Powell's recent statement doesn't serve as a global call to conscience, it is difficult to imagine just what will rouse the Security Council to action."[72] Caspar Weinberger, Reagan's Secretary of Defense, wrote in the *Wall Street Journal* on September 20:

> For those who, like John Kerry, believe that the proper foreign-policy course in Iraq and elsewhere is to turn everything over to the United Nations, events of the last week provided some highly dubious fodder: First, despite Colin Powell's correct description of the killings of African Muslims in the Darfur region of Sudan as "genocide," the UN did not leap into action . . . [I]f Kofi Annan had a vote on Nov. 2, which way would he vote? Now ask yourself the simple follow-up question, which way should I vote?[73]

### Conclusion

THE FACT that the genocide determination was dragged into the debate over the election seems particularly callous, but it illuminates the larger fact that in many ways most of the articles reviewed were not really about Darfur itself. They could have been written about any instance of mass violence that prompts a debate over humanitarian intervention. The narrative describing Darfur was an ideal vehicle for this debate. The coordinated campaign to target victims based on ethnicity recalled the shameful, repeated U.S. failure to stop the twentieth century's genocides. The Sudanese government, blamed for instigating the genocide, was both responsible for, and capable of, stopping it, meaning that an end to violence was imaginable if Khartoum reversed its policies. It was also agreed that only outside intervention could persuade Khartoum to do so—if not a full-fledged military intervention then at least punitive measures backed by a credible threat of the use of force. There was no debate over whether the U.S. *could* stop the violence if it were willing to use (or threaten to use) force to do so. Instead, the debate was over whether the U.S. *should* take such strong measures.

As a result, Darfur was the latest forum for the still-unresolved debate over what role the U.S. will play in the world when its values are in jeopardy but its interests are not at stake. Although it echoed previous debates over humanitarian intervention, it also revealed how the Iraq war had made the question of intervention more complex: by creating lingering fractures in the international community and further eroding the already-tenuous commitment to multilateralism embodied by the UN. In the case of Darfur, moral suasion and the memory of Rwanda proved to be powerful tools for attracting attention to the crisis, but were not strong enough to overcome the obstacles to action.

# 14

## *"Not On Our Watch"*
## *The Emergence of the American Movement for Darfur*

Rebecca Hamilton and Chad Hazlett

Breaking with the pattern of past genocides, the conflict in Darfur has been met by a vocal and resilient grassroots advocacy response in America. This was the result of several factors unique to the conflict, and some specific to the American context. Years of earlier American activism for south Sudan, especially from the Christian Right, had generated allies in Congress. These legislators understood Darfur in light of the government of Sudan's past brutalities, and were willing to call the conflict what they believed it to be: genocide. Invocation of that term stimulated tremendous grassroots activism, especially among Jewish groups and on college campuses. Darfur also had the benefit of coming after the Rwandan genocide and the guilt it produced, and of unfolding much more slowly, allowing time for organizing. This organizing was catalyzed by supportive and vocal writers and experts, expansive access to the internet and email; and the generosity of donors willing to support new, unproven organizations mobilizing around Darfur.

In this chapter we draw on interviews with key leaders in the movement and our first-hand experiences as activists to examine the American movement for Darfur, from its roots in 2003 through to the time of writing in September 2006.

## April 30, 2006

AN ORDINARY Sunday in downtown Washington D.C., with its closed storefronts and emptied streets, can be eerily quiet for a national capital. But by late morning on April 30, 2006, any subway passenger near the Federal Center Metro station would have discovered that this was no ordinary Sunday. That station was so crowded that stepping off the train and squeezing onto the edges of the platform proved a challenge. Chants of "Save Darfur!" filled the air, and the continuous arrival of protesters left the space congested for hours. Surrounded by this sea of students, religious groups, and ordinary citizens from across the country, even passersby who had never heard of Darfur would have realized they were witnessing something historic.

The crowd clogging Washington's underground passageways was matched by those entering the city overhead; on the roads via more than 200 buses, and by airplanes full of green wristband-wearing passengers. All were converging as planned to rally on the National Mall. There they would congregate to represent the largest and loudest American outcry against an African crisis since the anti-Apartheid movement two decades earlier.

Half a world away, Darfurian refugees gathered around short-wave radios listening to news of the rally. And it was not only refugees listening; "It is the first time in the history of genocide that a perpetrator so knows that America is watching them."[1] At the rally, dozens of religious leaders, human rights experts, students, members of Congress, movie stars, and a gold-medal Olympian spoke to the crowd. Scores of television cameras clustered to film the speakers against the backdrop of Capitol Hill, and to capture the intensity of the crowd. Peppered throughout the audience were people holding signs; "Make 'NEVER AGAIN' mean something!" "Americans care!" People attached consecutively numbered stickers to themselves; "I'm standing in for Darfur victim number 25,197."

Who were these people? An enormous contingent came from the Jewish community. The Manhattan Jewish Community Council alone chartered ninety buses. But the smaller organizing operations were no less inspiring. An interfaith coalition from the town of Glen Rock, New Jersey, population 12,000, filled seventeen buses for the event.[2] Enduring the thirteen-hour road trip, 110 students from the University of Illinois took an overnight bus to get there.[3]

Although the Washington rally was the largest, tens of thousands congregated at the same time in 29 other U.S. locations.[4] In San Francisco, 5,000 people formed a mile-long human chain spanning the Golden Gate Bridge. Activists gathered in other major American cities, as well as in small towns like Ipswich, Massachusetts, and Appleton, Wisconsin.[5] The web-based left-leaning political organization, MoveOn.org, even brought the event to cyberspace, creating a parallel "virtual march" that attracted some 95,042 online participants by Sunday afternoon.[6]

Toward the end of the rally, Assistant Secretary of State for African Affairs, Jendayi Frazer, attempted to explain that resolving the conflict was a priority for the Bush Administration. When she claimed "the strategy is working," the crowd, unconvinced, grew restless and began chanting back, "We Want More! We Want More!"[7]

### Three Years Earlier

THERE WAS A stark contrast between the surging rallies that day and the deafening silence on Darfur three years earlier. In mid-2003, there were no speakers, no television cameras, and certainly no crowd. Few members of the American public had heard of a place called Darfur, and reports by human rights organizations documenting atrocities there received no mainstream U.S. media coverage (International Crisis Group 2003; Amnesty International 2003).

However, one analyst was preparing to heighten public awareness of the unfolding crisis. A professor of English literature, Eric Reeves seemed an unlikely candidate to ring the alarm on Darfur. But by 2003, he had five years experience advocating for the people of Sudan—a passion that began in 1998 after Doctors Without Borders (MSF) sent him the first of its now-annual list of the "Top Ten Underreported Humanitarian Stories." Second on the list was famine in south Sudan. Reeves was not only shocked by the details in the report, but that he had not previously heard of the events it documented.[8]

Reeves' quest for information quickly grew into an obsession with Sudan. Over just a few years, he built a vast network of on-the-ground contacts, and began producing a weekly electronic publication for Sudan-watchers across the globe. By 2003 he had seen what the government of Sudan was capable of, so when atrocities in Darfur began to surface, he readily connected the dots. In December 2003, Secretary General Kofi Annan's Special Envoy, Tom Eric Vraalsen, reported the systematic denial of humanitarian access to areas of Darfur on the basis of ethnic affiliation.[9] For Reeves, this was the last piece in the puzzle: "I was completely convinced we were staring at genocide in December 2003."[10]

He penned an op-ed stating what to him was obvious: "Immediate plans for humanitarian intervention should begin. The alternative is to allow tens of thousands of civilians to die . . . in what will be a continuing genocidal destruction."[11] Reeves did not think he would have difficulty getting his warning published by the *Washington Post,* which had run his pieces before. They rejected his piece three times before finally printing it three months later on February 25, 2004.[12]

Soon after, another writer who would become a legend in the Darfur movement began reporting from the Chad-Sudan border. On March 24, 2004, veteran *New York Times* columnist, Nick Kristof wrote "Ethnic Cleansing, Again." It was the first of what would be over thirty columns—and counting—eventually leading to a Pulitzer Prize for his coverage of Darfur. His activist approach was clear from the outset; "[I]f we turn away simply because the victims are African tribespeople . . . then shame on us."[13] In the years to follow, Kristof's reporting of voices from the ground and specific suggestions for action would be the most widely read source of motivation and legitimacy for the Darfur movement.[14]

Yet as passionate and committed as they were, Reeves and Kristof failed to generate any visible public response in those first months of 2004. How then did this apparent public indifference give way to what would grow into a sweeping outcry for Darfur over the next three years? The answer begins with a legacy of activism on Sudan prior to the Darfur conflict, and the early impact this would have on moving Darfur into the spotlight.

## Early Foundations: The "G-word"

A CRITICAL FACTOR in Darfur's rapid rise to prominence in America was the groundwork laid by the coalition of groups, primarily-Christian organizations that had advocated for southern Sudan since the mid-1990s, and had helped bring an end to twenty-one years of Khartoum-orchestrated terror in the South (Hertzke 2004, chapter 7). The vast majority of Darfur activists who would later emerge knew little or nothing about south Sudan or about the Americans who had been advocating on its behalf. However it was that activism that created not only a pool of experienced and well-connected advocates, but also a contingent of Congressional "champions" for Sudan. These committed legislators quickly saw the conflict in Darfur as a repeat of the brutal scorched-earth campaigns the Sudanese regime had conducted in the South, and thus provided a ready source of allies for Darfur activists. Without their leadership, legislative action on Darfur would have been much delayed—or may never have occurred at all.

While not all southern Sudan activists would add Darfur to their portfolio—and some continue to shun it—a handful were among the first to act on Darfur. In order to attract attention, they turned first to members of Congress they had already engaged on South Sudan, particularly the Congressional Black Caucus (CBC).

The "Sudan Campaign" emerged in June of 2004, led by the Sudan Coalition and Christian Solidarity International (CSI)—two groups heavily involved in south Sudan advocacy. Together with members of the CBC, they held daily protests in front of the Sudanese embassy, allowing themselves to be arrested for obstructing the embassy entrance as an act of civil disobedience.[15] The protesters demanded that the U.S. take the lead in pushing for international intervention, impose targeted sanctions, and declare the conflict in Darfur to be genocide. The nongovernmental organization, Africa Action, was also early to the scene. They focused on pressuring then-Secretary of

State Colin Powell to declare the conflict to be genocide, launching a June 2004 petition with the help of the CBC.

CBC member Donald Payne (D-NJ) was among that Congressional group who had already been engaged in Sudan policy for several years, largely as a result of meetings with Sudanese former slaves and trips to Sudan arranged by south Sudan activists.[16] Accordingly he came to a quick appreciation of the situation, "What good is it to sign a peace agreement in the South if you engage in ethnic cleansing in Darfur?"[17] Similarly situated were Frank Wolf (R-VA) and Sam Brownback (R-KS), who had been engaged on south Sudan before Darfur made its way onto the agenda, and who would rapidly become leaders on Darfur.[18] In early July 2004, Payne visited Darfurian refugee camps in eastern Chad with Ted Dagne of the Congressional Research Service. Upon their return to the U.S., Payne and Dagne discussed what Congress could do to stop the killing. Recognizing that Darfur could become "another Rwanda," they resolved to get Congress to call the conflict by its "rightful name"—genocide.[19]

The focus on naming the conflict a genocide reflected widespread assessments that the refusal to give the legal name of "genocide" to the massacre of 800,000 in Rwanda while President Clinton was in office, was causally associated with the United States' accompanying failure to act. Early advocates believed that naming the situation in Darfur genocide would commit the U.S., to action.

On June 24, Payne and Brownback, flanked by a host of CBC members, introduced concurrent resolutions in the House and Senate, declaring that genocide was occurring in Darfur.[20] To the world's surprise on July 22, 2004, the House and the Senate passed the resolutions unanimously.[21] While Congress' genocide determination was encouraging, it would have little policy impact unless the Administration followed suit. The State Department had begun preliminary studies of the Darfur conflict at the same time as Payne had visited the region. After a subsequent visit to Darfur, then-Secretary of State Colin Powell commissioned the Center for International Justice to further investigate the atrocities (Center for International Justice 2004). On September 9, 2004, Powell stood before the Senate Foreign Relations Committee and concluded that "genocide has been committed in Darfur . . . the government of Sudan and the Jingaweit bear responsibility and genocide may still be occurring."

For the burgeoning Darfur movement, getting the U.S. government to use the "G-word," as activists referred to it, was an unimaginable coup. It seemed incomprehensible that the U.S. government could label a situation genocide and then fail to employ whatever means necessary to end it—and yet this is exactly what transpired. Use of the "G-word" may have been an early attempt by the Administration to assuage activists—but if so, the strategy had the opposite effect. Calling it genocide elevated Darfur above other atrocities with high death tolls, seemingly highlighting it as the crisis most deserving of attention. The legitimacy the term gave to Darfur advocacy emboldened a fresh and growing pool of activists, convinced that the "worst crime imaginable" demanded an uncompromising response.

### A New Coalition

BY MID-2004, a critical mass of individual activists and organizations realized a coalition was necessary to coordinate their advocacy efforts. In reality, the Darfur advocacy community would remain only intermittently organized in the years to follow, and efforts to broaden the coalition by taking non-committal policy positions ironically left many potential partners unsatisfied. Unlike the recently successful International Campaign to Ban Landmines (Cameron, Lawson, and Tomlin 1998) the movement did not begin with a serious effort to build an international coalition—a decision many would later regret. Nevertheless, the "Save Darfur Coalition" would play an important role as a central organizing point for nationally-coordinated campaigns such as the April 2006 rallies.

Crucial to the coalition-building effort was the United States Holocaust Memorial Museum (USHMM). Founded in 1980, the USHMM's mission was to make the lessons of the Holocaust relevant to the contemporary context. On Darfur, it was to pursue this mission wholeheartedly. It halted regular operations to issue a "genocide warning" for Darfur in January 2004, upgrading to a "genocide emergency" in July.

Focused in part by USHMM's work, Ruth Messinger, President of the American Jewish World Service (AJWS), took notice of the unfolding crisis.

Messinger and the director of the Committee on Conscience at USHMM, Jerry Fowler, organized a Darfur Emergency Summit at the City University of New York on July 14, 2004.[22] Speakers included the International Crisis Group's John Prendergast, who would soon become one of the most ubiquitous Darfur experts, and Holocaust survivor Elie Wiesel who was present "to lend gravitas to the meeting."[23]

Attendees were primarily faith groups, many of them Jewish. This was not strictly a reflection of the natural responsiveness of Jewish organizations to the specter of genocide, but also the result of the pre-existing connections that Messinger and Fowler had to organizations within the Jewish community. The urgency with which the meeting was arranged precluded time for the kind of broad outreach that might otherwise have occurred. The organizations produced a unity statement with the understanding that those signing on would constitute themselves into the "Save Darfur" coalition.[24] Former non-profit consultant David Rubenstein took on the role of coordinator. Only a handful of the original organizations did not sign the unity statement, mostly humanitarian groups worried about jeopardizing their operations in Sudan by publicly advocating on Darfur.[25]

Subsequently, Save Darfur composed a "Call to Action" that sidestepped consideration of politically difficult policy solutions, such as a Chapter VII intervention. Rubenstein explains that "after many difficult hours of mulling [over] policy alternatives, we realized that the closer we could get to a bumper sticker, the better we'd be as an organization."[26] The wisdom of the strategy has been sharply criticized. "They seemed more interested in merchandizing, and establishing their claim as the default organization—than in making any of the necessary policy decisions," notes Reeves.[27] Notwithstanding such criticism—which continued and intensified thereafter—Save Darfur would eventually emerge as a central forum for spreading awareness, organizing major events, and occasionally gaining access to the highest levels of the Administration.

## The Unexpected Constituency

ONE OF THE most prominent features of the Darfur movement is that much of its numerical strength, resilience, and even policy successes can be attributed to the overwhelming contribution of students—initially from colleges and universities, but later from high schools as well. This student movement engaged a generation whose parents may have participated in campus campaigns against the Vietnam War in the late 1960s. But in the intervening decades American students had become increasingly apolitical. No one expected them to be the first and loudest grassroots voices on Darfur.

Here again, USHMM would play a founding role. During the summer of 2004, recent college graduate Lisa Rogoff was interning at the Museum. From a family of Holocaust survivors, the concept of genocide had particular salience for Rogoff, and she found herself wondering if other students could become as passionate about the issue. With Fowler's endorsement, she organized a meeting for student leaders in the Washington D.C. area.[28]

On the evening of September 14, 2004, ninety students came to a panel discussion on Darfur at the Museum. Only days after Powell had made his genocide declaration, the gravity of the situation weighed on the students. The contingent from Georgetown University was by far the largest, due mainly to the efforts of their Jewish Student Association's President, Ben Bixby. Bixby and fellow students Martha Heinemann and Nate Wright were already well aware of the situation in Darfur before that evening's panel, having attended a talk by Sudanese Bishop Macram Max Gassis earlier that summer. They recruited forty students to attend the USHMM panel, hoping that once others knew about what was happening, they too would want to act.

The following week, fifteen of those students met in a Georgetown classroom and divided into three committees: awareness raising, political advocacy, and relief fundraising.[29] Bixby recalls believing they could stop the genocide within a few months—"an activity for the fall semester"—and thus tried to ensure they did not create a permanent structure.[30] Despite this breathtaking naivety, they produced something of lasting value—a brand name. Heinemann was fielding suggestions for an organizational name, experimenting until eventually Students Take Action Now: Darfur (STAND) came into being.[31]

Meanwhile in Philadelphia, Swarthmore College students Mark Hanis and Andrew Sniderman were working on another plan. Both were international students; Hanis from Ecuador and Sniderman from Canada. As with the student leaders at Georgetown, Hanis already knew more about Darfur than the average college student, having spent the summer interning at Res Publica, a non-profit organization that had tasked Hanis with compiling information about Darfur for their website.[32] Like Bixby and Heinemann, he was Jewish, and the grandson of four Holocaust survivors.

Both Hanis and Sniderman had read what was to become the veritable bible of the anti-genocide movement: Samantha Power's *A Problem from Hell: America and the Age of Genocide.* Hanis absorbed the book's critique of how genocides get mislabeled as humanitarian crises. "We would think it was absurd to have thrown bags of rice to the people suffering in [Nazi] concentration camps," notes Hanis.[32] Sniderman had also read Lt. Gen. Romeo Dallaire's account of the international community's failure to support his peacekeepers as they tried to protect civilians during the Rwandan genocide. The two started thinking about the need to support the African Union peacekeepers, who were the only force tasked with protecting civilians in Darfur.

That afternoon they conceived of the audacious idea that if governments weren't funding the AU sufficiently, then private citizens should. They wrote an op-ed entitled "Can You Spare Some Change for a Flak Jacket? Facilitating Private Funding to A.U. Troops in Darfur."[33] The idea was that by funding peacekeepers, American citizens would demonstrate their desire to stop the genocide, shaming the U.S. government to increase their own funding of the AU force. "We had an iron certainty that this idea could change the discourse about Darfur. We vowed that if the idea ever got big, we would not have our photos taken, nor tell anyone which one of us had the idea" recalls Sniderman.[34] They called the initiative a Genocide Intervention Fund.

Armed with Google and canned soup, the two embarked on a series of sleepless nights sending their proposal to anyone who might help. After countless rejections, former Senior Director of African Affairs for the National Security Council, Gayle Smith, said "let's make this happen."[35] Although plagued with logistical difficulties, the idea caught on quickly among everyday citizens. Among the thousands who would eventually help raise over $350,000 for the Fund, a piano teacher in Salt Lake City donated two weeks of her earnings, and a high school in Mamaroneck, New York, held a battle of the bands competition, contributing $5,000.

Despite these novel developments, students across the country were realizing that wanting to do something about Darfur and knowing what to do were very different things. However, it wasn't long before students latched onto some helpful organizing tools. One was to adopt the STAND structure for themselves. Another was a gift from Hollywood.

Hotel Rwanda was released in American theaters on September 11, 2004. Ten and a half years after the Rwandan genocide, it was the first time a mainstream audience saw the tragedy portrayed. Students quickly recognized this as an invaluable hook for convincing a broader audience that Darfur demanded their attention.

Another awareness-raising tool arose when Rogoff walked into Fowler's office one morning wearing a yellow Livestrong wristband. The wristbands had been created by Lance Armstrong and Nike to raise money for cancer research, but had acquired that intangible quality of "cool" due to the parade of Hollywood stars seen wearing them. Fowler asked if there was any reason not to create a wristband for Darfur. The eventual product was a green band saying "Save Darfur: Not on our watch." They quickly became a permanent fixture on activists' wrists.

In November 2004, the Washington Post decided to run a story featuring Rogoff, for which they needed a photo of student activists. By chance, students at George Washington University had a candlelight vigil scheduled that week. The Washington Post ran a closely cropped shot of students lighting candles with the title "Violence in Darfur Inspires Surge in Student Activism."[36] What the story didn't say was that on the evening of the vigil it was pouring rain and the five students in the photo comprised the sum total of students in attendance.[37] It didn't matter—the media had found a new story in the burgeoning Darfur movement: student activism was back in style.

President Bush had infamously scribbled "not on my watch" in the margins of a report about President Clinton's failure to respond to the Rwandan genocide (Power 2002, 511). But students rapidly co-opted "Not On Our Watch" as the mantra of their generation. Without the virtue of hindsight, it was a surprising development. They had been labeled as apathetic on social issues; the iPod generation selectively tuned to their own private worlds.

Almost none of the student leaders had a background in activism, and for most Darfur was the first issue to spur them to action. When asked to explain what transformed them from self-described non-activists into forces of social change, one reason predominates: genocide. Many preface their response guiltily, "I know [D.R.] Congo has a higher death toll—and it's not that crimes against humanity are run of the mill—but there's something uniquely morally repugnant about genocide."[38]

A twenty-first century genocide attracted attention from other unlikely quarters. The music television channel MTVu launched a campaign to promote activism for Darfur. It ran a competition whereby the winning students traveled to Chad to meet Darfurian refugees, with MTVu cameras in tow. The resulting documentary aired on the eleventh anniversary of the Rwandan genocide.[39] MTVu later launched a video game design competition, and the winning game idea, "Darfur is Dying" was spread online through a "viral" marketing campaign. The idea was to raise awareness by placing players in the role of a Darfurian teenager attempting to evade the deadly Janjawiid.[40]

Students' attempts to build awareness were also bolstered by high-profile speakers availing themselves for on-campus panels. In January 2005 actor Don Cheadle, who portrayed hero Paul Rusesabagina in *Hotel Rwanda*, joined Prendergast on a visit to Darfur. Upon their return they teamed up, writing several op-eds.[41] The pair leveraged Prendergast's expertise and Cheadle's fame, soon magnified by his Oscar nomination, to draw crowds to speaking engagements at countless campus events. On March 2, 2005, Kristof used his column to introduce the story of former U.S. Marine, Brian Steidle, who had returned from Darfur with a devastating photographic record of the ongoing atrocities.[42] The twenty-eight-year-old quickly became a hero on college campuses, speaking at twenty-seven different locations during his 21,000 mile "Witness to Genocide" tour organized by USHMM, ICG, and STAND.[43]

## April 2005: A Tangible Impact

STUDENT ACTIVISM was making impressive strides in generating interest and turnout at campus events. However, the actual ability to pressure the Sudanese regime awaited a new step. On April 4, 2005, Samantha Power announced to the crowd at Harvard's Kennedy School Forum, "This is the first week anything tangible has been done that would cause the Sudanese government to think twice about their genocidal campaign."[44] She was referring to the success of the divestment campaign led by Harvard students.

The principle of divestment is simple. The government of Sudan relies on revenues from foreign companies. Those revenues do not support hospitals, roads, or civil service salaries in Darfur, but they do buy helicopter gunships, arms, and ammunition, much of which is used to attack civilians. U.S. corporations play no part in this: in 1997, President Clinton issued Executive Order 13067, prohibiting U.S. firms from doing business with the government of Sudan, and President Bush renewed the order. However, non-U.S. corporations operating in Sudan are listed in U.S. financial markets, accessing U.S. capital. The goal of a divestment campaign is to withdraw capital from those companies, causing their share prices to fall while uncertainty and controversy rise. The hope is that companies are forced into a choice: stop doing business with Sudan, or lose investors and share value. Harvard students started locally, with investments held by their university's own endowment.[45]

The seeds of their campaign were sown six months earlier, during another Darfur panel in the same Kennedy School Forum. In the crowd that night sat Dan Hemel, a college student and reporter for the Harvard student newspaper, the *Crimson*. That night Hemel went back to his dorm room and soon came across Reeves' website, which documented key companies providing revenue for the Government of Sudan's activities. Hemel scribbled down ABB, TotalFinaElf, PetroChina, SiemensAG, and Tatneft, then called classmate Zach Seward, then the *Crimson's* finance reporter. Together they scanned Harvard's SEC filings and soon spotted 72,000 shares—roughly $3.9 million—held in Petrochina.

Hemel and Seward published their findings in the Harvard *Crimson* days later.[46] "Somewhat-embarrassingly," recalls Hemel "we failed to include, or solicit, student reaction for the initial story... though that certainly didn't stop Manav and Ben from reacting on their own."[47]

The article was a call to action for Harvard College roommates Manav Bhatnagar and Ben Collins. With rudimentary web skills—and almost no history in organizing—they built an online divestment petition asking the university to divest from Petrochina. Expecting the university to quickly resolve the problem once raised, they emailed friends and professors encouraging them to sign the petition.[48] It was a seemingly haphazard campaign that could have just as easily fizzled out in the coming days and weeks. However, they soon found that an army of fellow students would ensure the issue never fell from the spotlight.

Weeks before divestment surfaced as a potential strategy, students had formed the Harvard Darfur Action Group, which had begun to mobilize the campus for Darfur.[49] Campus activism soon spread, and a broad array of groups participated in campaigns targeting the university's holdings. Finally, at that April 2005 panel, Power read aloud the Harvard Corporation's decision to divest its shares in Petrochina. Echoing students' arguments virtually word-for-word, the Harvard Corporation justified its decision on the grounds that "Oil is a critical source of revenue and an asset of paramount strategic importance to the Sudanese government, which has been found to be complicit in what the U.S. Congress and U.S. State Department have termed 'genocide' in Darfur."[50]

### Turning to the U.S. Government

DIVESTMENT ENABLED students to pressure Khartoum without relying on the U.S. government. But students and advocacy organizations focused their efforts on changing U.S. policy as well.

On March 17, 2005, Payne had introduced the Darfur Genocide Accountability Act (H.R. 1424) in the House. If passed, the act would have granted President Bush the authority to use "unmanned armed planes and other military assets" in order to neutralize the Janjawiid and other militias intent on attacking civilians, as well as to destroy Sudanese aircraft and intelligence/military headquarters. The bill also called for capital market sanctions preventing any entity engaged in any commercial activity in Sudan from raising capital or trading securities on U.S. capital markets. Despite acquiring 138 co-sponsors in the House, the bill never received a mark-up in the International Relations Committee. Instead, that committee's chairman, Henry Hyde (R-IL), replaced it with the weaker Darfur Peace and Accountability Act (H.R. 3127) (DPAA). This bill still called for targeted sanctions on Sudanese leaders, but it removed the authorization for the use of U.S. military assets and the capital market sanctions. The net result was that these tough provisions were stripped from the subsequent policy debate entirely.

Even the weaker DPAA would require pressure to get through Congress. By mid-2005, students were collaborating with existing advocacy organizations, and a natural division of labor resulted. Established organizations provided their expertise, reputations, and high-level connections; students provided the noise and numbers required to focus Congress' attention. Illustrating such collaboration was a national call-in day on October 18, 2005, organized by the Friends' Committee on National Legislation (FCNL). With the DPAA stalling in Congress, FCNL coordinated language for action alerts and invited grassroots partners to use their phone-lines to call members in key congressional districts.[51] STAND leaders drafted lists of campuses to be mobilized, and organizers at each school set up tables in high-traffic areas, offering their cell-phones to fellow students willing to call their respective members of Congress.[52] The next week, eleven Representatives and six Senators added themselves as co-sponsors of the DPAA, the largest jump since the bills were introduced.

## Upping the Ante

SUCH LEGISLATIVE success evidenced the movement's ability to influence Congress on limited occasions. However, its impact on the Administration was far less impressive.[53] For this, the movement would look to elite advocates, and particularly religious community leaders.

On September 21, 2005, Save Darfur brought a delegation of primarily religious community leaders to meet Deputy Secretary of State Robert Zoellick, who had by then taken charge of the Darfur portfolio at the State Department. After a brief presentation he asked each attendee for comments. As several participants would later recall, Reverend Cizik most emphatically "took on the Administration" in that meeting, arguing "it doesn't matter what you're doing... the killing hasn't stopped."[54] The meeting left the group energized to apply greater public pressure to the Administration—but unsure how to do so.

The answer came when Tim Nonn, a veteran grassroots activist, made it his personal mission to get the disparate and uncoordinated community of Darfur activists talking to each other. "Organizing 101 is you should sit down face-to-face to strategize... it's different emailing or on the phone... trust can't occur without personal relationships." His organization, Dear Sudan, began with a project raising $10,000 from his hometown of Petaluma, California to feed Darfurian refugees for one day. But like Hanis, he soon realized it would take more than food to stop genocide.

Having developed relationships with a wide range of activists, he organized a meeting on November 4, 2005, in Washington D.C. In the last minutes of the meeting Nonn called for a vote to make April 2006 a coordinated month of action, culminating in rallies across the country. The largest rally would be in Washington D.C., but other rallies would take place nationwide, with the west coast's principal rally in San Francisco. Not everybody agreed—but nobody voted against it.[55]

The idea of large rallies was hotly contested on the conference calls that followed that meeting. Did Darfur have strong enough a grip on the American public to make such events successful? Rubenstein and others didn't think so. But Messinger and Martin Raffel, Executive Director of the Jewish Council on Political Affairs, had a different perspective. Both knew well the organizing abilities of the Jewish community. "I was sure we could get about 5,000 people from New York and Boston [to a rally in Washington]," Messinger recalls, "and I assumed others could get 5,000, so that's 10,000."[56] Reflecting lingering skepticism, planning began on the basis that they would be lucky to get 5,000 attendees to the Washington rally. However, a combination of timely support from celebrities and rigorous grassroots organizing, especially in the Jewish community, would show this estimate to be conservative.

### Confounding Expectations

BY SEPTEMBER 2005, students had been engaged with Darfur for a full year. This is typically the point when student campaigns falter; student leaders graduate and summer vacation interrupts momentum. But the student campaign for Darfur was not typical. New leadership was fostered, and graduating students worked out how to remain activists beyond the campus walls.

Hanis and three classmates graduated from Swarthmore and moved to Washington D.C., while Sniderman completed his studies. The Genocide Intervention Fund team of Hanis, Sam Bell, Ivan Boothe, and Rajaa Shakir pooled their resources to rent a rundown apartment, taking turns between who got to sleep on the couch and who got the floor. Their initial supporter, Gayle Smith, was a director at the Center for American Progress, which lent them a ground floor corner of their plush building, blocks from the White House. From there they set about creating a permanent organization. Keenly aware that their novel idea needed backing from "establishment" players, they successfully recruited a list of a high-profile endorsers that now includes the UN Special Advisor for the Prevention of Genocide, Juan Mendez; ICG President Gareth Evans; and Nobel Peace Prize nominee Lloyd Axworthy—as well as the ideological parents of the Fund, Power and Dallaire. In September 2005, the Fund was re-launched as the Genocide Intervention Network (GI-Net) with 501c3 status and enough funding to see them through the next six months.

In early 2006, a three-year capacity building grant from Humanity United, founded by Pam Omidyar, heralded GI-Net's entrance into the professional advocacy community. The GI-Net team started thinking strategically about what it would take to make "never again" actually mean something. Again taking their cue from *A Problem from Hell* they set about fixing the issue Power identified to be at the root of every failed response to genocide: a lack of domestic political will in countries with the power to act (Power 2002, 509).

The GI-Net team reasoned that building domestic political will would require more than the usual "elite" advocacy that *informs* policymakers—it would require a domestic "anti-genocide constituency" to *influence* policy-makers. Undaunted by the schemas that constrain more experienced human rights activists, they looked to unconventional sources for inspiration. The National Rifle Association and the American Association of Retired People, with their tremendous political influence, were models to emulate. Starting from the assumption that genocide will occur again, the GI-Net team decided that a constituency to fight genocide ought to be permanent—to ensure that the next crisis generates a speedier and more politically influential response than ad hoc organizing permits.[57] GI-Net is in the early stages of building this permanent anti-genocide constituency, the backbone of which is a nation-wide membership with members responding to action alerts, meeting with their representatives, and organizing in their home communities.

This approach of "getting political" about genocide is paying off. When high-level advocates found themselves unable to convince Senator Lugar, chairman of the Senate Foreign Relations Committee, to schedule the DPAA for mark-up, GI-Net tested their strategy. Using OpenSecrets.org, they identified the 550 individuals who contributed over $1,000 to Lugar's previous campaign. They organized student members to call donors directly and ask them to press the Senator to schedule the bill for mark-up. Two weeks later, on November 18, the bill was released by the Foreign Relations Committee, passing the Senate by unanimous consent.

In August 2006 GI-Net launched legislative scorecards in order to hold policymakers accountable for their actions while giving members a focus for their activism. These scorecards grade all members of Congress on their responses to Darfur. Congressional offices took their scores to heart to a degree that surprised even GI-Net. Many staffers and members themselves have called to argue that their grades should be changed, and several have even requested meetings just to talk about what can be done to improve their grade next time around.

Meanwhile STAND leaders came to realize this would be a longer battle than their initial optimism indicated. In August 2005, they established a National Steering Committee to create a centralized leadership structure.[58] Save Darfur supported the transition by funding a fulltime staff member to coordinate student activity. At the time of writing, students have established

600 STAND chapters on campuses throughout the country, creating a formidable collective voice.

The impact of student action was also evident as ripples of the Harvard divestment decision grew into waves never imagined by Harvard students. Twenty-six other universities followed suit: Stanford, Brown, Yale, Amherst, Dartmouth, Princeton, and UCLA, to name a few.[59] In the process, new student divestment gurus were created as students from Brandeis and UCLA pooled their skills to create a nationwide Sudan Divestment Taskforce.

The Taskforce used their on-campus experiences to lobby state governments to divest from their pension funds—which invest an estimated $91 billion in companies that do business in Sudan.[60] Producing scores of meticulously researched reports, their work began to pay off in mid-2005 with Illinois,[61] Oregon,[62] and New Jersey[63] divesting state pension funds from these companies. Maine, Connecticut, and California followed the next year.[64]

One of the powerhouses behind the Taskforce is Brandeis University student, Daniel Millenson. Younger-looking than his nineteen years, Millenson observes that "one of the nice things about being young is that people have very low expectations of you."[65] Millenson and fellow Taskforce students Adam Sterling and Jason Miller rapidly became the "go-to" people on divestment legislation. When Providence, Rhode Island, wanted to become the first city to divest from Sudan, they asked the Taskforce to draft legislative language by the following day. "We weren't lawyers, so we thought we would write out bullet points and then find an attorney to turn it into legal language—but nobody wanted to do it."[66] Undaunted, Millenson and Sterling drafted their first piece of legislation: "By that time we'd read enough bills to make it look right."[67] More than making it look right, the team had also developed a well-researched model of "targeted" divestment, rigorously justifying why some companies should be divested from while others should not. As Millenson notes, the model has attracted attention: "Tonight I have to write a bill for the U.S. Congress . . . to prohibit federal contracts going to companies doing business with the Government of Sudan. They asked for language by tomorrow morning."[68] Low expectations indeed.

### "A Million of Anything is a Lot"

AS THE STUDENT movement matured, the prospect of the upcoming rallies pushed religious and community groups to get serious about grassroots organizing. The most impressive example was the mobilization of Jewish communities. Jewish representation in the rallies represented the interaction of an infrastructure well-suited for organizing—Hillels, Jewish Community Councils, and congregations—with a conscious effort to make Darfur a priority. Through weekly conference calls with local organizers, AJWS situated itself at the helm of a carefully organized groundswell, registering 12,050 confirmed attendees for the D.C. rally by late April.[69]

Although Christian leaders including Richard Cizik, Richard Land, Bob Edgar, and Deborah Fikes had expanded beyond South Sudan to become Darfur activists, Christian organizations did not whole-heartedly engage in grassroots mobilization, and some Christian leaders have been hesitant to throw their weight into Darfur. One controversial explanation for this is that in South Sudan, Christians were under attack; in Darfur all the victims are Muslim. Perhaps there is "a subtle factor that motivates people when their own religious community is persecuted," as Cizik explained while trying to account for the lackluster interest of some evangelical Christians.[70] However, to the extent this bias exists, it may have less to do with any differential valuation of human life based on religion, and more to do with institutional connectivity. Unlike in Darfur, long-established "sister church" programs and exchanges with south Sudanese Christians deepened the connection between Christians in south Sudan and in America.

In addition, some evangelical leaders were hesitant to criticize Bush, especially in the build-up to the 2004 elections. Hertzke observes that "there was a sense among the south Sudan activists that there was gratuitous criticism of Bush."[71] Furthermore, key south Sudan activists worried that Darfur activism would jeopardize the peace deal for southern Sudan that they had so vigorously supported.[72] Aside from the policy implications, the general "lack of recognition of the genocidal dimensions of what happened in south Sudan," was off-putting to south Sudan activists.[73]

By late 2005, Save Darfur realized that many South Sudan advocates had been alienated. A colleague of Messinger's put her in touch with Boston-based community leader, Dr. Rev. Gloria White-Hammond. Messinger met White-Hammond and immediately knew she was the ideal person to help organize the rally. "She had connections to all the communities that we didn't have connections to."[74] White-Hammond had two conditions for coming onboard. "Number one was to acknowledge that the South had faced their own genocide, which meant we could involve Southerners and the Christian Right . . . Number two was that we refrain from 'Bush-bashing.'"[75] The stipulations paid off, "tweaking the message like that I started getting emails from [South Sudan activists] around the country saying, 'thank you; we're coming to the rally.'"[76] Some questioned whether it was possible to advocate effectively with limited freedom to criticize the president.[77] But White-Hammond would soon show that she, at least, felt no such constraint.

In the build up to the rallies, Save Darfur launched a "Million Voices for Darfur" campaign, aiming to get one million Americans to send postcards to President Bush. Some in Save Darfur's leadership were skeptical about the impact that mere postcards could have, but were ultimately persuaded by Raffel: "A million of anything is a lot."[78] Beyond numerical signaling, the campaign was a much-needed organizing tool: it gave activists something to *do*. With a parallel postcard campaign running online, the number of Americans signed up to receive email updates from Save Darfur increased from 50,000 in January 2006 to over 400,000 by April.[79]

Citizens were encouraged to add personal messages to the postcards. A teenager in Ohio wrote "I wake up every morning, go to school, and come home to a warm house and warm food . . . all the while these families in Darfur are being torn apart."[80] A school teacher from Maine wrote "I may not know everything about Sudan and the genocide, but I know people need our help."[81] The campaign exceeded its target. On June 29, 2006, Senate Majority Leader Republican Bill Frist and Democratic Senator Hilary Clinton signed the one millionth postcard to the President. It was a sizeable accomplishment, to which Rubenstein wryly observed "A million [Americans] sent postcards—that leaves 279 [million] more."[82]

### "On Darfur We Are Together"

AS PUBLIC INTEREST in Darfur surged, Congress felt the pressure. However slightly, the usual political considerations that determine policy outcomes began to recalibrate around this unlikely show of grassroots support.

Congressional engagement was already uncharacteristically energetic, illustrated by the resolutions declaring Darfur to be genocide,[83] House Resolution 1268 providing $55 million for peacekeeping operations in Darfur,[84] and the House and Senate versions of the DPAA.[85] On February 17, 2006, Representatives Joe Biden (D-DE) and Brownback introduced Senate Resolution 383, calling for significant NATO assistance to the AU, and transition to a UN force under a Chapter VII mandate. The proposal passed unanimously.[86]

Shortly after returning from a trip to Darfur, Representative Michael Capuano (D-MA) introduced an amendment to the Fiscal Year 2006 Emergency Supplemental Funding Request, proposing an additional $50 million for the AU force. Like Payne, Wolf, and other congressional champions for Darfur, Capuano's commitment to Sudan arose years earlier, in his case, after the American Anti-Slavery Group organized a meeting between him and an escaped Sudanese slave. When asked about the impact of the Darfur movement, Capuano explains "I have 635,000 constituents. Even if you can get me 500 letters, I can easily walk away from 500 votes. And in truth 499 of those people are going to vote the same anyway, because they agree with me on most other issues. *But they get my attention.*"[87]

While true that genocide is not an "electoral" issue, public noise was eventually able to do more than just garner attention. Capuano's amendment ran counter to entrenched political interests that might otherwise have prevented even him from approving it. The amendment was attached to a request for substantial additional funding for the war in Iraq, which ordinarily would have prevented some Democrats from voting for it, Capuano included. The amendment also failed to identify an offset for its proposed appropriation. Thus even Sudan champions like Tom Tancredo (R-CO), a deficit hawk,

would have been hard-pressed to approve the amendment if not for the public support. Capuano's amendment passed on the morning of March 16, 2006,
though its razor-thin margin of 213 to 208 indicated that there were still many
in Congress for whom Darfur took a backseat to other political priorities.

Those Congressional champions willing to deviate from "politics as usual"
over Darfur have come from both sides of the aisle, initially giving the movement a bipartisan flavor. As Capuano, a liberal Democrat, noted, "I disagree
with Tancredo on almost everything. When I see we voted the same way, I
stop and ask myself what just happened. But on Darfur we are together."
However this bipartisanship has had a limit. While both sides of the aisle have
their champions, bipartisanship has not been apparent throughout the
Congress as a whole. Support for Darfur legislation has come far more consistently from the left.[88]

### April 2006: "The Biggest Shove"

ACTIVISM VISIBLY intensified in the days before the April rallies.
Revisiting the civil disobedience demonstrations of two years prior, five
members of Congress,[89] five religious community leaders,[90] and one student
leader[91] were arrested in front of the Sudanese embassy in Washington on
April 28.

The same day, GI-Net and STAND organized 850 students from forty-six
different states to travel to Washington. They arranged more than 300 meetings with congressional staff, whom they pushed to support the deployment
of a larger multinational force to protect civilians. As these "student lobby-
ists" gathered, the words of STAND Coordinator Bryan Collinsworth captured the mood: "Never before, in the face of mass atrocities, have we heard
such a forceful and immediate outcry from everyday students ... if we've
been inching the world closer to stopping genocide, we come here this week-
end to give it the biggest shove it's ever had."[92]

Finally, the pieces were coming together: the grassroots groundswell, congressional action, and some high-profile media attention. American speed-
skater Joey Cheek had won gold at the 2006 Winter Olympics. He caught the

world by surprise when rather than the usual patter of thanks, he announced he would donate his $25,000 prize money to Darfurian refugees.[93] Save Darfur recruited him to speak widely on the crisis. "I am doing CNN, NBC, ABC, C-SPAN, all of these major news outlets. . . It has legs, as they say in the media world."[94]

Eight weeks later another story "with legs" hit the scene. Oscar-wining actor George Clooney and his father Nick traveled to Darfur on their own funds. Oprah Winfrey invited them to her talk show to screen their footage. Images of Darfurian child refugees shouting, "Hi Oprah! Oprah!" made many activists cringe. But after years of struggling for access to mainstream American media, activists could not have hoped for better exposure than when Winfrey told her ten million viewers that Darfur was something they must respond to, directing them to act through organizations such as Save Darfur and GI-Net.

As students lobbied on Capitol Hill, other advocates met with President Bush and his team in the Roosevelt Room of the White House. Bush's team included Assistant Secretary of State for African Affairs Jendayi Frazer; National Security Advisor Stephen Hadley; and Mike Gerson, the president's trusted senior policy advisor, speechwriter, and the man considered to be the "conscience of the White House" on Darfur.[95] On the advocates' side of the table, Rubenstein, Fowler, and White-Hammond represented Save Darfur. Keith Roderick of CSI and David Saperstein, Director of the Religious Action Center of Reform Judaism, were also among those present, as was Sudanese former slave, Simon Deng—who had just completed his twenty-one-day "Freedom Walk" from New York to Washington.

Scheduled for twenty minutes, the meeting lasted an hour, and Bush was keen to assure these advocates that far from resisting the growing support for Darfur, the Administration was on their side. "I just had an extraordinary conversation with fellow citizens from different faiths," Bush reported after the meeting. "They agree with thousands of our citizens—hundreds of thousands of our citizens—that genocide in Sudan is unacceptable . . . For those of you who are going out to march for justice, you represent the best of our country."[96]

Bush's demonstration of concern impressed several attendees, but most did not lose sight of the need to keep pressure on the Administration. If

White-Hammond was convinced by the Administration's show of commitment or concerned about "Bush-bashing," it wouldn't weaken her resolve as she rallied the crowd that Sunday, "We will not back up, George Bush! We will not back down, Kofi Annan! We are not going to shut up until the genocide and rapes stop and justice reigns throughout all of Sudan!"[97]

### Why Darfur?

THE NATIONWIDE rallies that extraordinary Sunday in April 2006 were a reflection of more than two years of constant engagement by students, interfaith leaders, and ultimately regular citizens. America has never seen such a public commitment to stop a genocide—let alone one taking place on a continent so often sidelined in the discussion of American national interest. The first three years of the movement's growth suggest a number of factors responsible for the phenomenon.

The pool of American advocates—many of them evangelical Christians—who had worked on south Sudan before Darfur hit the headlines, had fostered the development of a group of Congressional champions. These legislators went on to give the Darfur movement an enormous head start, generating a level of passion in Congressional circles that remains crucial today. As noted, south Sudan advocates did not shift seamlessly, or in some cases at all, into advocacy for Darfur, partly due to concerns that Darfur activism would distract from or somehow endanger the CPA. However, those south Sudan advocates who did take up the Darfur cause early on undoubtedly fast-tracked the first accomplishment of Darfur advocacy: the genocide determination.

The "G-word" had an enormous effect, especially in the Jewish community. The psychological commitment to Darfur that the invocation of genocide created was strengthened by the Jewish community's organizational structure. Their hierarchical system of national organizations, regional community centers, local synagogues, and college Hillels (Jewish organizations) could be efficiently mobilized. The Jewish community was a readymade constituency.

Darfur also had the benefit of coming after Rwanda—and the guilt it created—and of progressing much more slowly, providing three years for activists to organize, compared to Rwanda's mere one hundred days. Ironically though, activism for Darfur was distorted by having learned the "wrong lesson" from Rwanda. The early confidence activists had that if only the government would call this new crisis "genocide," a policy to stop it would follow—turned out to be unwarranted. Once again, people had fallen into the trap of viewing a current genocide through the lens of an earlier one.

Students were the unexpected driving force behind the resilience of the movement. For many students, the world's failure in Rwanda weighed heavily on their minds, though they were too young at the time of its occurrence to feel a personal sense of blame or failure. Thus when Darfur was declared to be genocide, they believed they could and should do better than their predecessors, as represented in their catchphrase "Not On *Our* Watch."[98]

The framing of the conflict was another important factor. The predominant description of a cruel government and its Arab proxy forces slaughtering mostly innocent "black" civilians, if severely oversimplified and almost ignorant of the rebel movement, gave an apparent moral clarity to the situation that put it ahead of more perplexing conflicts elsewhere. Equally critical was the somewhat ahistoric belief most activists held that unlike other crises of similar magnitude that have been festering for years, Darfur presented a new and hence not "intractable" problem. They felt there was something they could "do" about it, calling for divestment, diplomatic pressure, and a force to protect civilians.[99]

Key individuals have been vital to the movement's incubation. Kristof, Reeves, Prendergast, and Power were among those offering continual encouragement of activists' efforts, providing information and legitimacy, and expanding knowledge of Darfur to an ever-widening audience. Support from donors too, while less visible, has been vital. Individuals as well as foundations with a willingness to fund young, unproven organizations focusing on Darfur allowed these groups a relatively quick startup and the resources necessary to expand.

Widespread access to the internet also enhanced the movement's growth. Nowhere was this more evident than among students. Email allowed activists across the country to coordinate events and trade tactics. Websites allowed even small student groups to post materials such as petitions and organizing toolkits, and attract online surfers. The availability of news and analysis on Darfur through the web allowed students and other activists to build expertise quickly and stay abreast of recent developments. An unanticipated outcome of this technology was that the ability to communicate and take action from any location with an internet connection enabled the movement to develop in a remarkably decentralized fashion. This allowed the movement to grow into a larger and more diverse coalition than it could have otherwise been. However, these benefits of technology came at a cost, lessening activists' reliance on central coordination, thereby permitting the proliferation of an often confusing array of organizations with incoherent messaging. The movement's reliance on communications technology has also generated a constituency that exists to a large degree as names on email lists, with relatively little social interaction among members. While this may be a legitimate strategy for organizers to pursue, one must also question the depth and sustainability of commitment within such a constituency. The adoption of Darfur as an issue by organizations that do involve higher levels of social interaction—such as campus chapters and pre-existing community and religious organizations—may ultimately serve as the foundation for the movement's persistence into the future.

### To What Effect?

AT THE SAME TIME as thousands rallied, the April 30 deadline for the Darfur Peace Agreement (DPA) being negotiated in Abuja came and went, with no rebel groups signing on. Those who attended the rallies were more focused on advocating for a protection force than for a peace agreement. Still, after their Herculean efforts, the negative news coming out of Abuja was disappointing. However, by Monday, the deadline for negotiation was extended and Zoellick departed for Abuja in an effort to stitch the pieces together.[100] In a commentary reflective of discussions among advocates, Jill Savvit of Human Rights First asked "Can it be a coincidence that a deal is at hand after a major peace rally in Washington, D.C. and in other U.S. cities?"[101] By Friday, the DPA had been signed by the government of Sudan and Minni

Minawi's faction of the Sudanese Liberation Army, described by the U.S. as the most militarily powerful.[102]

However, six months later, none of the remaining rebel groups present at Abuja have joined the agreement. More troubling for the advocacy movement has been its inability to adapt to such changes in the policy environment. After the partial signing of the DPA, advocates were unable to determine how this would influence their policy position.[103] And as a result each missed deadline for implementation has passed without visible reaction from the American public, government, or media.[104] The August 31, 2006, UN Security Council Resolution 1706, authorizing 17,500 UN peacekeepers for Darfur, would seem a great victory for those who have been advocating for the deployment of a multilateral force. Yet if the government of Sudan ultimately does not consent to the deployment of such a force, activists must confront the serious challenge that a "non-permissive" intervention in Darfur may be a political, if not military, impossibility. Adding to the policy confusion, key U.S. policymakers working on Sudan have resigned. On June 15, Gerson confirmed he would be leaving the White House with the now ironic remark, "It seemed like a good time . . . Some of the things I care about are on a good trajectory."[105] Four days later, Zoellick announced he was leaving his post to work in the private sector.[106]

Of particular concern from an advocacy standpoint is the possibility that despite the movement's ability to influence Congressional activity, public pressure may not be able to compete with the traditional national security interests that ultimately guide the Administration's foreign policy choices. Much as the specter of American soldiers being killed in Somalia spoiled the Clinton Administration's appetite for intervention during the Rwandan genocide (Burkhalter 1994, 48), so the quagmire in Iraq casts a shadow over the Bush Administration's policy towards Darfur, depleting the political and military resources required for tougher action.

Yet it would be an oversimplification to suggest that in the absence of war in Iraq, the U.S. would pursue whatever means necessary to end the genocide in Darfur. Numerous countervailing national interests must also be considered. Sudan's cooperation in the war on terror appears to have earned it a measure of protection from the U.S. intelligence community.[107] Likewise, few expect the U.S. to expend the political and economic capital required to dramatically alter China's willingness to remain Sudan's most important financier. At this stage in the evolution of American activism against genocide, it remains an open question as to whether such interests will always take precedent over humanitarian concerns, or if increasing the scale of public outcry still further will eventually alter U.S. foreign policy priorities. To date, the movement's efforts to pressure the U.S. government may have, somewhat perversely, forced the Administration to place a higher priority on "managing" activists than finding a workable solution for Darfur.[108]

There is an increasing awareness within the Darfur movement that America-centric activism is not enough to successfully improve conditions on the ground.[109] Unilateral policy actions by the U.S. generate far less pressure than could be generated if China and European, African, and Arab countries were also willing to use their political and economic clout to raise the cost of genocide or choke off Sudan's financing or flow of arms. Accordingly, the American movement has begun to turn its attention overseas, where activism is comparatively non-existent.[110] Save Darfur, USHMM, the National Association of Evangelicals, Physicians for Human Rights, STAND, and Human Rights First, among others, are working in earnest to build coalitions abroad. They are talking with human rights organizations in Egypt,[111] evangelicals in Switzerland,[112] and students in Ghana.[113] The first example of this shift in focus has been the "Day for Darfur" on September 17, 2006, which involved dozens of rallies around the world. Although the largest turnout was in New York, meticulous attention was paid to ensuring it was pitched as an international campaign.[114] Of course, it is uncertain how successfully the movement will be able to adapt to the different social and political contexts of other nations.

With the declassification of documents, historians will render a more thorough assessment of the impact that the American groundswell has had on the U.S. policy towards Darfur. To date, the movement has been fairly successful in engaging Congress—with one considerable failure being that the only legislation authorizing the president to use U.S. military assets to stop the genocide was not even brought to a vote. Furthermore, important provisions within the DPAA, such as a clause that would have protected the constitutionality of state-level divestment, did not survive into the final bill now awaiting the president's signature.[115] The picture is worse with respect to the movement's impact on the Administration. In only two instances to date have advocates significantly pushed the Administration beyond mere rhetoric: the renewal of U.S. sanctions already in place against Sudan, and the decision to abstain rather than veto the UN Security Council referral of Darfur to the International Criminal Court. Regarding all other items on the advocacy agenda, the Administration's actions fall strikingly short.[116] No punitive measures were imposed against any perpetrator until sanctions against four individuals in April 2006, only one of whom was related to the government.[117] At present the major test is whether the Administration is willing to engage in the serious level of diplomacy required to restart the political process and get Sudan's consent to a UN force.

With the distance of time the historical record will determine the ultimate impact for the people of Darfur. At the very least it is safe to say that "but for" the Darfur movement, the plight of Darfurians would have remained side-lined from mainstream discussion, along with the suffering of countless other African civilians facing violence. Without the movement's persistent noise-making, it seems inconceivable that the U.S. would have abstained from vetoing the UN Security Council referral of Darfur to a court that the U.S. refuses to recognize. Nor does it seem likely that Bush would have renewed the economic sanctions on Khartoum after the signing of the CPA. And public pressure was undoubtedly a key factor at the Congressional level, from their declaration of genocide—the first time such a determination had taken place during an ongoing crisis—to the $225 million of funding appropriated for the African Union so far. Public support has also been critical to divestment taking hold in universities and states throughout the country. Nevertheless, at this juncture, our prediction is that the movement's ultimate contribution will be measured less in terms of its impact on the people of Darfur, and more in terms of the foundation it has established and precedents it has set for responding to subsequent twenty-first century atrocities.

# 15

## Darfur's Elusive Peace

ALEX DE WAAL

D ARFUR'S PEACE IS NO LESS complicated than its war. The negotiating chamber in Abuja corralled Darfur's complexity into a rectangular seating arrangement: delegations from the government and the armed movements faced each other across a table, flanked by African Union (AU) mediators on one side and international diplomats on the other. Simplification is essential if a complex conflict is resolved. But in Darfur the parties, mediators, and international community did not even agree on what would constitute "peace."

### Whose Peace?

FOR SALIM AHMED SALIM, the AU chief mediator of the formal negotiations in Abuja, "peace" was implicitly defined as an agreement that both sides would honor. This conception of peace was based on formulas for power sharing, wealth sharing, and security arrangements in Darfur, agreed by the warring parties and endorsed by the international community, which would buttress Sudan's Comprehensive Peace Agreement (CPA). Indeed the three-fold division of issues, augmented by the Darfur-Darfur Dialogue and Consultation, was precisely modeled on the talks between Khartoum and the Sudan People's Liberation Movement (SPLM) held in Naivasha, Kenya, that led to the CPA. The AU mediation was established on the premise that such an agreement was necessary and possible.[1]

However, the warring parties did not trust or respect each other and shared low expectations that any agreement would be honored. Implicitly, they defined "peace" differently—as the ability to pursue the political objectives behind their war aims without being condemned for waging war. This kind of "peace" would not end violence, but rather allow for any continuing violence to be described as enforcing the agreement or police action. Government and armed movements had, of course, different and contradictory hopes for how politics would unfold and violence be used after a peace agreement.

The de facto definition of "peace" by the ruling National Congress Party (NCP) and the northern Sudanese security chiefs is a series of political bargains with individual Darfurian leaders which incrementally isolates, weakens, and de-legitimizes those who continued to fight. Those leaders include resistance commanders, opposition politicians, and native administrators. This we may describe as "retail peace." Under this conception, the pattern of how a dominant center manages its peripheries, as described in chapter one, resumes, with the center exercising greater control over the provincial elite. In the best case, large-scale organized violence between the Sudan armed forces and the Darfur armed movements ceases, to be replaced by small-scale actions against "outlaw" groups. In the worst case, this fighting is labeled as eliminating outlaws and policing the peace. The population of Darfur is quiescent, not because its aspirations have been fulfilled, but because its administrative and political leaders are dependent upon Khartoum's patronage. This political management reaches across Sudan's international frontiers to include deals with governments, security officers, and insurgents in neighboring states, especially Chad, Central African Republic, and Eritrea.

In negotiating the CPA, John Garang had a converse definition of what peace entailed: a democratic transformation in which Sudan's marginalized majority is politically awakened and organizes to create a "New Sudan." For him, the CPA enabled this transformation to proceed through political struggle instead of armed struggle. Garang acknowledged that his vision of the New Sudan, undiluted by the compromises contained in the peace agreement with his adversary, ultimately involved the ruling elites surrendering power, but he confidently averred that the NCP had no choice in the matter. History, he said, was on his side. While the leaders of the Darfur armed movements—

the Sudan Liberation Movement (SLM) and Justice and Equality Movement (JEM)—often echoed Garang's phrases, they showed few signs of grasping how an agreement for Darfur could become part of such a transformational process. They did, however, see a peace agreement as the basis for continuing coercion—in this case the forcible disarming of the Janjawiid and the apprehension of its leaders, preferably by international troops.

Darfur's peace talks were conducted while fighting continued and the humanitarian crisis remained unresolved. The negotiations were often intermittent and always appeared agonizingly slow. Darfur burned while Sudanese leaders talked, or talked about talking, or refused to talk. Darfurians died while the negotiations remained stuck on agreeing on the movements' representation or adopting an agenda for the security arrangements track. The urgency of concern manifested by humanitarian workers and activists did not seem matched by the slow pace of the talks and—as recounted by Laurie Nathan in this volume—foreign leaders constantly demanded quicker progress. Such directives to accelerate had not featured in talks to end previous wars (including in south Sudan) and were a new phenomenon for African peacemakers.

This international humanitarian concern also drove another concept of peace: security for ordinary people in the villages and displaced camps of Darfur. In most peace talks in Africa (including South Sudan) mediators and negotiators assumed that a deal between the belligerents would automatically end human suffering, but that before any agreement was reached, little could be done except provide humanitarian aid. Darfur was different, both in the assumption that killing and hunger should be halted *before* a peace agreement was reached, and in the belief that a peace agreement in itself would be insufficient to end violations. As described by Rebecca Hamilton and Chad Hazlett, also new was the volume of clamor from the American Darfur activists for an international military presence that could protect civilians.

Rather than envisioning a peacekeeping force as a buttress to a political agreement, the logic of the activist campaign was that an international protection force was the main goal and a peace agreement was both secondary and improbable. Such a foreign military intervention would provide safety for the people of Darfur, at the expense of the Sudan armed forces and

Janjawiid. If the Sudan government was ready to agree to such a force, so much the better, but few activists held out much hope for this. Across North America the debate was not on whether there should be international troops in Darfur, but what form that presence should take. This had a direct impact on U.S. policy and from the middle of 2005, U.S. diplomatic energies were primarily directed into the handover of the African Union Mission in Sudan (AMIS) to a United Nations force.

In March 2007, ten months after the conclusion of the Abuja negotiations that resulted in the Darfur Peace Agreement (DPA), it is the NCP's version of peace by political bargain that is most likely to be realized. Efforts to achieve by agreed formal text and to bring international troops to Darfur have not succeeded, chiefly because the belligerent parties (especially the government of Sudan) have seen this as against their interest, partly because of the complexity of the task, and partly because international approaches were confused and inconsistent. This concluding chapter examines why Darfur has failed to achieve peace.

## A Formal Agreement and Its Limits

THE ATTEMPTS BY the AU mediation and its international partners to achieve a fair and inclusive peace agreement for Darfur had limited success. The mediator's first task is to provide a venue in the hope that the simple proximity of the negotiators will encourage them to discuss and reach agreement. This was the AU's "plan A." In January and February 2006, it looked as though this might succeed, as secret talks between the government and Abdel Wahid al Nur came close to an agreement. Another try was made in the middle two weeks of April 2006, when vice president Ali Osman Taha and a group of senior NCP politicians, SPLM leaders, and security officers stayed in Abuja. Ali Osman had made the breakthrough with Garang in Naivasha in 2003 and the AU and U.S. hoped for a repeat of that performance. Only when this failed did the AU present a comprehensive mediation paper on April 25, in the form of an 87–page, 510–article text that covered all the issues that had been under discussion. This text had been shared with and approved by the international representatives in Abuja and was intended to form the basis for further give-and-take discussion. This was a bold step: it is exceptional for mediators to present such wide-ranging proposals. Bolder still was the demand that the parties agree to the text immediately—a mediation paper was transformed into an arbitrator's ruling.

How did it come to this? Why were the parties so unwilling to negotiate a compromise? Why did the AU and the internationals try to become arbitrators rather than mediators?

The political context for the Darfur peace talks was never favorable and became less so as the talks continued into late 2005 and 2006. Developments in Sudanese and Chadian politics and the internal politics of the NCP and the armed movements were all critical determinants of the prospects for success.

The Darfur Peace Agreement only made sense as a buttress to CPA. The international community saw the CPA as the "mother agreement" which not only addressed Sudan's biggest and longest war but provided for national democracy. However, Darfurians were skeptical about the CPA when it was signed, seeing it chiefly as a ceiling on their immediate political claims rather than a charter for national transformation.[2] The common Darfurian interpretation was that the southerners had achieved their aspirations and were now denying Darfurians their equally legitimate demands for a self-governing region, a vice president, and fair representation in national institutions. That skepticism increased while the Abuja talks were in session. In early 2005, the movements' leaders hoped that the appointment of John Garang as first vice president would allow him both to pursue energetically their shared vision of a New Sudan and also become personally involved in resolving the Darfur conflict. Garang's death in July 2005 killed those hopes and the new SPLM leadership engaged little in Darfur.

The progress made in the wealth-sharing commission in Abuja showed what might have been possible with greater confidence in the CPA. During the seventh round, the wealth-sharing commission addressed and resolved almost every issue on the agenda, with the important exception of the initial government payment into the compensation fund. One reason for this progress was that the mediation and the World Bank organized a number of specialist workshops on wealth-sharing issues. In addition, the head of the government wealth-sharing team, the SPLM minister of state for finance and economic planning, Dr. Lual Deng, who had also been an SPLM wealth-sharing negotiator in Naivasha, spent much of his time explaining the strengths and weaknesses of the CPA's wealth-sharing provisions to the movements. He served as much as an advisor and resource person for the Darfurians as a representative of central government. But his opposition to the Darfurian demand for compensation slowed agreement on that issue. A final reason for the success of the wealth-sharing track was the hard work, patience, and attention to detail of the acting chair of the commission, Boubou Niang. He showed that the skills of a mediator—listening and understanding the positions of the parties and bringing them closer—are very different to the skills of a negotiator, and that the former was what was required in Abuja.

Nothing comparable took place in power sharing. The commission was chaired by ambassador Berhanu Dinka, an experienced and sharp negotiator who rapidly became frustrated by the intransigence of the parties and their unwillingness to negotiate seriously. Abdul Mohammed, an adviser to the mediation, attributed some of the rebel delegates' hard-line stand to their limited understanding of the transformative potential of the CPA and he invested much time and effort in helping them explore how they could best benefit from the democratic opening. This was insufficient. What the SLM needed was sustained, detailed, and direct assurances from the SPLM that the DPA would be followed by a common political project pursued jointly by the two parties. But energetic political engagement by the SPLM during Abuja was conspicuously lacking. One reason for this was the disarray in the SPLM following the death of Garang, which was especially marked over the SPLM policy for northern Sudan. Another reason was that NCP distrusted the SPLM over Darfur and was determined to minimize its role there.[3]

Possibly the most important political determinant of the outcome of the Abuja talks was the war in Chad. During 2005–2006 there was a race between the Darfur peace process and the escalation of the Chadian war. The Chad war won. Chadian president Idriss Déby was never neutral over Darfur but in 2003–2005 he had strong interests on both sides of the conflict, giving him a strong reason to support efforts for peace. By December 2005, Déby realized that he was in a fight to the death with opposition groups backed by Sudan, and in reaction decided to give open and unlimited support to the Darfur rebels. He succeeded in winning over the JEM leadership to his cause, to the extent that JEM fighters were heavily involved in defending N'djamena from a rebel attack in April 2006.[4] Déby had no intention of giving up his strongest political card—his ability to support rebellion in Darfur—until his own political future was assured. During the last weeks of the Abuja talks, JEM delegates showed little interest in engaging in any discussions and much of the international engagement with JEM on May 2–4 was pro forma, expecting no agreement.

The dominant dynamic in the negotiations was distrust. The Sudan government, the SLM-Minni, and the JEM did not consider that their military options were exhausted and were ready to continue fighting to improve their positions. If compelled to sign an agreement, they wanted to preserve the integrity of their forces and preserve their ability to resume fighting if necessary. Only Abdel Wahid saw that his military option had closed, but he hoped for third party military intervention in his favor. Lacking any trust in the Sudanese (or indeed Darfurian) political system, Abdel Wahid looked for guarantees from abroad.

The movements' leaders did not trust each other and indeed while the talks proceeded, there was serious fighting among them. The only way in which the two SLMs and JEM could adopt a united position at the peace talks was to agree on the most hard-line stance. None of the leaders had sufficient authority to offer a compromise. When Abdel Wahid delinked his negotiating position from Minni and JEM in January 2006, not only did he incur their wrath (and further military attacks from SLA-Minni) but he also lost the support of nineteen commanders and delegates who had been aligned with him. There was also distrust *within* each of the rebel camps. In April and May, Abdel Wahid's camp was divided into several factions. Most of the delegates were in favor of Abdel Wahid signing either on May 5 or in the following week, but two of his advisors[5] energetically and successfully sabotaged their efforts. Minni feared that if he signed he would lose the support of many of his commanders. At no point during the entire negotiations was any one resistance leader sufficiently confident or powerful to be able to make an offer of a compromise on the main planks of the movements' shared platform. Any such offer would have been seen as a sign of political weakness or betrayal and fastened upon by his political rivals. This is precisely what happened when Minni signed.

The government was not united either. The head of the government delegation in Abuja, Majzoub al Khalifa, refused to entertain any significant concessions and dismissed them as "not possible."[6] One reason he gave was that if he made a concession to Darfur, then other groups elsewhere in Sudan would make similar demands and raise arms in pursuit of their goals. Majzoub exaggerated but his reasoning contained an important truth. As a senior party organizer, Majzoub could not offer a compromise that entailed sacrificing the posts occupied by party officials. He had to calculate his internal rivals' options for weakening him. Majzoub saw Ali Osman Taha as one of his principal internal rivals and threats. Every time Ali Osman made a move on Darfur—for example meeting with Khalil Ibrahim and Minni in Tripoli in March 2006—Majzoub made a counter-move. Others in the NCP and security were also conspiring against Ali Osman. For that reason, when Ali Osman came to Abuja in April, he was tightly constrained in what political offer he could make to the Darfur movements without exposing himself to the accusation of weakness or betrayal. When Ali Osman met with the AU mediation he indicated that he could only entertain some very modest compromises on power sharing—much more limited than the mediation had expected.

Only a mediation paper could break this double deadlock. The April 25 proposals did so. For example, the AU asked the movements to compromise on their demands for a single region for Darfur at once and for a vice president. Both Minni and Abdel Wahid accepted these. The proposals asked the government to give up more posts than Ali Osman had said was politically possible and to concede on some key security demands, and Majzoub accepted.

The mediation strategy of a producing a comprehensive set of proposals was born of frustration with the lack of progress in reaching agreed compromises. During February and March 2006, the mediation pushed the parties to agree a ceasefire first, on the grounds that this was within reach and so could be achieved quickly, and would increase confidence on all sides. By early April it was clear that this was not working and the strategy shifted instead to a comprehensive mediation paper to form the basis of give-and-take discussions. The mediation team expected that the parties would focus their negotiations on a handful of key issues so that the gap could be closed over the following weeks. The focused discussions of May 2–4 and the modest and specific demands formulated by Abdel Wahid the following week suggest that this strategy was working. But this approach faced one critical problem: there was no mechanism for closing the deal. The outstanding issues might be substantively small but the political leap necessary to bridge them remained huge. There had been no proper face-to-face negotiations on the central power sharing or security issues and so there was no established process whereby the leaders took steps to agree. The gap of distrust had not narrowed at all.[7]

In response to this problem, the U.S. and Nigeria proposed that the AU mediation text of April 25 be "enhanced" by international partners (all of whom had, incidentally, agreed to the original version), and then become an arbitration proposal which would be presented sequentially to the parties to obtain their separate agreement.[8] This was a highly unorthodox approach and a gamble. Pulling it off would rely on the incentives, pressures, and negotiating skills that the international community—specifically the U.S.—could provide. Robert Zoellick demonstrated why he was ranked one of the world's most experienced and skillful negotiators in securing two commitments to sign an enhanced text. His exercise did not involve mediation.

The very short period of time available for the movements to examine the mediation text, discuss it, and formulate their responses, was critical to Abdel Wahid's failure to sign and the failure of Minni to obtain widespread support for his signature. Why was the Abuja process, which had creaked along at less than walking pace lurching from rut to rut over many months, suddenly jet-propelled to a conclusion in just a few days?

One rationale for doing it rapidly was that the constraint on the parties was not time but political calculation, and that the sooner the attempt was made the better. Another was that the UN Security Council had set a deadline and that if this deadline were missed then future deadlines would carry no weight—if the pressure-cooker effect of working under a looming deadline were ever going to function it would be now. The internal logic of the mediation process, which dictated at least another month of talking, was brushed aside by these considerations.

Having abandoned the attempt to mediate the conflict, the U.S. and the other members of the quartet adopted a logic that required them to treat the text as completely non-negotiable, the deadline as fixed,[9] and to threaten the non-signatories.[10] This logic baffled the Sudanese. As Minni and Abdel Wahid resisted signing, the threats intensified. Minni submitted. He said the next day, "I calculated the balance of forces and I knew I had to sign."[11] Abdel Wahid did not calculate the consequences of his actions and did not respond to threats—if he had done either he would not have become chairman of the SLM in the first place.

Arbitration can only work if the ruling is enforced. The AU and U.S. had no capacity to enforce the DPA without the consent of the parties. They did not even try.

The political circumstances surrounding the Abuja process were so adverse that it is remarkable that the peace process enjoyed any credibility with and respect from the parties. The movements came to Abuja because it gave them recognition, a platform and an opportunity to build their internal political infrastructures. The government was there because it needed the international legitimacy that would come from signing a DPA. For both sides, it was the presence of the Leviathan—America—that determined their engagement at Abuja. Throughout the seventh round, the mediation, the warring parties and the U.S. delegation shared an unspoken assumption, that the final deal would be brokered by the U.S. But while Abuja process was made possible by American power, American priorities also made it more difficult for it to succeed. The following section explains how the vision of international troops bringing safety to Darfurian victims of genocide complicated the search for peace.

### Bringing International Troops to Darfur

THE AFRICAN UNION Mission in Sudan (AMIS) deployed in Darfur on the basis of the N'djamena Humanitarian Ceasefire Agreement of April 8, 2004.[12] From the start it was mission impossible because the ceasefire agreement was fatally flawed. President Déby was impaled on the dilemma of trying to please both Khartoum and the armed movements and under pressure for a quick deal. His mediation cut corners and deceived the parties.

The N'djamena ceasefire contained neither maps of the areas controlled by the parties' armed forces nor processes for determining the locations of those forces, making it impossible to monitor the ceasefire. Government and SLA agreed to the neutralization of armed militia without defining either what the term "militia" referred to or what "neutralization" might mean. Worst of all, the text exists in contradictory versions. Immediately after the parties had signed the Khartoum delegation approached the Chadian foreign minister saying that a mistake had been made and a provision for the cantonment of the rebel forces had been omitted. They demanded that an extra line be included. The foreign minister instructed an AU official to write the cantonment of the rebels into the text by hand. The addition was stamped and endorsed by the Chadians but not agreed with the SLA. N'djamena was not an agreement at all. The UN would never have sent peacekeepers under these circumstances. The AU had the enthusiasm of a novice and sent its military observers and troops into the middle of an ongoing war. Nonetheless, in the twelve months after its initial deployment in July–August 2004, AMIS helped bring increased stability to most areas of Darfur. Its mandate expanded from monitoring the ceasefire to protecting civilians in the immediate vicinity of its forces.

These months also saw much increased coverage of Darfur in the U.S. press and mounting activism among American advocacy groups. Although the pattern of the war was now changing, the underlying narrative in the U.S. still followed the model detailed by Deborah Murphy in chapter 12—Darfur was described as genocide warranting American military intervention.

As the crisis unfolded in 2004–2005, the U.S. government had several different policies towards Darfur. Despite Secretary of State Colin Powell's statement that genocide had occurred in Darfur, the State Department was primarily committed to making the CPA work and therefore to supporting a complementary deal for Darfur. The CIA was enjoying the cooperation of Khartoum's security agencies on counter-terrorism. USAID was focused primarily on humanitarian operations in Darfur and its staff in the field quickly developed sympathies for the rebels. Congress had a remarkable bipartisan consensus of hostility to Khartoum's rulers. Popular opinion demanded military intervention but the

Pentagon had no intention of sending troops, aircraft, or any other assets to Sudan. In the second quarter of 2005, the White House extracted a policy priority from these competing demands: AMIS should be handed over to the UN.

The UN troops proposal began as a piece of political spin. It deflected the activists' ire from the White House to the UN and those Security Council members not ready to support tough action against Khartoum. More troops, more armor, and a tougher mandate would be a visible step that had the potential to bring tangible security benefits, while stopping short of the kind of armed attack called for by some liberal hawks.[13] There was an element of deception in the proposal. No UN mission would be able to deploy quickly (six to nine months is the typical lead time), disarm the Janjawiid by force,[14] or provide physical protection to more than a small minority of Darfurian civilians. Its task would have been to monitor and occasionally enforce the security arrangements of a peace agreement, with the mandate and firepower to deal forcibly with local situations that ran out of control, but no more than that. Although mandated under the UN's Chapter VII, such a force would be better described as "chapter six-and-a-half"—a classic peacekeeping mission with extra capacity to deal with lawlessness. It could only operate with Khartoum's consent. The UN mission would have consisted of mostly African soldiers and would have included at most some specialist support from NATO countries. Perhaps it is not too cynical to assume that President Bush's advisors calculated that once a UN force had been approved, any disappointments could be placed at the door of the UN and the troop contributing countries, not the U.S.

The UN deployment became an end in itself. The proposal won the support of the Darfur activists in the U.S., who demonstrated an extraordinary ability to mobilize enormous demonstrations in favor of peacekeepers. It was uncritically endorsed by the International Crisis Group. Senior officials at the UN Department of Peacekeeping Operations (DPKO) were pleasantly surprised at how fashionable their activity had become, but dismayed at the unrealistic expectations for what they could achieve.

However, the UN handover proposal did not enjoy widespread international backing and the U.S. needed to work hard to get it accepted. The AU Commission and AU Peace and Security Council (PSC) were both well aware of the shortcomings of AMIS but feared that a plan to wind down the operation would lead to it being starved of resources and blamed for failure. Their misgivings were justified because both of these duly happened. The morale of the AMIS troops suffered as soon as the UN handover proposal was floated—no soldier on a difficult mission likes to be told he is the second-best option and his best efforts are not going to be good enough. Even before the AU had approved the transition in March 2006, after considerable arm-twisting by the U.S., AMIS funds began to dry up and a few months later its troops went for eight weeks without pay and sometimes without rations and fuel. Instead of the AU PSC discussing how to improve AMIS's mandate and operations, it was asked to discuss its demise. Rather than being expanded and made more effective, the mission began to wither. The UN DPKO did not want to take on Darfur. It was already overstretched by its existing peacekeeping commitments (including in other parts of Sudan) and feared another mission impossible. The UN DPKO officials could not say no to their political masters but they could (and did) argue in support of their basic rule—before peacekeepers are sent there must be a peace to keep.

Obtaining these commitments from the AU and UN took up the majority of the U.S. administration's diplomatic efforts on Darfur. Pushing the Sudan government to agree consumed much of the remaining time and energy. Just as the U.S. was lining up support at the AU and UN, on March 8–9, 2006, Ali Osman Taha signaled to the Americans that should there be a peace agreement in Darfur, he would ensure that the Sudan government looked favorably on the transition to the UN. On March 12, in a marathon ten-hour session, the AU PSC voted to hand over AMIS to the UN. Sudan lobbied hard against the proposal and won a slight reprieve—the handover would take place after six months. A month later, at the U.S.'s initiative, the UN Security Council endorsed the handover and called for a peace agreement by the end of that month—April. The "deadline diplomacy" so deplored by Laurie Nathan in this volume did not appear from the diplomatic ether. It arose because the primary goal of American policy on Darfur was UN troops, and a peace agreement was a tool in support of that.

Along with American activists, Darfurians had inflated hopes and fears for what UN troops might be able to do.[15] When Abdel Wahid al Nur demanded guarantees "like Bosnia" in the early hours of May 5, this is what he had in mind. Some members of the Sudan government feared the possibility (however remote) that UN troops would be mandated to execute arrest warrants on behalf of the International Criminal Court, or see their mission expanded in some other direction. They were fearful that the UN special representative would accrue even more power in his hands. However, others were more sanguine, aware that a UN force would only be an increment on AMIS and on this latter assumption, most of the Sudanese generals were ready to accept UN troops. Internal distrust within the ruling clique clouded the issue—the fact that Ali Osman supported UN troops raised suspicions among his rivals. The government prevaricated and on September 3, President Bashir came out categorically against UN troops. Whatever the original rationale for this decision, Bashir soon realized he had scored a cheap political win by calling the American's bluff. He could portray himself as a defiant nationalist with no real risk to himself. Others in the government soon discovered that they had gained a tactical advantage by locking the Americans and UN into an unwinnable confrontation that would keep international attention diverted from the politics of Darfur and leave the AU weak.

The AU PSC met on May 16 to welcome the DPA. Under other circumstances, it would also have given a new mandate to AMIS to enable it to fulfill the various functions and tasks assigned to AMIS in the DPA. The AU mediation's security arrangements commission included an implementation task force which had drawn up estimates for the numbers of troops and civilian police required. In line with the three stages of the ceasefire, a three-stage deployment was envisaged, beginning with 14,000 troops and civilian police and rising to over 20,000. Troops were needed to verify the positions of the parties' military forces, to monitor the disengagement and withdrawal of the parties, and to monitor the limited arms control. Troops and civilian police were needed for the demilitarization of the displaced camps and the training of a "community police force" drawn from among the displaced communities. Troops were required to monitor the demilitarization of humanitarian supply routes, to monitor the government's staged plan for restricting, containing, and disarming the Janjawiid, and to monitor airfields in order to ensure that the government was complying with its obligation to halt offensive military flights. New staff and capabilities were needed for the Ceasefire Commission. This would have been a very complicated and challenging mission for an organization with extensive peacekeeping experience—which the AU was not. Nonetheless, the possibility of building up AMIS's capability was not even considered. No action was taken to begin the implementation of the DPA security arrangements. Some steps could have been taken with AMIS's existing capability but in accordance with the rationale was that the mission was about to be handed over to the UN, the minimum was done.

In June, a joint UN-AU planning team visited Darfur and the implementation task force's estimates were refined but not substantially changed. In turn this formed the basis for the troops and mandate called for by UN Security Council resolution 1706 of August 31, 2006, which asked the Sudan government to consent to the deployment of 20,000 UN soldiers and civilian police.

In assessing the value of the proposed UN force for the protection of Darfurian civilians it is tempting to compare the troop strengths and mandate of resolution 1706 with the actual deployment of 7,000 demoralized AMIS soldiers. The fair comparison would be between the proposed UN force and an AMIS force that had continued to be fully supported during 2005–2006 and which had its mandate and numbers revised in accordance with the DPA's ceasefire implementation plan. This comparison is between an AU force of about 20,000, tasked to implement the DPA's ceasefire, and a UN force of about 20,000 mostly African troops, tasked to implement the DPA's ceasefire.

United Nations peacekeeping was invented at the time of the Suez crisis in November 1956. In the subsequent half century, much has been learned about the dispatch of troops to conflict zones. The most important lesson is that international peacekeepers can succeed if their function is to support a peace agreement (at best) or a disciplined ceasefire (at minimum). They are not a substitute for a political settlement. United States policy on Darfur ignored this lesson, making the peace process an adjunct to peacekeepers rather than the other way round. American efforts to obtain a peace agreement and efforts to bring UN troops to Darfur cancelled each other out.

### Retail Peace

FROM THE BEGINNING of the crisis, the Sudan government's preferred solution was to destroy or intimidate the resistance and then buy off the Darfurian elites one by one. Its approach to the external sponsors of the rebellion—Chad, Eritrea, and the SPLM—was an extension of this: to maneuver them into a position of dependence on Khartoum. It also needed to manage the monster that it had unleashed, the Janjawiid. International mediation was a major inconvenience. Once the Abuja process was under-way, however, Khartoum had to operate within its constraints. Majzoub al Khalifa at first sought to do a bilateral deal with Abdel Wahid. This would have brought him Darfur's largest constituency and would have split the resistance. After this failed, his strategy was to use the DPA as the imprimatur of legitimacy for the government and then revert to retail politics—buying or co-opting the movements' leaders on an individual basis.

Majzoub did not sit idly in the Chida Hotel waiting for the process to con-clude. He and his team compiled a file on every member of the Darfur resist-ance and tried to calculate what would be needed to purchase their dependence. Majzoub was quite explicit about this and claimed that some of the commanders and delegates were seeking positions in the army or execu-tive, others were looking for trading opportunities, and others would be con-tent with a simple cash payment. When Ali Osman visited Abuja, each of the movement leaders who visited him explored whether the vice president could offer a better personal deal than Majzoub, and each went away dissatisfied.

At the signing of the DPA, Majzoub was visibly disappointed that Minni had signed but Abdel Wahid had not. He was cheered up by the arrival of Abdel Rahman Musa and his group of thirteen, who split away from Abdel Wahid's camp to declare their support for the DPA. President Olusegun Obasanjo embraced Abdel Rahman at the signing ceremony and welcomed them to the peace, thereby requiring the AU to extend recognition to them. Over the fol-lowing month the band of aspiring signatories was joined by Ibrahim Madibu, formerly power-sharing negotiator for Abdel Wahid, and a breakaway group from JEM. In June, the AU drew up a "Declaration of Commitment" for them to sign and organized a low-key signing ceremony in Addis Ababa. However, Minni Minawi refused to recognize them and described the Declaration of Commitment as "illegal."[16] Over the following six months, a handful more joined, including one of Abdel Wahid's commanders, Abul Gassim Imam.

During and after the process of signing the DPA, Minni faced strong dissent from within his own group and suffered many desertions. He entered Khartoum a reduced figure. His strategy for bolstering his authority was to deny legitimacy to others rather than to try to broaden his support base. Lacking political skills and political confidence, he soon became a pawn in the hands of the NCP and specifically Majzoub, who became the de facto head of implementation of the DPA. All the key appointments were made by Majzoub. He put in Abdel Rahman Musa as state minister for cabinet affairs, Ibrahim Madibo as commissioner for rehabilitation and development, Abul Gassim Imam as governor of West Darfur, and General Mohamed al Dabi as head of the security arrangements implementation commission. All of these appointments were supposed to have been made by Minni and one of them— Gen. al Dabi—is not even a member of the movements but on the contrary an army officer long engaged in the suppression of the Darfur rebellion. The most important institutions of the Transitional Darfur Regional Authority— envisaged as the centerpiece of implementing the DPA—simply do not exist.

The other side of this coin was military action against the groups that refused to sign. Khartoum declared the non-signatories "outlaws" and insisted that they be expelled from the Ceasefire Commission. No steps were taken to control or disarm any militia. Units from SLA-Minni were brought in to serve as the vanguard of attacks. However, the non-signatories repelled the government offensives.[17] The fact that the AU complied with the expulsion of the non-signatories from the CFC, failed to take any measures on the Janjawiid and provided assistance to evacuate wounded members of SLA-Minni, compromised the organization's neutrality. The AU was facing two distinct and contradictory mandates: it was supposed to be neutral in order to monitor the ceasefire and talk with the non-signatories to encourage them to join the DPA, and it was also supposed to be a partner in implementing an agreement that was not accepted by most Darfurians. It was unable to do either properly.

Khartoum's strategy for dealing with Chad was a similar mixture of force and manipulation. The security chiefs had lost confidence in Déby in 2005, convinced that even if he promised not to support any Darfur rebels, he no longer had any control over his Zaghawa kinsmen. Sudanese military intelligence began arming the Chadian opposition and dispatching them into Chad, anticipating that they would bring down Déby.[18] If the April 16, 2006, assault on N'djamena had succeeded in installing a new ruler for Chad, loyal to Khartoum, the dynamics of the last weeks in Abuja would have been very different. However, not only did that attack fail but the immediately subsequent efforts also did not succeed.

Khartoum began to utilize its parallel channel, of seeking Chadian compliance through regional intermediaries. In March 2006, the Libyan government had convened a meeting and obtained a paper agreement for a normalization of Chadian-Sudanese relations including placement of a monitoring force on the border. The Tripoli Agreement was principally a piece of diplomatic theater to stop the AU adding border monitoring provisions to the DPA and AMIS mandate.[19] Nothing was implemented. Eleven months later the Tripoli Agreement proved its value to Khartoum. As part of the follow-up to Security Council resolution 1706, the UN sent a mission to Chad to explore the possibility of a UN protection force in eastern Chad. Déby at first opposed this, expecting that the announcement of a forthcoming UN troop deployment would provoke Khartoum to send the Chadian rebels to attack him. Then he changed his mind and agreed. This was a ploy: it prompted Libya to convene a meeting and invite the signatories to the Tripoli Agreement to discuss how to implement their plan for policing the border. This time, the "brother leader" Muammar Gaddafi also invited Eritrea. The outcome was that Eritrean troops would monitor the border. An Eritrean contingent was promptly flown to Geneina and Déby told the UN he had decided not to accept UN troops after all.

Eritrea had emerged as a pivotal intermediary in the strategy for managing Darfur. President Isseyas Afeworki's only aim is to stay in power. His country is small, isolated from its neighbors, and economically prostrate. He is fearful that Ethiopia will overrun Eritrea. His assets are a formidable army and a reputation for military chutzpah. His strategy has been to sponsor insurgents to keep his two big neighbors—Ethiopia and Sudan—weak and unstable. For this to work Isseyas needs to keep out the international community because once UN, AU, or other international troops take on the role of guaranteeing the stability of the region's hotspots, Eritrea becomes strategically irrelevant. Asmara's strategy is to be indispensable in Darfur by being the sponsor of the armed movements.

The Eastern Sudan Peace Agreement (ESPA), concluded in October 2006 brought an end to the twelve-year insurgency of the Beja Congress and its smaller ally, the Rashaida Free Lions, organized under the banner of the Eastern Front. The ESPA consisted of a deal between Khartoum and Asmara in which the latter sold out the Sudanese insurgents in return for security guarantees and economic assistance (an open border and oil shipments). This agreement had been cooked many months before. As early as April, the Eritreans were working closely with Sudanese security on Darfur. Their supposed common strategy was for Eritrea to centralize the Darfur armed movements under a new umbrella, the National Redemption Front (NRF) and then deliver it to Khartoum as part of the same package that provided for the ESPA. Khartoum knew that the Eritreans were as likely to divide as to unite the Darfur armed movements and was happy to go along—either outcome was in its favor. Asmara hoped that unifying the Darfur resistance would increase its leverage on Sudan and make it the key player in implementing any political settlement—to the extent of having its troops on the ground.

The strategy was unworkable because Asmara could never deliver the Darfurians in the same way that it could control the Beja and Rashaida based in its own territory. Abdel Wahid came to the meeting in Asmara to found the NRF in June 2006 but went back on his promise to sign up. He would not accept having Khalil Ibrahim, president of JEM, imposed as leader. Abdel Wahid's quarrelling lieutenants foolishly followed him there and were detained by the Eritrean authorities and one of them (Babiker Abdalla) was tortured in prison.

In September the Eritreans finally let the SLA commanders leave Asmara and instead tried to corral them together in Chad. The Eritreans hoped that by offering Déby security guarantees—troops to monitor the border and probably a security detail for N'djamena as well—they would entice him to unify the Darfurian resistance under the NRF which would then become their client.

Meetings in Abéché and N'djamena failed to bring the Darfurian commanders together. The commanders simply did not trust either Eritrea or the NRF leadership, and by this time they had re-armed themselves from failed Sudan army offensives and were not dependent on arms supplies routed through Chad. Also, Déby knew his Zaghawa politics better than the Eritreans did—he took the Eritrean guarantees but let the Darfurian commanders decide for themselves. Déby was as fearful of the threat of Zaghawa discontent as he was concerned about the Khartoum-supported armed groups. The commanders dispersed back to Darfur, shunning the NRF. In March 2007, the Eritreans enticed the president of South Sudan, Salva Kiir, to N'djamena as a bigger incentive for the SLA commanders to come to N'djamena. That didn't work either.

The Eritrean and Sudanese security chiefs understand each other well. They will continue to work together, each trying to double cross the other. But Khartoum has far more cards to play. It has much more money. It also knows that Eritrea's attempts to unite the Darfur resistance will only succeed in dividing the armed movements. So Sudanese security is happy for Asmara to expend its efforts on the Darfurian resistance, expecting that this will keep the international community out, keep the Darfurians divided, and contain any threat from Déby. Meanwhile, should Eritrean military support to the Darfur commanders become too generous, Khartoum can cut Asmara's economic lifeline at a moment's notice.

Khartoum is also managing the SPLM role in Darfur. It wants to minimize the possibility that the SPLM will gain a political constituency among Darfurians in advance of the 2008/2009 elections. It wants to prevent SPLA military links with the Darfurian commanders in case there should be a resumption of war with the SPLA. Until the time of writing, the SPLM has yet to organize a political infrastructure to engage with Darfur and so the NCP and security chiefs have not been challenged. Allowing the Eritreans to take the lead with the SPLM serves them well in the short term. Khartoum's greater concern is that Asmara will also try to build up the SPLA in southern Sudan as a means to weaken Khartoum. That, however, is a different story.

Khartoum's biggest challenge in Darfur in 2007 is managing the Arab tribes. Arab militia leaders are acutely conscious of the way in which they have been exploited as the vanguard of the government's counterinsurgency.

They took casualties. They were able to make short-term economic gains from looting and were able to settle in some areas, but they also lost the social and economic interconnectedness with their now-displaced neighbors that had sustained their livelihoods. Above all, their reputation was badly sullied and the label "Janjawiid" achieved an international notoriety that was applied indiscriminately to all Darfur Arabs. In many parts of Darfur, the Arab militia are stronger than the army and can dictate government appointments and security policy. Opinion is divided among Darfur's Arab leaders as to whether to be loyal to the government, switch to an alliance with the non-signatory SLA, or remain neutral. Their choice also depends on whether the discontent among the Arabs of south and west Kordofan translates into insurrection, and what form such a rebellion might take.

Thus far the government has managed the Arabs by absorbing many of the militia into the army, Popular Defense Forces, and other paramilitaries, and continuing to give individual leaders money and political positions. This is the pattern of how it has tried to manage powerful militia since the 1980s. It has had limited success. The Baggara *murahaliin* militia of south Kordofan and south Darfur, armed in the 1980s, came to distrust the government in the 1990s and refused to join the Darfur counterinsurgency in 2003. Many of the southern militia organized under the umbrella of the South Sudan Defence Force later joined the SPLA. In Darfur, the government has exactly the same fears. The numbers are too large to absorb into the armed forces and most of them have been integrated into paramilitaries as formed units with their own loyalties. The government is working hard to prevent any coordinated defection or rebellion among the Arabs. It is buying time.

Underpinning the approach of the NCP and the security chiefs is the utilization of the native administration system, local government, and where possible the management of the displaced camps, to control the population of Darfur. A controlled and quiescent population constitutes peace.

For Khartoum, the year following the DPA has demonstrated that Darfur can be managed on a retail basis, mostly directly but also using the Eritreans as an intermediary. The precise tactics will change according to circumstance but there is little reason for the NCP and security leaders to alter their strategy. The Darfur resistance is not an immediate political threat and unless it becomes so—perhaps through a much wider rebellion including Arabs or Kordofan groups—Khartoum has every reason to continue business as usual. A robust peace agreement that leads to a cohesive Darfurian bloc in Sudanese politics, or a strong international presence in Darfur, would introduce new and difficult-to-manage factors into the Sudanese political equation, which would destabilize the ruling group.

## Coda

THE POLITICAL ALIGNMENT for a robust peace was most favorable in the first six months of 2005, when Garang, Ali Osman, and Déby were actual or potential partners for peace. The Darfur armed movements were less disunited than subsequently, with JEM playing a role of coordinating the positions of the SLM factions. The AMIS force was on the ground and enjoyed the respect of both sides. But the internal dynamics of the peace process had hardly begun and the only product from Abuja during those months was the Declaration of Principles. That favorable alignment began to slip in the final months of 2005 and 2006, with Garang dead, Ali Osman eclipsed, and Déby a spoiler.

The best chance for a negotiated peace with a semblance of fairness and international guarantee was the DPA of May 2006. Once that opportunity had been missed, Sudanese politics returned to business as usual. The ruling cliques of the NCP and security services have no grand strategy and do not agree among themselves. Nonetheless they are habitual masters of managing crisis through retail politics, purchasing their internal stability and survival at the cost of allowing Darfur to remain divided, unstable, and violent indefinitely.

While Darfur remains in this way, the Sudanese political environment changes. The CPA has a timetable for elections and the referendum on self-determination for southern Sudan. When the political alignments for a negotiated peace recur—which could be a few months' hence or, more likely, many years into the future—the players, the issues, the context, and the solutions could all be different. Meanwhile, Darfurians continue to face a miserable existence.

NOTES

BIBLIOGRAPHY

INDEX

# NOTES

## 1. Sudan: The Turbulent State

1  See Deborah Murphy in this volume.

2  See http://www.sudanjem.com. Also see Ahmed Kamal in this volume.

3  See Jérôme Tubiana in this volume.

4  See Musa Abdul-Jalil, Adam Azzain Mohammed, and Ahmed A. Yousuf in this volume.

5  See Musa Abdul-Jalil, Adam Azzain Mohammed, and Ahmed A. Yousuf in this volume.

6  Note that the central blocs also do this: Libya has often supported the Umma, Egypt the Unionists, etc.

7  Also organized under the banner of the Eastern Front in alliance with the Rashaida Free Lions.

8  See Roland Marchal and Julie Flint, both in this volume.

9  See the contributions of Dawit Toga, Laurie Nathan, and Alex de Waal in this volume.

10  See Ahmed Kamal El-Din in this volume; also El-Affendi 1990.

11  The phrase is from Abdullahi el Tom.

12  See Musa Abdul-Jalil, Adam Azzain Mohammed, and Ahmed A. Yousuf in this volume.

13  David Hoile, apologist for the Sudan government, develops this approach (Hoile 2005).

14  See Ali Haggar in this volume.

15  See Jérôme Tubiana in this volume.

16  See Julie Flint in this volume.

17  See Roland Marchal in this volume.

## 2. Native Administration and Local Governance in Darfur: Past and Future

1  The popular story goes that a wise stranger arrived in North Darfur and was given homage by Sultan Shaw of the Tunjur, who was ruling most of the region. The

stranger was subsequently married to the Sultan's daughter, Keira, who bore him Sulayman (so named because of his light complexion). Because of the matrilineal rule of succession Sulayman became the next sultan of Darfur.

2   Ahmed Rijal is a retired local government administrator and has a reputation for refusing to act according to government directives regarding the current conflict in Darfur. He was told not to talk to foreign diplomats who visit Nyala but he refused to abide by this order.

### 3.  Darfur: A War for Land?

1   This chapter is an updated version of a French article (Tubiana 2006), and based on fieldwork carried out in Darfur in 2004 and 2005 on behalf of the French non-governmental aid agency Action contre la faim (ACF). The author is grateful to Victor Tanner for his English translation of the article and for his informed comments and advice.

2   The figure of two million IDPs does not account for the many who have fled to other parts of Sudan, mainly the large cities, or the large number who have not returned from seasonal labor on the farms of central and eastern Sudan (OCHA 2005).

3   The author prefers the term "non-Arab" to "African," "black," "black African," or "indigenous"—all carryovers from the war in South Sudan, spread by Western media, and frequently used by the rebels themselves. These terms are, at best, misleading. Many of the "Arab" populations have been in the region for centuries. They have widely intermarried with their "African" neighbors, and are often indistinguishable from them in skin color and physical features. They are, in truth, as African as the other ethnic groups (de Waal 2005a, 181–205).

4   These groups speak Arabic and often perceive themselves as Arab, but are sometimes referred to, with irony, by other non-Arabs, as the "Arabs of 2005." Even the Fallata of Tulus in South Darfur, who still speak their original West African language, consider themselves, and are considered by others to be Arab (Tanner 2005a; Jérôme Tubiana 2005, 168).

5   These genealogies are thought to have been mostly created *ex post* in the eighteenth and nineteenth centuries. Their authenticity, however, is no doubt greater that of that of the Arab lineages boasted by some non-Arab groups, like the Tunjur and some clans of the Fur and Zaghawa, whose decidedly non-Arab sense of self does not preclude their claiming Arab ancestors—an ancient tradition that sought the prestige linked to Islam rather than Arab-ness.

6   These conflicts include the Fur-Arab war of 1987–1989 and the Arab-Masalit war of 1994–1998, mentioned above. Also of note was the resurgence, in the 1990s, of a thirty-year conflict in northwestern Darfur between Zaghawa and the camel-herding northern Rizeigat (Rizeigat Abbala) over the Jineik water hole. The Zaghawa consider another micro-conflict with Rizeigat Abbala from western Darfur as having triggered their entry into the war, which came later than that of the Fur and the

Masalit: a series of reciprocal camel-rustling incidents that grew increasingly murderous in the area of Abu Gamra (south of Kornoy), all against the backdrop of
government support for new Arab migratory routes deep inside Dar Zaghawa
(Tubiana 2005, 184–186).

7   Minni Minawi and Suleiman Jamus, interviews, SLA-controlled areas of Darfur,
September 2005; interviews with various SLA leaders in Sudan and abroad,
2004–2005.

8   In Darfur, as elsewhere in Sudan, Khartoum has manipulated the so-called native
administration (*idara ahlia*) set up by the British, by empowering local strongmen
and undermining the system in general.

9   This includes the Zaghawa families of the sultan of Tine and the *shartai* of
Kornoy, who educated their children in the schools set up by the British. Khalil
Ibrahim, for instance, hails from the royal house of Tine.

10  The Arab group that has most successfully refrained from getting dragged into the
violence is the Rizeigat Baggara of ed Da'in, under the leadership of their *nazir,*
Said Mahmud Musa Madibu. The neutrality of the dar-holding Arabs has become
widely recognized. But while there is no discounting how important the "neutrality" of these groups is to Darfur's future, it is also important not to underestimate
the large numbers of members of these groups who took part in the violence as
individuals.

11  The term "militia" may overstate the degree of organization of groups that were
often little more than bands of armed villagers, composed of traditional groups of
young men gathering for collective agricultural works, house building and war.

12  For the symbolic importance to Darfurians of the oft-promised but never built
road, see Tanner 2005a, 14.

13  A UN map of Darfur's ethnic groups refers to these two areas as the "original
homeland" of the northern Rizeigat and Zayadiya respectively. "Homeland" is a
powerful term, the Arabic translation of which could well be *dar.* The reality is,
however, that the Kutum area is made up of different dars, all non-Arab, controlled
mostly by Tunjur chiefs, while the Mellit-Abu Ku area is the heart of Dar Berti.
Furthermore, both the settled and transhumant Arab groups of these areas are
newcomers compared to the non-Arab dar-holders—many of the northern
Rizeigat have come from Chad in the course of the past half-century or so, while
the Zayadiya came from Kordofan. One cannot overstate how dangerous such
maps can be. While official in appearance, they are hastily drawn and based on
tendentious sources, and thus prone to political manipulation.

14  Ereigat (sometimes also called Zabalat) are actually a "sister branch" of the
Rizeigat, their ancestor, Zabali, being the brother of the one of the Rizeigat,
Rizeige. But in Darfur, they have been for a long time tied to the northern
Rizeigat, and are often considered as Rizeigat.

15  Following the genealogies I obtained in Chad and Darfur, Awlad Rashid, who live
mostly in Chad, constitute one of the four big branches of the Juhayna Arabs, the

others being Atiya (Rizeigat and Misirya), Salamat, and Hemat. But in Darfur, Awlad Rashid have been for a long time tied to the northern Rizeigat.

16  Although in some cases the Arab versus non-Arab clashes only began during the current conflict. This includes the case of Korma, where the Ereigat had settled since as early as the sultanate.

17  Interview, Khartoum, September 2004.

18  Some observers say the 2000–2001 resurgence of Arab militancy in Wadi Salih was due to the arrival of former Darfurian and Chadian Arab members of Gaddafi's Islamic Legion (interviews with West Darfur leaders, Khartoum, September 2004).

19  The Sudanese understand "statutory" law to be that of the post-independence republic, especially the Nimeiri period onward, starting in 1969. By "customary" law, we mean the traditional judiciary system of the sultanate. However, the simplistic and idealized terms with which the traditional system is often remembered today in Darfur have little to do with the fluid and highly localized system described so well by O'Fahey and Salim 1983, 12–21.

20  Interview with non-Arab traditional leader, al Fashir, August 2005.

21  Predatory mechanized farming schemes allowed absentee landlords backed by the state—and by foreign donors such as the World Bank—to deprive local communities of access to their own land, while at the same time strip-farming the land to environmental oblivion. Subsequent legislation by the post-1989 regime reinforced the power of the Islamist state as the earthly custodian of God's land. The areas that have suffered most from mechanized farming have been Kordofan and especially the Nuba Mountains and Blue Nile, Gedarif, and Kassala states, as well as those areas of South Sudan under Khartoum's control, especially Upper Nile (Coalition for International Justice 2006, 46–60; Ajawin and de Waal 2002; African Rights 1997).

22  Interview with SLA representative from Abuja, Paris, March 2006.

23  The plurals are: *salatin, muluk,* and *sharati,* respectively.

24  In the case of the Zayadiya, their leader kept on being called Sheikh for some time.

25  Interview with a Fur intellectual, al Fashir, October 2004.

26  Interview, al Fashir, October 2004.

27  Interview, al Fashir, August 2005.

28  Interview, Khartoum, August 2005.

29  Interview, Khartoum, August 2005.

30  Article 2 of the Declaration of Principles, established in Abuja on July 5, 2005, states, "Tribal land ownership rights (*hawakeer*) and other historical rights shall be affirmed within their historical borders."

31  Interview, SLA-controlled area of Darfur, September 2005.

32  Interview, Nyala, September 2004.

33  Interview, al Fashir, October 2004.

34  The HRW text refers to Abu Noba variously as "Mustaba Abu Nooba," "Mustapha Abu Nouba," and "Mustapha Abu Nuba," but the author is confident it refers to the same individual (Human Rights Watch 2005, 34–35).

35  Interview, Nyala, September 2004.

36  Interview, Khartoum, September 2004.

37  That is, that statutory law takes precedence (Food and Agriculture Organization 2004, 13).

38  Interview, Paris, March 2006.

39  Interview with Awlad Rashid leader, Bor Said, August 2005.

40  Interview with SLA commander, Shangal Tobay, September 2005.

41  Interview with SLA representative in Abuja, Paris, March 2006.

### 4. Islam and Islamism in Darfur

1  Muhamad bin Omar al Tunisi's book, in Arabic, documenting his visit to Darfur is entitled "Exerting the Brains with Reports on the Lands of Arabs and the Sudan." It has been edited by Dr. Khalil M. Asakir and Dr. Mustafa M. Hussein and is published by Egypt House for Authorship, Translation and Publishing, Cairo, 1960. Al Tunisi spent over seven years in Darfur, starting from 1803. Also cf. Al Zain 1998.

2  The Dali Code was issued by Sultan Shao Dor Sheit's brother, Daleel Al Bahr, or Dali. The Code formed the basis for legislation in the Sultanate until its demise in 1916 (Trimingham 1946).

3  Ma jallatul Ahkam Al Adliyah was the full name of this Ottoman compendium of rules of law, especially civil law. The Dali Code, however, was more comprehensive, covering all criminal, civil, public, and private divisions of Darfur national legal system.

4  Al Ma'quor was an Abbasid prince, from Beni Hilal, who left Baghdad with other relatives upon the downfall of their dynasty in 1421 CE (823 ADH) and settled shortly in Tunis before traveling to Darfur upon a conflict with his elder brother. His son from Sultan Dor Sheir's daughter would be the famous Sultan Suleiman Solonj (meaning the "red" or the Arab); cf Shuqeir 1981, 149–151.

5  *Tijaniyya* seems to be the first *Sufi* order in Sudan. The currently most populous *Qadiriyya* order in central Sudan, it came from Baghdad with Tajuddin al Baghdadi towards the end of the sixteenth century. *Sammaniyya* order was introduced by Ahmed al Tayeb Bashir al Jumou'ee (1793–1853); cf. bin Dhaifallah 1985.

6  And for that purpose it equally suited the whole of the Sudanese population who were exposed to *Sufi* Islam.

7  Dr. M. Nageeb A. Eisa recorded in his unpublished manuscript, "A Brief History of contemporary Darfur Vestibues (*Rewaq Darfur*) at Al Azhar," an interview he conducted with Amin Hassan Abdallah, the then (2003) Sheikh of Darfur Vestibules since 1995.

8  Cf. Trimingham 1946.

9  Tassel 2005; also posted on Daniel Pipes' weblog http://www.danielpipes.org/article/2300. Other relevant articles on the same weblog include "The Challenge of Islamism in Europe and the Middle East," by Daniel Pipes, delivered as a speech at The First International Coptic Symposium, September 23, 2004.

10 The Quran: Chapter V Al Ma'idah (The Table) verses V:44, V:45 and V:47.

11 1951 is the year when the first Darfurian (Suleiman Mustafa Abbakar) was recruited into the Sudanese Muslim Brothers movement, according to interviewee Yassin Omar al Imam, current editor-in-chief of the opposition Islamist Popular Congress Party's newspaper, *Rai al Sha'b* (People's Voice).

12 Dr. Gibril Ibrahim Mohammed, JEM co-founder and current leading member, interviewed on October 14, 2006.

13 The Economic Department of the National Congress Party: The Economic Sector Conference: The Final Report on the Works of the Economic Sector Conference, held at the Friendship Hall, Khartoum, September 11–12, 2005.

14 The Final Report, op. cit, Part (2) Third Assumption: The Future of Investment during the Interim Period.

15 The relevant Popular Congress Party resolution was passed late in July 2006 in favor of a conditional acceptance of a UN deployment (later formalized in UN Security Council Resolution 1706 of 2006), based on rules of necessity to save the lives of innocent civilians. The resolution was supported by thirty-seven and opposed by twenty-two votes with fourteen abstentions, cf. Akhbar al Youm, online version, posted 7.7.1427 AH (1 August AD), http://www.akhbaralyoumsd.net/modules.php?name=News&file=article&sid=3458.

### 6. Darfur's Armed Movements

1 Mohamed Issa of the Darfur Forum, interview above, Abuja, December 2005.

2 Abdel Wahid Mohamed al Nur, interview, Abuja, October 2005.

3 Hafiz Yousif, interview, Abuja, October 2005.

4 Daud Taher Hariga, interview, Abuja, December 2005.

5 Estimates of the dead range from fifty-six to seventy-seven. Wildly different dates are cited. The date used comes from Minni Minawi, who gives a very detailed chronology of the early years of the rebellion.

6 Commander Kamal Imam Gasy, interview, Muzbat, January 2005.

7 Hariga, interview.

8 Interviews in Abuja, December 2004.

9 Interview in Abuja, December 2005.

10 Khamis Abdalla, interview, West Darfur, February 2004.

11 Minni Minawi, interview, Abuja, November 2005.

12 Sudan Organization Against Torture, press release, August 23, 2002.

13 Mustafa Mahmoud al Tayyib, interview, Abuja, November 2005.

14 Abdel Wahid dates the first arms shipments from south Sudan to October 2002. Those who were in the south to dispatch them say they began in January 2003.

15 Hariga, interview.

16 Abdel Wahid Mohamed al Nur, interview, Abuja, September 2005.

17 Babiker Abdalla, interview, Abuja, December 2005.

18 Commander Suleiman Marajan, interview, Abuja, October 2005.

19 Interior Minister Gen. Abdel Rahim Mohamed Hussein, report to parliament, May 2003.

20 Interview with senior SLA official, Abuja, October 2005.

21 Interviews with rebel commanders and western diplomats, London and Abuja, April and October 2005.

22 Interviews with JEM leaders, London and Abuja, 2004–2005.

23 JEM General Coordinator Abubakr Hamid Nur, interview, Abuja, December 2004.

24 JEM Secretary-General Bahr Idriss Abu Garda, interview, Abuja, October 2005.

25 Bahr Idriss, interview.

26 Abdalla, interview.

27 Adam Ali Shogar, interview, N'djamena, January 2005.

28 Interviews with Fur and Zaghawa, 2003–2005.

29 Shogar, interview.

30 Minni Minawi, interview, Abuja, December 2005. Despite denials by some of his family, Minawi admitted to the author that his men "tortured and killed" Malik Abdel Rahman. He claimed they did not know the identity of their prisoner.

31 Minawi claimed publicly that he released Marajan. He acknowledged privately that he gave no such order.

32 SLA Commander Suleiman Marajan (one of those sent to close the JEM office), interview, Abuja, October 2005.

33 Hafiz Yousif, interview, Abuja, November 2005.

34 Most of JEM's political documents are available, often only in Arabic, on its website: www.sudanjem.com.

35 See "Resolving the Issue of Religion and the State," www.sudanjem.com

36 Military Statement no. 1, issued in Jebel Marra on December 6, 2006 and signed by Cmdr. Yassin Yousif.

37 Interviews with G-19 commanders, Abuja, January 2006.

38 Suleiman Marajan, interview, Abuja, February 2006.

39 Suleiman Jamous, telephone interview, September 2006.

40 Confidential email to the author, July 24, 2006.

### 7. The Unseen Regional Implications of the Crisis in Darfur

1 The first version of this text was commissioned by the CPPF in July 2005. The updating has been made possible thanks to fieldwork in Chad and Sudan.

2 Among many publications, see the various International Crisis Group reports on Darfur that underplay this transnational dimension.

3 See Reports of the United Nations panel of experts S/2006/65 and S/2006/795.

4 For background information, visit : http://www.columbia.edu/itc/sipa/martin/chad-cam/index.html

5 Borogate speak Daza and Beri and could be associated with the Gorane as well as with the Zaghawa.

6 Among diplomatic circles, other reasons were provided: the French Ambassador

pushed for massive support to civil society organizations and free media, and was vocal against the plundering of the state assets by Déby's inner circle.

7   See other chapters of this book.

8   One of the staunchest supporters of the JEM was Daoussa Déby, who actually grew up in the same house as Khalil Ibrahim. Beyond kinship, there were others cultural developments that explained this mobilization in favor of the Sudanese insurgency. Beyond what is quoted here, see Marchal 2006.

9   This point is actually inadequately studied in the history of the Chadian civil war. Relationships between the traditional and modern elites in Chad are more complex and contentious than in Sudan, where cooptation was the overwhelming scenario. This refers to a discussion by Jean-François Bayart 1993.

10  Chad recognized Taipei in 1997 at a time its president was short of cash. This was a perfect illustration of the "dollar diplomacy" pursued by Taiwan to get support from poor or indebted states.

### 10.  The Making and Unmaking of the Darfur Peace Agreement

1   This chapter is an updated version of Laurie Nathan, "No Ownership, No Peace: The Darfur Peace Agreement," Working Paper, no. 5 (series 2), Crisis States Research Centre, London School of Economics, September 2006.

2   The author joined the AU mediation team in December 2005 and was a member of the Security Arrangements Commission and the Coordinators' Forum until mid-March 2006.

3   See, for example, the comments by Said Djinnit in African Union, "The AU Commissioner for Peace and Security Meets the Sudanese Parties and the International Partners," press release no. 29, Abuja, February 10, 2006; and the comments by Hilary Benn, the UK's Secretary for International Development, in *Africa Confidential* 2006, 4.

4   These concerns related to compensation for victims of the violence in Darfur, the involvement of the SLM in monitoring the disarmament of the Janjawiid, the protection of IDPs and refugees as they returned to their homes, and stronger provisions on political representation (*Sudan Tribune* 2006j).

5   For an account of the mediators' efforts after the signing ceremony, see "AU Reacts to ICG Report," and chapter 11 in this volume.

6   Dawit Toga (political analyst in the Conflict Management division of the African Union), interview, July 30, 2006. See also Watts Nyirigwa, "Darfur Peace: Does It Meet Legitimate Aspiration of the People?" *Sudan Tribune*, June 12, 2006.

7   These problems were greatest in the Power Sharing Commission and the Security Arrangements Commission. In the Wealth Sharing Commission, the parties' negotiators were able to reach a number of agreements (AU 2006).

8   On the government's poor performance in relation to the Comprehensive Peace Agreement, see International Crisis Group 2006a.

9   For accounts of the rebel divisions and their negative impact on the negotiations ,
    see "Briefing by Dr. Salim Ahmed Salim," 2–3; and International Crisis Group
    2005c.

10  In July 2006 a group of Abdel Wahid's commanders announced that they had over-
    thrown him because of his failure to maintain the unity of the SLM and consult its
    leadership; the commanders expressed opposition to the DPA and support for a
    negotiated settlement (*Sudan Tribune* 2006q).

11  The shortage of funds also led periodically to the non-payment of per diems to
    the rebel delegates, generating much tension with the mediators, whom the rebels
    expected to solve the problem.

12  Abdullahi Eltom interview, "Darfur: Inside the Crisis," May 15, 2006, available at
    http://www.democracynow.org (accessed September 5, 2006).

13  The letter was published in the *Sudan Tribune* on May 9, 2006 under the heading
    "AU Mediators Address Open Letter to Reluctant Darfur Rebels."

14  See, for example, Ken Silverstein, "Official Pariah Sudan Valuable to America's War
    on Terrorism," *Los Angeles Times*, April 29, 2005, retrieved from the website of the
    Global Policy Forum, www.globalpolicy.org on September 13, 2006.

15  On the international community's failure to respond adequately to the Darfur
    killings and humanitarian catastrophe see, for example, Prunier, 2005. See also
    http://www.sudanreeves.org, the website of Eric Reeves, who writes prolifically
    on this topic.

### 11. Darfur's Deadline: The Final Days of the Abuja Peace Process

1   He also instructed Abdul Mohammed to begin working on proposals for the
    Darfur-Darfur Dialogue and Consultation.

2   This corresponds to paragraph 417 of the final DPA.

3   Khalil Ibrahim is a member of the ruling lineage of the Kobe Zaghawa.

4   Letter from Abdel Wahid al Nur, Chairman of the SLM, to Dr. Salim Ahmed
    Salim, Chief Mediator of the African Union, May 10, 2006.

5   Letter from Salim Ahmed Salim, Special Envoy and Chief Mediator, to Abdel
    Wahid al Nur, Chairman of the SLM, May 13, 2006.

6   Author's notes from the meeting.

7   "Memorandum of Understanding between the Government of Sudan (GoS) and
    the Sudan Liberation Movement/Army (SLM/A)," May 14, 2006.

8   Government of Sudan response to SLM/A Memorandum, May 14, 2006.

### 12. Darfur After Abuja: A View from the Ground

1   Personal observation and personal communications with local residents and local
    leaders, Nyala, Tulus, Geneina, and Zalingei, May–June and September–October
    2006.

2   Personal communications from al Fashir residents (in person and by phone),
    Khartoum, October 2006.

3 Displaced Fur sheikh from the Shattaya area, location withheld (Darfur), May–June 2006.

4 Email communication, Sara Pantuliano (Overseas Development Institute), February 2007.

5 Author interviews and conversations in Khartoum and North, West, and South Darfur, May–June and September–October 2006.

6 Personal communications, Fur elder from al Fashir, Khartoum, October 2006, and former SLA field commander, Khartoum, October 2006; Masalit leaders from Gereida interviewed in Nyala (South Darfur), September 2006; personal communication, senior SLA-Minni commander, Nyala (South Darfur), October 2006.

7 Personal communication, Jérôme Tubiana, November 2006 (based on his fieldwork in Chad in October 2006).

8 Former SLA field commander, interviewed in al Fashir, September 2006.

9 Email communication, Theo Murphy (Centre for Humanitarian Dialogue), who has been in regular phone contact with rebel commanders on the ground, January 2007.

10 Personal communication, former Sudanese special forces officer, Khartoum, October 2006.

11 Personal communication, former Sudanese armored cavalry officer, Khartoum, October 2006.

12 Polgreen, Lydia, "Sudanese Soldiers Flee War to Find a Limbo in Chad," *New York Times*, October 18, 2006.

13 Personal communication, Khartoum, October 2006.

14 Personal communications, al Fashir residents, September-October 2006.

15 The second author carried out five weeks of field research in mid-2004, speaking to dozens of Darfurians in North, South, and West Darfur, as well as in Khartoum, about the roots causes of the conflict.

16 Fur *omda*, interviewed in Nyala (South Darfur), June and September 2006. His home area is not mentioned for security purposes.

17 Displaced Fur leader, Kas area (South Darfur), June 2006.

18 Mararit *omda*, interviewed in Nyala (South Darfur), June 2006. His precise home area is not mentioned for his security reasons.

19 Senior Masalit traditional leader, interviewed in Geneina (West Darfur), June 2006.

20 Displaced Fur man, interviewed in Saraf Omra (North Darfur), June 2006.

21 Displaced Hausa man, interviewed in a larger group in Tulus (South Darfur), May 2006.

22 For example, these are some of the reconciliation meetings that took place in South Darfur in 2005 and early 2006: Rizeigat-Birgid (2005); Miseriya-Birgid (2005); Dajo-Miseriya (2005); in Buram and Gereida, Habaniya-Masalit (2005); in Kas, displaced Fur and Arab tribes (2005); in Malam, Fur and Bani Mansur (2005); in Hamada, Birgid, Tarjam, and Rizeigat (2006); in Buram, Habaniya-Fallata (2006).

23 Masalit tribal elder, interviewed in Geneina (West Darfur), June 2006.

24  South Darfur state official, office of the Wali, interviewed in Nyala, May 2005.

25  See Dawit Toga in this volume for an explanation of the Darfur-Darfur Dialogue and Consultation within the DPA.

26  Fur traditional leader, interviewed in Nyala (South Darfur), May 2006.

27  Senior Masalit leader, interviewed in Geneina (West Darfur), June 2006.

28  Northern Rizeigat (*abbala*) traditional leader, interviewed in North Darfur (location withheld for security reasons), June 2006.

29  Tama *omda*, interviewed in North Darfur (location withheld for security reasons), June 2006.

30  Dar (pl. *diar*), tribal homeland; *hakura* (pl. *hawakir*), estate. See Jérôme Tubiana in this volume.

31  See Musa Abdul-Jalil, Adam Azzain Mohamed, and Ahmed A. Yousuf in this volume.

32  Interview with al Hadi Issa Debaka, Idd al Ghanam / Idd al Fursan (South Darfur), May 2006. He did, however, deny that any real violence had occurred in his nazirate, dismissing any incidents that occurred as local problems.

33  Leading Fur activist and politician, interviewed in Khartoum, May 2004.

34  Interviews with Fur cultivators in Zalingei (West Darfur), October 2006. For in-depth research on the move to *wadi* cultivation in the 1990s, see El Amin 1999a, 31ff; El Amin 1999b, 25–38. One of the consequences of the withdrawal of aid programs in Darfur in the 1990s was the progressive decrease in social research and systematic data collection. What little solid analysis existed was often hard to access outside of Sudan. Khalid El Amin's two excellent papers are cases in point.

35  Group of Hausa internally displaced, interviewed in Tulus (South Darfur), May 2006.

36  See Roland Marchal in this volume.

37  Personal observation and personal communications with local residents and local leaders, Nyala (South Darfur), May, June, September, and October 2006; Tulus (South Darfur), May 2006.

38  The authors follow the reasoning of Dr. Abdel Ghaffar M. Ahmed (Ahmed 2002).

39  Former Sudanese political activist, interviewed in Sudan (location withheld), January 2007.

40  State government official and career administrator, interviewed in Kadugli (South Kordofan), December 2006.

41  Based on field work in Tawila and Sese, June 2004. For a more detailed description of the positive role played by police in those periods in Tawila and Sese camp, see Tanner 2005, 38–39.

42  Interviews, Kutum, Kabkabiya, and Geneina, June 2004.

43  Mornei police commander, interviewed in Mornei (West Darfur), June 2004.

44  Meidob leaders, interviewed in Sudan (location withheld), September–October 2006.

45  Fallata men, interviewed in Tulus, May 2006.

46  Gimir traditional leader, interviewed in Katila, May 2006.

47  Gimir state official, interviewed in Nyala, May 2006.

48  The name "SLA-Free Will" was also used by a breakaway group from SLA-Abdel Wahid, headed by Abdel Rahman Musa, his chief negotiator in Abuja, who signed an agreement with the government. This group has support among the Tunjur.

49  Jérôme Tubiana, email communication, August 2006.

### 13. Narrating Darfur: Darfur in the U.S. Press, March–September 2004

1  A few exceptions to this were: concern that Islamist leader Hassan al-Turabi was affiliated with the rebel Justice and Equality Movement (*Washington Times* 2004, "Remember Rwanda, Act on Sudan," A14, April 13); criticism of the rebel's own human rights record (*Washington Post* 2004, "300,000 Deaths Foretold," A22, June 7; *Washington Post* 2004, "Next Steps on Darfur," A18, September 1); and concern that the rebels translated the outcry against Khartoum as support for their cause and would become intransigent (Dealey, S. 2004, "Misreading the Truth in Sudan," *New York Times*, A11, August 8; Abramowitz, M. and S. Power 2004, "A Broken System," *Washington Post*, A21, September 13).

2  Kristof 2004, "Will We Say 'Never Again' Yet Again?" *New York Times*, A15, March 27; Fowler 2004, "In Sudan, Staring Genocide in the Face," *The Washington Post*, B02, June 6.

3  The one explicitly stated exception to this viewpoint appeared in an editorial by journalist Sam Dealey, who criticized the "three myths of one of the worst humanitarian crises—that the Janjaweed are the sole source of trouble and are acting only as proxies for Khartoum; that the conflict pits light-skinned Arabs against black Africans; and that the Sudanese government can immediately end the war whenever it wishes . . . It may be clear to Washington that Khartoum controls the conflict, but in Darfur the situation is more complex" ("Misreading the Truth in Sudan").

4  By September, the relief effort was improving, but some were beginning to realize it was inadequate. Morton Abramowitz and Samantha Power wrote, "The delivery of humanitarian aid lets us off the hook . . . It has helped reduce the death toll, but it is a stopgap solution that keeps the media at bay and allows lawmakers and policymakers to do good deeds while avoiding the political problem at the heart of Darfur's destruction" ("A Broken System"). Senator Jon Corzine and Richard Holbrooke agreed, "The disaster in Darfur . . . is man-made, and if the outside world continues to treat it simply as a humanitarian crisis without addressing the underlying causes, it will not end" (*Washington Post* 2004, "Help the African Union," A27, September 9).

5  Mufson, S. 2004, "How a Tragedy Became a Cause: Why We Read About Darfur and Not Burundi," *Washington Post*, B05, August 15.

6  Examples include: Power, S. 2004, "Remember Rwanda, but Take Action in Sudan," *New York Times*, A23, April 6; *Washington Times*, "Remember Rwanda, Act on Sudan," A14, April 13; Hentoff, N. 2004, "Stop a Repeat of Rwanda," *Washington Times*, A23, May 31.

7   *New York Times* 2004, "Peril in Sudan," A20, April 7.

8   "Remember Rwanda, but Take Action in Sudan."

9   *New York Times* 2004, "Witness to Genocide," A23, September 6.

10  *Washington Post* 2004, "300,000 Deaths Foretold," A22, June 7.

11  "Remember Rwanda, but Take Action in Sudan."

12  *Washington Post* 2004, "How Did 'Never Again' Become Just Words?" *Washington Post*, B02, April 4.

13  *Washington Post* 2004, "The Darfur Catastrophe," B07, May 30.

14  *New York Times* 2004, "Reign of Terror," A15, September 11.

15  Traub, J. 2004, "Never Again, No Longer?" *New York Times*, 6:17, magazine desk, July 18.

16  *Wall Street Journal* 2004, "A No-Fly Zone for Darfur," *Wall Street Journal*, A12, August 31.

17  *Washington Post* 2004, "The Stakes in Darfur," A20, July 22.

18  *New York Times* 2004, "Saying No to Killers," A19, July 21.

19  "Never Again, No Longer?"

20  *Washington Post* 2004, "End the Genocide Now," A31, September 22.

21  *Washington Times* 2004, "Don't Just Sit There," A17, September 14. In this context, "divest" refers to withdrawing investments in companies that do business with Sudan.

22  Khartoum also decided the "war on terror" was the best angle for its propaganda campaign in the U.S. On May 20, a *Washington Times* editorial urged the U.S. to engage Sudan in the war on terror: "According to information provided solely to the *Washington Times* by Sudan's Washington embassy, Khartoum has arrested nearly 600 members of Al Qaeda. It has also conducted seven joint operations with the CIA against Al Qaeda and affiliated groups in the Horn of Africa." Regarding Darfur, "While the crisis is real, what is untold in most press accounts is how the misery is being spread by terror groups . . . Militias loyal to radical Islamist leader Hasan al-Turabi are waging a revolt to try to topple the pro-American government" ("Engaging Sudan," A18, May 20). Khartoum soon ceased to find a home for its propaganda on the *Washington Times* editorial page. On July 22, on the same day it printed a letter from the government defending its conduct, the *Washington Times* wrote in an editorial, "Khartoum fails, in its lengthy defense of itself, to address the gathering storm of evidence illustrating its complicity in what has been, at best, homicidal ethnic cleansing and, at worst, genocide," and recommended the deployment of AU peacekeepers ("Sudan in Denial," A20, July 22).

23  "Misreading the Truth in Sudan."

24  "'Realism' and Darfur," B06, August 1.

25  *New York Times* 2004, "Dithering as Others Die," A13, June 26.

26  *Washington Times* 2004, "Pure Evil in Sudan," A17, August 2.

27  "'Realism' and Darfur," B06, August 1.

28  "How Did 'Never Again' Become Just Words?"

29  "The Stakes in Darfur."

30  "Will We Say 'Never Again' Yet Again?" A few observers did call for a more robust international response right from the start, notably Samantha Power, who called for ten thousand international peacekeepers to the region on April 6 ("Remember Rwanda, but Take Action in Sudan"), but there would not be a general consensus that peacekeepers were needed for months.

31  Kristof, N. 2004, "Cruel Choices," *New York Times,* A27, April 14; Hentoff, N. 2004, "Opening Their Eyes: The World Awakens to Atrocities in Darfur," *Washington Times,* A17, April 19.

32  *Washington Post* 2004, "Stalling in Sudan . . ." A22, April 26; Bogert, C. 2004, "SOS Sudan," *Wall Street Journal,* A16, May 26.

33  *Washington Post* 2004, ". . . And in Geneva," A22, April 26.

34  *Wall Street Journal* 2004, "The U.S. Cavalry," A10, July 2.

35  *Washington Post* 2004, "Next in Darfur," A14, July 2.

36  The French Ambassador responded with a letter published July 12, denying the charge and touting France's diplomatic efforts in the region (Levitte, J. 2004, "Relief for Darfur," A16, July 12). On July 25, the *Post* responded with another editorial criticizing France's failure to supply the UN relief operation with requested helicopters or enforce a no-fly zone from its military base in Chad (*Washington Post* 2004, "Mr. Powell's Mistake," B06, July 25). France eventually supplied troops to oversee the relief effort in Chad, and the Netherlands donated the six requested helicopters.

37  "Reign of Terror."

38  "Countdown on Darfur," A16, August 24.

39  "A Broken System."

40  "As Genocide Unfolds."

41  "The Stakes in Darfur."

42  "The Darfur Catastrophe."

43  "See No Evil in Sudan," A18, May 18.

44  "The U.S. Cavalry."

45  "End the Genocide Now."

46  "Another Triumph for the UN," A15, September 25.

47  *New York Times* 2004, "Still Dying in Darfur," A14, August 16.

48  "Countdown on Darfur"; Prendergast, J. 2004, "Sudan's Killing Fields," *Washington Times,* A17, September 7; "Help the African Union."

49  One interesting recommendation was made by Senate Majority Leader Bill Frist, following a suggestion by John Garang, who recommended the deployment of the joint SPLA-government of Sudan forces envisioned in the North-South peace agreement to augment the AU forces (*Washington Post* 2004, "Steps for Saving Lives in Sudan," A21, August 11).

50  "Dithering as Others Die."

51  "The U.S. Cavalry."

52  "Regime Change in Sudan," A15, August 23.

53  "See No Evil in Sudan."

54  "End the Genocide Now."

55  "How Many More Deaths?" A18, July 28.

56  "Sudan's Killing Fields."

57  "Help the African Union."

58  "Misreading the Truth in Sudan."

59  "Crisis in Darfur," B06, April 4.

60  "Cynical in Sudan," A12, July 28.

61  "Silence on the Arab Street," A10, July 2.

62  *New York Times* 2004, "The Genocide Next Door," A23, April 6.

63  *New York Times* 2004, "Starved for Safety," A23, March 31.

64  "Politics of Misery," A25, August 19.

65  "Will We Say 'Never Again' Yet Again?"

66  "As Genocide Unfolds."

67  *New York Times* 2004, "Sudan"s Final Solution," A17, June 19.

68  Fowler, J. 2004, "In Sudan, Staring Genocide in the Face," *Washington Post*, B02, June 6. While several editorials said that victims were targeted because of their black skin, often on the basis of refugee testimony, most editorials (even those saying the conflict is Arab-African) did not mention skin color. A few stressed the fluidity of ethnic boundaries in the region ("Sudan in denial;" "Misreading the Truth in Sudan").

69  "Time for Action on Sudan," A30, June 18.

70  "Remember Rwanda, but Take Action in Sudan."

71  "Genocide," B06, September 12.

72  "Calling it Right in Sudan," A18, September 14.

73  "Kofi Votes Kerry," A20, September 20.

### 14. *Not on Our Watch: The Emergence of the American Movement for Darfur*

1  Samantha Power quoted in Shannon Baker, "Rally against Darfur Genocide Prods Sudanese Government," *Baptist Press*, May 2, 2006.

2  Farah Stockman, "Americans Rally for Darfur; Protests Push US Action on Genocide," *Boston Globe*, May 1, 2006.

3  "D.C. Rally Condemns Darfur Genocide: We Refuse to Be Silent," *Chicago Sun-Times*, May 1, 2006.

4  Complete list of rallies available at http://www.genocideintervention.net/advocate/rally-apr06/

5  http://www.genocideintervention.net/advocate/rally-apr06/

6  Jim Doyle, "Tens of Thousands Rally for Darfur," *San Francisco Chronicle*, May 1, 2006.

7  "Tens of Thousands Rally for Darfur."

8  Hamilton interview with Reeves, June 26, 2006.

9   Tom Vraalsen, "Note to the Emergency Relief Coordinator; Sudan: Humanitarian Crisis in Darfur," December 8, 2003.

10   Hamilton interview with Reeves, June 26, 2006.

11   Eric Reeves, "Unnoticed Genocide," *Washington Post,* February 25, 2004.

12   Hamilton interview with Reeves, June 26, 2006

13   Nicholas Kristof, "Ethnic Cleansing, Again," *New York Times,* March 24, 2004.

14   One novel feature of Kristof's Darfur writing is his inclusion of links to advocacy organizations, through which he encourages his readers to take action. See, for example, Nick Kristof, "Darfur: A Village Waiting for Rape and Murder," *New York Times,* March 12, 2006.

15   See, for example, "NCC General Secretary Arrested in Protest Outside Sudan Embassy," *National Council of Churches News Service,* July 14, 2004; Tom Sullivan, "Rangel Arrested in Sudan Protest," *The Hill,* July 14, 2004.

16   Hazlett interview with Roger Winter, July 17, 2006.

17   "Congressional Black Caucus Joins Africa Action in Call for US Intervention to Stop Genocide in Darfur," *Africa Action Press Release,* June 23, 2004.

18   Hazlett interview with Ted Dagne, August 25, 2006

19   Hazlett interview with Ted Dagne, August 25, 2006

20   H. Con.Res. 467 and S. Con. Res. 133. *See* http://thomas.loc.gov/cgi-bin/bdquery/z?d108:h.con.res.00467.

21   Charles W. Corey, "U.S. Congress Terms Situation in Darfur 'Genocide'," *U.S. Department of State Press Release,* July 23, 2004.

22   Hamilton interview with Fowler, June 29, 2006.

23   Hamilton interview with Fowler, June 29, 2006.

24   Hamilton interview with Fowler, June 29, 2006.

25   Hazlett interview with Rubenstein, July 13, 2006. As generally occurs, humanitarian organizations found themselves wishing to condemn Khartoum but justifiably concerned as to the effect this would have on their ability to provide services in the country. For example, Samaritan's Purse, whose committed Christian constituency in the U.S. could have been powerful advocates, has hospitals operating in Khartoum. Other organizations did not participate in advocacy efforts but served an important role by providing in-the-field information of use to analysts and advocates.

26   Hazlett interview with Rubenstein, July 13, 2006.

27   Hamilton interview with Reeves, June 26, 2006.

28   Hamilton interview with Rogoff, June 29, 2006.

29   Hamilton interview with Bixby, July 21, 2006.

30   Hamilton interview with Bixby, July 21, 2006.

31   Hamilton interview with Bixby, July 21, 2006.

32   Res Publica was an early mover on Darfur issues. Their website, DarfurGenocide.org, was one of the first websites on Darfur, and its email list grew to 50,000 activists. This remained the largest email list of Darfur activists

until Save Darfur surpassed that number early in 2006. Hazlett interview with Ricken Patel, July 14, 2006.

33  Hamilton interview with Hanis, July 17, 2006.

34  Available at http://www.genocidewatch.org/
SudanStudentsProposeGenocideInterventionFund26oct2004.htm

35  Hamilton interview with Sniderman, July 20, 2006.

36  Hanis quoting Smith in Drake Bearden, "Swarthmore Students Help Bring News of Genocide to Light," *News of Delaware County*, August 11, 2005.

37  Valerie Strauss, "Violence in Darfur Inspires Surge in Student Activism," *Washington Post*, November 23, 2004.

38  Hamilton interview with Sara Weissman, June 24, 2006.

39  Hamilton interview with Millenson, June 27, 2006.

40  The student winners were: STAND co-founder Nate Wright; Swarthmore student Stephanie Nyombayire; and Boston student filmmaker Andrew Karlsruher.

41  *MTVu Sudan Campaign Backgrounder*, on file with authors.

42  See, for example, Don Cheadle and John Prendergast, "Seven Deadly Trends in Darfur," *Washington Times*, February 10, 2005; Don Cheadle and John Prendergast, "The Darfur Genocide," *Wall Street Journal*, March 24, 2005.

43  Nicholas Kristof, "The American Witness," *New York Times*, March 2, 2005.

44  See http://www.savedarfur.org/steidle/

45  Another victory occurred days earlier on March 31, when the UN Security Council referred the Darfur case to the International Criminal Court. It is noteworthy that the UN achieved this despite never having actually referred to the situation as genocide.

46  Students and the advocates they collaborated with, including Reeves and AASG's Jesse Sage, drew inspiration and legitimacy for divestment from historical successes, most notably against apartheid in South Africa, and in Reeves' earlier campaign pressuring TIAA-CREF to divest from Canadian oil company Talisman, ultimately forcing Talisman to withdraw from Sudan.

47  Daniel Hemel and Zachery Sewed, "University Bought Shares in Oil Firm That Activists Say Helped Fuel Genocide," *Harvard Crimson*, October 25, 2004.

48  Hazlett email correspondence with Hemel, July 19, 2006.

49  Hamilton interview with Ben Collins, July 9, 2006.

50  Harvard Darfur Action Group co-founders were the authors and Harvard College student Sabine Ronc.

51  "Harvard Announces Decision to Divest PetroChina Stock," *Harvard Gazette*, April 4, 2004.

52  Hazlett interviews with Bridget Moix and Laura Weis, July 12, 2006.

53  Hazlett interview with Patrick Schmitt, July 13, 2006.

54  "Why Darfur?"

55  Hamilton interview with Messinger, June 30, 2006.

56  Hazlett interview with Tim Nonn, August 23, 2006.

57 Hamilton interview with Messinger, June 30, 2006.

58 The authors were personally involved in early discussions about building a perma-nent "anti-genocide" constituency and aspects of its initial implementation.

59 "STAND Proposed Bylaws," National Student Conference, August 11, 2005, on file with authors.

60 At the time of writing, twenty-two universities have divested and campaigns are underway on an additional sixteen campuses. See Sudan Divestment Taskforce, *State of Sudan Divestment*, June 20, 2006, 5.

61 "Sudan-linked Pension Fund Holdings Under Fire," *Associated Press*, November 14, 2004.

62 Nick Timiraos, "Sudan-Divestment Activists Get Act Together," *Wall Street Journal*, July 19, 2006.

63 "Sudan-Divestment Activists Get Act Together."

64 "Sudan-Divestment Activists Get Act Together."

65 Sudan Divestment Taskforce, *State of Sudan Divestment*, June 20, 2006, 5; Matthew Garrahan, and Guy Dinmore, "California Rushes in Where Washington Fears to Tread," *Financial Times*, October 6, 2006.

66 Hamilton interview with Millenson, June 27, 2006.

67 Hamilton interview with Millenson, June 27, 2006.

68 Hamilton interview with Millenson, June 27, 2006.

69 Hamilton interview with Millenson, June 27, 2006.

70 Email correspondence with Gitta Zomorodi, AJWS.

71 Hazlett interview with Cizik, July 18, 2006.

72 Hamilton interview with Hertzke, June 26, 2006.

73 Cizik interview. See also Allen Hertzke, "The Shame of Darfur," *First Things*, 2005, 16–22. While some south Sudan activists had argued that a military victory by the south was the most desirable outcome of the north-south conflict, the CPA was broadly accepted as the best hope for peace.

74 Hamilton interview with Hertzke, June 26, 2006. See also Faith McConnell, "The Cost of Reconciliation," *National Review Online*, May 8, 2006.

75 Hamilton interview with Messinger, June 30, 2006.

76 Hazlett interview with White-Hammond, June 19, 2006.

77 Hazlett interview with White-Hammond, June 19, 2006.

78 For example, Hamilton interview with Reeves, June 26, 2006.

79 Hazlett interview with Rubenstein, July 28, 2006.

80 Hazlett interview with Rubenstein, July 28, 2006.

81 Hazlett interview with Rubenstein, July 28, 2006.

82 Hazlett interview with Rubenstein, July 28, 2006.

83 Hazlett interview with Rubenstein, July 28, 2006.

84 H. Con. Res. 467 and S. Con. Res. 133. See http://thomas.loc.gov/cgi-bin/bdquery/z?d108:h.con.res.00467.

85 H. Res 1268 (Emergency Supplemental Appropriations Act," 109th Congress), signed into law May 11, 2005.

86 S. Res. 1462, passed November 8, 2005, and H. Res. 3127, passed April 5, 2006.

87 S. Res. 383, "Calling on the President to take immediate steps to help improve the security situation in Darfur, Sudan, with an emphasis on civilian protection." Available at http://thomas.loc.gov/cgi-bin/query/D?c109:2:./temp/~c109ZeBqtk::

88 Hazlett interview with Capuano, March 21, 2006.

89 110 members of Congress sponsored or co-sponsored the major Darfur legislation in 2006 (S. 495, S. 1462, and S. 383 in the Senate; H.R. 723, H.R. 3127, H.R. 4939, and H.R. 5522 in the House). Only ten of those 110 were Republicans. For more information, see www.darfurscores.org

90 Tom Lantos, Sheila Jackson, Jim McGovern, Jim Moran, and John Olver.

91 Ruth Messinger, Rabbi Steve Gutow, Rabbi Michael Namaht, and Rev. Dr. Terence H. Allen.

92 Georgetown student Patrick Schmidt, then Executive Director of STAND.

93 "The Unprecedented Student Movement for Darfur," GI-Net press release, April 30, 2006.

94 "Cheek Wins Speed Skating Gold, Donates His Bonus," *Associated Press,* February 14, 2006.

95 Joey Cheek, "Voices on Genocide Prevention," USHMM podcast, available at http://www.ushmm.org/conscience/analysis/details.php?content=2006–04–27

96 Nicholas Kristof, "When Genocide Worsens," *New York Times,* July 9, 2006.

97 "President Meets with Darfur Advocates," White House press release, April 28, 2006.

98 Jim Doyle, "Tens of Thousands Rally for Darfur," *San Francisco Chronicle,* May 1, 2006.

99 Another surprising element of the student movement was that many student leaders did not end their engagement with Darfur upon graduation, but rather found ways to build or participate in the new organizations advocating for Darfur.

100 Hamilton interview with Ben Collins, July 9, 2006, and Hamilton interview with Bixby, July 21, 2006.

101 "Deputy Secretary Zoellick: Travel to Abuja, Nigeria," U.S. Department of State, May 1, 2006.

102 Jill Savitt, "Pressure on Darfur," May 5, 2006, available at http://www.tompaine.com/articles/2006/05/05/pressure_on_darfur.php

103 "Main parties sign Darfur accord," *BBC News,* May 5, 2006.

104 Hamilton interview with Sirkin, June 29, 2006.

105 A handful of organizations have written letters to the Administration urging the enforcement of DPA deadlines, principally under the leadership of Physicians for Human Rights. However, substantial pressure from a large coalition of groups has been absent, as has any response whatsoever from grassroots actors.

106 Peter Baker, "Top Aide Michael Gerson Knew Just How to Address the President," *Washington Post,* June 15, 2006.

107 Christine Hauser, "Rice's Deputy to Join Goldman Sachs," *New York Times,* June 19, 2006.

108  Allegations of cooperation between the CIA and Sudan on counterterrorism intelligence were first argued in Prendergast and Cheadle, "Our Friend, and Architect of the Genocide in Darfur," *Los Angeles Times*, February 14, 2006. This article detailed how Salah Gosh, Sudanese intelligence chief and partial architect of Darfur's horrors, has been protected by the U.S. to ensure he continues providing information on Al Qaeda.

109  One serious concern is that U.S. activism resulted in a premature conclusion to the DPA negotiations, producing an untenable agreement while making future attempts at settlement more difficult. See Laurie Nathan in this volume.

110  See Samantha Power, "The Void," *The New Republic*, May 10, 2006.

111  See Samantha Power, "The Void," *The New Republic*, May 10, 2006.

112  Hamilton interview with Sirkin, June 29, 2006, and Hazlett interview with Rubenstein, July 13, 2006.

113  Hazlett interview with Cizik, July 18, 2006.

114  Hazlett interview with Patrick Schmitt, July 13, 2006.

115  Paul Majendie, "Global Protests Call for U.N. Intervention in Darfur," *Washington Post*, September 18, 2006.

116  "Turning to the U.S. Government."

117  Despite the rather surprising level of attention paid to Sudan by the State Department, the Administration has missed many policy opportunities. At the time of writing these include imposing targeted sanctions and leading more aggressive action such as establishing a no-fly zone, or coordinating the deployment of a robust UN force.

118  Security Council Res. 1672, UN Doc. S/RES/1672, April 25, 2006. However, these sanctions were not imposed for human rights violations directly, but rather for "obstructing the peace process."

### 15. *Prospects for Peace in Darfur*

1  Salim tried to obtain greater participation from civil society and women in the peace talks and, addressing a Darfurian civil society workshop in Khartoum on March 26, 2007, regretted that he had not succeeded in this regard.

2  See Adam Azzain Mohamed in this volume.

3  The NCP accused the SPLM of secretly sending arms and military officers to escalate the rebellion in 2003 at exactly the same time as it was negotiating for peace in the south.

4  See Roland Marchal in this volume.

5  Both of them Canadians of Darfurian origin.

6  De Waal 2006b.

7  An additional problem was the question of implementation. Would the parties have the will to implement an agreement that they had not worked out among themselves? They might have signed the paper but they would not have internalized the logic of the agreement. In the event, this issue never arose.

8  The detail of this is described in chapter 11.

9  The only speaker from the international side on May 4–5 to ask for more time was the UN's General Henry Anyidoho.

10  Unspecified threats were also made against the Sudan government, especially on the evening of May 2, but Khartoum chose not to complain publicly about them. The question is not whether the U.S. or other internationals were "biased" but whether an approach based on arbitration could work.

11  Speaking to Alex de Waal, May 6, 2006.

12  See Dawit Toga chapter 9 in this volume.

13  Susan Rice, Anthony Lake, and Donald Payne, "We saved Europeans. Why not Africans?" *Washington Post,* October 2, 2006, A19.

14  Contrary to the assumptions of the International Crisis Group 2006b.

15  Abdul Jabbar Fadul and Victor Tanner chapter 12 in this volume.

16  The AU Commissioner for Peace and Security, Said Djinnit, presided over the ceremony for signing the Declaration of Commitment. He made it a precondition that the AU special representative, Baba Gana Kingibe, obtain the express consent of Minni to this procedure. In the presence of this writer, Kingibe assured Djinnit that Minni had given his consent. Minni subsequently denied this.

17  See Abdul-Jabbar Fadul and Victor Tanner chapter 12 in this volume.

18  Note that one of the Sudan government's main objections to the DPA was the provision for disarming foreign combatants in Darfur (see de Waal, chapter 11 in this volume).

19  Khartoum's tactic worked in part. The DPA makes reference to the Tripoli Agreement and does not include a border monitoring function for AMIS or its successor. But provisions for disarming foreign combatants remain in the DPA.

# BIBLIOGRAPHY

Abdel Halim, Rajab M. 1991, *Arabism and Islam in Darfur during the Middle Ages*, Cairo, Al Thaqafah.

Abdel Salam, A. H. and Alex de Waal (eds.). 2000, *The Phoenix State: Civil Society and the Future of Sudan*, Trenton NJ, Red Sea Press.

Abdel Salam, A. H. and Alex de Waal. 2004, "Islamism, state power and *jihad* in Sudan," in A. de Waal (ed.), *Islamism and Its Enemies in the Horn of Africa*, London, C. Hurst & Co.

Abdul-Jalil, Musa. 1984, "The Dynamics of Ethnic Identification in Northern Darfur, Sudan: A Situational Approach," *The Sudan: Ethnicity and National Cohesion (Bayreuth African Studies Series)*, Bayreuth, Bayreuth University Press.

———1985, "From Native Courts to People's Local Courts: The Politics of Judicial Administration in Sudan," *Verfassung Und Recht in Ubersee (Law and Politics in Africa, Asia and Latin America)*,18.2, 139–152.

Abuelbashar, Abaker Mohamed. 2006, "On the Failure of Darfur Peace Talks in Abuja," *Sudan Tribune*, August 25.

AFP. 2005, "Sudan Patience Wearing Thin," October 4. http://www.news24.com (accessed July 14, 2006).

———2006, "International Envoys Push Rebels to Back Darfur Peace Deal," May 4. http://www.sudan.net (accessed July 10, 2006).

Africa Action, "Congressional Black Caucus Joins Africa Action in Call for US Intervention to Stop Genocide in Darfur," press release, June 23, 2004.

*Africa Confidential*. 2005, "Who's Who in Darfur." 46.4.

——— 2006. "Sudan: It's the Government, Stupid." 47.10.

African Rights. 1995, *Facing Genocide: The Nuba of Sudan*, London, African Rights.

———1997, *Food and Power in Sudan: A Critique of Humanitarianism*, London, African Rights.

African Union. 2005, "Press Statement by Ambassador Baba Gana Kingibe, Special Representative of the Chairperson of the African Union Commission, on the Deteriorating Security Situation in Darfur, Khartoum, 1 October 2005," Khartoum, African Union.

————2006a, "Briefing by Dr. Salim Ahmed Salim, AU Special Envoy and Chief Mediator for the Darfur Conflict, to the U.N. Security Council on 13 January 2006," Addis Ababa, African Union.

————2006b, "Communiqué," Peace and Security Council, 46th Meeting, March 10, Addis Ababa, African Union.

————2006c, "African Union Presents Ceasefire Proposal to Sudan Government and Darfur Movements: AU Tells the Sudanese Parties in Abuja—Time is Up," press statement, Abuja, African Union.

————2006d, "The Current Chairman of the African Union Holds High Level Consultations with the Sudanese Parties and Other Stakeholders in Abuja," press release 44, Abuja, African Union.

————2006e, "Statement by Dr Salim Ahmed Salim, AU Special Envoy and Chief Mediator, 30 April 2006," press statement, Abuja, African Union.

Ahmed, Abdel Ghaffar M. 2002 "'Tribal Elite': A base for social stratification in the Sudan," in Abdel Ghaffar M. Ahmed (ed.), *Anthropology in the Sudan: Reflections by a Sudanese Anthropologist*, Utrecht, International Books, and Addis Ababa, Organization for Social Science Research in Eastern and Southern Africa.

Ahmed, Mustafa Babiker. 1988, "Primary export crop production and the origins of the ecological crisis in Kordofan: the case of Dar Hamar," in Douglas Johnson and David Anderson (eds.), *The Ecology of Survival: Case Studies from Northeast African History*, London, Lester Crook.

Ajawin, Yoanes and Alex de Waal. 2002, "Land Rights, Natural Resources Tenure and Land Reform," in A. Yoanes and A. de Waal (eds.), *When Peace Comes: Civil Society and the Future of Sudan*, Trenton NJ, Red Sea Press.

Al Tayeb, al Tayeb M. 1991, *Al Maseed*, Khartoum, Khartoum University Press.

Al Zain, Qaisar Musa. 1998, *The Sultanates and Spreading of Islam Era*, Omdurman, Al Haram.

Alsikainga, Awad. 1996, *Slaves into Workers: Emancipation and Labor in Colonial Sudan*, Austin TX, University of Texas Press.

Amnesty International. 1989, "Sudan: Human Rights Violations in the Context of Civil War," London, Amnesty International.

————2003, "Looming crisis in Darfur," London, Amnesty International, July 1.

————2006, "Sudan: Korma: Yet more attacks on civilians," London, Amnesty International, July 31.

Asad, Talal. 1970, *The Kababish Arabs: Power, Authority and Consent in a Nomadic Tribe*, London, C. Hurst.

Barnett, Tony and Abbas Abdelkarim (eds.), 1988, *Sudan: State, Capital and Transformation*, London, Croom Helm.

Bayart, Jean-Francois. 1993, *The State in Africa: The Politics of the Belly*, London, Longman.

Bin Dhaifallah, Mohamed al Nour. 1985, *Kitab ul Tabaqaat*, third ed., Khartoum, Khartoum University Press.

Brown, Richard. 1992, *Sudan: Public Debt and Private Wealth: Debt, Capital Flight and the IMF in Sudan*, London, Macmillan.

Buijtenhuijs, Robert. 1978, *Le Frolinat et les révoltes populaires du Tchad, 1965-1976*, The Hague, Mouton.

———1987, *Le Frolinat et les guerres civiles du Tchad (1977-1984)*, Leiden, Afrika-Studiecentrum, and Paris, Karthala.

———1998, *Transition et élections au Tchad (1993-1997)*, Leiden, Afrika-Studiecentrum, and Paris, Karthala.

Burkhalter, Holly. 1994, "The Question of Genocide: The Clinton Administration and Rwanda," *World Policy Journal* 11.

Cameron, M. A., Lawson R. J., and Tomlin B.W. (eds.). 1998, *To Walk Without Fear: The global movement to ban landmines*, New York, Oxford University Press.

Center for International Justice. 2004, "Documenting Atrocities in Darfur," Department of State Publication 11182.

Chabal, Patrick and Jean-Pascal Daloz. 1999, *Africa Works: Disorder as Political Instrument*, London, James Currey.

Clanet, Jean-Charles. 1994, "Géographie pastorale au Sahel central, thèse de doctorat d'Etat," 2 vols., Paris, Université de Paris IV-Sorbonne.

Coalition for International Justice. 2006, "Soil and Oil: Dirty Business in Sudan," Washington, D.C., Coalition for International Justice.

Collins, Robert and J. Millard Burr. 1999, *Africa's Thirty Years War: Libya, Chad and the Sudan 1963-1993*, Boulder CO, Westview Press.

Corey, Charles. 2004, "U.S. Congress Terms Situation in Darfur 'Genocide'," U.S. Department of State, press release, July 23, 2004.

de Waal, Alex. 1989, *Famine That Kills: Darfur, Sudan, 1984–1985*, Oxford, Clarendon Press.

———1994a, "Some comments on militias in contemporary Sudan," in M. Daly and A. Alsikainga (eds.), *Civil War in the Sudan*, London, British Academic Press.

———1994b, "Starving out the South," in M. Daly and A. Alsikainga (eds.), *Civil War in the Sudan*, London, British Academic Press.

———2004, "Counter-insurgency on the cheap," *London Review of Books*, 26.15.

———2005a, "Who are the Darfurians?" *African Affairs*, 104, 181–205.

———2005b, *Famine that Kills: Darfur, Sudan*, New York, Oxford University Press.

———2006a, "I will not sign," *London Review of Books*, 28.23.

———2006b, "Explaining the Darfur Peace Agreement," www.justiceafrica.org.

de Waal, Alex and Bridget Conley-Zilkic. 2007, "Reflections on how genocidal killings are brought to an end," SSRC webforum *How Genocides End*, http://howgenocidesend.ssrc.org; accessed January 5, 2007.

de Waal, Alex and Helen Young. 2005, "Steps Towards the Stabilization of Governance and Livelihoods in Darfur, Sudan," USAID, March. Available at http://pdf.usaid.gov/pdf_docs/PNADC782.pdf.

Deng, Francis. 1995, *War of Visions: Conflict of Identities in Sudan*, Washington D.C., Brookings.

Djinnit, Said. 2006, "The AU Commissioner for Peace and Security Meets the Sudanese Parties and the International Partners," press release, Abuja, African Union.

Doornbos, Paul 1988, "On Becoming Sudanese," in T. Barnett and A. Abdelkarim (eds.), *Sudan: State, Capital and Transformation*, London, Croom Helm.

Duffield, Mark. 2001, *Global Governance and the New Wars*, London, Zed Books.

El-Affendi, Abdelwahab. 1990, "Discovering the South: Sudanese Dilemmas for Islam in Africa," *African Affairs*, 89, 371–389.

————1991, *Turabi's Revolution: Islam and Power in Sudan*, London, Grey Seal.

El Amin, Khalid A. 1999a, *Drought, Adjustments in Economic Activities, Changes in Land Use and Land Tenure Forms in Darfur, Sudan*. Development Studies Research Centre Monograph Series No. 42, Khartoum, Khartoum University Press.

————1999b, "Some Environmental Consequences of Human Responses to Drought in Sudan, Darfur Region," Development Studies Research Centre, University of Khartoum, June.

Eltom, Abdullahi. 2006, "Darfur: Inside the Crisis," *Democracy Now*, http://www.democracynow.org, accessed September 5, 2006.

Flint, Julie. 2006. "Without Foreign Chancelleries and Hollywood's Finest, Can Darfur Peace Deal Succeed?" *Pambazuka News* 254, May 11.

————2006b. "Where Is the African Union in Darfur?" *Daily Star* (Lebanon), July 12.

————2006c. "Pursuing an Illusion of Peace in Darfur," *Daily Star* (Lebanon), May 23.

Flint, Julie and Alex de Waal. 2005, *Darfur: A Short History of a Long War*, London, Zed Books.

Food and Agriculture Organization, UN High Commissioner for Refugees and Norwegian Refugee Council 2004, "Land and Property Study in Sudan," Nairobi.

Evans, Gareth. 2006, "Letter to Ambassador Said Djinnit, African Union Commissioner for Peace and Security," http://www.crisisgroup.org, accessed July 11, 2006.

GI-Net. 2006, "The Unprecedented Student Movement for Darfur," press release, April 30.

Government of Sudan (GoS) and Sudan People's Liberation Movement (SPLM). 2004a, "Framework Agreement on Wealth Sharing During the Pre-Interim and Interim Period, Between the Government of the Sudan (GoS) and the Sudan People's Liberation Movement/Sudan People's Liberation Army (SPLA)," Naivasha, Kenya.

————2004b, "Protocol Between GOS and SPLM/A on Power Sharing," Naivasha, Kenya.

————2004c, "Protocol on the Resolution of Conflict in Southern Kordofan (Nuba Mountains) and Blue Nile States," Naivasha, Kenya.

Haggar, Bichara Idriss. 2003, *Tchad: témoignage et combat politique d'un exilé*, Paris, L'Harmattan.

Harir, Sharif. 1994, "'Arab Belt' versus 'African Belt,' Ethno-Political Conflict in Darfur and the Regional Cultural Factors," in S. Harir and T. Tvedt (eds.), *Short-Cut to Decay: The Case of the Sudan*, Uppsala, Scandinavian Institute for African Studies.

Hasan, Yusuf Fadl (ed.). 1971, *Sudan in Africa*, Khartoum, Khartoum University Press.

Hertzke, Allen. 2004, *Freeing God's Children: The Unlikely Alliance for Global Human Rights*, Lanham, Rowman and Littlefield.

Hoile, David. 2005, *Darfur in Perspective*, London, European Sudanese Public Affairs Council.

Howell, John (ed.). 1974, *Local Government and Politics in the Sudan*, Khartoum, Khartoum University Press.

Human Rights Watch. 1999, *Famine in Sudan: The Human Rights Causes*, New York, Human Rights Watch.

———2003, *Sudan: Oil and Human Rights*, New York, Human Rights Watch.

———2005, *Entrenching Impunity: Government Responsibility for International Crimes in Darfur*, New York, Human Rights Watch.

Hutchinson, Sharon. 1996, *Nuer Dilemmas: Coping with Money, War and the State*, Berkeley CA, University of California Press.

International Crisis Group. 2003, *Sudan's Other Wars*, Africa Briefing 14, June 25, Brussels

———2005a, *A New Sudan Action Plan*, Africa Briefing 24, Brussels.

———2005b, *Darfur: The Failure to Protect*, Africa Report 89, Brussels.

———2005c, *Unifying Darfur's Rebels: A Prerequisite for Peace*, Africa Briefing, 32, Brussels.

———2006a, *Sudan's Comprehensive Peace Agreement: The Long Road Ahead*, Africa Report, 106, Brussels.

———2006b, *Darfur's Fragile Peace Agreement*, Africa Briefing, 39, Brussels.

International Labour Organization (ILO). 1978, *Growth, Employment and Equity: A Comprehensive Strategy for the Sudan*, 2nd ed., Geneva, International Labour Organization.

International Rescue Committee. 2006, "Increased Sexual Assaults Signal Darfur's Downward Slide," August 23. http://www.theirc.org/news/latest/increased-sexual-assaults.html, accessed February 2007.

Johnson, Douglas. 2003, *The Root Causes of Sudan's Civil Wars*, Oxford, James Currey.

Jok, Jok Madut. 2001, *War and Slavery in Sudan*, Philadelphia, University of Pennsylvania Press.

Jullien de Pommerol, Patrice. 1999, *Dictionnaire arabe tchadien–français*, Paris, Karthala.

Kaldor, Mary. 1999, *New and Old Wars: Organized Violence in a Global Era*, London, Polity.

Karadawi, Ahmed. 1999, *Refugee Policy in the Sudan 1967–1984*, Oxford, Berghahn.

Keen, David. 1994, *The Benefits of Famine: A political economy of famine and relief in southwestern Sudan, 1983–1987*, Princeton, Princeton University Press.

———. 2005, *Conflict and Collusion in Sierra Leone*, Oxford, James Currey.

Khalid, Mansour. 1985, *Nimeiri and the Revolution of Dis-May*, London, KPI.

Kristof, Nicholas D. 2006, "Genocide in Slow Motion," *New York Review of Books*, 53.2.

Lavergne, Marc. 2005. "L'analyse géographique d'une guerre civile en milieu sahélien." *Afrique contemporaine*, 214, 154–155.

Leitenberg, Milton. 2006, "Deaths in Wars and Conflicts in the Twentieth Century," *Occasional Paper* no. 29, Peace Studies Program, Ithaca NY, Cornell University.

Lesch, Ann Mosely. 1999, *Sudan: Contested National Identities*, Bloomington IN, Indiana University Press.

Mahmoud, Fatima Babiker. 1984, *The Sudanese Bourgeoisie: Vanguard of Development?* Khartoum, Khartoum University Press.

Mahmoud, Ushari and Suleiman Baldo. 1987, "El Diein Massacre and Slavery in the Sudan," Khartoum, mimeo.

Mail&Guardian Online. 2006. "UN Becoming Anxious Over Darfur," April 20. http://www.mg.co.za. (accessed April 21, 2006).

Marchal, Roland. 2004a, "Le conflit au Darfour, point aveugle des négociations Nord-Sud au Soudan," *Politique africaine*, 95, 125–146.

———2004b, "Le Soudan d'un conflit à l'autre," *Les Etudes du CERI*, 108/109.

———2006, "Chad/Darfur: how two crises merge," *Review of African Political Economy*, 109.

Médecins Sans Frontières. 2004, "Emergency in Darfur, Sudan: No Relief in Sight—Focus on Mornay Camp, West Darfur State," Khartoum/Paris, Médecins Sans Frontières/Epicentre, June 21.

Mekki, Yousif Kuwa. 2002, "Things would no longer be the same," in S. Rahhal (ed.), *The Right to be Nuba*, Trenton NJ, Red Sea Press.

Mohamed, Adam Azzain. 1998, "Native administration and societal change: The case of Darfur Region," in M. M. Ahmed (ed.), *Current Studies on the Sudan*, Omdurman, Mohamed Omer Beshir's Center for Sudanese Studies.

———2005. "The Views of Darfur Communal Elites on Darfur Crisis." Khartoum, Institute for the Study of Public Administration and Federal Governance.

Morton, James. 1994, *The Poverty of Nations: The Aid Dilemma at the Heart of Africa*, London, British Academic Press.

———2004, "Conflict in Darfur: A Different Perspective," A Resource Paper for HTSPE Limited, http://www.htspe.com.

Morton, John. 1993, "Pastoral decline and famine: The Beja case," in John Markakis (ed.), *Conflict and the Decline of Pastoralism in the Horn of Africa*, London, Macmillan.

Nachtigal, Gustav. 1971, *Sahara and the Sudan, Vol. IV, Wadai and Darfur*, A.G.B. Fisher, H. J. Fisher, and R. S. O'Fahey (eds.), London, C. Hurst.

Nathan, Laurie. 1999, "When push comes to shove: The failure of international mediation in African civil wars," *Track Two*, Occasional Paper, 11.3.

———2004, "Mediation and the African Union's Panel of the Wise," in S. Field (ed.), *Peace in Africa: Towards a Collaborative Security Regime*, Johannesburg, Institute for Global Dialogue.

———2006, "No ownership, no peace: The Darfur Peace Agreement," Working Paper, no. 5 (series 2), Crisis States Research Centre, London School of Economics.

O'Fahey R. S. 1980, *State and Society in Darfur*, London, C. Hurst.

O'Fahey, R. S. and M. A. Abu Salim, with Joseph and Marie-José Tubiana. 1983, *Land in Dar Fur*, Cambridge, Cambridge University Press.

Office for the Coordination of Human Affairs. 2005, "Darfur Humanitarian Profile 13," April 1.

Palmer, Monte. 1980, *Dilemmas of Political Development: An Introduction to the Politics of the Developing Areas*, Itasca IL, Peacock Publishers.

Popular Congress Party. 2005, "The Darfur Crisis: A Vision for Solution," Khartoum.

Power, Samantha. 2002, *A Problem from Hell: America and the Age of Genocide*, New York, Harper.

Prendergast, John. 2006. "A Dying Deal in Darfur," *Boston Globe*, July 13.

Pronk, Jan. 2006. "Darfur Agreement is Severely Paralysed," *Sudan Tribune*. July 1.

Prunier, Gérard. 2005, *Darfur: The Ambiguous Genocide*, London, C. Hurst & Co.

Rahhal, Suleiman. 2002, *The Right to be Nuba*, Trenton, NJ, Red Sea Press.

Reeves, Eric. 2006a, "Why Abuja won't save Darfur," *The New Republic*, May 10, 2006; http://www.sudanreeves.org/Sections-article565-p1.html (accessed February 26, 2007).

———2006b. "Darfur's Downward Spiral," August 11. http://commentisfree.guardian.co.uk, accessed August 31, 2006.

Roden, David. 1974, "Regional Inequality and Rebellion in the Sudan," *The Geographical Review*, 64.4.

Ruay, Deng A.1994, *The Politics of Two Sudans*, Uppsala, Scandinavian Institute for African Studies.

Reuters. 2006, "AU Warns Aid Needed for Darfur Peace Pact to Hold," April 18. http://www.alertnet.org, accessed April 21, 2006.

Ryle, John. 2004, "Disaster in Darfur," *New York Review of Books*, 51.13.

Salih, Globawi Mohamed. 1974, "The Heritage of Local Government," in John Howell (ed), *Local Government and Politics in the Sudan*, Khartoum, Khartoum University Press.

Salih, M. A. Mohamed. 1999, *Environmental Politics and Liberation in Contemporary Africa*, Dordrecht and Boston MA, Kluwer.

Salih, M. A. Mohamed and Sharif Harir. 1994, "Tribal Militias: The Genesis of National Disintegration," in S. Harir and T. Tvedt, *Short-Cut to Decay: The Case of the Sudan*, Uppsala, Scandinavian Institute for African Studies.

Satya. 2006, "A Rebel Walks Out for Peace: The *Satya* Interview with Tadjadine Bechir Niame." June/July 2006. http://www.satyamag.com/jun06/niame.html (accessed August 11, 2006).

Schatzberg, Michael. 2001, *Political Legitimacy in Middle Africa: Father, Family, Food*, Bloomington IN, Indiana University Press.

Shils, Edward. 1965, *Political Development in the New States*, New York, Mouton.

Shuqeir, Naom. 1981, *The History of Sudan*, Cairo, Dar el Jeel.

Straw, Jack. 2006, "Darfur at the Crossroads: Foreign Secretary's Speech to the Peace Talks on Darfur, Abuja, 14 February 2006," http://www.gnn.gov.uk (accessed March 15, 2006).

Sudan Divestment Taskforce. 2006, *State of Sudan Divestment*, June 20, http://www.sudandivestment.org/position.asp#state, accessed July 20.

Sudan Organization Against Torture. 2002, press release, August 23.

*Sudan Tribune*. 2006a, "UN Envoy Slams Darfur Rebels Position in Abuja Talks." January 24.

———2006b, "AU's Nguesso Urges Sudanese Parties to Conclude Darfur Peace Deal." April 10.

———2006c, "Sudanese Parties Resume Direct Negotiations over Darfur Conflict." April 11.

———2006d, "SLM/JEM Say Sudan's Taha Adopts a Rigid Position in Darfur Peace Talks." April 15.

———2006e, "AU to End Darfur Peace Talks If No Agreement by End of April." April 24.

———2006f, "SLM's Menawi Threatens to Suspend Darfur Peace Talks." April 24.

———2006g, "Darfur Rebel SLM Rejects Integration of Its Forces in the Army." April 30.

———2006h, "Darfur SLA/JEM Joint Press Statement on Proposed Peace Deal." May 1.

———2006i, "AU's Salim Reveals Abuja Handicaps, Last-Minute Compromise." May 22.

———2006j, "SLM's Nur Urges UN's Annan to Intervene in Darfur Peace Process." May 24.

———2006k, "Text—Darfur SLM Says AU Deal 'Incomplete', Demands UN Mediation." June 4.

———2006l, "After 5 May Deal, SLM Minawi Faces Divisions and Defections." June 19.

———2006m, "AU Reacts to ICG Report on Darfur Peace Deal." June 25.

———2006n, "Tension Mounts within the Darfur SLM-Minawi Streams." July 1.

———2006o, "Sudan Military Reported To Be Aiding Rebel Attacks." July 12.

———2006p, "Peace Implementation Panel Condemns Ceasefire Violations in Darfur." August 6.

———2006q, "Newly Appointed Darfur Rebel Leader Ready for Negotiated Solution." August 19.

Tanner, Victor. 2004, "Darfour: racines anciennes, nouvelles virulences, " *Politique étrangère*, 4, 715–28.

———2005a, "Rule of Lawlessness: Roots and Repercussions of the Darfur Crisis," Washington D.C., Sudan Advocacy Coalition report.

———2005b, "In Just Ten Months, 700,000 People Were Brutally Driven From Their Homes—How is it the World Hardly Noticed?" *Parliamentary Brief*. August 19–20, London.

Tanner, Victor and Jérôme Tubiana. 2007, "Divisions and Continuity—the Rebels of Darfur," a Small Arms Survey working paper, forthcoming.

Tassel, Janet. 2005, "Militant about 'Islamism': Daniel Pipes wages 'hand-to-hand combat' with a 'totalitarian ideology,'" *Harvard Magazine*, January–February, 107.3.

Trimingham, J. Spencer. 1946, *Islam in the Sudan*, F. Akoud (trans.), Cairo, Higher Cultural Council.

Troutt-Powell, Eve. 2003, *A Different Shade of Colonialism: Egypt, Great Britain and the Mastery of the Sudan*, Berkeley CA, University of California Press.

Tubiana, Jérôme. 2005, "Le Darfour, un conflit identitaire?" *Afrique contemporaine*, 214, 165–206.

———2006, "Le Darfour, un conflit pour la terre," *Politique africaine*, 101, 111–131.

Tubiana, Joseph. 1984, "Tunjur," in R. V. Weekes (ed.), *The Muslim Peoples' Encyclopaedia*, Westport, Greenwood Press.

Tubiana, Marie-José. 2006, *Carnets de route au Dar For (Soudan), 1965–1970*, Saint-Maur, Sépia.

Tubiana, Marie-José and Joseph Tubiana. 1977, *The Zaghawa from an Ecological Perspective*, Rotterdam, A. A. Bakelam.

Tuchman, Barbara. 1984, *The March of Folly: From Troy to Vietnam*, New York, Abacus.

United Nations. 2005, "Report of the International Commission of Inquiry on Darfur to the United Nations Secretary-General, Pursuant to Security Council Resolution 1564 of 18 September 2004," New York, United Nations.

UN News Center. 2006a, "Security Council Calls for Smooth Transition to UN Operation in Darfur." April 11.

———2006b. "Secretary-General Voices Concern about Worsening Situation in Sudan."

UN Office for Humanitarian Affairs. 2006a, "Darfur Humanitarian Profile," 24 (July 1).

———2006b, "Darfur Humanitarian Profile," 25 (October 1).

VOA News. 2006. "Civil Rights Activist Dubious of Darfur Deal." May 5. http://www.voanews.com, accessed August 2, 2006.

*Vigilance Soudan.* 2000, website, April, http://www.vigilsd.org.

*Washington Post.* 2006, "Darfur Peace Accord a Battle of Its Own," May 9.

White House 2006, "President Meets with Darfur Advocates," press release, 28 April 2006.

Woodward, Peter. 1990, *Sudan 1898-1989: The Unstable State*, London, Lester Crook. 1957, *Countries Almanac*, Vol. IV, Beirut, Sader House.

Young, Helen, A. M. Osman, Y. Aklilu, R. Dale, B. Badri and A. J. A. Fuddle. 2005, *Darfur: Livelihoods Under Siege*, Somerville MA, Feinstein International Famine Center, Tufts University, and Omdurman, Ahfad University for Women.

Zartman, I. William. 1989, *Ripe for Resolution: Conflict and Intervention in Africa*. New York: Oxford University Press.

——— 2001, "The Timing of Peace Initiatives: Hurting Stalemates and Ripe Moments," *Global Review of Ethnopolitics*, 1.1, 8–18.

# INDEX